# Critical Writings
## 1953–1978

**Theory and History of Literature**
**Edited by Wlad Godzich and Jochen Schulte-Sasse**

*For other books in the series, see p. 247*

# Critical Writings, 1953–1978

## Paul de Man

Edited and with an introduction
by Lindsay Waters

Theory and History of Literature, Volume 66

University of Minnesota Press, Minneapolis

Published by the University of Minnesota Press
2037 University Avenue Southeast, Minneapolis, MN 55414.
Published simultaneously in Canada
by Fitzhenry & Whiteside Limited, Markham.
Printed in the United States of America.

**Library of Congress Cataloging-in-Publication Data**

De Man, Paul.
  Critical writings, 1953–1978 / Paul de Man; edited and with an introduc-
tion by Lindsay Waters.
    p. cm. – (Theory and history of literature; v. 66)
  Bibliography: p.
  Includes index.
  ISBN 0-8166-1695-7
  ISBN 0-8166-1696-5 (pbk.)
  1. De Man, Paul—Contributions in criticism. 2. Criticism—20th cen-
tury. I. Waters, Lindsay. II. Title. III. Series.
PN75.D45A25    1988    88-31595
809–dc19    CIP

# Contents

# Preface

Shortly before he died I persuaded Paul de Man to allow the essays in this volume to be collected, and shortly after his death was myself persuaded by the editors of the Theory and History of Literature series to pull the volume together and write an introduction to it that would give a brief account of de Man's life and intellectual itinerary. The introduction was to be based on my discussions with him over a number of years as his editor and on interviews to be conducted with colleagues, friends, and associates of his.

This book collects the writings that belong to Paul de Man's "critical" phase, the first stage of his maturity. Paul de Man was, as Dan Latimer has suggested, the embodiment of Lukács's ironic essayist as described in *Soul and Form*, a writer who deals with ultimate questions in the guise of book reviews. Journalism's occasional nature, he felt, challenged him to keep his mind focused on central issues, and in these essays he discussed many issues that were to preoccupy him throughout his career. The volume includes all the essays he and I had agreed to include in the book, as well as an introduction in which I suggest how the critical phase of de Man's career fits into his career as a whole. I have included, in the notes to my introduction, a number of letters de Man wrote that pertain to his work. All along my effort has been to make as coherent a picture as possible of de Man's work, to make the pieces fit into a story that is both the same and different from the usual stories we have heard about Paul de Man.

In the preceding sentence I should have said "the usual stories we *had* heard about Paul de Man." I had finished one version of my introduction a year ago, before the news broke that de Man had written for the Brussels daily *Le Soir*, as well as for a number of other collaborationist publications produced during the German occupation of his country. In my research I had come upon nothing that hinted at this aspect of his past. The news of de Man's wartime writings forced me to discard my original introduction and write a new—and substantially different—one.

What I have learned about de Man in the last year has changed my sense of the first steps he took in his career. Even before learning about the articles in *Le Soir*, I had been puzzled by the strength of his thoughts about figures like Sartre and other "engaged" intellectuals of the thirties as he had expressed those thoughts in some of his essays and conversations. Now I understand better: he, too, had been an engaged intellectual and still felt the need to distance himself from any such stance.

All of this positioning I have tried to lay out in some detail here. As will become clear, I find the ideas he espoused in 1941 and 1942 indefensible and his evasiveness afterward far from admirable. But there is much, much more in de Man's career and critical practice that merits our closest attention. I hope this book will be a useful aid in the effort to come to terms with the man and his work.

I owe thanks to many people who have helped me prepare this book. In the first place come those who have given me valuable testimony about Paul de Man: his wife, Patricia de Man; his cousins Jan Buschmann and Elisabeth de Man; Robert Martin Adams, Peter Dodge, Fred de Vos, Harry Levin, John Hollander, Harold Bloom, Geoffrey Hartman, J. Hillis Miller, Tom Keenan, David Braybrooke, Yves Bonnefoy, Alain Seznec, Robert Silvers, and Vincent Crapanzano. Next are those who translated essays for this book: Richard Howard ("Montaigne and Transcendence," "Poetic Nothingness," "The Situation of the Novel," "Madame de Staël and Jean-Jacques Rousseau," and "Jacques Derrida, *Of Grammatology*"), Dan Latimer ("The Temptation of Permanence" and "Thematic Criticism and the Theme of *Faust*"), and Kevin Newmark and Andrzej Warminski ("Process and Poetry"). My special thanks are due those who read the introduction in one or both of its forms and provided valuable commentary: Wlad Godzich, Jochen Schulte-Sasse, Jim Miller, Denis Hollier, Rachel Jacoff, Hayden White, Richard Rorty, Terry Cochran, Neil Hertz, Dominick LaCapra, Fredric Jameson, Dan Latimer, Walter Kendrick, Thomas Pavel, Barbara Johnson, Peter Brooks, Jim Conant, Cynthia Chase, Gerald Graff, and Shoshana Felman.

L. W.
Cambridge, Massachusetts
September 1988

# Introduction
# Paul de Man: Life and Works
*Lindsay Waters*

## A Brief Life

Paul de Man was born in Antwerp on December 6, 1919, the second son of a well-to-do Flemish bourgeois family. His most notable ancestor was his grandfather, the popular Belgian poet Jan van Beers (1821–88). The de Man family was both liberal and nonreligious, and a number of them were Freemasons. De Man's family was "flamingant" but at the same time of some social standing. It was customary for members of the high bourgeoisie in Flanders such as de Man's family to differentiate themselves from the general populace by the assimilation of French culture. Moreover, the de Mans were decidedly cosmopolitan: fluency in four languages was taken as a matter of course among them. De Man's father was a manufacturer of X-ray machines. His only sibling, a brother, died in an accident at a train crossing as a teenager. His mother committed suicide when de Man was an adolescent.

De Man began his academic studies in 1937 at the francophone Free University of Brussels, which distinguished itself in part from the other great university in Belgium, the Catholic University of Louvain, by its anticlericalism and freethinking. De Man had passed his admission exams from the Ecole Polytechnique at the University of Brussels in 1936, but after a year there had switched to the Free University, where he had won a degree of second "candidature" in the academic year 1939–40. (This is roughly the equivalent of a bachelor's degree.) He then switched to the "première license" program in social sciences for the year of 1940–41, but in November 1941, the university closed its doors because it would not cooperate with the German occupying forces, which had been in control of Belgium since the spring of 1940. De Man began his writing career at the Free University, where he was a contributing editor and then chief editor of the literary journal *Les Cahiers du Libre Examen*. The politics of the journal were explicitly anti-Nazi—its editors had proclaimed themselves as early as 1937 to be "democratic, anticlerical, antidogmatic, and antifascist." The journal ceased publication soon after the German invasion.

De Man married Ann Baraghian, a Romanian who had settled in Belgium with a Belgian husband whom she later divorced. Her marriage to de Man took place before the German invasion. Many in de Man's family fled Belgium for the south of France when the Germans attacked, and de Man and his wife got as far as the Spanish border but were unable to cross over and returned to Belgium.

When de Man returned to Belgium, his most prominent relative, Hendrik de Man, helped (through Raymond de Baecker, its chief editor) to get him a job on what is still the leading French-language daily in Belgium, *Le Soir*. De Man's job was to write a column entitled "Chronique littéraire," as well as notices of concerts, recitals, artistic exhibitions, and the like. The editors of *Le Soir* followed the Nazi line, and during the occupation it was renamed by many citizens of Belgium *Le Soir Volé* (The stolen evening). De Man also wrote at this time for a Flemish-language journal, *Het Vlaamsche Land*. He wrote for *Le Soir* from December 1940 through November 1942 when (as he wrote in a letter years later to the Harvard Society of Fellows) he resigned his position to protest German control of what was being published in the newspaper.

After he resigned his position at *Le Soir,* Paul de Man went to work for a book distributor and publisher called Agence Dechenne. He wrote book notices for their "Bibliographie." The Agence Dechenne is mentioned by de Man in a number of his articles for *Le Soir* and seems to have been involved in the publication of paperback editions of classics as well as of translations. During the latter part of the Occupation, de Man worked on a Flemish translation of *Moby Dick,* which was published in 1945. He also worked on translations of Goethe and arranged for others to translate books.

After the war ended in 1945 all Belgians who were suspected in any way of collaborating with the Germans were brought before the tribunal called the Auditeur Générale. Paul de Man went before the tribunal and all charges against him for his work at *Le Soir* were dismissed, although many others who had worked at *Le Soir* were convicted and sentenced to jail.

After the war de Man, along with a number of colleagues, started a publishing firm called Editions Hermès. Hermès was not in business for long. A number of factors conspired to bring the house down. Hermès was meant to publish well-illustrated and authoritatively written books in art history. One side of de Man's family, the Buschmanns of Antwerp, had been in the printing business since the nineteenth century. With financial support from many sides de Man and his colleagues—all contemporaries—started publishing. The key to making a book work financially was arranging for it to be exported into a number of other countries, with texts in the language of the destined country to be slotted in by Hermès for the copublisher. It seems likely that only two books were published: Jean de Beucken's *Vincent van Gogh: A Portrait* and Paul Haesert's *Renoir: Sculptor.*

Paul de Man made his first trip to the United States in 1947 to try to arrange quickly for an English-language publisher to do the book on Renoir after Clement Attlee suddenly declared as an austerity measure the importing of books to England would have to be restricted to one title per day and a previously made deal fell apart. In the end the book did appear from Reynal and Hitchcock in New York, but the prospects for Hermès did not significantly improve. Finances were terrible. Neither de Man nor his colleagues seemed to be good managers. De Man—his cousin Jan Buschmann reported to me—was more of an artist than a commercial director, and in the end he had (in Buschmann's words) "too much hay on his fork." Hermès went bankrupt.[1]

The year 1948 was a decisive one for de Man, and it was a very difficult one for most Europeans. Americans remember the Berlin blockade and the threat the Soviets posed to the West in that situation. The mysterious death of Jan Masaryk in Prague in 1948 made evident to Europeans who harbored hopes that the Russian model could be democratically introduced elsewhere in Europe that such hopes were groundless and that the Soviet Union was an imperialist power. The same year also presented the spectacle of all the Western Communist parties (with the exception of the Italians under Togliatti) kowtowing to the Soviets. Many Western Europeans thought they were on the verge of a Soviet invasion and that they would soon be thrown back into the same situation of being occupied from which they had been freed three or four years previously. In this context, then, de Man's choice to go to America makes some sense. He had studied English and American literature, and he suspected—according to his Hermès colleague Fred de Vos—that in America there would be some possibilities for a person well trained in arts and letters. The country was technically very advanced and there was little a European could expect to offer in that regard, but the arts were a different matter.

And so it was in 1948 that de Man decided to take his chances in America. But still the question arises: why America and not France? De Man's orientation was indeed French. When he worked for the Agence Dechenne during the war he had had a number of occasions to travel to Paris and work with French writers, publishers, and journalists. (He may have even been involved in arranging to print in Belgium a volume of poetry by Resistance writers.) Moreover, his close friend from Belgium, Georges Lambrichs, was on his way to Paris, where he was to lead a distinguished career at Editions de Minuit, the great French house started as an act of resistance, and then at Gallimard, where in time he assumed the mantle of the most prestigious literary editor in France, Jean Paulhan, and became editor of the *Nouvelle Revue Française.* In Paris he also had ties through Hermès with the avant-garde publisher Girodias, and he had a number of connections with the journal *Critique,* whose chief editor was Georges Bataille. Nonetheless, de Man decided against Paris.

His first plan was to start another publishing firm when he arrived in New York. But instead, de Man ended up working as a clerk in the Doubleday book-shop in Grand Central Station. He had hoped to pursue parallel lives as a pub-lisher and a critic. He followed the suggestion of colleagues at *Critique* and else-where and through them offered his services to William Phillips, editor of *The Partisan Review.* A letter he wrote in 1948 to Phillips touches upon both aspects of his work when he first reached the States:

> "This year I came over to the USA with the intention to stay here permanently. The publishing business has become almost completely impossible in Europe, and my main commercial purpose here is to con-tinue and develop the publication of illustrated books (especially on art) partly manufactured in Europe. In the meanwhile, I took a job with Doubleday bookshop in order, first of course to secure myself a living, and to get acquainted with the technique of American book distribution.
> . . . I wanted to give you an article I wrote and which might in-terest *Partisan Review.* At least the quotations it contains reveal what seems to be an important aspect of contemporary French writing, an as-pect which your review has not yet covered as it deserves to be. My contribution on this subject is in the same direction as a series of simi-lar articles I wrote on American literature, which will appear in the French review *Critique.* It could eventually be followed by articles of French writers like Bataille, Blanchot, Michaux, etc., belonging to this movement and who all expressed to me their willingness to contribute to *Partisan Review.* Anyway, all this might be worth talking about."[2]

De Man became for a while one of those who, as he wrote in 1964, "lived on the subway circuit between uptown Columbia and downtown Astor Place in the New York of the forties" (see the essay "Heidegger Reconsidered"). His contacts were Dwight Macdonald, Alexander Calder, Fred Dupee. He tried to see whether there were ways to set up the distribution of *Partisan Review* in Europe. In the end his efforts to participate in *Partisan Review* were as fruitless as his efforts to set up shop as a publisher. His only article for *Partisan Review* was published sixteen years after his arrival in the United States. He did, however, manage to place an essay by Georges Bataille, "On Hiroshima," in a special issue of Dwight Macdonald's *Politics* dedicated to "French Political Writing."[3] And thanks to knowing Macdonald, Dupee, and Mary MacCarthy he managed to get a job teaching at Bard College in New York.

De Man taught at Bard for the academic years 1949 to 1951. There he met his second wife, Patricia Woods. After he left Bard, work was not so easy to locate.

One summer the de Mans picked strawberries. After that he secured a position teaching French at the Berlitz School in Boston. While in Boston he attended some of the informal gatherings of graduate students in comparative literature at Harvard, where he met Harry Levin and Renato Poggioli, the chief professors of comparative literature at Harvard, who invited him to study there.[4] Because of his age (he was older than the typical graduate student), his need for financial support, and his experience and knowledge, they did after some time encourage him to apply for a position as a junior fellow of the Society of Fellows. He had continued working at the Berlitz School and earned extra money translating articles from three languages for Henry Kissinger's journal, *Confluence*. The Society of Fellows was set up by James Conant as a route to teaching that would be an alternative to the doctorate. Now almost all the junior fellows hold a Ph.D. or are on the way to getting one. It has always been a place where only those who are considered exceptional are accepted. In the end de Man decided to take a Ph.D., which he earned in 1960 with a dissertation called "Mallarmé, Yeats, and the Post-Romantic Predicament." A third part of the dissertation was to have been on Stefan George. During the time he was connected with Harvard, de Man also spent a year away in Paris (where he delivered the essay entitled "Process and Poetry," included here, to Jean Wahl's Collège de Philosophie)[5] and another six months in Ireland working on Yeats. (The portion of the dissertation that deals with Yeats is now included in *The Rhetoric of Romanticism*. A précis of the part of the dissertation that deals with Mallarmé is available here in the chapter entitled "Poetic Nothingness." The 125 pages in the dissertation that are devoted to Mallarmé are interesting but very dated, given the great deal of work that has been done since 1960 on the manuscripts of Mallarmé. That is why those pages are not included here. Moreover, this volume includes only published work.)

De Man's position at Harvard his last few years had been as a lecturer in a non-tenure-track position. He had in those years taught courses both in the General Education program and in the Department of Comparative Literature. When he was nearing the end of his dissertation, an effort was led by Reuben Brower with whom de Man had worked on the "Hum 6" course in the General Education program to persuade Dean McGeorge Bundy as well as Harry Levin and Renato Poggioli to retain de Man in a tenure-track post at Harvard. Brower wrote Levin and Poggioli a letter on January 13, 1960, that gives some notion of how one senior and very admired professor at Harvard considered de Man. I quote from the letter:

> "He is simply one of those people who carry on the process of education constantly by their presence and conversation. . . . I have felt and do feel most grateful to you both for making all sorts of extraordinary arrangements so that he could continue to work in my course [Hum 6]. As far as the past is concerned, I feel unusually lucky. I am

thinking rather of the future of Harvard College and of the Department in its relation to exceptional undergraduates and exceptional young teachers of literature.

"I am really saying, can't Harvard occasionally take a glorious risk? And can't we consider the full-range abilities of the man? For Paul has what I can only call *soul*: for him aesthetic and moral choices are not separable, he has some of the fine Gallic feeling that a critical position is a position of combat. This means of course that he is sometimes obstinate, sometimes 'prickly.' But aren't all good men 'prickly' at his age?

"Well, such are my thoughts as I start the day. I think they are worth taking into account, somewhere, somehow, if the University is to continue to be a live and rich community of men possessing both intelligence and character.

"Sincerely,
"Ben"[6]

Brower's letter was unsuccessful. Given de Man's performance in his oral exams and the overphilosophical nature of his dissertation (as it was perceived), Levin and Poggioli felt that a special effort to retain de Man would have been out of order.

De Man's itinerary after 1960 is much better known. He moved from Harvard to Cornell in 1960 and remained associated with Cornell until 1969. He was made Ordinarius for Comparative Literature at the University of Zurich, where he taught with Emil Staiger, the leading figure of German Studies in this period, and fellow Belgian and professor of French Georges Poulet. He held this post from 1963 to 1970. He also held the position of Professor of Humanities at Johns Hopkins University from 1968 to 1970, after which he moved permanently to Yale University, where he was made Sterling Professor of Comparative Literature and French in 1979. Yale University had had a noted program in literary studies— perhaps the most prominent program in literary studies in North America— for most of the twentieth century. The group of scholars with whom Paul de Man worked most closely at Yale formed a sort of strategic combination of forces that was to be called the Yale School, thanks to some notable publicity efforts (not by de Man) and despite the serious disagreements between some of the parties about the goals and methods of literary studies.[7] Paul de Man died of cancer in December 1983.

## Aesthetic Nationalism

It is hard at this distance to understand the temptation of National Socialism for intellectuals. Czeslaw Milosz argues in *The Captive Mind*—his study of how totalitarian political thinking in Eastern Europe won the allegiance of many intellectuals—that leftist totalitarianism at least has its attractions whereas "the rightist totalitarian program was exceptionally poor. The only gratification it offered came from collective *warmth:* crowds, red faces, mouths open in a shout, marches, arms brandishing sticks; but little rational satisfaction. Neither racist doctrines, nor hatred of foreigners, nor the glorification of one's own national traditions could efface the feeling that the entire program was improvised to deal with the problems of the moment."[8] Thin, nasty gruel perhaps, but the movement—unfortunately—did have its idealists. The historian Fritz Stern has recently written a number of essays exploring what he calls—it's the title of a powerful essay— "National Socialism as Temptation."[9] It simply and sadly is not true that terror was the only force keeping the Nazi regime in power in Germany and throughout the occupied territories. Fascism had its intellectual disciples just as the communism of which Milosz speaks did.

The young Paul de Man was a cultural nationalist. In some of his writings for *Le Soir* and *Het Vlaamsche Land* he espoused a form of national aestheticism that was complicit with National Socialism. There is no escaping this distasteful, ugly fact. A liberal humanist might attempt to separate a philosopher's or a critic's ideas or a poet's verses from his or her life and political opinions. But the writer, as Paul de Man understood the act of writing, cannot be so easily let off the hook. Jean-Paul Sartre says in *What Is Literature?* that "once you enter the universe of significations, there is nothing you can do to get out of it."[10] We cannot blot any of de Man's words from the record, and they cannot now be shunted aside. They tell us so much more than we ever knew before about where de Man came from and, I would argue, explain why he so adamantly states his opposition in some of the essays included in this volume to the very type of the thirties writer, the engaged intellectual who put mind and pen in service of state or party. The man he attacks when he disparages Malraux, Hemingway, Jünger, and Sartre in the pages in this volume is just as much the kind of intellectual that he himself had been.

But if the early texts cannot and should not be expunged from the record for all they have to tell us, they have to be understood carefully. If they contextualize Paul de Man, we must be careful to contextualize them when we consider them. A brief account must be given of them here because they clearly form the first part of de Man's complex intellectual journey.

I will echo Fritz Stern's caveat to the readers in his writings on why intellectuals in Germany fell prey to the fascist temptation of right-wing authoritarianism: I do not mean to pass any facile judgments here; rather, I want to take de Man seriously and bear in mind the remark of the poet Gottfried Benn: "We were not all opportunists."[11] De Man seems, alas, to have been not just an opportunist. To some considerable extent he was probably an idealistic believer, though even the notion that someone could have been an idealist in such a situation may be hard to stomach. But more recent works such as those of Stern as well as Zeev Sternhell's various books (the most relevant in this case being *Neither Right nor Left: Fascist Ideology in France*)[12] have helped us see better than we could years ago the variety in the positive responses to National Socialism and thus understand the mechanics of how some people came to feel they could work with the Nazis. Old activists like de Man's uncle and young idealists like de Man himself did get caught up in what they perceived was revolutionary fervor.[13] For them time was off its hinges. For them 1940 presented the opportunity of a revolution in a society in which change was otherwise blocked.

What change in society was being sought? Some backtracking is necessary to understand the crisis of the spirit that gripped many Europeans in the 1930s and made them eager for some (any) change. Talk of revolution was the most pervasive discourse of the decade on the left, right, and in between. The 1930s were seen as a time of crisis for liberal democracy, in Europe and in North America. All intellectuals were looking on the fringes of political life for ideas that would transform political life. This quest had really begun many years before. The years 1870 to 1914 were the heyday of liberalism and democracy in Europe. But the behavior of those in power was thoroughly discredited during the Great War, and democracy as a form of political arrangement was never much admired from that point on. The collapse of the League of Nations and the Abyssinian situation only gave further evidence of the "failure" of the democracies.

The feeling prevailed that democracy had run its course. The best among the democrats got bogged down in bureaucratic "nonsense" and the worst were decadents and plutocrats who know how to manipulate the system to their own advantage. In the minds of many the choice was between nationalism and cosmopolitanism, and nationalism stood for something more noble than cosmopolitanism. Cosmopolitanism compelled people to become more and more specialized while at the same time tempting them with a "sham" universality. Modern cosmopolitanism left (supposedly) no room for reverence for tradition, one's own heritage, the matrix of human nobility. Nationalism was superior to the constructs of legalists based on abstractions like "society" and dedicated to soulless goals like "growth."[14] Antimodernism had great appeal to those who found modern Europe false to the core. "Call us not tragic," wrote Auden of the bourgeoisie in a poem of the period, "Falseness made farcical our death."[15] Georges Sorel and Carl Schmitt were leading thinkers who became critics of democracy. Schmitt argued that "the bourgeois ideal of peaceful agreement, an ongoing and prosperous business that has advantages for everyone," was no better than "the monstrosity of cowardly intellectualism." Endless discussion without decision was a common view of parliamentary government, but—said Schmitt already in 1923— "openness and discussion have become an empty and trivial formality" and the nineteenth-century parliament had "lost its previous foundation and its meaning."[16]

Against this vision of humdrum, gray, bourgeois life a set of thinkers and writers began to project in the 1920s and 1930s a cult of revolutionary spirit that would sweep away the doomed and decadent liberal order. Action, any action but especially radically revolutionary action, was better than the constant chitchat of the democrats that never led anywhere.

The cult of action over analysis had as many manifestations as it had promoters; and it had many promoters on left and right, ranging from the coarsest advocate of brutality on to a philosopher like Heidegger. It was in this context, for example, that in the 1920s interest in Kierkegaard's existentialism continued to build.[17] He was seen as an advocate of decisiveness, one who made a virtue of getting beyond abstract and endless rationalization.

Carl Schmitt, once again, was one of the notable advocates of action. Schmitt promoted what was called "decisionism." For him the power to decide, not reason or nature, was the source of the legitimacy of the state. In his *Concept of the Political* he celebrated Hobbes as the only major political theorist to have recognized in the rule of the sovereign the "decisionist" substance of the politics of states. Sovereign is he who decides. The ruler who uses rational discourse has no sovereignty, for rationalism (as he wrote in *The Crisis of Parliamentary Democracy*) "falsifies the immediacy of life."[18] Parallel views were occasioned by the existentialist reading of passages of Heidegger's *Being and Time* like the following: "If Dasein, by anticipation, lets death become powerful in itself, then, as free for death, Dasein understands itself in its own *superior power,* the power of its finite freedom, so that in this freedom, which 'is' only in its having chosen to make such a choice, it can take over the *powerlessness* of abandonment to its having done so, and can thus come to have a clear vision for the accidents of the Situation that has been disclosed."[19] Heidegger's notion of "Dasein's fateful destiny" probably remained opaque to most readers, except after 1933 when in his Rectoral Address Heidegger took the precipitous step of connecting the fateful choice to a heinous politics. Heidegger speaks at a very abstract level with the sort of generality that would allow Marxists such as Lucien Goldmann, Georg Lukács, and Herbert Marcuse to be inspired by such an emphasis on action even as Heidegger himself hoped such writing in 1933 would help inspire the national "renewal" that was developing in Germany at the same time.

Between the coarse formulation of the call to action and Heidegger's complex words came many other voices, most notably writers of literature. This aspect of the aesthetic ideology of the 1930s is very important for understanding Paul de Man's ideas as presented in the essays in this volume and elsewhere. He himself in the essays of 1941 and 1942 subscribed to a version of this notion of the health of decisive action over analysis; but he rejected action in a good number of his essays thereafter, although instead of dispensing with the notion of action altogether, he reformulated it in more critical terms.

We are dealing here with cultural stereotypes, but in the 1930s cultural stereotypes were coming to rule the day and they would come to dominate entirely by the end of the decade. Literary promotion of the cult of action took many forms in the 1920s and 1930s and it appealed broadly. The most popular forms for the man of action were the bullfighter and the airplane pilot. Henri de Montherlant's first novel, *Les Bestiaires* (1926), was based on his effort to learn bullfighting. Hemingway in the same year published *The Sun Also Rises,* and in it and other works he seemed to suggest that the bullfighter led a kind of authentic existence because his body and spirit were made one in the tragic bloodletting into which he pushed himself. This rude, violent life in Spain was surely more compelling than the scene of Americans learning to mime French customs in Paris. The challenge was to get anywhere out of this world of bourgeois shilly-shallying. Writers took it as their task to enable their readers to see the limits of bourgeois order. For Auden a clinical detachment was possible if you removed yourself to the height of the pilot. He began one strong poem of the 1930s this way:

> Consider this and in our time
> As the hawk sees it or the helmeted airman:
> The clouds rift suddenly — look there
> At cigarette-end smouldering on a border
> At the first garden party of the year.[20]

Without themselves becoming fascists and often while expressing great distaste for Nazism, a set of writers did begin to praise the strong ruler, the man of few words and swift action. They were led to Germany: "We wanted," said Stephen Spender, "to see the crudeness of Germany. It excited us more than the stylishness of France."[21] Christopher Isherwood tells in his thinly disguised autobiographical novel *Lions and Shadows* how he and his contemporaries like Auden and Spender came to idealize the "Truly Strong Man," who is the antithesis of themselves, Truly Weak Men, the coddled products of bourgeois culture: "The Truly Strong Man travels straight across the broad America of normal life, taking always the direct, reasonable route."[22]

This was a period when American culture became popular in Europe because it was seen as an antidote to the decadence of European culture. Charles Lindbergh was seen as a quiet, sure man of action, and became a type of the Truly Strong Man who would appear in Renoir's *Rules of the Game* and have his own European avatar in Saint-Exupéry. Faulkner was first translated into French in 1933. The book was *Sanctuary* and it received an introduction by Malraux. In America now the name Faulkner immediately calls to mind the cerebral, hesitant, Truly Weak Man, Quentin Compson. But the French saw violence, alcohol, an atmosphere that was like that of a criminal novel, and Faulkner seemed a healthy break from the overrefined aesthetics of the European tradition and especially Proust. We might have directed them to Henry James to give them a more balanced picture of American culture, but they would not have been interested because then as always extraliterary concerns had a lot to do with what sort of heroes they wanted to read about. And what they were interested in was the bull-fighter. The bullfighter had a long and illustrious career in European literature in the first half of this century. Even the refined Michel Leiris admits in his autobi-ography, *Manhood,* that he was enamored of the bullfighter: the afterword to *Manhood* is called "The Autobiographer as Torero," and he recounts that as he looked at the urban bustle from his desk where he composed the afterword that he could not stop himself from daydreaming:

> I was dreaming, then, of a bull's horn. I found it hard to resign myself to being nothing more than a *litterateur.* The matador who transforms danger into the occasion to be more brilliant than ever and reveals the whole quality of his style just when he is most threatened: that is what enthralled me, that is what I wanted to be.[23]

The Truly Strong Man. He appears to us now in the image of the inescapably reac-tionary Dirty Harry, but the Clint Eastwood persona may provide a clue to what enthralled the mind of literary writers across the political spectrum in the 1930s. After all, Clint Eastwood's persona was produced by Europeans in the 1960s who had no doubt been influenced by the image of the Tan, Silent, Strong American that emerged for them in Europe in the 1930s.

Eastwood never pauses, never reflects. Such an image of the man of action is particularly compelling for intellectuals. Nicola Chiaramonte, a literary figure of some prominence in the 1930s and 1940s and a political activist in Italy who was compelled by his antifascist activities to go into exile in 1934 and later fought in the Spanish Civil War on the Republican side, gives a brilliant, if ultimately dis-heartening, analysis of the tendency of intellectuals in the 1930s to misunderstand politics and the realm of action in an essay entitled "Malraux and the Demon of Action." He finds that this tendency begins with "the rejection of what Kier-kegaard called 'inwardness.' " For such people, well-meaning people to be sure, "history is made into a faith that leads to material and moral liberation." The sad fact is that "we in the West are incapable of believing that there is a more convinc-ing test for ideas than the act. . . . History, the event, the situation, transcends all truth." The great thing is to overcome inaction. Europe without religion "has been deprived of any spiritual aim," says Malraux.[24] The solution to overcoming the nihilism that threatened Europe was to throw oneself into battles and the strug-gle for power. Chiaramonte, who was a colleague of Malraux's in Spain in the air corps, calls this the true nihilism, more destructive of value than any aesthetic that severs politics from action.

All of this is not to say that one can condemn Malraux easily but that through his plight and that of others one can see the desperation of those times. Roger Shattuck calls his essay reevaluating Malraux, "Malraux, the Conqueror," and writes that his virtues are very different from those of a Montaigne who exemplifies "moral comprehension."[25] Shattuck also writes in the same volume of essays about the Writers Congress in Paris in 1935 and how confused and foolish the participants revealed themselves to be, but I think their confusion was a measure more of desperation than sheer foolishness. The notion that those assembled at the congress could have had much impact on politics may have been a delusion, but those who gathered there were surely not wrong to worry about what could be done.

The worries and dreams of writers in the 1930s in France and in other countries took certain forms and one was this effort to praise action as the alternative to analysis. One more sign of the times that is in some ways in line with the cult of action is Sartre's article of January 1939 in which he shouts "Eureka!" because he has found the philosophy that will enable Europe to escape from the exaggerated emphasis on the self and return to the world outside:

> Husserl has reestablished the horror and the charm of things. He has restored the world of artists and of prophets: frightening, hostile, dangerous, with havens of grace and love. He has made a distinct place for a new treatise on the passions that will be inspired by a truth so simple and so profoundly misunderstood by our refined sensibilities: if one loves a woman, it's because she is lovable. We are, then, liberated now from Proust. We are also at the same time liberated from the "interior life."[26]

Sartre, who in his "L'Enfance d'un chef" revealed himself very aware of the sort of problem that Auden and Company and Malraux were susceptible to in their glorification of action over analysis, declared himself the enemy of the Proustian tradition of introspection.

Given the way issues that pertain to the relation of literature to politics became confused in the 1930s and the considerable difficulty of distinguishing between left and right opposition to democracy and capitalism, it becomes all the more easy to see how certain ideas led to a climate in which, as Fritz Stern and Zeev Sternhell point out, some fell prey to fascist ideas. They admired what Bertrand de Jouvenal called "the great historical phenomenon of our times: the seizure of power by young groups animated by anti-bourgeois spirit."[27]

But would not the violence of the Nazis have been a sign of the true nature of the beast unleashed when Hindenburg made Hitler his chancellor in 1933? Georges Bataille had noted in 1937 that it was a failure of Nazism to adopt violence as its main instrument: "Even in fascism itself authority has been reduced to founding itself on a so-called revolution—a hypocritical and forced homage to the only imposing authority, that of catastrophic change." Failed strategy or not, violence was an essential part of the revolution.[28] Sternhell argues that the idealists among the Nazi sympathizers probably did not approve of the murders, imprisonments, and beatings that accompanied the revolutionary storm but that they rejected liberal opinion for its opposition to the revolution.[29] De Man himself wrote in *Le Soir* for March 25, 1941, that the propaganda system of the democracies created an image of the German army as barbarians but that now that people have experienced "the perfect conduct of the highly civilized invader" they will be able to make their own choices and that they will be "revolutionary" compared to the convictions of yesterday: "The lesson of the events [the euphemism for the invasion and defeat] has been so clear that good sense is able to interpret them in only one way." Beyond such grotesque propaganda was a belief that the pervasive violence of an oppressive, colonialist class society could only be met with violence. The Europeans of this time were the first generations to have lived through a total war waged by professionals on a defenseless civilian population. There was little sympathy for the ruling classes in Europe. The self-styled revolutionaries thought that it was not only necessary but proper to oppose a righteous revolutionary violence to the violence of the establishment and thus there were few scruples about violence by those who knew that it was being used wantonly. And even the thinkers foresaw the need for violence. Carl Schmitt quoted approvingly Sorel's *Réflexions sur la violence.* Only the cowardly, intellectual bourgeois believes in stalling decisions until a peaceful agreement can be made. Democrats need to be reminded—as Trotsky reminded Kautsky—that "the awareness of relative truths never gives one the courage to use force and to spill blood." Beyond that, Schmitt writes in 1923—and these horrible words look forward to the war and concentration camps—that "the revolutionary use of force by the masses is an expression of immediate life, often wild and barbaric, but never systematically horrible and inhuman." How wrong can one be? Hitler figured out well how to channel mass support into an occasion for the use of a horror next to which the errors of the leaders in Europe during World War I pale by comparison.[30]

What most poignantly reveals the difficulty of neatly separating left and right in the 1930s is the case of Paul de Man's uncle, Hendrik de Man (1885–1953). In fact, a number of key figures on the right in the twentieth century had migrated there from the left. Mussolini himself started as a Marxist and identified himself with Marxism from 1902 to 1914. To recall that Mussolini was once a Marxist evokes surprise,[31] but Georges Sorel followed this route, and Hendrik de Man traces this intellectual destiny in a singular way.

De Man's swerve was a very important one to many Europeans because he was one of the major thinkers of Western socialism in the period after World War I. He wrote many books, some of which are still in print in English, and he has been the subject of a fair amount of scholarly discussion.[32] He had become the leader of the Belgian socialist party in 1939. Although he was not formally a member of a collaborationist government—in fact there was not, properly speaking, a collaborationist government in Belgium—Hendrik de Man was very influential in convincing many Belgians that cooperation with the invaders might lead to a socialist future that was better than the democratic past. He was the only important

Belgian political leader to support King Leopold II in his decision to surrender to the German army. Hendrik de Man came from the opposite side of the political spectrum from the Rexists, the extreme right-wing party that operated in Belgium thoughout the late thirties and put itself at the service of the Nazis when they took over the country. Peter Dodge, de Man's chronicler, asks some difficult questions about de Man's behavior:

> How are we to understand [the] actions and pronouncements [of de Man in 1939–40] on the part of a man whose books had been burned by the Nazis in 1933, whose entire life had been devoted to the construction of a social order in which coercion and inequality would be minimized, whose most notable political leadership in the "planiste" movement had been explicitly and emphatically justified in the name of anti-fascism?[33]

The answer, says Sternhell, is nationalism. Hendrik de Man lost faith in the revolutionary virtues of the proletariat and rejected the notion that a class could be the agent of change that transformed capitalism into socialism. De Man wrote in *Le Travail* on May 6, 1941, that the "socialism of tomorrow will no longer be a thing of one class, but of a whole nation, nay, even of all Europe."[34] Once he came to believe this de Man had traveled from the left to a position where he could cooperate with the Nazis. Their vile creed in its entirety may not have been his, but there was a basic agreement that nation and nation alone was the only agent capable of sweeping Europe of liberalism's bias toward the greedy individual and enable the world to rid itself of cultural despair. Sorel and Schmitt before de Man had already come to the conclusion that, as Schmitt puts it, "the energy of nationalism is greater than the myth of class conflict."[35] Such a switch was probably not very easy for Hendrik de Man and it came only after many years of slow change, but it came at the end of the 1930s and so just in time to benefit the Nazis, who would have found most supportive his urging the king of Belgium to neutrality and the explicit endorsement of the Nazi occupation in his manifesto to the members of the Belgian Workers' Party:

> . . . Do not believe that it is necessary to resist the occupying power; accept the fact of his victory and try rather to draw lessons therefrom so as to make of this the starting point for new social progress.
>
> The war has led to the debacle of the parliamentary regime and of the capitalist plutocracy in the so-called democracies.
>
> For the working classes and for socialism, this collapse of a decrepit world is, far from a disaster, a deliverance. . . . [T]he verdict of the war . . . condemns the systems where speeches take the place of action, where responsibilities are dissipated in the babble of meetings, where the slogan of individual liberty serves as a cushion for conservative egoism.

Social justice has not been able to develop from a system calling itself democratic but in which money powers and the professional politi-
cians in fact predominate. . . .

For years the double talk of the warmongers has concealed from you
that [the Nazi system], despite everything in it that strikes our mentality
as alien, had lessened class differences much more efficaciously than the
self-styled democracies, where capital continued to lay down the law.[36]

By all the other indices Hendrik de Man seems to have been a well-meaning
man. He never took a post in the Nazi regime. And he fled Belgium in November
1941 when he had no doubt figured out that the Nazis had used him to bring prestige to themselves but that they were not looking for colleagues who would be
equals in the task they had set for themselves of revolutionizing Europe. He was
convicted in absentia by the Belgian military tribunal, the Auditeur Générale, in
1945, and sentenced to twenty years in prison.

It remains difficult to understand Hendrik de Man's move from left to right,
and the difficulty we have says something no doubt about the inadequacies of our
categories and about the complexities involved in his and others' actions. But how
could left and right get so thoroughly mixed up? One possible avenue to understanding this problem is to consider the two-pronged attack on liberalism that is
being waged in our day by those on the left who feel that liberalism and
democracy place more of an emphasis on what is procedural within politics rather
than on developing a sense of the good life that might be led under its regime,
and those who feel that liberalism privileges the autonomous individual over the
community and who are searching for a communitarian philosophy that will replace the Rawlsian regime of individual rights. Such people are not "right
wingers," but they have begun a critique of democracy from within that has given
solace to a critique of democracy from without, and it is not entirely surprising
that there is a renewal of interest at this time in the works of Carl Schmitt, whom
I have quoted on a number of occasions. Perhaps it is difficult to understand Hendrik de Man in terms of our labels, but it would not be so difficult if we considered
the similarity of thinkers like de Man and Schmitt to contemporary demagogues
on left and right who distrust institutions.[37]

We cannot doubt that Hendrik de Man's example would have mattered greatly
to his nephew, a nephew with whom he was in any case very close personally.
They ate dinner together weekly. He had long been of great personal help to Paul
de Man, having supported him emotionally after his mother's death. The uncle
put in the word that got the nephew a job, and the nephew began to write.

Before laying out some of de Man's themes in *Le Soir*, one more caveat to the
reader. Ralf Dahrendorf warns that "no one who has not himself been led into
temptation has the right to pass moral judgment on others."[38] Even more relevant
to our problem of understanding are Sartre's thoughts in *What Is Literature?* He

speaks for all those of his generation who were "abruptly situated . . . brutally reintegrated into history." He says that the older generation was lucky. It was able to ignore all the tough decisions that were thrust upon his generation. He says that later generations will look back at this period and it will seem simple to judge. Things will have fallen into place and all will look inevitable, and in looking at history this way we the people to come whom Sartre addressed will have deprived him and his contemporaries of their freedom, argued Sartre, the freedom to be heroes or knaves: "The irreversibility of our age belonged only to us. We had to save or lose ourselves gropingly in this irreversible time. These events pounced on us like thieves and we had to do our job in the face of the incomprehensible and the untenable, to bet, to conjecture without evidence, to undertake in uncertainty and persevere without hope. Our age would be explained, but no one could keep it from having been inexplicable to us. No one could remove the bitter taste, the taste it will have had for us alone and which will disappear with us."[39]

Sartre was wrong, of course. The bitterness remains—even in the accounts of the war and its cost, and especially in reading the words with which some people sought at the time to justify it—but it should not blind us to the wisdom of what Sartre says. The events and decisions took place in a way those who have not experienced such a calamity cannot imagine. But the task of imagining it *is* ours. Walter Benjamin argued to the effect that the tendency of historians to empathize with the victor is a failure of the imagination that has a consequence: "Empathy with the victor invariably benefits the rulers."[40] When we read these lines we normally think: Right, the good people are always the losers and so it would be more virtuous to be on the side of the losers. But what about a case in which the losers are in fact the villains? In World War II the losers were the villains, yet by letting the texts of the villains drop out of the picture we are unfortunately blinding ourselves to the dialectic of history, a dialectic according to which, sadly, no document of barbarism is not at the same time a document of civilization. Reviewing the de Man papers of 1941–42 forces us to attend to both sides of this dialectic.

In its grandest moments the Nazi ideology "aimed at bringing about a total spiritual revolution."[41] How could one believe such a thing? De Man, by the evidence of his writings in 1941 and 1942, did. Philip Larkin in a poem that is a sort of secular prayer petitions that he might be one of the "less deceived"—less deceived by history, by one's place in life, and so on. De Man in this period, despite his intelligence and no doubt largely but not only because of family influences, was one of the more deceived. Saying this in no way mitigates the harm he may have caused others, however indirectly, by lending his intelligence to the service of those occupying Belgium. And in Belgium, as in Germany, elite support of the regime must have contributed to the consolidation of power.[42]

From the evidence of his writings de Man felt at ease and at home in the discourse of Nazi ideology and most damnably when he adopted the language of race and exclusion in the essay "The Jews in Contemporary Literature" (*Le Soir,*

March 4, 1941), which advances the notion that European literature would not be harmed were the Jews to be removed from Europe because the Jews have had little effect on that literature, which has remained pure in any case:

By preserving, despite the Semitic intrusion [*l'ingérence sémite*] into all aspects of European life, an originality and a character that have remained intact, our civilization has shown that it is healthy in its deep nature. Moreover, we can anticipate that a solution of the Jewish problem that would envisage the creation of a Jewish colony isolated from Europe, would not result, for the literary life of the West, in regrettable consequences. The latter would lose, all in all, some people of mediocre value, and would continue as in the past to develop according to its own great laws of evolution.

Arguing that it is no loss to literature to remove the Jews because they could not harm it anyway may be a tame form of anti-Semitism, a far cry from what he calls in the first lines of the essay "vulgar anti-Semitism" (referring possibly to Celine's *Bagatelles pour une massacre* and *Ecole pour cadavres*). This is still, in March 1941, months before the Wannsee Conference in January 1942 during which the plans for the Final Solution were laid out for the ministers of all the states of the Reich,[43] but the acceptance of the notion of exclusion is very clear. In propounding this notion he is working at the heart of the nationalist ideology.

If we think of the Nazi regime simply as a rule of terror we miss an important, even central, aspect of its way of working. At its core is the sense of community. Its effort is to restore the organic community, Gemeinschaft, to a world that has lost a sense of what community is all about thanks to modernization and its attendant evils. Anti-Semitism and the effort to exclude those who do not belong to the community is not an optional feature of the Nazi ideology. It is crucial. The legitimacy of the liberal state is based on the rule of law before whom all are equal. The Nazi state rejects liberalism lock, stock, and barrel and bases its legitimacy on group, that is, racial, membership. Peter Pulzer's *The Rise of Political Anti-Semitism in Germany and Austria* makes clear the historical link between nationalism and anti-Semitism.[44] In 1933 Georges Bataille saw very clearly that the awful brilliance of the Nationalist Socialist approach to legitimacy was its recourse to the notion of race: "National Socialist Germany . . . has not been afflicted with the theoretical difficulties [that afflict Mussolini's Italy]. . . . the mystical idea of race immediately affirmed itself as the imperative aim of the new fascist society; . . . Even though the conception of race lacks an objective base, it is nonetheless subjectively grounded, and the necessity of maintaining the racial value above all others obviated the need for a theory that made the State the principle of all value."[45] The Nazis put in the place of the social contract between so many autonomous monads a charismatic force that displaces the thin, abstract ties that so weakly bound the autonomous individuals of the liberal order.

There is a strong aestheticist, communitarian dimension of the appeal of Hitler's version of fascism. The recourse to nation solves with brutal simplicity a set of problems that are much too complex to be given such a single overarching solution. With their mass rallies and festivals the Nazis offered the simulacrum of a reconciliation of the two opposing poles of the modern political order, the individual and the collective. The Nazi aesthetic seems both to preserve and to overcome the isolation of the individual in modern life. This is one of the reasons why the nation becomes so important in order. We see in many of the texts of de Man from this period how important nationalism was. Two essays give voice to explicit anti-Semitism, but many are pervaded with cultural nationalism. Such nationalism differs from National Socialism in certain ways. For the National Socialist, race, blood, is the most important factor in politics. For the aesthetic nationalist—this is a way of thinking that goes back to Herder and the romantics—it is aesthetics, culture, that determines national politics because it is the source of identity, but it can be as anti-Semitic as Nazism.

Belief in this kind of nationalism has a number of consequences that we see in de Man's writings of 1941 and 1942. First is that it allows him to promote Flemish nationalism. In the early years of the Occupation the Germans allowed those who would sympathize with them to believe that German nationalism would foster the nationalism of other Caucasian nationalities. De Man, who would not have subscribed to the extreme right-wing nationalism of the Rexist party, still strongly supported Flemish nationalism and probably saw the Germans as allies against the hegemonic power of francophone culture in Flanders. He writes that "cultural division . . . governed these last years of the liberal era" (*Het Vlaamsche Land* [*HVL*] June 1, 1942) and this led to chaos, but now the situation has changed. Now Europeans can see that "the national essence of the nation" is "one of the foundations of all civilizations" (*HVL*, March 29–30, 1942). The paradox, as he sees it, of "the present revolution" is that national values of individual nations need to be encouraged as well as the spiritual values of a united Europe. The paradox can be solved by understanding that "European unity is possible only if national sentiments can freely come to expression and if every nation is fully conscious of its own worth and originality" (ibid.). This effort will best be furthered if people understand "the fundamental significance of Germany for the life of the entire West. . . . The entire continuity of a Western civilization depends on the unity of the people who are at its center" (*Le Soir*, May 16, 1942).

In order to promote his propagandistic view of the significance of Germany, de Man wrote a number of reviews of German books, novels in particular, that praised the German spirit, especially by way of contrast with the spirit of the French. This may have all been done with the sense that what hurts the French helps the Flemish, but that impulse does not seem to exhaust what is at work in these texts. There are a number of such reviews. A typical one is a review of *La Servante du pasteur,* a translation of a German novel by Ernst Wiechert. The basic constrast worked out here is that between the egocentric spirit (*une nature égocentricque*) of the typical French novelist versus the universal nature (*une nature universelle*) of a German novelist:

> *La Servante du pasteur* is sufficiently characteristic of the German novel so that its traits abstracted from context can represent the general aspects of German literature of the day. The atmosphere of this novel plunges us into a climate entirely different from that of the French novel. The contrast is between a spirit that features poetic, symbolic meditation rather than lucid clarity of analysis and in its verbal expression a spirit that privileges metaphorical and symbolic forms over precision of statement. But the main feature of the German novel that enables it to touch an entirely different part of our sensibility than a Proust, a Gide, or a Valéry touches is that instead of being the scene for the depiction of psychological details it rather dramatizes ethical behavior. The French novel studies and observes the manner in which appetites and inclinations develop within characters without preoccupying itself with judgments about morals or instincts. Driven in this regard by a praiseworthy care for objectivity, the French novelist always carefully avoids revealing the least preference for the behavior of any one of his characters or condemning them for any one of their acts. . . . The French novel is not, then, simple, since it sets itself forth within a form of speculation that is often complex, and it brings to life characters who are often unusual and whose actions and feelings are far from normal. Everything is different in a novel like *La Servante du pasteur*. It is not, as we have said, a psychological study, but a conflict between good and evil. . . . All is made sublime within this symbolic vision. . . . It is not surprising then that the men and women in this novel are very different from the ones one meets in a French novel. They are of extreme simplicity, all of one piece and always the same. They are like forces of nature.

The story and the conflict are both conducted on the exterior, not inside the characters. De Man then argues that

> what this rude and elementary art loses in rigor, it makes up for in poetry. The qualities of this novelist are those then of a poet: originality of vision, depth of emotion, and the musical virtue of language. . . . This tendency to depth, to love to search beneath exterior appearances for a hidden sense and then reveal its surrounding material objects with a climate of dreamy reverie is above all one of the eternal constants of the German artistic mentality. (*Le Soir*, August 5, 1941)

De Man never thoroughly disparages the French novel; he seems rather to be trying to make the best case for the German novel as such. And what may be more significant than the way he seeks to characterize the literary products of the different nations is that he thinks it is important and possible to define essential traits of nations at all. It is true that the way he characterizes the French associates them with the bourgeois order that is supposedly being swept away at that time. He contrasts in another review André Gide and Ernst Jünger. In Gide one gets "an incessant coming and going of characters, of psychological problems, and sentimental conflicts." Gide pursues endlessly "the search for the Self within the Totality." Gide emphasizes people. Jünger emphasizes things, "primitive forces," and his books move within the spheres where only primitive forces interact, "creating a serenity that is all the more pure the more black the chaos" (*Le Soir,* June 23, 1942). In another review of a book by Jünger he contrasts the French tradition, which since Stendhal has been a "work of explication, of intelligence," with the German tradition that creates narratives that are the "site of an encounter betweeen the eternally antagonistic forces of Good and Evil" (*Le Soir,* March 31, 1942).

De Man explains what is at stake in his contrast between the two traditions in an article entitled "French Literature since the Events" (*Le Soir,* January 20, 1942). There he remarks on the "persistence of the individualist spirit in France, a spirit given more to analysis than organizing others, and which is still not ready to abandon itself to the rapture of communal effort without staying to look at the past." Then he goes on to conclude: "Individualism survives, but it can no longer play a dominant role. . . . One sees the need finally in France of organizing power, and one senses that the future state will have to pass beyond that preoccupied with egoism." De Man shows himself to be fully in accord with a totalitarian, communitarian politics.

Another aspect of de Man's beliefs at this time is his adherence to historicism. The nationalist, anticapitalist, antidemocratic ideology that led to Nazism was based on the politics of cultural despair. That despair was in part based on historicist doctrine that history was either linear or cyclical and in any case continuous but that the trend was negative. Europe was a *Spätkultur,* a society in decline. When the hope for renewal emerged, the notion of history as regress was dropped for that of history as progress and evolution, but the notion of history as a teleology was retained. De Man uses the terminology of historicism on numerous occasions in the essays in *Le Soir* and *Het Vlaamsche Land.* In one review he gives expression to this belief by arguing that literary history is not "constituted by a dispersed and divided number of isolated works without the least unity. After all, literary history is the product of a people with one and the same historical and temporal alignment. . . . There exists an aesthetic determinism of which artists themselves are not conscious, the same determinism that is expressed in the course of history, which, after all, does seem to move around a number of constants" (*HVL,* June 7–8, 1942). In another article he states that "creative art does not run its course completely erratically and arbitrarily, but appears to arrange itself in certain forms — styles — that vanish and return in cyclical fashion" (*HVL,* March 29–30, 1942).

I have called attention to the historicist nature of de Man's thought at this time for three reasons: (1) it gives one more indication that his frame of mind in those years was formed by the historicist doctrine that permeated National Socialism; (2) the question of history is an important one for de Man early and late, but his way of dealing with the question from his earliest writings to his latest ones have some considerable differences; and (3) an awareness of the early de Man's implication in historicist thinking puts to rest the notion that the knowledge of history is an antidote to the fascism of the early de Man. He was himself a historicist. A different sort of historical consciousness is what is necessary to counteract what goes on in the earliest writings of de Man. De Man was not, even at this age, the sort of historicist who thought an age could be reduced to a single quality. In his critique of a book by noted French collaborationist Drieu La Rochelle he argued that whole ages cannot be reduced to a single aspect because they are too complex. There are, he says, many ways to characterize the present revolutionary age — an economist would say that it marks the definitive end of liberal economics, a politician would describe it in terms of the affirmation of national values against a sterile internationalism, and so on. But you cannot "consider history as if it were the faithful image of the abstract thought of philosophers" (*Le Soir,* December 9, 1941).

At the same time as he espoused these various elements of aesthetic nationalism, he also did not entirely toe the line. In fact, his aestheticism often overpowered his nationalism. Given what he frequently says in contrasting the French and German novel, he ought to have had few kind words to say when Paul Valéry came to a conference at the Beaux-Arts in Brussels. But in an article (*Le Soir,* January 11, 1942) he defended Valéry, a man "whom some might depict as frivolous and light," for precisely what he had otherwise criticized as negative in the French tradition — his analytic ability, his concern for language. He spoke of the considerable charm Valéry displayed when he interviewed him and then continued:

> From this conference and this conversation, the auditor saw what a curious impression Valéry makes on minds that are open and clearheaded because he confronts them with a multitude of problems that arise even in the most unsuspected places. All is subject to reflection for an attentive spirit who refuses to admit without verifying it himself any of the formulas already made that language puts at one's disposal. This continual necessity to reverify, to place in doubt, to find grounds for reservation, is a characteristic of all thought that is rigorous. And this characteristic is everywhere manifest in Valéry in his extreme care for exactitude and his constant preoccupation (evident in his written word and his eloquent speech) to make precise and circumscribe the sense of the words he uses. There is here not the true mark of a fastidious aesthete, but an inherent need for all who can claim intellectual probity.

He ends by saying that we cannot without disastrous consequences lose all respect for certain forms of human intelligence that are able to labor only within calm and serenity—and presumably far away from the revolutionary storm.

In other reviews he came to the defense of the French novel that had appeared so poor in comparison to the German novel. He judged various novels, Flemish and English ones, against the standard of the French novel and most often found them wanting. It is the French tradition of Gide and Proust that has established an *"esthétique nouvelle"* based on its concern with psychology, with interiority, and seen compared to the French tradition those non-French novels (other than German) are lacking precisely to the degree that they emphasize what is external to the characters as opposed to what is internal (*Le Soir,* June 10, 1941). The novel at an earlier stage—that of the realist and naturalist novel—emphasized the description of externals. The backward Flemish novel is still too much influenced by this earlier stage.

De Man reveals in these essays and reviews from 1941 and 1942, besides the nationalistic bias, that he is already on the way toward his great theme of the 1950s and early 1960s—inwardness, interiority. His aesthetic experience is primarily that of the novel, not poetry. It must be said that although he may have an inkling here of his great theme the essays are simply not comparable in quality or complexity with his later work. They represent the same person, a very smart person, working at a great rate (an essay or more per day) at a very early stage in his life. They are marginal texts and would be of no more interest than his slight essays for the student literary review *Les Cahiers du Libre Examen* were it not that they are part and parcel of a whole aesthetic politics that is de Man's starting point and that he hoped to have moved beyond in his writings in the 1950s and 1960s, but not without indirect comment as some of the essays included in this volume reveal.

## Inwardness

Much of romanticism is founded upon enchantment. The nationalism, political and aesthetic, that dominated Germany and other parts of Europe in the 1930s and 1940s was a consequence of certain aspects of romanticism. It brought with it its enchantments, and we now know that the young Paul de Man fell under the sway of these enchantments. For the romantic writers, as Harold Bloom has argued, enchantment was caught up in the dialectic with the resistance to enchantment, and "the most intense effort of the Romantic quest is made when the Promethean, Titanic stage is renounced and the purgatorial crisis that follows moves near to resolution."[46]

For Paul de Man, developing the resources for resistance was his main study throughout the rest of his career, and it is hard to understand the thrust of his work unless one knows how deep was the kind of enchantment from which he hoped to enable himself and others to extricate themselves. De Man was, like Daniel Bell, one of the "twice-born" intellectuals who came of age in the 1930s or early 1940s in an era of political absolutes and saw what those absolutes made themselves and others do, and tried to make themselves over afterward into different sorts of thinkers. They had seen the attractions of living "heroically" as ideologues, as people who exist at extremes and criticize ordinary folk for failing to live at the level of grandeur and who believe, as Bell says, that there is a genuine possibility that "the next moment could be actually a 'transforming moment' when salvation or revolution or genuine passion could be achieved." But they come to believe that "such chiliastic moments are illusions" and that "one's role can only be to reject all absolutes."[47]

For such people it became crucial to reject the ideology of action that dominated the 1930s and that had its representatives on left and right, and to set themselves the task of understanding what would be new bases of action, for only such an understanding could possibly enable one to resist the temptation offered by enchantment when it recurred, as it was bound to do. Such an effort to understand is what led de Man to his concern after the war with what he called inwardness.

It is conventional to separate de Man's intellectual career into two parts— before and after the turn to rhetoric. With the turn to rhetoric he seems to dispose of an existentialist concern for subjectivity and to espouse something like the notion of the death of the author by replacing the author with the famed mobile army of tropes and metaphors. This separation of his career takes the form of a narrative of progress, and it has fostered in a way that is all too familiar the idea that the latest stage not only supersedes but is superior to what came before it. But just as it greatly helps our understanding of de Man to see how his writings of 1941 and 1942 anchor him, if only to reveal that mind-set against which he worked the rest of his days, so the critical writings up through the essays in *Blindness and Insight* are useful, crucial, knowledge. They represent an effort to deal with a set of issues that would remain germane to his later writings.

The decentering effort of de Man's deconstructive phase is part and parcel of his concern in the 1950s and 1960s with inwardness. Decentering is not the alternative to inwardness; it is its complement.[48] In the late work of de Man we are, as he says, "no longer within a thematic context dominated by selfhood but in a figural representation of a structure of tropes," and this "radical negation of the self is in fact its recuperation," but importantly a recuperation without "pathos." The effort represented by his late work may undo selfhood, as he says in *Allegories of Reading,* but it replaces it with "the knowledge of [the self's] figural and epistemologically unreliable structure." De Man cannot tolerate the pathos of the self but must understand the structure of self-understanding (*AR,* pp. 186, 187, 175). The first essay in this volume, a term paper written for the great Diderot scholar, Herbert Dieckmann, at Harvard, and later published in Bataille's journal, *Critique,* concerns one of the great figures in the tradition of inwardness, Montaigne. In it de Man writes that

> Montaigne introduced a turn of mind whose originality and validity are forever admirable. Intuitively, without entering into the metaphysical ramifications of this decision, but with the vigor of an intelligence so beguiled by its own exercise that it cannot tolerate for a moment the notion of its own destruction, Montaigne escaped the impasse in which his axiomatic Pyrrhonism might have imprisoned him. If his subjectivity interposes an impassable screen between object and mind, then mind will be exercised on the level of this very screen and will find in the acknowledgment of its failure its only positive function. The main object of knowledge becomes the knowledge of its failure. Not of its limits; that would be a banal attitude. The limitation of knowledge is total, in simple as well as in complex problems, for that limitation is inscribed in the very constitution of knowledge, colors its every activity, great or small. But the lucid mind can know its own subjectivity, precisely at the point where subjectivity destroys its functioning. It recognizes that its life consists in an endless series of failures of this order, and it finds that it retains the power to take stock of them all. This power is asserted, thanks to an amazing change of sign, as a positive force; just when the mind falls into the despair of its impotence, it regains all its elasticity in perceiving this very impotence.

De Man's effort has been all along to understand "subjectivity, precisely at the point where subjectivity destroys its functioning." The consistency with which de Man dramatizes this very question illustrates what he calls "The recurrent symbiosis of the problems of understanding with those of selfhood" (*AR*, p. 175). This is not the place to lay out in full detail the lines connecting early and late de Man, but merely to suggest that within the body of his mature work there is a fair degree of continuity and that that continuity has to do with his concern for the structure of self-understanding and self-representation.

And the concern excludes that of the "pathos of the self." He writes those words in *Allegories of Reading,* but even from the very beginning de Man's turn inward was not toward an "existential self." On the contrary, it takes us beyond the self as usually understood, and to a fragmentation of experience that calls our ordinary notions of identity into question. To help understand why this might be so it is crucial to understand more about the context in which de Man's mind matured in the 1940s.

The intellectuals of the 1930s in France had attacked subjectivity, interiority. In his 1931 preface to the French translation of *A Farewell to Arms,* Drieu La Rochelle had celebrated the barbarian vitality of Hemingway as a welcome antidote to French decadence. Malraux in his 1933 preface to Faulkner's *Sanctuary* had praised American writing as a means to shake off the Proustian legacy of introspection and psychologizing. Sartre in lines I have already quoted praised Husserl's philosophy as a way of thinking that would allow people to confront things in themselves and no longer be imprisoned within their consciousnesses like Proustian characters. Thanks to Husserl we will be "delivered from Proust," says Sartre, "and delivered at the same time from the 'interior life.' " [49] But many thinkers came to feel well before the war ended that more attention was owed precisely to the interior life. If politics and philosophy and literature were to be relinked in some healthy way it could not be by subordinating literature and ideas to politics as the ideology of action so favored in the late 1930s and early 1940s did. The attack on interiority—an attack in which the young de Man himself had engaged—was part of the problem.

In texts like *The Transcendence of the Ego*, Sartre and other thinkers had been trying to reconceptualize the notion of the subject in a way that would separate subjectivity from subjectivism, from the personal self. The key text being studied at this same time in Paris to work out this problem was Hegel's *Phenomenology of Mind*, and the key figure in the Hegel revival was of course Alexandre Kojève. Kojève was working under the influence of Heidegger, whose *Being and Time* strongly directed Kojève's reading. In the thought of the mature Hegel subjectivity came to play a role it had not earlier. It was this emphasis on subjectivity that Kojève's lectures highlighted.

De Man may not have been a Hegelian straight down the line, but he acknowledged early and late his debts to Hegel. Foucault in 1970 asserted "Our entire epoch struggles to disengage itself from Hegel."[50] But de Man never associated himself with the effort to go "beyond Hegel." For him the claim to have left Hegel behind was no better than a delusion. "Whether we know it, or like it, or not," he said, "most of us are Hegelians and quite orthodox ones at that. . . . Few thinkers have so many disciples who never read a word of their master's writings."[51]

For de Man, following Kojève, Hegel was "the theoretician of internalization"; "the commanding metaphor that organizes the entire system is interiorization." Kojève had argued that "philosophy cannot content itself with being a philosophy of nature" and that "human reality, or the I, is not then a natural or an immediate reality but a dialectical or mediated reality," for "man differs essentially from nature, and he differs not only in the realm of thought alone but in his activities as well." Kojève conceived of Hegel in a very Heideggerian way, not as the thinker of Absolute Spirit, not of the totality, but rather as a thinker of "negation" and separation, and so for him the emphasis fell on the moment of the "unhappy consciousness."[52]

Kojève taught his courses on Hegel at the Ecole des Hautes-Etudes from 1933 to 1939. By the end of the war Hegel was being discussed more and more. Jean Wahl's *Le Malheur de la conscience dans la philosophie de Hegel* had appeared in 1929 and his lectures, along with Kojève's, led many readers to Hegel. (De

Man had considered writing a thesis on Hegel and Hölderlin under Wahl before deciding to come to America, and de Man delivered his paper "Process and Poetry" [collected here] to Wahl's seminar, the Collège de Philosophie, in Paris in the mid-1950s.) The major treatise on Hegel at this time was Jean Hyppolite's *Génése et structure de la Phénoménologie de l'esprit de Hegel,* which appeared in 1946 and marked a great advance in Hegel scholarship in French. Hyppolite noted in 1946 that "most contemporary thinkers . . . criticize Hegel's system as a system. They generally prefer what Hegel calls 'unhappy consciousness' to what he calls 'spirit.' "[53] The contemporaries Hyppolite mentions certainly included de Man, who even in the 1980s reflected his early training and disposition to take Hegel seriously as indicated in the following words: "If there ever was a philosophy of necessary separation, it is Hegel's; to assimilate the notion of Absolute Spirit with idealist reconciliation is to simplify all the way to misprision."[54]

De Man in the lines I have just quoted is following here not just Kojève, Heidegger, and Wahl but also that diverse set of literary figures that includes Georges Bataille, Maurice Blanchot, Pierre Klossowski, and others. It was they who even during the war were working out the consequences of the Heideggerian version of Hegel for the writing and reading of literature. What they developed was first of all a thematic of separation, death, and temporality that might well have seemed to some to be inflected with pathos (as even de Man recognized in *AR*). It is a thematic one can see at work in Blanchot's *The Gaze of Orpheus* and *The Space of Literature* as well as in de Man's essays up to *Blindness and Insight*. It permeates the part of his dissertation that is devoted to connecting Mallarmé and Hegel. But beyond the thematic there is the preoccupation with the problem of the self that appears very clearly in the texts Bataille wrote during the war, *L'Expérience intérieure* (1943) and *Le Coupable* (1944).[55]

There seem to be within our modernity at least two grand avenues for thought to follow. One identifies spirit or mind with nature and the other separates the two realms. One adheres to and follows out the implications of the Principle of Identity and the other the Principle of Negation. Hegel and Coleridge and other exponents of totality populate the first camp. Heidegger's Hegel, the Heidegger not of *Geist* but of *Riss* (conflict), Adorno, and the followers of the French Hegel of the 1940s inhabit the second camp. Convinced that death considered in the abstract separates us forever from nature, exponents of negation believe we can do no better than to try to understand the structure of our failure to know, to connect with nature, to make word and object cohere. It is for this reason that such thinkers may become proponents of interiority. It is interiority that such people feel we must come to understand, and they seek to represent the struggle for such self-understanding in their literary texts and philosophical treatises. It is for this reason that one of the most significant aesthetic efforts imaginable in our modern times is Proust's attempt to represent "cette perpétuelle erreur, qui est précisément la 'vie' " (the epigraph to the first edition of *Blindness and Insight,* dropped by mistake I daresay, speaking as one of those responsible, from the second edition).

Sartre remained the adamant enemy of Proustian introspection after the war just as he had been before it. For him the lesson of the war seemed to be that the analytic cast of mind associated by de Man in his texts of 1941 and 1942 with the cerebral and decadent culture of France still needed to be overcome. Sartre wrote these sharp words in the manifesto announcing his journal of the postwar years, *Les Temps modernes:*

> The legend of the irresponsibility of the poet . . . derives its origin from the analytic cast of mind. Since bourgeois authors themselves think of themselves as peas in a can, the solidarity binding them to other men seems strictly *mechanical* to them—a matter, that is, of mere juxtaposition. Even if they have an exalted sense of their literary mission, they think they have done enough once they have described their own nature or that of their friends: since all men are made the same, they will have rendered a service to all by teaching each man about himself. And since the initial postulate from which they speak is the primacy of analysis, it seems quite simple to make use of the analytic method in order to attain self-knowledge. Such is the origin of intellectualist psychology, whose most polished exemplar we find in the works of Proust. As a pederast, Proust thought he could make use of his homosexual experience in depicting Swann's love for Odette; as a bourgeois, he presents the sentiments of a rich and idle bourgeois for a kept woman as the prototype of love, the reason being that he believes in the existence of universal passions whose mechanism does not vary substantially when there is a change in the sexual characteristics, social condition, nature, or era of the individuals experiencing them. Having thus "isolated" those immutable emotions, he can attempt to reduce them, in turn, to elementary particles. Faithful to the postulates of the analytic cast of mind, he does not even imagine that there might be a dialectic of feelings—he imagines only a mechanics. Thus does social atomism, the entrenched outpost of the contemporary bourgeoisie, entail psychological atomism. Proust chose himself to be bourgeois. He made himself into an accomplice of bourgeois propaganda, since his work contributes to the dissemination of the myth of human nature.
>
> We are convinced that the analytic spirit has had its day and that its sole function at present is to confuse revolutionary consciousness and to isolate men for the benefit of the privileged classes. We no longer believe in Proust's intellectualist psychology, and we regard it as nefarious. [56]

For Sartre the psychologistic novel is an exercise in narcissism and little better than a *New Yorker* ad for bourgeois life. He has rejected the emphasis on "l'expérience intérieure" in Proust and in others as his uncomprehending 1943 review of Bataille's book of that name reveals.[57]

The task many writers set for themselves in the 1930s and 1940s was the same: to answer the question posed baldly by Michel Leiris in his 1947 autobiography *Manhood:* "Can the fact of writing ever involve, for the man who makes it his profession, a danger which if not mortal is at least positive?" Leiris sought in *Manhood* "to write a book that is an act."[58] Those who followed Sartre believed that the notion of engagement in some way solved the question. But many argued with Sartre, from Adorno to Bataille to Blanchot and on to the young Roland Barthes whose *Writing Degree Zero* was meant to rebut the claims of Sartre. Heidegger, whom Sartre claimed as an authority, rejected Sartre's idea that existentialism is a humanism in the rebuke, *Letter on Humanism* (1947): "The basic tenet of 'existentialism' has nothing at all in common with the statement from *Being and Time*."[59]

Derrida commented much later on the contretemps between Heidegger and Sartre that "it is astonishing and highly significant that at the moment when the authority of Husserlian thought was asserted [as it was in Sartre] and then established in postwar France, even becoming a kind of metaphysical mode, the critique of anthropologism remained totally unnoticed, or in any event without effect."[60] Derrida's point in part is that Sartre so emphasized the person, the manhood of the writer or thinker that he could not see the point of Husserl's or Heidegger's philosophy of reflection, which was to emphasize not the person but rather "the reflexivity or 'specular' freedom of human consciousness to reflect on its own engagement with the world and on the mirroring mind's necessary, if frequently occluded, structural limits."[61]

These structural limits were exactly what Hyppolite emphasized in his interpretation of the unhappy consciousness of Hegel, what Hegel calls "a consciousness absolutely entangled in its confusions and self-reversals." Hyppolite presents Hegel's notion of consciousness this way:

> Changeable, having no essence, "it is the consciousness of its own contradiction." The consciousness of life which discovers that life as presented to it is not genuine life but only contingency is here identified with the consciousness of contradiction, that is, the consciousness of the I that is internally rent. . . . This unhappy consciousness is subjectivity, which aspires to the repose of unity; it is self-consciousness as consciousness of life and of what exceeds life. But it can only oscillate between these two moments.[62]

This abstract consciousness is exactly what the heterodox tradition de Man emulated (and whose proponents he worked with on *Critique* and elsewhere) would focus upon, even though the difficulties of keeping clear the distinction between the ontological self and the personal self and keeping the notion of consciousness strictly impersonal would prove difficult given the pathos inherent in phrases like "unhappy consciousness" and the use of the idea of death, which however universal an occurrence tends to be read existentially. It is such circularity that would give rise to the anthropologism that is the subject of de Man's 1966 essay on Blanchot. Blanchot himself was not guilty of anthropologism, but even his austere work showed what difficulties attended this way of thinking.

De Man in the essay on Blanchot as well as elsewhere aligns himself with those who had been seeking since the 1930s to understand interiority in an impersonal sense. The language one used presented a problem. Bataille had tried to explain things in a critique of Sartre's book on Genet by stating that

> Finally, what is, for us, is scandal. Consciousness of being is the scandal of consciousness, and we cannot—indeed, we must not, be surprised. But we must not be taken in by words. Scandal is the same thing as consciousness: a consciousness without scandal is alienated consciousness—a consciousness, experience proves it, of clear and distinct objects, intelligible, or thought to be so.[63]

In the end the difficulty of getting straight such a point would lead some thinkers to conspire to kill the author and thereby to the so-called death of the author in order to make absolutely clear that a critique of "anthropologism" was being advanced. The goal of understanding subjectivity in the abstract in order to render clear the negative implications of such a way of thinking for the naive understanding of how word and object and word and deed connected made it necessary to generalize and depersonalize the notion of consciousness. (This is anything but *Newsweek* existentialism.) Just as subjectivity became inflected, the individual subject began to lose significance. But the language still led those who did not appreciate the thought behind the ideas to personalize. So the polemic of the "death of the author" was developed to remove the physical person of the author from the scene of writing. The polemic has not been altogether successful, since those who do not appreciate the thought behind it take it literally, as if those who argued for the death of the author wanted to kill off individual authors, shirk personal responsibility, and lead the populace to embrace nihilism. The point of the polemic is best captured by a few rare poets—poets like Celan, who wrote

> es sind
> noch Lieder zu singen jenseits
> der Menschen.

> [there are
> still songs to be sung on the other side
> of Mankind.][64]

Or John Ashbery, who writes of the scandal that is consciousness when he says in "Self-Portrait in Convex Mirror" that the scandal is

that the soul is not a soul,
has no secret, is small, and it fits
into its hollow perfectly: its room, our moment of
attention.[65]

De Man's primary aesthetic experience before 1945 was that of the novel. Coming of age for a second time as a twice-born intellectual amidst Wahl, Hyppolite, Bataille, and others gave him a much larger framework for understanding the experiments in exploring consciousness that the novels of Proust, Woolf, Kafka, Faulkner, and others constituted. It provided thereby a way for changing his direction and allowing him to see the point of a set of literary works that he had no doubt appreciated but had been willing to criticize as a young ideologue. It gave him the chance to clarify the reasons he might not want to emulate Sartre, who seemed in de Man's eyes too eager after the war to become the ideologue he had not been in the 1930s. It also gave him the chance to develop himself, thanks to the ideas of Hegel as mediated and rendered more problematic in a productive way by Kojève and Heidegger, and to reinvestigate the gap that the ideologue tends to ignore between idea and act. At the heart of what he learned from these thinkers was a form of dualism that made him see the realm of spirit and the world of objects (to use very broad terms) as related only indirectly. This dualism is called in Hegel and Heidegger negation. Negation, said Heidegger in *What Is Metaphysics?*, "permeates all thought."[66] Negation does not undermine all connections but it problematizes them and it makes the highest priority the understanding of the structure of subjectivity, as de Man says in his Montaigne essay. This is an intellectual imperative, the imperative to understand the world from the vantage point of inwardness, but it is also more than that, as de Man suggests at various points in this book. It is for him a moral and political imperative. The essay in this volume entitled "The Inward Generation" confronts this issue, but a long footnote in de Man's 1960 dissertation on Mallarmé might usefully be cited here since it comes back to Sartre and some of the issues we have been touching upon:

Thus confronted with his times, the writer can legitimately ask whether his effort should not be primarily directed towards the times rather than towards the work, whether political action should not take precedence over poetic speculation. In our own age, this has become the very familiar problem of "literature engagée"—a problem which should indeed be considered in relation to dramatic media rather than, as in Sartre's *What Is Literature?*, in relation to the novel, itself a confusingly ambiguous genre. Contrary to what is often assumed to be the case, Mallarmé was very seriously concerned with this choice. He had the advantage of facing the problem when he had reached a considerable degree of intellectual maturity. This made it possible for him to avoid the mistake committed by many in our own, political half-century, who have recourse to collective, historical aspects of reality as a means to dodge the problems of their own, individual consciousness. (I am not thinking so much of Marxist or pseudo-Marxist attitudes as in Sartre of Lukács—for there, occasional and obvious bad faith is often merely strategic and, hence, philosophically harmless—but rather of the veiled exploitation of existential historicism in Jaspers and in Heidegger.) Mallarmé's attitude on this point is admirably uncompromising: the way to be present to one's time begins in total inwardness, certainly not out of indifference towards history, but because the urgency of one's concern demands a lucid self-insight; action will follow from itself, when this insight has been gained:

"Aussi garde-toi et sois là.

La poésie, sacre; qui essaie, en de chastes crises isolément, pendant l'autre gestation en train." ("L'Action restreinte")[67]

Thus, be there and stand back.

Poetry, that sacred trust, assays, in chaste crises, in isolation, while the other gestation proceeds.

In 1983 de Man projected writing a book on the aesthetic ideology that would have centered on Hegel.[68] The critique of the aesthetic ideology, of aesthetic nationalism, of romantic anticapitalism began here with inwardness and more generally with the notion of negation, the noncoincidence of self (understood in the abstract sense only) and world. In Kojève's words: "Man differs essentially from Nature, and he differs from it not only because of his thought but also because of his action."[69] If this is the case, then it followed for de Man, mutatis mutandi, that literature could not and should not be brought in alignment with either state or ideology. Literature was not "beyond ideology," but its relation to ideology had to remain problematic lest ideology work to enchant literature and people as it had in the 1930s and early 1940s.

For this reason de Man, following Bataille and others, felt Sartre was taking exactly the wrong tack after the war. De Man reveals little sympathy for Sartre and Camus in the essays included here, and the rebuke he delivered to both was one he might have felt his earlier self deserved to receive, but even more strongly. He speaks in "The Inward Generation" of the political writers of the 1930s— Malraux, Ernst Jünger, Pound, Hemingway—in a way that pertains just as well to his earlier self: "All these men were forcefully committed politically, but their convictions proved so frail that they ended up by writing off this part of their lives altogether, as a momentary aberration, a step toward finding themselves." So frail *and* so factitious, but the large point is that in de Man's later way of regarding things he comes to approximate another thinker influenced by Hegel, Adorno, who wrote in his essay "Commitment" that "it is not the office of art to spotlight

alternatives, but to resist by its form alone the course of the world, which permanently puts a pistol to men's heads" and argued against Sartre that "this is not a
time for political art, and nowhere more so than where it seems to be politically
dead."[70] Such, indeed, is the art of Mallarmé that de Man defends in these pages.
Sartre in his essay "Mallarmé: The Poetry of Suicide" had argued that we find
in Mallarmé little more than "the outline of a metaphysics of despair."[71] The
Beckett Adorno defended in his critique of Sartre's committed literature may appear to many as writer of the same nihilist sort. De Man presents Mallarmé as
the poet who has indeed solved the problem Leiris posed of how to write literature
that is an act because he has "a conception of the poetic as a privileged action,
the only one by which the possibility of a new innocence and of a possible future,
beyond negation, can still be conceived." In this sense Mallarmé writes truly
historical poetry. Here de Man may be following Heidegger, who had written:
"Only authentic temporality which is at the same time finite, makes possible
something like fate—that is to say authentic historicality."[72]

De Man's concern for "inwardness" links him to the heterodox tradition of dis-
sident French critics and philosophers, and it also stands behind his late project
to set out in detail a critique of the aesthetic ideology, but it does more than that.
The experience of inwardness is a specifically "romantic" experience, and his understanding of self and consciousness enabled what was his most successful academic achievement and that was—working in concert of course with many others,
most notably Geoffrey Hartman and Harold Bloom—the simultaneous disposal of
the New Critics and the reestablishment of the centrality of the romantics from
Rousseau, Wordsworth, and Keats onward. He remarks in his 1966 "Introduction
to Keats" (included here) that "our criticism of romanticism so often misses the
mark: for the great romantics, consciousness of the self was the first and necessary step toward moral judgment." We hear in these words the emphasis on inwardness and self that motivates de Man's early work, but we also hear him learning to apply them to a body of literature. With his writings on the romantics de
Man's American work truly begins, and the role he will play, not as a follower
of Bataille and Blanchot but as a practical critic, becomes more apparent.

## America and the New Criticism

In America there was no sense of the tradition of thought that derived from
the new French Hegel, from Husserl, Heidegger, Kojève, and Hyppolite, of the
tradition that had been given literary articulation by Bataille, Blanchot, and
others. For those Americans who were concerned with it, French thought in the
postwar period meant Sartre and then Camus. The philosopher Jean Wahl had
taught during the war at Smith College, but Sartre's brand of existentialism—the
"humanistic" version rejected by Heidegger—dominated American views of
French intellectual life. The way was not prepared for de Man. He could, per-

haps, convince Dwight Macdonald to print one essay by Bataille in *Politics,* but that was all.[73] The literary philosophical concern for interiority that flourished among certain writers in France had no analogue in America. But although the way was not prepared for de Man, the situation was one where he could have some considerable effect, especially among the literary, given the nature of the resistance to the category of subjectivity — his preoccupation — in the Anglo-American world of literary criticism.

The year 1957 was probably the apogee for the literary modernism that was fostered by Eliot and Pound and the critical school of New Criticism that sprang up to promulgate, as it were, the ideas and values that the modernists espoused. It was in that year that Northrop Frye published his *Anatomy of Criticism,* a book that more than anything by I. A. Richards gave the luster of science to the literary profession while not failing to capitalize on the religious motivation that inspired so many of the writers and scholars who wrote after Eliot. Even though 1957 may have been the apogee of New Criticism, the whole of the 1950s were the glory years for the movement. Even those like Kenneth Burke who know that its ideas were wanting had to recognize its ascendance in the field. A certain cockiness is even evident in the writings of some New Critics who doubted that any other Western countries had reached such a level of sophistication as the critics of England and America.[74]

Although the modernists and the New Critics had triumphed, there was real dissatisfaction with the emerging orthodoxy. Another set of voices, from William Carlos Williams to the Beats and on to — even amidst the modernists — Randall Jarrell, protested the systematizing of literature. The tragedy of Delmore Schwartz is relevant here. It is hardly an exaggeration to say that this young man, who could craft wonderful first lines of poems but could not make what followed them much more than a pastiche of Auden, Eliot, Yeats, and so on, died of asphyxiation in the oxygen-depleted room that was created by the combined triumph of modernist poetry and New Criticism. John Berryman could at least joke about the situation: "I didn't want my next poem to be *exactly* like Yeats or exactly like Auden since in that case where the hell was *I* ? But what instead *did* I want it to sound like?"[75]

Randall Jarrell delivered the most eloquent of the protests launched against the enslavement of poetry in his essay "The Age of Criticism." In his lament he asked rhetorically, "How many of us seem to think that the poem or story is in some sense 'data' or 'raw material' which the critic cooks up into understanding, so that we say, 'I'd never *read* "We are seven" till I got so-and-so's analysis of it for Christmas!' " Then he answered: "The work of art is as done as it will ever get, and all the critics in the world can't make its crust a bit browner." The critic insists on turning poetry into image patterns or ideas despite (and in spite of) the experience of readers. Jarrell contrasted two groups: "Readers, real readers, are almost as wild a species as writers; most critics are so domesticated as to seem institutions."[76]

Criticism in the heyday of New Criticism had tamed poetry. Yves Bonnefoy in an acute essay from 1958, "Critics—English and French," contrasted English and American criticism with that of the French by claiming that the anglophone critics, despite professed interest in ambiguity and metaphor in language, were primarily interested in meaning, the public meaning of a literary work.[77] This all may have worked to the advantage of teaching students communication arts (as I. A. Richards had argued it would), but it was dispiriting for poets who were just as interested, if not more so, in words as in ideas. The problem for poets was that the critical industry threatened to co-opt every single line of poetry and recycle it for its own purposes. What was lost in this process, some argued, was the poetry, poetry whose capacity to give rude pleasure vanished under the scrutiny of the professors and their diligent students.

New Criticism is often dismissed as a mere formalism because of its attention to the specifics of image patterns and its well-noted rejection of "extrinsic" matters such as history, the life of the writer, and so on. But New Criticism had an appeal and an agenda that went far beyond that of sheer abstract formalisms. It included a social critique that originated on the right with T. S. Eliot, Pound, and the Agrarians but that migrated to the liberal left in the *Partisan Review* crowd. It connects to a long tradition in the modern world that has sought to give poetry dignity among those who care little for it as well as to have it fulfill the social function of religion. Major figures in the tradition from Coleridge on to Eliot, Frye, and Wimsatt have been moved by religious conviction. So the appeal of the movement was broad even though there may have been those who were dissatisfied with it.

Because its appeal was complex and in some ways hidden, it would have been difficult to attack let alone grasp by a newcomer like Paul de Man. One conviction that might have linked many modernists and New Critics and that would have also made his new situation all the more foreign to de Man was the long-term hostility in American criticism to notions of subjectivity and inwardness. Eliot and Pound made it a criterion of good poetry that it be impersonal. "Poetry is not a turning loose of emotion, but an escape from emotion; it is not the expression of personality, but an escape from personality," wrote Eliot.[78]

When he arrived in America de Man might have discovered that the problem his European mentors had been struggling with for decades had been solved to the satisfaction of many literary Americans years before. The way to separate subjectivity from subjectivism, the transcendental consciousness from the personal one, was by rejecting both. The key figure in this effort was not Eliot but his teacher at Harvard, Irving Babbitt, who had argued that one entailed the other; and so baby and bathwater were both tossed out. The New Humanism Babbitt promoted needed to base itself, he thought, on something more solid than the subjectivist thought of Rousseau. Babbitt's New Humanism rejected all the residues of the revolutionary impulse. Eliot simply traced out the consequences of such a move when he declared himself a royalist and a classicist and became a High Church Anglican. The young Robert Lowell got the point and converted to Catholicism. Delmore Schwartz may have come to realize that the club was intended to exclude him. T. S. Eliot in 1933 in his lectures at the University of Virginia explicitly stated his doubt that the West need do more to accommodate "free-thinking" Jews. The club was certainly not set up to give comfort to the non-believer.

Babbitt's great ally, his student T. S. Eliot, rewrote literary history to undermine the periods in which the emphasis on subjectivism he and Babbitt found in Rousseau had any dominance. The great thing for a poet was to find an "objective correlative" for his or her ideas to subordinate feeling to "wit." The result was an organic wholeness, in which "wit is not only combined with, but focused into, the imagination" and gives the reader "a direct sensuous apprehension of thought." The alternative was the dreaded "dissociation of sensibility,"[79] the failure to subordinate feeling to reason that sets in when there is any undue emphasis on the person of the poet. Eliot believed he could rather precisely date time periods in which this dissociation of sensibility was acutely felt, and notable among them were the moments of the English Revolution and romanticism. This allowed him to write off vast tracts in literary history and such troubling figures as Milton and Shelley. During the heyday of New Criticism one pursued an interest in such unfashionable poets as Shelley at one's own peril.

The key doctrine for New Critical pedagogy was that of the literary symbol, the metaphor that incarnated an idea. Incarnation was the right word, given the religious conviction that underlay this notion. In 1960 de Man wrote that "the priority of the natural object remains unchallenged among the inheritors of romanticism" (*RR*, p.9). De Man argued against Eliot that the "spirit cannot coincide with its object" (*BI*, p. 237). Many in those days blamed language for this failure. They trusted ideas, but distrusted words. Their experience was like the one recounted by Hugo von Hofmannsthal in his "Letter to Lord Chandos." Far preferable to Lord Chandos would have been communication by means of inanimate objects rather than slippery words.

Twentieth-century poetry and criticism present all too many instances of writers seeking a whole set of halfway solutions, out-of-court settlements by means of a plea bargaining that would have, they hoped, reconciled them with the world of things. They feared language would obstruct justice, and so took justice in their own hands. The schoolbooks, the poetry primers, are full of talk of objective correlatives, epiphanies, apotheoses, incarnation, concrete universals, literary symbols. All are compromises rigged up by one or another poet or critic from Coleridge to Eliot on down who hoped he or she could escape the human condition, hoped possibly out of religious conviction that his or her poetry could provide a straight way through to things themselves, to the really real. But as

Valéry says, "Hope is only man's mistrust of the clear foresight of his mind."[80] Some unfortunately were deprived of that foresight.

John Crowe Ransom advertised in the title of a noted essay, "Wanted: An Ontological Critic." All he had to do was look all around him. Since the time of the imagists poetry had been promoted as a form of ontology. The imagist May Sinclair stated in 1915: "What the Imagists are 'out for' is direct naked contact with reality."[81] T. S. Eliot was no naive adherent of imagist doctrine. Yet he too argued that the truest poetry is the most transparent: "Language in a healthy state presents the object, is so close to the object that the two are identified." Eliot praised John Donne and other poets in whose language, he argued, "sensation became word and word was sensation."[82] The predicament that developed is described well in the 1950s by Jarrell and also usefully surveyed by Robert Pinsky in his 1976 book *The Situation of Poetry*. Modern poets sought an escape from abstraction and recurrence—characteristics of poetry that are also essential aspects of language—by attempting to give their poetic words the status of things. Pinsky wrote, "Modern poetry often expressed or implied certain persistent ambitions, ambitions which have to do with giving the poem some of the status of an object or phenomenon, rather than a statement. . . . Pound tells us to go in fear of abstractions."[83] But Eliot, Pound, and their followers are the victims of a false dichotomy. The choice is not between the abstract diction of Pope and the concreteness espoused by Pound. Poetry (because it is language) can never be reduced to a proposition, nor can poetry (because it is language) ever escape the fate of words. Robert Creeley writes:

> . . . I hate the metaphors,
> I want you.[84]

Here is a paradox: a poet who wants to be anywhere outside the confines of the poem. He hates the fuss with words. For such a poet every word is a problem because it is the opposite of a sensory particular. The most pressing task of the poet becomes the effort to write lines in which word and object can coincide. The criticism that is written in line with such an assessment of poetry will praise reconciliation as Lionel Trilling does when he praises the "imaginative reason" of Matthew Arnold that "closed the gap between head and heart, between feelings and intellect,"[85] and as M. H. Abrams does when he calls Wordsworth's poetry "an attempt . . . to overcome the sense of man's alienation from the world by healing the cleavage between subject and object."[86]

For de Man the separation of subject from object was absolute. This separation was one of Hegel's great themes, one that had been highlighted by Kojève. De Man had a different sense of the "power of the mind over the universe of death," to use Wordsworth's words, because of his appreciation of interiority. He had certainly read Sartre's *Transcendence of the Ego* and *The Psychology of the Imagination,* which date from the 1930s and represent Sartre under the influence of Husserl and with a more complex notion of subjectivity than he would develop later. In *The Psychology of the Imagination* de Man would have read about the "intentional structure of the image" and that we must "rid ourselves of the illusion of immanence. . . . the object of the image is not itself an image. . . . The object is, therefore, a correlative of a certain synthetic act, which includes among its structures a certain knowledge and a certain 'intention.' The intention is at the center of consciousness: it is the intention that envisages the object, that is, which makes it what it is." In other words, "consciousness is of course not in bondage to objects but to itself."[87] The emphasis falls on the world as directly presented to or constituted by the subject with no idea of a communion of subject and object. De Man might also have learned of these ideas directly from Husserl himself either in German or in the 1931 French translation of *Cartesian Meditations* by Gabrielle Peiffer and Emmanuel Levinas. The ideas Sartre stated were those of Husserl. It was Husserl who strenuously emphasized, following Franz Brentano, that " 'intentionality' is the fundamental characteristic of 'psychic phenomena.' The 'object' is 'given' to us only in 'consciousness.' And every grounding, every showing of truth and being, goes on wholly within myself." And it was Husserl who first stated the notion of significance of subjectivity that Derrida has famously stated in the line "Il n'y a pas de hors texte": "Transcendency in every form is an immanent existential characteristic, constituted within the ego. Every imaginable sense, every imaginable being, whether the latter is called immanent or transcendent, falls within the domain of transcendental subjectivity, as the subjectivity that constitutes sense and being. The attempt to conceive the universe of true being as something lying outside the universe of possible consciousness, possible knowledge, possible evidence, the two being related to one another merely externally by a rigid law is nonsense. . . . If transcendental subjectivity is the universe of possible sense, then an outside is precisely—nonsense."[88] When de Man talks about Montaigne and transcendence in the essay of that title included in this volume, he means "transcendence" in the sense that Husserl uses the word. In his essays "Form and *Intent* in American New Criticism" (in *Blindness and Insight*) and "The *Intentional* Structure of the Romantic Image," (emphasis added), he is pointing to Husserl just as surely as Derrida does in his famous line calling into question the clichéd distinction between inside and outside.

Such concern for the mediating effect of language and of consciousness on our appropriation of the objects of the world would make de Man particularly appreciative of Heidegger's text "The Origin of the Work of Art," an essay no doubt in part inspired by Husserl and an essay that had a great effect on de Man and must have made him particularly sensitive and critical of the incarnationalist aesthetic of the New Criticism with its organicist notions of the literary symbol.

In his decisive critique of the form/matter distinction, "The Origin of the Work of Art," Heidegger argued that art has been so far helpless against the forces that privilege representation and think of art as representing objects because "representation has at its command a conceptual meaning that nothing is capable of withstanding." Form and matter may be clichés, hackneyed concepts, but they dominate all art theory and aesthetics. Nonetheless we have to stop thinking of the materiality of the text as if it were some sort of defect. If we think of the poem as something that is just supposed to produce a state of mind in us, we will be thinking of it instrumentally, and its materiality will have very little significance for us. However, the medium of art is not a mere instrument. The purpose of art is to privilege its medium. The work of art "does not cause the material to disappear, but rather causes it to come forth for the very first time." Poetry "sets (language) free to be nothing but itself."[89] Heidegger orients his theory toward the materiality of the medium. What proposition, after all, could adequately take the place of the artistry of a Grecian temple? The poem, like the temple, is not a self-consuming artifact. The paraphrase of a poem is no substitute for the poem itself. As long as form and matter are neatly distinguishable, and form and meaning are privileged over language, the task of poetry will seem to be making language subordinate and having work and object coincide. Against this view Heidegger argued that the work of art should be an "instigation" to "strife." The goal of art is not to harmonize our experiences of the world in some "insipid agreement," to resolve the so-called tensions, but rather to let strife remain strife. Heidegger argues that the work of art can set forth this strife, thereby winning its purchase on truth. What de Man took from Heidegger on art is a principle of negation or incommensurability that would stipulate that in art idea and medium can never so perfectly cohere that the medium can drop out of the picture rendering transparent the idea, but the principle of negation is at the same time an affirmation, an affirmation of the crucial import of the medium itself.

De Man's education in the ideas of Husserl and Heidegger made it impossible for him to accept many of the tenets of New Critical practice. He could admire the New Critics' attention to the text, their commitment to reading, but at the same time—as the foreword to Carol Jacobs's book makes clear—he felt there were real limitations in New Critical practice. And so he argued for the notion of intentionality:

> The intentional factor has been bypassed. A clarification of the notion of "intent" is of great importance for an evaluation of American criticism, for at the rare moments when the New Critics consented to express themselves theoretically, the notion of intent always played a prominent part, although it was mostly a negative one. . . . If such a hypostasis, which changes the literary act into a literary object by the suppression of its intentional character, is not only possible but necessary in order to allow for a critical description, then we have not left the world in which the status of literary language is similar to that of a natural object. This assumption rests on a misunderstanding of the nature of intentionality. . . . the concept of intentionality is neither phys-

ical nor psychological in its nature, but structural, involving the activity of a subject regardless of its empirical concerns. (*BI,* pp. 24–25)

He lays all this out in this 1966 essay on the inability of American critics to appreciate intentionality:

> The partial failure of American formalism, which has not produced works of great magnitude, is due to its lack of awareness of the intentional structure of literary form. (*BI,* p. 27)

What critics and poets claim about the uses to which they put poetic imagery obscures and represses intentionality:

> The image is inspired by a nostalgia for the natural object, expanding to become nostalgia for the origin of this object. [What Hölderlin says] is a perfect definition of what we call a natural image: the word that designates a desire for an epiphany but necessarily fails to be an epiphany, because it is pure origination. For it is in the essence of language to be capable of origination, but of never achieving the absolute identity with itself that exists in the natural object. Poetic language can do nothing but originate anew over and over again; it is always constitutive, able to posit regardless of presence but, by the same token, unable to give a foundation to what it posits except as an intent of consciousness. The word is always a free presence to the mind, the means by which the permanence of natural entities can be put into question and thus negated, time and again, in the endlessly widening spiral of the dialectic. (*RR,* p. 6)

As for the objective correlative and its perfect fusion of word and object, de Man says:

> Poetics of "unmediated vision," such as those implicit in Bergson and explicit in Bachlard, fuse matter and imagination by amalgamating perception and reverie, sacrificing, in fact, the demands of consciousness to the realities of the object. Critics who speak of a "happy relationship" between matter and consciousness fail to realize that the very fact that the relationship has to be established within the medium of language indicated that it does not exist in actuality. (*RR,* pp. 7–8)

For this reason de Man found it crucial — and he was not alone at this time in arguing this point — to return to the repressed tradition of the romantics in French and English literature:

> This is why an effort to understand the present predicament of the poetic imagination takes us back to writers that belong to the earlier phases of romanticism such as, for example, Rousseau. The affinity of later poets with Rousseau — which can well be considered to be a valid

definition of romanticism as a whole—can, in turn, be best understood in terms of their use and underlying concept of imagery. (*RR*, p. 10)

Eliot may have seen the romantics as weak poets because of their perceived inability to subordinate words and objects to wit. Their defenders fell into a different trap of claiming that they were "nature poets" who sought to fuse their minds with nature. The evaluation may have differed from Eliot's, but the mechanism they saw at work and its implicit ontology were much the same as his. De Man saw— following what Descombes calls the terrorist version of Hegel, the Hegel of the 1940s, the Hegel of "separation" and death—a radical separation between "the plastic power that abode" within the poet Wordsworth and nature. Objects and images exist for the poet only *within* a structure of intentionality. Inner and outer are not neatly differentiated but subject to a great tension: this is a poetry not of reconciliation, wholeness, and organic unity, but rather of conflict, of what Heidegger calls *Riss:*

> One feels everywhere the pressure of an inner tension at the core of all earthly objects, powerful enough to bring them to explosion.
> The violence of this turmoil is finally appeased by the ascending movement recorded in each of the texts, the movement by means of which the poetic imagination tears itself away, as it were, from a terrestrial nature and moves toward this "other nature" mentioned by Rousseau, associated with the diaphanous, limpid, and immaterial quality of a light that dwells nearer to the skies. (*RR*, p. 14)

The romantics uncover, according to de Man, "a fundamentally new kind of relationship between nature and consciousness" (*RR*, p. 14). Writing in 1960, at the height of the quest for image patterns that were to reveal the fundamental structures of meaning within texts, de Man argued that the "imagination" of Wordsworth

> . . . has little in common with the faculty that produces natural images born "as flowers originate." It marks instead a possibility for consciousness to exist entirely by and for itself, independently of all relationships with the outside world, without being moved by an intent aimed at a part of this world.

It was the romantics, the poets themselves, who undercut New Critical theory and practices; for they were "the first modern writers to have put into question, in the language of poetry, the ontological priority of the sensory object" (*RR*, p. 16).

The lucidity of Montaigne is revealed in his determination to come to terms with the structure of our failure to know. The wisdom of the poet is revealed in his or her ability to understand not just the importance of consciousness but more particularly the "formal structure of representing as such" (Heidegger's words quoted by de Man, *AR*, p. 175) and the necessary failure to appropriate and represent in words the object or image itself. De Man wrote in 1960 in his dissertation on Mallarmé that

> the poet knows that he cannot live within the plenitude of a natural unity of being; he also knows that his language is powerless to recapture this unity, since it is itself the main cause of the separation. But he surmounts despair at this discovery by objectifying his negative knowledge, and making it into a form which has this knowledge for its content. In so doing, the poet hopes to safeguard the future possibility of his work by substituting the contemplation of his failure to a useless quest for unity.[90]

In coming to this realization in those moments of inwardness in which a conciousness confronts its own true self, "the organic analogy between subject and object reveals itself as false" (*BI*, p. 58).

Again and again in his work in the 1950s and 1960s de Man grapples with the problematic that he designated by the words "inwardness," "self," "consciousness." It is a tricky issue, and he had to be wary — as he repeatedly reveals himself to be — of the dangers of letting these words suggest psychologism. He follows Husserl in rejecting psychologism; but it is harder to enforce the sorts of distinctions Husserl makes when you are dealing with literary texts, a field where so much has been made of the life of the author and where so often criticism has been practiced by people who see it as their job to identify with the mind, the "genius," of the author and let the mediating words fall away as so many obstructions to the communion of true spirits.[91]

Looking back at his work of the 1950s and 1960s, de Man said he saw "someone most uncomfortably stuck in ontologism."[92] This is true to the extent that he pursued then a line of inquiry that was Husserlian and Heideggerian in its basic thrust. At the same time, however, it could be said that his work was itself a critique of the ontological compulsion of so much New Criticism, its notion that poetic practice and criticism revolved around the literary symbol that somehow gave access to reality. De Man's work criticized this notion and did so primarily by reference to the poetry of the romantics, from Wordsworth, Hölderlin, and Keats up to Yeats and Rilke.

The idea that governed much criticism of the romantic poets at that time was one that argued that romantic poetry was "nature poetry." There was no division within the mind of the poet. The division fell between the poet and nature, and thus the poet's task was to mend the rift and somehow to identify himself (usually) with nature. The goal of the poet might be to have a mind open to nature and thus be able to grasp things as a living process, for the highest function of imaginative art is to touch and share "a unity of being," as W. J. Bate argued. Poet and world are to be reunited. "Romantic philosophy is thus," argued M. H. Abrams, "a metaphysics of integration, of which the key principle is that of 'reconciliation,' or synthesis, of whatever is divided, opposed, and conflicting."[93] Against the commonplaces about romantic literature de Man held that romantic poetry is not nature poetry, nor is it the scene of some attempted reconciliation of the mind of the poet and nature. It would have been difficult for de Man to agree with the received opinion about romantic and modern poetry. His complex idea of intentionality guaranteed that "reconciliation" of the sort most scholars and critics sought signs of in romantic poetry was a problematic notion for de Man, and the phenomenological split between consciousness and nature was absolute and would have made him doubt the very possibility of reconciling mind and nature.

In his concern to propound a new way of reading literature by reference to romantic texts de Man was not alone. On the one hand there was Geoffrey Hartman, whose 1964 book on Wordsworth was a radical departure from accepted ways of thinking about Wordsworth as a nature poet, as Robert Langbaum understood best of all the reviewers of that book: "Mr. Hartman . . . is interested in Wordsworth's conflict with imagination itself—in his fear of imagination as an apocalyptic force that threatens to overwhelm the external world, to destroy it as a counterpart to imagination."[94] Hartman's focus, like de Man's, was on the inner divisions and ruptures in the mind of the poet and not on some ontological split between the self of the poet and the world. And like de Man he was very interested in Continental criticism and poetry—Blanchot, Rilke, and on. His starting point was different from that of de Man; it was Erich Auerbach and his dichotomy between realistic writing and literary language, a dichotomy foreign to de Man.

Another ally in the cause for romantic poetry was Harold Bloom. Bloom shared de Man's suspicion of the fundamentally religious and specifically Christian character of much American criticism and scholarship. In the "days of my youth," writes Bloom, "professors of literature were a secular clergy."[95] Such professors espoused what de Man called "salvational criticism . . . [which is] a trend in which formalist techniques are overlaid with intentions of a mythical and religious order. . . . It aspires to an ultimate reconciliation on a cosmic scale" (*BI*, pp. 242–43). Both Bloom and de Man began work in the 1950s with no allegiance whatsoever to T. S. Eliot. In this, of course, they were anomalies. In retrospect we can see that they began in opposition to his religiously inspired critical and educational program. Bloom and de Man also had in common a general approach to literature by means of problems of the self. That they shared this perspective may not be obvious, especially since Bloom's interest in psychoanalysis is in marked contrast to de Man's refusal (following Husserl) to brook psychological categories. However, both Bloom and de Man emphasize the consciousness of the poet, the interior as opposed to the exterior, and the impossibility of reconciling self and nature. Bloom argued that "subjectivity or self-consciousness is the salient problem of Romanticism" and "modernist poetry in English organized itself, to an excessive extent, as a supposed revolt against Romanticism, in the mistaken hope of escaping this inwardness." "It is evident," he wrote in 1968, "that we still need to clear our minds of Eliotic cant on this subject." Part of that effort was coming to realize that, in Bloom's words, "Most simply, Romantic nature poetry, despite a long critical history of misrepresentation, was an antinature poetry." De Man's work was salutary because—again, according to Bloom—"more powerfully than any other critic [he] emphasized the Romantic renunciation of the natural object and enhances our awareness of the intentional separation between consciousness and nature in Romantic vision."[96] The link between Hartman, Bloom, and de Man as readers of romantic literature who wanted to reassert its importance against Eliot and Company by stressing the very subjectivity that Eliot had sought to remove from his own poetry and had encouraged others to suppress in theirs is strong. J. Hillis Miller also proved an ally, having his own reasons to emphasize the consciousness of the writer given his ties to the Geneva School of literary criticism.

It is wrong to give the impression that de Man found American criticism deplorable or otherwise in lamentable shape except for the few allies he developed. He stated on a number of occasions his admiration for American criticism, primarily because—and this was something he missed in French criticism—it gave such close attention to the text. But more specifically he believed that the New Critics focused on those moments of negativity in a text that would concern de Man all of his scholarly career. What limited what the New Critics could do with close reading was the way they rapidly categorized those moments or understood them all too quickly in mythic and religious terms and thus smoothed things over. This was not what he wanted to do.

Is there, then, it might be asked at this point, a "Yale School"? Would it make any difference if there were? The links between de Man and his colleagues were real enough. He was perhaps instrumental in nudging them all in a certain direction. All three of the Yale colleagues I have named were to some extent invoking, before they came into contact with de Man, nonliterary terms to explain things that de Man suggested could very well be understood in literary terms—creativity, genius (Bloom), consciousness (Miller, following Geneva), materiality and transcendence (Hartman). De Man may have shown his colleagues that there were distinct advantages to be gained by dropping such categories. But beyond that Yale was no united front, and we only make it more difficult for ourselves to understand the contributions of these scholars if we think of them that way. I fear that the perception that Yale was a single-minded avant-garde of criticism was due in no small measure to the publicity effort that led to various articles in the *New Republic* in the mid-1970s and the *Georgia Review* in the late 1970s and even as soon as 1980 was backfiring, causing more resentment than envy. Beyond that, the notion of a neatly defined Yale School leads us perhaps to ignore de Man's close working relationship with a number of scholars at Yale whose work seems to differ from his. I think here of a scholar de Man brought to Yale when he was chair of the French department, Fredric Jameson, and another whose work he fostered when he was chair of French, Shoshana Felman.

## The Turn

Very little of the last stage of Paul de Man's career is represented in this book, just the review of Derrida's *Of Grammatology* that he did for Jean Starobinski and the foreword to Carol Jacobs's book. The Derrida review is short and straightforward and gives only a hint of what de Man would achieve in "The Rhetoric of Blindness: Jacques Derrida's Reading of Rousseau." The preface for Carol Jacobs's book, with its focus on the question of paraphrase, is his last substantial statement about New Critical practice. The last stage of de Man's career, the academically published stage of his career, is inaugurated with the essay "The Rhetoric of Temporality" that was the outgrowth of his Christian Gauss Seminars in 1967 at Princeton and was delivered at a conference at Johns Hopkins University in 1968.

With his title "The Rhetoric of Temporality," de Man gestured two ways, backward with the Heideggerian word "temporality" and forward with the word "rhetoric." In this essay he still employed the Heideggerian terminology, but it was being displaced by that of rhetoric. His effort would increasingly be to develop a terminology that was strictly, as he saw it, in line with language in its very materiality and thus to avoid bringing a metalanguage to bear upon literature.

In "The Rhetoric of Temporality" we can see him, then, taking a turn in direction. De Man wrote in the foreword to the revised edition of *Blindness and Insight* that "The Rhetoric of Temporality" "with the deliberate emphasis on rhetorical terminology . . . augurs what seemed to me a change, not only in terminology and in tone but in substance." He went on to say that "this terminology is still uncomfortably intertwined with the thematic volcabulary of consciousness and of temporality that was current at the time, but it signals a turn" (*BI*, p. xii).

That a turn took place was evident in de Man's adoption of rhetorical terminology. What is less evident is what was at stake in the turn. I am only going to give this subject the most cursory of treatments, but some examination of it is necessary to complete in however sketchy a manner my account of de Man's intellectual itinerary. A great deal has been wrtten about what some have hastened to call de Man's deconstructive phase, but one key aspect of it has not been pointed to, and some focus on that aspect will help complete the narrative of his career by allowing me to suggest how he handled in this last phase the issue that is key to his earlier work, inwardness.

Some understand de Man's work since 1968 by reference to the ideas of Derrida and what has come to be called deconstruction, but this is inadequate. De Man met Derrida at the 1966 conference at Johns Hopkins University that marked the arrival on these shores simultaneously of structuralism and poststructuralism some twenty-five years or so after Jakobson and Lévi-Strauss came to New York and created the possibility for the development of the international movement called structuralism. After the 1966 conference in Baltimore de Man and Derrida became crucial allies. De Man, shortly thereafter the chair of French and Comparative Literature at Yale, was able to arrange for Derrida's appointment as an annual visiting professor at Yale, thereby creating a situation that allowed for the training under the cooperative tutelage of de Man, Hartman, Bloom, Miller, Derrida, Jameson, and Felman of a number of doctoral students. De Man and Derrida shared a philosophical tradition that included Hegel, Nietzsche, Husserl, and Heidegger — a tradition they both felt was limited in serious ways but enabling in others. Derrida's "influence" on de Man is misunderstood if it is exaggerated, and influence is in any case the wrong word. Derrida has, I think, little direct influence on de Man beyond what he says in the key suggestive pages at the beginning of "The White Mythology" on the materiality of the "inscription." I would suggest that Derrida and de Man were crucial to each other in the way Bloom and de Man were crucial to each other, but for different reasons. As ally, Derrida's effect on de Man was considerable. He energized de Man, enabling him to refocus his efforts.

To subsume de Man under the rubric of deconstruction is misleading in the obvious way in which all vague labels are misleading as well as for more specific reasons. Rodolphe Gasché has written a number of essays that distinguish the projects of de Man from those of Derrida, and they bear consideration in this regard. Much misunderstanding is also caused by taking literally as if there were no calculation behind them various assertions of the late de Man attacking the Holy Trinity of conventional literary criticism — Reference, Person, Unity. De Man intended to provoke. He wanted to rip away what he no doubt saw as the delusive appearance of harmony and totality from the ideology of culture that had dominated literary studies since Coleridge, Arnold, and Eliot. He knew that readers always have tried and always will try to connect the literarySo work to reality, to the person of the author or the reader, or to make sense of it in terms of accepted notions of wholeness. He knew they would do this. Yet he wanted to make it difficult for them to do so, to slow them down so that they would not jump to conclusions that would cause their attentiveness as readers to relax. He wanted to short-circuit our natural tendencies to stop the reading process too early and too easily. He was a modern avant-gardist, what with his emphasis on the materiality of the text seemingly at the expense of morality and adherence to the "unities." He was a pedagogue with his desire to slow down our reading. He had a strategy that we miss when we highlight and abstract his more outlandish statements about literature from his strategic emphasis on the process of reading, that we miss when we read him literally instead of taking him rhetorically.

So, isolating de Man's more flamboyant statements about literature is as misleading a guide to what he was all about as labeling him a deconstructionist, even though he himself used the word for what he did. A closer approach to what he was doing is possible, I believe, if we attend to his similarities to a thinker who I think had a decisive impact on the last stage of his career, Walter Benjamin. Benjamin is the thinker whose influence accounts for the turn we can see in "The Rhetoric of Temporality." Both de Man and Benjamin worked within the framework of German idealist philosophy, and both worked very hard to shake themselves free of the extraordinary emphasis on subjectivity that is the burden of all who are Hegel's students.

Freeing his work from the notion of subjectivity became crucial for de Man in the late 1960s. He had been working in the tradition of "interiority" since after the war. He knew the limits of that line of thinking very well. The main problem, as he saw it, was its circularity. "Intentionality" had been created as a concept in order to overcome any possible psychologism or naturalism, but it had in fact invented a new psychologism and a new naturalism.[97] The transcendental subjectivity of Husserl, despite all his efforts, could not avoid getting caught up in notions of personal subjectivity. De Man's essay on Blanchot in *Blindness and Insight* is an analysis of the problem of circularity that he saw Blanchot caught up in but that he himself was experiencing as well. Much more was at stake than mere problems of logical consistency. De Man was also concerned that the set of ideas he had derived from the idealist tradition — selfhood, death, separation, time, division — were not so much analytic tools as a set of themes, so that the criticism he had been writing was in fact the sort of criticism he had been at pains to attack.

The turn de Man took can be dated with some accuracy to the years 1967–69. In April 1967 de Man gave a Christian Gauss Seminar on Wordsworth that was full of careful analyses and sharply rejected the tried-and-true interpretations of Wordsworth while celebrating the arrival on the critical scene of Geoffrey Hartman's treatise on Wordsworth, but the essay was most remarkable for its adherence to a metalanguage derived from Heidegger. The essay has recently come to light in manuscript, and it is all too apparent why de Man decided not to publish it. He was in the process at just this moment of changing his thinking about a number of key issues, and the Wordsworth lecture was indicative of where he had been rather than where he wanted to be going. In it he wrote, for example, that "temporality characterizes the consciousness of beings capable of reflecting on their own death." He uses the phenomenological distinction between consciousness and nature and the notion that consciousness is directed away from nature toward death and pure nothingness. It is this situation that allows, he argues, consciousness to grasp history and thus have a true sense of temporality.[98]

It was in the late 1960s in France, Germany, the United States, and elsewhere that many of Walter Benjamin's texts were republished, newly published, and translated. Although dead since 1940, he was received as a new and most vivid contemporary by many. Suhrkamp Verlag issued a large number of his texts in Germany. Already in 1955 Suhrkamp had published two volumes entitled *Schriften*, edited by Theodor and Gretel Adorno. And in the mid-1950s, even before the appearance of *Schriften*, Peter Szondi (later a friend of de Man's) began to refer to the texts of Benjamin in his own writings. De Noël published a two-volume selection of essays in French. The key text for de Man was, I believe, *The Origin of the German Tragic Drama*. What de Man derived from Benjamin's book on the tragedy of the seventeenth century can be most simply designated by the word "allegory," but saying that does not say enough as de Man suggested himself in his citation of Benjamin's book at the end of "Form and Intent in the American New Criticism," where he wrote that Benjamin defined allegory as a void "that signifies precisely the non-being of what it represents."[99] In the *Origin* we can learn as de Man did about allegory, not as a way of handling certain themes, but as a process of signification, the motor of which is negation. "Death," as presented by Kojève following Hegel, named negation too, but only as a theme. Allegory names it as a process. Benjamin also focused upon death, to the same degree Kojève did, but he spoke of death strikingly in terms of the death mask, a degraded physiognomy that expresses but cannot mediate the gulf between mortality and redemption. Benjamin argued that the expressiveness of allegory is distinct from that of the symbol. Allegory does not point beyond itself toward some point of transcendent realization. The task, then, of understanding a text does not involve synthesizing it into a whole but *mortifying* it, shattering it into pieces. Benjamin suggested to de Man the power there might be in the use of the figures of rhetoric to mortify the text by disfiguring it in order to see how it works, not as something guided by an animating spirit, but as a mechanism. Such analysis could be conducted by seeing how the rhetoric of figures and the rhetoric of thought are at odds with one another in every text, how syntax and grammar are at odds in every text.

Benjamin is present in de Man's essays "The Rhetoric of Temporality" and "Conclusions: Walter Benjamin's 'The Task of the Translator,' " but I suggest that he is present in many other late essays of de Man's and perhaps no more so than in a key late work, "Shelley Disfigured," where he is not mentioned at all. The case of Shelley and the circumstances surrounding his death allowed de Man to pick up and develop Benjamin's own image of the death mask in a particularly macabre way playing upon both literal and figurative significances. The poem is a fragment, a ruin, as Benjamin suggests that allegory is, but so too was Shelley's body. The erasure or effacement, the disappearance of the author that de Man discussed in the essay was literally the loss of a face. The figures into which de Man disfigures Shelley's poem are—and here I allude to Neil Hertz's fine essay on de Man—"lurid figures."[100] In the essay, de Man worked out in terms of Shelley's "Triumph of Life" the implications of what Benjamin had to say about the triumph of death in his pages on the *facies hippocratica* of history in the *Origin*. And it is there that de Man made good, if he ever made it good, his claim in some of his early essays collected in this book that "far from being anti-historical, the poetical act (in the general sense which includes all the arts) is the quintessential historical act: that through which we become conscious of the divided character of our own being, and consequently, of the necessity of fulfilling it, of accomplishing it in time, instead of undergoing it in eternity" (see "The Temptation of Permanence").[101]

Benjamin provided a decisive critique of the literary symbol, the notion that empowered a certain form of romantic criticism from Coleridge on through Eliot and the New Critics. "Intentionality," as de Man employed that phenomenological concept, had provided some strong basis for criticizing the romantic aesthetic ideology, but it was insufficient to complete the task. My sense is that with the addition of Benjamin's critique of the organic symbol and his positive notion of allegory de Man felt he had the tools he needed to achieve what he knew was impossible before. It is for this reason the "The Rhetoric of Temporality" is rightly (I think) felt to be his most fully achieved essay. His target is clear, the means he mobilizes to attack are multiple, its suggestiveness is great, and it summarizes a great amount of research and reflection on his part. In it he argues against two dogmas that have shaped critical thought about literature since the very end of the eighteenth century and the beginning of the nineteenth: the conception of irony as a fixed perspective and of the symbol as a fusion of image and idea that cannot be found in allegory. In the essay we find him betwixt and between Heidegger and Benjamin. De Man had seen the considerable limits of Heidegger in the mid-1950s, as his essays "Heidegger's Exegeses of Hölderlin" and "The Temptation of Permanence" show, and yet he had felt it necessary to fall back on his categories in a fairly uncritical way as late as 1967. He was bogged down, and Benjamin provided the way forward.

Benjamin enabled de Man not just to substitute allegory for symbol and to adopt the language of rhetoric in the place of that of temporality; he also enabled de Man to reapproach the question of history that had always been central to his work but had previously been too heavily tied to what Heidegger said in *Being and Time*. In allegory the "false appearance of totality is extinguished." Allegory "thereby declares itself to be beyond beauty." The work of art as allegory stands as a ruin and therby bears the imprint of the progression of history inscribed within it. There is no apotheosis, no incarnation of time itself within allegory. This is not the realm of *The Four Quartets*. But although there is no apotheosis in allegory, this form, because it is a ruin, nonetheless has a function, and that is to make historical content into philosophical truth. The work as ruin acquires the very fluidity of time.

All of these ideas of Benjamin's have the strongest influence on the late de Man, given his own effort to develop a philosophical criticism that would be equal to the tasks set by Benjamin. I risk exaggerating the significance of Benjamin for the late de Man to make the point that a fuller exploration of the relationship of de Man's thought to Benjamin's will reveal more than comparing and contrasting it to the work of others. But what, finally, is the point of the Benjaminian turn? The point only becomes clearer, I think, with the essays of the 1970s collected in *Allegories of Reading*. The main point toward which Benjamin was moving with his work in the 1930s was to problematize and ultimately efface the distinction between the subject of idealism and the material object of knowledge. This was the goal of *The Arcades Project*.[102] It is also at the heart of what de Man hoped to achieve. In the end he rejected the notions of interiority and inwardness as tools of analysis and he also rejected the inner/outer dichotomy that he had derived from the tradition of German idealism. The Parisian arcades, both inside and outside, both edifice and street, were the "dialectical image" with which Benjamin hoped to blur the distinction between subject and object. Literature understood rhetorically in the very materiality of its functioning was meant to serve the same function for de Man that the arcades were meant to serve for Benjamin. Literature was important for de Man, not as a privileged mode of consciousness, but because it was betwixt and between. It was not inner, it was not spiritual; it was *material*. That is why he called late in his life for a return to philology in a polemical essay that asked scholars and students to attend to the materiality of the text and consider it *prior* to any effort to conceptualize. Such counsel warred directly with the Hegelian imperative to bring all objects of analysis "to a concept" (" *auf den Begriff bringen*"). He paused in another late polemical piece on the border between theory and the materiality of the text to make problematic any notion that the two territories were separate. The promotion of theory as the height of literary scholarship was suspect, according to de Man, because it reauthorized the subject/object and inside/outside binaries. His efforts were more in line with the Benjamin who wrote to Martin Buber in 1927 that he sought "to write a description of Moscow . . . in which 'all factuality is already theory' and which would thereby refrain from any deductive abstraction, from all prognostication, and even within certain limits, from any judgment."[103] The starting point for both Benjamin and de Man is Hegel. Their late work is in each case an effort to make such conceptual devices as that of the subject/object distinction less of a hindrance.

De Man refrained from the use of abstractions such as death, temporality, and intentionality in his later work to concern himself with the workings of texts. He devoted his attention to the mechanics of language, spurred on and guided by Benveniste, Jakobson, Austin, and others. By giving precedence to the figurative aspects of language over the referential, he believed he could call into question the binary opposition of subject to object. The question of the subject is the explicit concern of a number of chapters in *Allegories of Reading*. In it he attacked the notion of consciousness by reference to Nietzsche, who had made, he said, the "binary polarity of classical banality," the opposition of subject to object, the target of his analysis (*AR*, p.107). Belief that language was just a tool at the service of the subject was a source of great misunderstanding. Language is not just a tool, a set of keys (as it were) at the service of the soul. "One may well begin to wonder," he wrote, " whether the lock indeed shapes the key or whether it is not the other way around, that a lock (and a secret room or box behind it) had to be invented in order to give a function to the key" (*AR*, p.173). The self is a product, an effect of language, "a double structure held together by the connivance of words and deeds" (*RR*, p.102).

But the self remains—as a product of language, of the devices we know as prosopopoeia, apostrophe, and so on—and de Man devoted a great deal of his later work to trying to understand the function of figures that pertain to the self. Is this because in the end one cannot escape from the self and its problematic? Charles Taylor argues in his *Sources of the Self* that the modern concern for the self and the contemporary deconstruction of the self are flip sides of the same coin, and de Man's writings seem to bear this out. He argues the "necessity to escape the tropology of the subject" (*RR*, p.72), but he also wrote that "the rhetorical resources of language . . . are by no means, in themselves, incompatible with selfhood." He also stated that there is much that "illustrated the recurrent symbiosis of the problems of understanding with those of selfhood" (*AR*, pp. 173, 175). The question he set for himself was now to escape the Hegelian overemphasis on selfhood and consciousness. It is a task he shared with many other thinkers, especially those who, like Foucault, inherited the set of concerns that Bataille, Blanchot, Heidegger, and Husserl made salient at midcentury. De Man's contribution to the solution of the problem cannot be considered decisive, but the struggle apparent in his own writings to deal with the problem is instructive. The struggle in fact may well be without solution, may well be one (he might have said) we are fated to lose, but the nature of the failure can itself be a most fruitful subject for understanding.

It is in this context that one should consider de Man's inquiry into the aesthetic ideology. His research led him to believe that the source of some of our confused notions about what role literature should play in society was that set of thinkers who had taken up the critical philosophy of Kant and transformed it into idealism, and in the process had developed the ideology of the aesthetic that was responsible for concepts such as organic form and the symbol as well as for the notion that literature could be harnessed directly to political and moral ends. It is an ideology that requires that literature be dominated by the knowing subject who ascribes meaning and moral to the text. It is an ideology that monumentalizes literature by setting it up as a symbol of civilization. As such it needs to be contested, argued de Man, for "it is as apolitical force that the aesthetic still concerns us as one of the most powerful ideological drives to act upon the reality of history" (*RR*, p.264). This was yet another reason why the effort to dismember and disfigure the monuments was a crucial one for de Man. But the process of monumentalization that needs to be fought also needs to be understood historically, and it is what remains of de Man's efforts to do so that will be pulled together in the forthcoming volume entitled *The Aesthetic Ideology.*

## Conclusion

In my thoughts
There was a darkness . . .
Wordsworth, *The Two-Part Prelude* (1799)

Wallace Stevens in his seventies went looking for news of what Martin Heidegger might have had to say about his supreme poet, Freidrich Hölderlin. He acquired different German editions of Hölderlin's poetry in 1948 and 1949, and in 1952 asked his bookseller to find him a copy of Heidegger's critical writings about Hölderlin. Hölderlin and Heidegger seized upon Stevens's imagination at about the time that Paul de Man was traveling with wife and child up Route 15 in Connecticut past Hartford, where Stevens lived. The de Mans were on their way from New York to Boston, where de Man was going to teach French at the Berlitz School. It is odd to think of de Man, filled with news of Hölderlin and Heidegger, news that he would slowly learn to impart to American colleagues and students, traveling right past the doorway of the great American poet who was himself seeking to learn about the German poet and the German philosopher.

In the end it seems likely that Stevens never learned much about Hölderlin and Heidegger, but the few ties that do link them have provoked some very sensitive commentary.[104] And if it is only fanciful to imagine a meeting between de Man and Stevens in the early 1950s, nonetheless an affinity exists between them that goes beyond their obvious interest in Hölderlin and Heidegger. There is in both Stevens and de Man a certain prizing of poetry, to be sure. There is, moreover, a similar preoccupation with the theme of death, a similar effort (in Stevens's words) "to read the word 'death' without negation" in order, as it were, to reveal life in its true poverty, the nothing that is. But what is even more striking, because it is a deeper current in the writings of both men, is what might be called their antihumanism. Remember that it is Stevens who imagined that

A gold-feathered bird
Sings in the palm, without human meaning,
Without human feeling, a foreign sound.
("Of Mere Being")

De Man was influenced early by the critics of anthropologism who flourished in Paris in the mid-1940s and were teasing out the implications of what Derrida has remarked was "one of the inaugural motifs of Husserl's transcendental phenomenology." Late in his career he sought to understand the workings of literature without recourse to the old props of artistic creativity, subjectivity, and the imagination. He sought to understand Wordsworth as a "poet of sheer language," the very plainness of whose writing was its point. But the "plainness of plain things," as Stevens says, "is a savagery" ("An Ordinary Evening in New Haven"). And it is the savagery of de Man's antihumanism that has chiefly shocked people, and this is correct. This is as he intended. I do not mean by comparing him to the American poet to suggest a new way to domesticate de Man (because in fact that has been done by a good number of people already) but rather to suggest a new way to reconsider his legacy, a legacy he hoped would resist easy assimilation. The horror of what he proposed in suggesting what he called in his late essays on Kant an "a-pathetic criticism" may need reconsideration for reasons Stevens articulated better than many, because he knew that "the absence of the imagination had / Itself to be imagined" ("The Plain Sense of Things"). If the notion of poetic practice and of life itself without the control of the subject is appalling and makes it seem as if we "had come to the end of the imagination" and were "inanimate in an inert savoir" ("The Plain Sense of Things"), this is nonetheless what Stevens and de Man asked us to consider in their writings, and congruent with what Ashbery says in the poem I have already quoted:

> . . . that the soul is not a soul,
> has no secret, is small, and it fits
> into its hollow perfectly: its room, our moment
> of attention.

De Man schooled his soul in a chastening form of asceticism to free it from the old guardians of human pride and dignity, the old consolations. He wondered for a time whether the motor that propelled his work was an analytic principle or just a mechanism for exploring a set of themes (death, temporality, and so on). In the end I think it fair to say that there are themes that traverse his work and that he focused his attention on a set of themes in the works of others, but there is also a principle that runs through his works and that is the principle of negation, of noncoincidence. His emphasis on negation derives, of course, from his education with Hegel, Kojève, Hyppolite, and Wahl, and his work as a whole could be seen (uncharitably, I think) as a set of variations upon a theme of Hegel's until he came to appreciate the point of what Dieter Henrich has presented in a more compelling fashion than anyone else as the aporetic structure of Kant's thought. But considering de Man's work as a set of variations on one aspect of Hegel's thought does not adequately summarize what de Man was able to do with the principle of negation. It served many purposes for him. In the first instance it gave him grounds for a critique of the notion of salvation through action as it was held by Sartre, Malraux, and many thinkers in the 1930s and 1940s on the right and the left including himself in 1941 and 1942, thinkers who believed that there was some straight way through from literature to action. Against such a thought de

Man held that word and deed cannot coincide. In the second instance the principle of negation gave him ground for his critique of the incarnationalist aesthetic that ran from Coleridge through the Symbolists and on to T. S. Eliot and the New Critics. Against those who subscribe to that network of beliefs de Man held that word and object cannot coincide. Finally it is the principle of negation that gave him (and Walter Benjamin before him) the grounds for developing the concept of allegory for literary analysis, and it is allegory that motivates de Man's entire theory of rhetoric.

The principle of negation and noncoincidence runs through all his work, so it is odd and ultimately unfortunate (if in the end not very surprising) that so many students and colleagues came to identify with him the way they did. Identification counters negation. It was unfortunate that he became such an academic institution. It is not, however, as if he did not work toward that goal. He did. But he became in a way the victim of his own success. His ideas and procedures with all their avant-gardiste characteristics—coming as they did from Mallarmé, Leiris, Bataille, Blanchot, and so on—got turned into a set of academic techniques, rules for the Mechanical Operation of the Spirit. It is a contradiction in terms when the avant-garde becomes institutionalized. Yet de Man's career and influence provide an example of this paradox. I will suggest how this process took place. It was a hard-won achievement for de Man to begin to see how the subject/object dichotomy prevalent among all influenced by the tradition of idealist philosophy and literature could possibly be put into doubt. The understanding he reached in the later stages of his career was treated by those who followed de Man as if it were a most common sort of knowledge. It was not, and is not. The struggle to understand how this dichotomy might be rendered dubious and the sort of asymmetry that might be understood to obtain between the supposedly polar opposites was glossed over as de Man's approach to a whole set of problems was rendered into the routine business of "deconstructing" oppositions such as inside and outside and so on. The ease with which the insights he had earned were mimicked made him wince. He told me so.

Despite the "turn" represented by the adoption of rhetoric in the late 1960s and despite his statements (most notably in the preface to *The Rhetoric of Romanticism*) upon looking at his own work about the fragmented nature of his efforts over the years, de Man's writings since 1953 present us with a fairly unified picture of a writer pursuing a set of core problems. There are shifts and yet there are continuities as well. In 1953 he declared himself concerned with the structure of our failure to know, a failure about which he thought literature was our best instructor. In 1983 he was still concerned to understand the mechanism that underlies our failure to know. The main difference was that he saw that mechanism not as one that can be thought of as *inside* us, governed by intentionality, but as something neither inside nor outside, something that resides in language.

When he said failure he meant failure, including the failure of his own efforts.

Even the monumentalizing of artistic works that he sought to warn against in essays like "Shelley Disfigured" must inevitably go on—as he said, "monumentalization is by no means necessarily a naive or evasive gesture, and it is certainly not a gesture that anyone can pretend to avoid making" (RR, p. 121). But it goes on not as some inner necessity but because of the nature of language that is outside or rather both in and out in a way that breaks down the old polarities. He wrote: "The positing power of language is both entirely arbitrary, in having a strength that cannot be reduced to necessity, and entirely inexorable in that there is no alternative to it" (RR, p.116). Its operation is random but this is in any case preferable to the forces that unify, such as the unifying myths of nation and race that make sense of everything only to deprive each individual and every event of its freedom.

If he erred early in his career—and he surely did—he saw it as his task to continue to try to understand how he had erred. He came to know the power of language as well as the seductions of its delusions, as he said in his tribute to the noted critic Georges Poulet (brother, in fact, of a former colleague at Le Soir, Robert Poulet). He accepted the idea that "words cannot be isolated from the deeds they perform" (RR, p.102), words that condemn what he wrote in 1941 and 1942 for reasons he stated in however roundabout a way in the essays that begin this volume, "Montaigne and Transcendence" and "The Inward Generation," and for other reasons as well. When he wrote in 1941 and 1942, he had not sufficiently reflected on the power of words as performatives, something in which he became expert in his later years as he continued to pursue Michel Leiris's question of whether it is possible "to write a book that is an act." De Man's considered answer to the question is that we live out "the discrepancy between the power of words as acts and their power to produce other words" (RR, p.101). The relation of action to words is real but asymmetrical:"The sequence [of words] has to be punctured by acts that cannot be made a part of it" (RR, p.116).

His achievements were plural. They are frequently misunderstood because people tend to take him literally. He himself has been monumentalized, in ways that betray some naïveté and evasiveness. Theoretical practice, properly pursued, should leave itself open to constant critique, as he argued in "The Resistance to Theory." The effect of his practice may have been different from what he intended, but intention can serve little to constrain interpretation and adaptation, as he knew. Moreover, it cannot be denied, I think, that his provoking and challenging texts sometimes invite a certain misunderstanding. How, then, are we to consider him? Many questions come to mind, but at the conclusion of this discussion I think it would be well to attend to his own questions. I think he offers us some guidance in this regard in lines from Allegories of Reading that once again pick up the notion of consciousness at the same time they work to deconstruct the notion of the self. I think he speaks about himself and provides in these words one criterion for judging his continued usefulness:

The originator of this discourse [that of the critique of selfhood and of rhetorical analysis] is then no longer the dupe of his own wishes; he is as far beyond pleasure as he is beyond good and evil or, for that matter, beyond strength and weakness. His consciousness is neither happy nor unhappy, nor does he possess any power. He remains however a center of authority to the extent that the very destructiveness of his ascetic reading testifies to the validity of his interpretation. (*AR*, pp. 173–74)

Here all the dichotomies are neutralized, their aporias pointed out. An authority is asserted here, to be sure, but not the sort that would be an ultimate ground. This is an authority that cannot lead or guide but only remind. De Man signals here that he is beyond thinking of things in terms of Jean Wahl's "*malheur de conscience.*" And he also signals that he is one who sought, as Stevens sought, "to try to get as close to the ordinary, the commonplace, and the ugly as it is possible for a poet to get. It is not a question of grim reality. The object is of course to purge oneself of anything false."[105] If he can be sufficiently ascetic, if he can get to the plain sense of things, then he is to be valued. If not, his work should be discarded. De Man has set stringent conditions under which he is willing to retain any claim to authority over us as a critic. We should heed him. He would have expected us to be no less harsh on him.

## Notes

The following abbreviations have been used for works by Paul de Man cited in the body of my text: *AR, Allegories of Reading* (New Haven, Conn.: Yale University Press, 1979); *BI, Blindness and Insight* (Minneapolis: University of Minnesota Press, 1983); *RR, Rhetoric of Romanticism* (New York: Columbia University Press, 1984); *RT, Resistance to Theory* (Minneapolis: University of Minnesota Press, 1986).

1. I have spoken to two of de Man's partners at Editions Hermès, Fred de Vos and de Man's cousin Jan Buschmann. Both of them say that de Man was not guilty of any wrong doing in his work for the firm. The firm did go bankrupt, and the bankruptcy did mean that the supporters of the firm lost money. De Man's father lost the money he had lent his son, and de Man's aunt (Jan Buschmann's mother) lost her house as a result of the collapse of the firm. There were hard feelings but according to my sources no wrongdoing. The way the business of the firm was conducted did cause de Man trouble later on in his life when he returned to Europe in 1955 to do research after he had been selected to become a Junior Fellow of the Harvard Society of Fellows. Once he had left the United States and returned to Europe, he had difficulties with his passport because, as de Man put it in a letter of December 3, 1955, to Renato Poggioli at Harvard, "irregularities in the bookkeeping" at Hermès having to do with rules of foreign exchange and export licenses led to a legal action called an *instruction judiciare* against all the partners of the firm. The problem was settled during the time de Man was working in Paris, and he was allowed to return to the United States, but this problem extended his absence from Harvard, where he should have been attending regular meetings of the Society of Fellows.

2. Letter of June 22, 1948, from Paul de Man to William Phillips. This letter is in the archives of *The Partisan Review* at Boston University and is printed here thanks to the assistance of *The Partisan Review*.

Allan Stoekl of Yale University has also discovered a letter from de Man to Georges Bataille among the papers of Bataille at the Bibliothèque Nationale in Paris. The letter dates from 1948 and gives further indication of what de Man was doing at this period in his attempts to arrange for transatlantic intellectual interchange. The letter reads as follows:

"New York, le 3 juillet

"Cher monsieur et ami,
    "J'aurais voulu vous écrire plus longuement, mais j'en suis encore à émerger lentement de l'agitation du départ et des premières semaines de séjour ici. Mais je commence à organiser mon existence dans ce monde étranger (tellement plus étranger quand on y vient non pas en visiteur mais en aspirant-citoyen) et je compte bien vous parler prochainement de la partie de cette expérience qui peut vous intéresser.
    "Je vous envoie ce mot rapide pour vous dire deux choses:
    "(1) Ne renoncez surtout pas à m'envoyer dès que vous pourrez le faire, le ou les articles que vous préparez pour les Etats-Unis. Je crois plus que jamais à la possibilité et à la nécessité de vous voir publié ici et je peux avoir les moyens qu'il faut (relations, etc.) pour que cela se fasse dans les meilleures conditions—financièrement et du point de vue influence et retentissement.
    "(2) Je tiens à vous dire le grand bonheur que j'ai eu de vous rencontrer à Anvers quelques jours devant mon départ et d'emporter ainsi l'impression toute fraîche d'une manière d'être et de penser que vous représentez—et qui me rend ici la vie plus facile et peut-être féconde, dans la mesure où des contacts peuvent s'établir avec certains esprits que je n'ai aucune peine à reconnaitre à travers votre image.
    "Envoyez, je vous prie, d'éventuels articles à mon adresse provisoirement définitive: Paul de Man, 110 East 4 Street, New York, 21, N.Y. En tout cas, je vous écrirai à nouveau prochainement.
    "Mon meilleur souvenir à votre femme.
    "Croyez-moi bein votre
    "Paul de Man
    "Au cas où le sujet n'aurait pas encore été réservé, j'envisage pour *Critique* éventuellement une étude sur le livre de Kinsey, *Sexual Behavior in the Human Male*, en parallèle avec quelques autres ouvrages récemment publié ici. Je compte parler de la question uniquement sur le plan sociologique, utilisant le document comme un réactif très sensible pour l'étude d'une certain structure de la société américaine. (Rien ne s'oppose donc à ce que quelqu'un d'autre parle de l'ouvrage sur le plan éthique.) Cela ne serait en tout cas pas écrit avant 1 ou 2 mois d'ici et risque d'être assez long."

One more item to note at this point is that de Man's life in the first stage of his coming to America was the subject of a novel by Henri Thomas called *Le Parjure* (Paris: Gallimard, 1954). According to Yves Bonnefoy, Thomas learned of de Man's circumstances in the 1950s and decided that they could be the material upon which to base a novel. The account is highly fictionalized.
    3. Georges Bataille, "On Hiroshima," *Politics,* no. 4 (July–August 1947), pp. 147–50.
    4. The following letter helps date de Man's introduction to Harry Levin and also tells how he described his then current work:

"10 Blossom Street
Boston
October 10, 1951

"Dear Professor Levin,
    "Last summer, while you were in Wellfleet, I wrote you from Bard College. I suppose that Ted Weiss, chairman of the English Department at Bard, also wrote you about me.

"I am now living in Boston and would appreciate very much an opportunity to talk to you. For the last year, I have been working on a book on poetical theory, taking French Symbolism as a starting point. Perhaps you might be interested in this attempt to evolve a critical language that would fuse recent European with the American vocabulary.

"Whenever you can spare me a few minutes, would you please drop me a line — my phone is not connected yet. I can call you up then to make an appointment.

"Yours sincerely,
"Paul de Man"

5. The following letter to Harry Levin, the head of the Department of Comparative Literature at Harvard, gives a sense of de Man's interests in 1955 when he was in Paris:

"17, place de Panthéon, Ve
Hotel des Grandes Hommes
Paris
June 6, 1955

"Dear Harry,
"  . . . Paris is not bewildering enough to require one's total attention; as far as I am concerned, I find it conducive to withdrawal. . . . The main impression one gets, from the university as well as from the literary groups, is that people are truly tired of the ceaseless mood of polemics and 'prises de position' in which they have all lived for so long. . . .

"The main obsession remains, of course, political, but in a way, which, after the United States, seems rather childish. The long and painful soul-searching of those who, like myself, come from the left and from the happy days of the Front populaire, seems to have made less headway than in the States. It still takes on the form of an embarrassed and apologetic criticism of orthodox Marxism, in terms on which everyone, including the communists themselves, would readily agree. The last case in point is Merleau-Ponty, whom I saw and heard quite often, in private and at his courses at the Collège de France. It took him the reading of Max Weber to decide that, after all, one could simply no longer go along with total Marxism, so he wrote a short book, *Les Aventures de la Dialectique,* in which he breaks at last openly and publicly with Sartre. Sartre, on the other hand, keeps coming closer and closer to the party-line, praises communist self-criticism and poses as a victim because the *Figaro* refuses to take paid ads for his new play, which goes on for four hours and is called *Nekrassov.* So Camus and Merleau-Ponty find themselves together as the last heretics of note — and both publish journalistic articles in *L'Express,* the Mendès-France periodical which has hit upon the successful formula of combining techniques from *Time* magazine (the idol of Servan-Schreiber), *Harper's Bazaar* for the lower income brackets (the model of the lady editor, Madame de Giroud), and *Paris-Soir.* What one falls back on after leaving the fold seems worse than what one left — but then, the obvious mistake is that every intellectual thinks he should stand and express himself on Algeria, Tito, Mendès, the baccalariat, etc. Coming back to these exchanges after a long time is pleasant enough, especially with the prospect of not having to spend one's life among them.

"With the best will in the world, I could not say that the faculties of literature at the university have shown much sign of change; the same admirable historical and philological precision and, often enough, real erudition (especially, of course, on French subjects) but the same defensive and overcautious attitude regarding whatever, in the approach to literature, is even remotely problematic.

"Younger professors of literature—Nadal, Mme Durry, J. Scherer, etc.—admit that they are so intimidated by the pressure of historical erudition that they simply cannot afford to think about anything else. They give extremely detailed courses on such new subjects as Apollinaire (Durry) or "La jeune parque et ses variances" (Nadal) but make it sound as if they were talking about the *Chanson de Roland*—and not in too lively a manner at that. I was impressed by several 'defenses de thèse' I heard, but then the average age of the candidates was well over fifty and they generally turned out to have been schoolmates of the jury members at Normale. The funny thing is that the jury is almost always automatically divided between the bien-pensants et atheistes, and that each time the French Revolution is fought over again, à propos of Baudelaire, Racine, or even 'la formation du concept du réflexe au 18eme siècle,' So even the Sorbonne is not free from the troubles of the outside world, although all unite in condemning, perhaps with envy, the unacademic criticism of people like Blanchot or Bataille, or even Breton (on whom there will no doubt be a pretty thorough course ten years from now).

"More restless minds drift towards philosophy, the Ecole des Hautes Etudes, or the financially unrewarding but useful Centre National de la Recherche Scientifique. It is out of these places that come the best articles of an academic nature. The German influence is still extremely strong, among the students still more than among the professors. All the Hegel specialists from the thirties have made brilliant careers: Jean Hyppolite (who is director of Normale Supérieure), Kojève, Wahl (who is not a Hegelian but comes nevertheless from there); and the defenders of Descartes and Kant are fighting a lonely battle against the terrifying skill with which the advanced students handle Hegelian dialectics as if it were the table of two. I would not take *Time*'s report on the French youth too seriously. I heard several of them in action and they are amazingly articulate and informed, though more skilled than critical—which seems like a change.

"I had several useful contacts with Jean Wahl and Eric Weil and have written articles for both of them, which will appear in the *Revue de Métaphysique et de Morale* (on Hölderlin) and in *Critique* (on Heidegger). . . .

"This chaotic report on academic life in Paris should at least bring back some memories of your last year over here—the only excuse for its length. Please give our best regards and wishes to Mrs. Levin.

"Yours sincerely,
"Paul de Man"

I am grateful to Harry Levin for sharing this letter with me.

6. I am grateful to Harry Levin for showing me this letter. I am also grateful to Mrs. Reuben A. Brower for kindly giving me permission to reprint it. Brower's *Alexander Pope: The Poetry of Allusion*, originally published in 1959, has just been reprinted (Oxford: Clarendon Press, 1986).

7. The most notable publicity efforts I refer to are the essays in which J. Hillis Miller announced the Yale School, his survey of the year's work in literary criticism for *The New Republic*, November 29, 1975, pp. 30–33, and his article "Steven's Rock and Criticism as Cure, II," *Georgia Review* 30(1976); pp.330–48 (in which he states that de Man, Bloom, Hartman and Derrida "come together . . . in the way the criticism of each, in a different manner each time, is uncanny, cannot be encompassed in a rational or logical formulation, and resists the intelligence of its readers" (p. 343).

8. Czeslaw Milosz, *The Captive Mind,* trans. Jane Zielonko (New York: Vintage Books, 1981), p. 8.

9. Fritz Stern, *Dreams and Delusions: The Drama of German History* (New York: Knopf, 1987), pp. 175, 155. Also see Fritz Stern, *The Politics of Cultural Despair: A Study in the Rise of the Germanic Ideology* (Berkeley: University of Calif. Press, 1961).

10. Jean-Paul Sartre, *What Is Literature?*, trans. Bernard Frechtman (New York: Washington Square Press, 1966), p.15.

11. Stern, *Dreams and Delusions,* p. 151.

12. Zeev Sternhell, *Neither Right nor Left,* trans. David Maisel (Berkeley: University of California Press, 1986).

13. I do not want to minimize the differences between Hendrik de Man and Paul de Man. Hendrik de Man was an intellectual with a great deal of experience as a labor activist. He may have urged cooperation with the Nazis for a different sort of reason than his literary and philosophical nephew could have imagined. He might have thought as a socialist strategist that cooperation with the enemy was a historical necessity his party would survive and in the end overcome because history was on its side and it understood history much better than the enemy with whom it had made a temporary alliance. For more on Hendrik de Man, see Dodge and Sternhell.

14. A very useful text to read in order to understand the intellectual antimodernism that could be sympathetic to some of the goals of the Nazis is Leo Strauss's portrait of Kurt Riezler in his *What Is Political Philosophy? and Other Essays* Glencoe, Ill.: Free Press, 1959); see esp. pp. 235–38.

15. W. H. Auden, *The English Auden*, ed. Edward Mendelsohn (London: Faber & Faber, 1977), p. 144.

16. Carl Schmitt, *The Crisis of Parliamentary Democracy,* trans. Ellen Kennedy (Cambridge, Mass.: MIT Press, 1985), pp. 69, 50. A number of Carl Schmitt's books have just now been made available by MIT Press and should be consulted. See also Carl Schmitt, *Political Romanticism,* trans. Guy Oakes (Cambridge, Mass.: MIT Press, 1985), and *Political Theology,* trans. George Schwab (Cambridge, Mass.: MIT Press, 1985). There has also been a special issue of *Telos* (no. 72, 1987) devoted to Schmitt. Also read Jürgen Habermas's review essay of the recent Schmitt translations, "Sovereignty and the *Führerdemokratie, TLS,* September 26, 1986, pp. 1053–54.

17. I have found useful in understanding this development the article by John Stroup, "Political Theology and Secularization Theory in Germany, 1918–1939: Emanuel Hirsch as a Phenomenon of His Time," *Harvard Theological Review,* 80 (1987), pp. 1–48.

18. Schmitt, *Crisis of Parliamentary Democracy,* p.71.

19. Martin Heidegger, *Being and Time,* trans. John Macquarrie and Edward Robinson (New York: Harper & Row, 1962), p. 436. The most authoritative work on Heidegger and Nazism is that of Hugo Ott, who is preparing a book on the topic. Ott's work is summarized and added to by Victor Farias in his *Heidegger et le nazisme* (Lagrasse: Editions Verdier, 1987). A very useful study of the attitudes and actions of German philosophers during the Nazi regime is being prepared by Hans Sluga.

20. W. H. Auden, "Consider," in *The English Auden,* p. 46.

21. Stephen Spender, quoted in Herbert Mitgang, "Spender Novel Emerges After Six Decades," *New York Times,* January 11, 1988.

22. Christopher Isherwood, *Lions and Shadows* (Norfolk, Conn.: New Directions, 1947), pp. 207–8.

23. Michel Leiris, *Manhood,* trans. Richard Howard (Berkeley, Calif.: North Point Press, 1983), p. 155.

24. Nicola Chiaramonte, *The Paradox of History: Stendhal, Tolstoy, Pasternak, and Others* (1970; reprint Philadelphia: University of Pennsylvania Press, 1985), pp. 101, 102, 105, 108, 107.

25. Roger Shattuck, *The Innocent Eye: On Modern Literature and the Arts* (New York: Washington Square Press, 1986), p. 247.

26. Jean-Paul Sartre, "Une idée fondamentale de la phénoménologie de Husserl: L'intentionalité," in *Situations I* (Paris: Gallimard, 1947), pp. 31–35, 34.

27. Sternhell, *Neither Right nor Left,* p. 287.

28. Georges Bataille, *Visions of Excess*, ed. Allan Stoekl (Minneapolis: University of Minnesota Press, 1985), p. 200.

29. Sternhell, *Neither Right nor Left*, pp. 286–87.

30. Schmitt, *Crisis*, pp. 69, 64, 72. See also Hannah Arendt, *On Violence* (New York: Harcourt Brace Jovanovich, 1970).

31. Ernst Nolte, *The Three Faces of Fascism*, trans. Leila Vennewitz (London: Weidenfeld & Nicolson, 1965), p. 151.

32. See especially Peter Dodge, *Beyond Marxism: The Faith and Works of Hendrik de Man* (The Hague: Martinus Nijhoff, 1966), and Peter Dodge (ed.), *A Documentary Study of Hendrik de Man, Socialist Critic of Marxism* (Princeton, N.J.: Princeton University Press, 1979). Also essential is Zeev Sternhell's *Neither Right nor Left*.

33. Peter Dodge, "Post hoc, propter hoc: A critique of Sternhell on de Man," *Bulletin de l'Association pour l'étude de l'oeuvre d'Henri de Man*, no. 14 (May 1987), p. 26.

34. Dodge, "Post hoc," p. 25.

35. Schmitt, *Crisis*, p. 25.

36. Dodge, *A Documentary Study of Hendrik de Man*, pp. 326–27.

37. Many today criticize democratic institutions without considering the implications of such a stance, without seeing how the left-wing critique has in the past so easily tipped over to the right. It is worth noting at a time when Carl Schmitt is being revived in translations and in special issues of quarterlies what Jürgen Habermas wrote in a recent *TLS* article on Schmitt: "The manner in which [Schmitt] undertakes this mockery of parliamentary institutions is as instructive now as ever; not least for those left-wingers in the Federal Republic, and today above all in Italy, who drive out the Devil with Beezlebub by filling the gap left by the non-existent Marxist theory of democracy with Schmitt's fascist critique of democracy" (Habermas, "Sovereignty and the *Führerdemokratie*," *TLS*, September 26, 1986, p. 1054).

38. Stern, *Dreams and Delusions,*, p. 150.

39. Sartre, *What Is Literature?* pp. 147, 148, 156.

40. Walter Benjamin, *Illuminations*, trans. Harry Zohn, intro. Hannah Arendt (New York: Harcourt Brace Jovanovich, 1968), p. 256.

41. Sternhell, *Neither Right nor Left*, p. 27.

42. Stern, *Dreams and Delusions*, p. 175.

43. See, among others, Hannah Arendt, "The Wannsee Conference, or Pontius Pilate," in *The Banality of Evil*, 2d ed. (New York: Harcourt Brace Jovanovich, 1965), pp. 112–34.

44. Peter Pulzer, *The Rise of Political Anti-Semitism in Germany and Austria*, 2d ed. (Cambridge, Mass.: Harvard University Press, 1988).

45. Bataille, *Visions of Excess*, p. 155.

46. Harold Bloom, *Ringers in the Tower* (Chicago: University of Chicago Press, 1971), p. 23.

47. Daniel Bell, *The End of Ideology* (Cambridge, Mass.: Harvard University Press, 1988), pp. 301–2.

48. This point is made by Charles Taylor in *Sources of the Self* (Cambridge, Mass.: Harvard University Press, 1989).

49. See Arthur Danto, *Sartre,* (New York: Viking, 1975), pp. 15–16; Sartre, *Situations I*, pp. 31–35; John Atherton, "1933," in Denis Hollier (ed.), *History of French Literature* (Cambridge, Mass.: Harvard University Press, 1989).

50. Michel Foucault, *L'Ordre du discours* (Paris: Gallimard, 1971), p. 74.

51. Paul de Man, "Sign and Symbol in Hegel's Aesthetics," *Critical Inquiry*, 8(1982), p. 763.

52. De Man, "Sign and Symbol," p. 771; Alexandre Kojève, *Introduction à la lecture de Hegel* (Paris: Gallimard, 1947), pp. 528, 530, 534. Especially important is the essay by Kojève, "The Idea of Death in the Philosophy of Hegel," which is appendix 2 of the *Introduction* but which is not avail-

able in the English edition of the work, *Introduction to the Reading of Hegel,* ed. Allan Bloom, trans. James Nichols (Ithaca, N.Y.: Cornell University Press, 1969).

53. Jean Hyppolite, *Genesis and Structure of Hegel's "Phenomenology of the Spirit",* trans. Samuel Cherniak and John Heckman (Evanston, Ill.: Northwestern University Press, 1974), pp. 204–5.

54. De Man, "Sign and Symbol," p. 771.

55. An English translation of *L'Expérience intérieure* is now available as *Inner Experience,* trans. Leslie Anne Boldt (Albany: SUNY Press, 1988). *Le Coupable* will appear in an English translation with an introduction by Denis Hollier from the Lapis Press in Santa Monica, California.

56. Jean-Paul Sartre, "Introducing *Les temps modernes"* in Sartre, *"What Is Literature?" and Other Essays,* intro. Steven Ungar (Cambridge, Mass.: Harvard University Press, 1988), pp. 258–59.

57. Jean-Paul Sartre, "Un Nouveau Mystique," in *Situations I,* pp. 143–48.

58. Leiris, *Manhood,* p. 157.

59. Martin Heidegger, *Basic Writings,* ed. David Farrell Krell (New York: Harper & Row, 1977), p. 209.

60. Jacques Derrida, *Margins of Philosophy,* trans. Alan Bass (Chicago: University of Chicago Press, 1982), p. 118.

61. I use here John Sturrock's words in his review of Rodolphe Gasché's *Tain of the Mirror* in *The London Review of Books,* March 31, 1988, p. 18.

62. G. W. F. Hegel, *Phenomenology of the Mind,* trans. J. Baillie (London: Macmillan, 1909), p. 250; Hyppolite, *Genesis and Structure,* pp. 194–95.

63. Georges Bataille, *Literature and Evil,* trans. Alastair Hamilton (London: Calder & Boyers, 1973), p. 171.

64. Paul Celan, *Poems,* trans. Michael Hamburger (New York: Persea Books, 1981), p. 183.

65. John Ashbery, "Self Portrait in Convex Mirror," in Helen Vendler (ed.), *The Harvard Book of Contemporary American Poetry* (Cambridge, Mass.: Harvard University Press, 1985), p. 229.

66. Heidegger, *Basic Writings,* p. 107.

67. Paul de Man *"Mallarmé, Yeats, and the Post-Romantic Predicament"* (Ph.D. diss., Harvard University, 1960), p. 102.

68. De Man outlined this project to me in a letter of August 11, 1983, that also gave his plans for *The Resistance to Theory.* It might be useful to excerpt the letter as it pertains to both projects:

"Dear Lindsay,

"It was good to see you and your wife here in New Haven and subsequently to hear about my new-found popularity with the book clubs. They must really be hard up.

"I return the signed contract for *The Resistance to Theory.* In order to allow you to get an overview of the present state of my work, I include two tentative tables of contents for that and for the other one (on aesthetics, rhetoric and ideology) on which I am working. I also indicate what is ready and what still has to be done, to give you an idea of possible deadlines, and include the finished parts.

"This should give you a fair notion of what you can expect from me over the next one or two years. . . .

"All my best,
"Paul de Man

*The Resistance to Theory*
1. The Resistance to Theory *
2. Reading and History in H. R. Jauss *
3. Hypogram and Inscription in Michael Riffaterre *

4. The Ideology of the Body in Kenneth Burke and Roland Barthes o
5. Aesthetics and Society in Benjamin and Adorno o

"*Aesthetics, Rhetoric, Ideology*
1. Epistemology of Metaphor *
2. Pascal's Allegory of Persuasion *
3. Diderot's Battle of the Faculties o
4. Phenomenality and Materiality in Kant *
5. Sign and Symbol in Hegel's *Aesthetics* *
6. Hegel on the Sublime *
7. Aestheticism: Schiller and Friedrich Schlegel's Misreading of Kant and Fichte o
8. Critique of Religion and Political Ideology in Kierkegaard and Marx o
9. Rhetoric/Ideology (theoretical conclusion)"
Completed *      In progress o

69. Kojève, *Introduction à la lecture de Hegel*, p. 534.

70. Theodor Adorno, "Commitment," in Ernst Bloch et al., *Aesthetics and Politics* (London: Verso, 1977), pp. 180, 194.

71. Jean-Paul Sartre, *Between Existentialism and Marxism*, trans. Quintin Hoare (New York: Pantheon, 1974), p. 173.

72. Heidegger, *Being and Time*, p. 437.

73. Lionel Abel describes Wahl's connections to American intellectuals in *The Intellectual Follies* (New York: Norton, 1984).

74. For an example of this see Stanley Edgar Hyman, *The Armed Vision* (New York: Vintage Books, 1955), pp. ix–x.

75. Quoted in Mark Ford, "No One Else Can Take a Bath for You," *London Review of Books*, March 31, 1988, p. 20.

76. Randall Jarrell, *Poetry and the Age* (New York: Knopf, 1955), p. 80

77. Yves Bonnefoy, "Critics—English and French," *Encounter*, 11(1958), p. 40.

78. T. S. Eliot, *Selected Essays* (New York: Harcourt Brace, 1950), p. 10. On the question of impersonality in Eliot and Pound, see Maud Ellmann, *The Poetics of Impersonality* (Cambridge, Mass.: Harvard University Press, 1987).

79. Eliot, *Selected Essays*, pp. 255, 246, 247.

80. Paul Valéry, *Anthology*, ed. James Lawler (Princeton: Princeton University Press, 1977), p. 97.

81. Quoted in Louis Menand, *Discovering Modernism: T. S. Eliot and His Context* (New York: Oxford University Press, 1987), p. 58.

82. T. S. Eliot, *The Sacred Wood* (London: Methuen, 1948), pp. 149, 129.

83. Robert Pinsky, *The Situation of Poetry* (Princeton: Princeton University Press, 1976), pp. 4–5.

84. Robert Creeley, "Pieces," in *Collected Poetry* (Berkeley: University of California Press, 1982).

85. Lionel Trilling, *Matthew Arnold* (New York: Norton, 1939), p. 194.

86. M. H. Abrams, quoted in Hans Aarsleff, *From Locke to Saussure* (Minneapolis: University of Minnesota Press, 1981), pp. 350, 380.

87. Jean-Paul Sartre, *The Transcendence of the Ego*, trans. Forrest Williams and Robert Kirkpatrick (New York: Farrar, Straus, and Giroux, 1957); Jean-Paul Sartre, *The Psychology of the Imagination* (Secaucus, N.J.: Citadel Press, n.d.), pp. 7, 13, 63.

88. Edmund Husserl, *Cartesian Meditations*, trans. Dorion Cairns (The Hague: Martinus Nijhoff, 1973), pp. 41, 82, 83–84. On Husserl see Henry Staten, *Wittgenstein and Derrida* (Lincoln: University of Nebraska Press, 1984), pp. 33–58; John Llewelyn, *Derrida on the Threshold of Sense* (New

York: St. Martin's Press, 1986), pp. 16–31; and Jacques Derrida, *Edmund Husserl's "Origin of Geometry": An Introduction,* trans. John P. Leavey, Jr. (Stonybrook, N.Y.: Nicholas Hays, 1978).

89. Martin Heidegger, "The Origin of the Work of Art," in Martin Heidegger, *Poetry, Language, Thought,* trans. Albert Hofstadter (New York: Harper & Row, 1971), pp. 27, 46, 64.

90. De Man, "Mallarmé, Yeats, and the Post-Romantic Predicament," p. 92.

91. The role of notions of interiority and self in *Blindness and Insight* is pronounced. In chapter 1 he criticizes structuralism for its too hasty "suppression of the subject" and its failure to deal with "the larger question of the ontological status of the subject" (*BI,* p. 19). (De Man was not going to get swept up in the trend called structuralism, as his remarks in various places on Lévi-Strauss, Foucault, and Barthes reveal. I will pick up this issue in this note after I have discussed *Blindness and Insight.* Chapter 3, on Binswanger, deals with the confusion caused by the failure to appreciate the difference between the empirical self and the aesthetic self. "Art," he says, "originates in and by means of this divergence" (*BI,* p. 41), for the self has to be taken into account as the origin not of an anthropology but of an ontology. Chapter 4, on Lukács, argues that the considerable insight into literature Lukács had was due to his ability to free himself from preconceived notions about the novel as an imitation of reality. "This form can have nothing in common with the homogeneous, organic form of nature: it is founded on an act of consciousness, not on the imitation of a natural object" (*BI,* p. 56). Chapter 5 uses Blanchot to home in even closer on the literary implications of focusing on what Husserl calls the transcendental, not the personal, self. Attention to language is what allowed Mallarmé, according to Blanchot, to depersonalize his writing. This sort of attention and attentiveness to language suggested to de Man, I believe, a way of retaining the best aspects of New Criticism, its own attentiveness to language; for, although language cannot give people access to the "really real" realm of concrete things, it is itself such a material thing. He writes: "The double aspect of language, capable of being at the same time a concrete, natural thing and the product of an activity of consciousness, serves Mallarmé as the starting point of a dialectical development that runs through his entire work" (*BI,* pp. 69–70). This understanding of the materiality of writing will be taken up and developed in de Man's later writings. Chapter 6, on Poulet, addresses the question of the literary self but faults Poulet for thinking of language primarily as a means to the end of gaining access to "a deeper subjectivity." Self and language are parts of a dialectic; neither is anterior to the other (*BI,* pp. 100–101). Chapter 7, on Derrida and Rousseau, argues that Rousseau "interiorizes the object." "Presence" in Rousseau does not inhere in the world of external objects but is "transposed within the self-reflective inwardness of a consciousness" (*BI,* pp. 133–34).

Concerning de Man and Lévi-Strauss, Foucault, and Barthes: The critical comments on Lévi-Strauss appear at *BI,* pp. 9–12, 18–19; those on Foucault at *BI,* pp. 37–38, 49–50. His stringent criticism of Barthes appears in Richard Macksey and Eugenio Donato (eds.) *The Structuralist Controversy* (Baltimore: Johns Hopkins University Press, 1966) in the form of an intervention by de Man at the famous conference in Baltimore directed at Barthes. The statement reflects de Man's thinking about his two main topics, history and consciousness:

"I would like to speak a moment of Roland Barthes's treatment of history. I find that you have an optimistic historical myth (the same one I saw in Donato) which is linked to the abandonment of the last active form of traditional philosophy that we know, phenomenology, and the replacement of phenomenology with psychoanalysis, etc. That represents historical progress and extremely optimistic possibilities for the history of thought. However, you must show us that the results you have obtained in the stylistic analyses that you make are superior to those of your predecessors, thanks to this optimistic change which is linked to a certain historic renewal. I must admit, I have been somewhat disappointed by the specific analyses that you give us. I don't believe they show any progress over those of the Formalists, Russian or American, who used empirical methods, though neither the vocabulary nor the conceptual frame that you use. But more seriously, when I hear you refer to facts of literary history, you say things that are false within a typically French myth. I find in your work a false conception of classicism and romanticism. When, for example, concerning the question of the narrator or the "double ego," you speak of writing since Mallarmé and of the new novel, etc., and you oppose them to what happens in the romantic novel or story or autobiography—you are simply wrong. In the romantic autobiography, or well before that, in the seventeenth-century story, this same complication of the ego (*moi*) is found, not only unconsciously, but explicitly and thematically treated, in a much more complex way than in the contemporary novel. I don't want to continue this development; it is simply to indicate that you distort history *because* you need a historical myth of progress to justify a method which is not yet able to justify itself by its results. It is in the notion of temporality rather than in that of history that I see you making consciousness undergo a reification, which is linked to this same optimism which troubles me" (p. 150) It is interesting that Barthes was also the occasion of de Man's break with *The New York Review of Books*. De Man was asked to review the English translation of *Mythologies*. He argued that "the actual innovations introduced by Roland Barthes in the analytic study of literary texts are relatively slight" (MS, "Roland Barthes and the Limits of Structuralism"). The review was declined by the editors of *The New York Review of Books*.

92. Letter of Paul de Man to Wlad Godzich, March 10, 1982. The passage of the letter reads—de Man is referring to the essays "The Dead End of Formalist Criticism" and "Heidegger's Exegeses of Hölderlin"—as follows: "I certainly know what it is I was struggling with, but the terminology all too often gets in the way. Be this as it may, the two pieces are certainly typical and properly contrastive versions of someone most uncomfortably stuck in ontologism. Maybe they can still have some use as 'das warnend ängstig Lied' to those tempted to go the same way."

93. W. J. Bate, *The Burden of the Past and the English Romantic Poet* (Cambridge, Mass.: Harvard University Press, 1972), pp. 124–25; M. H. Abrams, *Natural Supernaturalism: Tradition and Revolution in Romantic Literature* (New York: Norton, 1971), p. 182.

94. Geoffrey Hartman, *Wordsworth's Poetry, 1787–1814* (1964; reprint Cambridge, Mass.: Harvard University Press, 1987). Robert Langbaum, "Magnifying Wordsworth," *ELH*, 33 (1966), p. 273.

95. Harold Bloom, *Ruin the Sacred Truths: Poetry and Belief, the Bible to the Present* (Cambridge, Mass.: Harvard University Press, 1989).

96. Harold Bloom (ed.), *Romanticism and Consciousness: Essays in Criticism* (New York: Norton, 1970), p. 1; Bloom, *Ringers in the Tower,* pp. 16–17, 19, 2.

97. Gilles Deleuze, *Foucault,* trans. Sean Hand (Minneapolis: University of Minnesota Press, 1988), p. 108.

98. Paul de Man, "Time and History in Wordsworth," MS. J. Hillis Miller kindly shared this MS with me. In the mean-time, Tom Keenan of Princeton University working with Patricia de Man has discovered the texts of the set of Christian Gauss Seminars minus this one, that de Man delivered at Princeton in April and May 1967. This lecture, read on April 27, 1967, was the fourth of a series of six entitled "Contemporary Criticism and the Problem of Romanticism."

99. See *BI*, p. 35, citing Walter Benjamin, *The Origin of the German Tragic Drama,* trans. John Osborne (London: Verso, 1977), p. 233.

100. Neil Hertz, "Lurid Figures," in Lindsay Waters and Wlad Godzich (eds.), *Reading de Man Reading* (Minneapolis: University of Minnesota Press, 1989).

101. De Man's interest in history as a category has received little attention. It may be that the concept as he employed it in the 1950s and 1960s is Heideggerian in origin, and reveals the influence of what Heidegger says about "authentic historicality" in *Being and Time* (p. 437), and that is all there is to say; but matters may be more complicated. In texts like "Mallarmé and Poetic Nothingness" he seems to make some of the same claims Julia Kristeva, coming from the same intellectual background, makes for the historical significance of poetry in *The Revolution in Poetic Language.* A useful document pertaining to de Man's professed interest in history is the following letter to Wlad Godzich of August 30, 1982. De Man is responding to Godzich's introduction to the Minnesota edition of *Blindness and Insight*:

"Dear Wlad,

"Please forgive me for replying so late to your kind letter and outstanding introduction, but I am only slowly recovering some of my physical strength, though the intellectual one doesn't seem as impaired (but who am I to know? — at least the illusion is intact). I have been (and indeed am) seriously ill, but especially since I got home from the clinic, I have made considerable progress. I find the entire experience quite fascinating and of great interest.

"As a matter of fact, your preface is the first thing I read on coming home and is forever associated (metaphorically?) to that blessed moment. The epithet 'surgical' on page one seemed particularly apt, but the text gave me much deeper satisfaction, as I fully expected after your previous text on the Derrida essay in *BI*. What a relief to be understood and to be, at long last, *technically* (and not existentially or polemically) understood and considered. I find your text impeccable in all respects, entirely responsive to yet independent from what I try to do. And your own 'solar' version of the (double motion) in lightning ('Jetzt aber tagt's' or 'Mir hat Apollo geschlagen' in Hölderlin) and in the light (as mediated Geist) is original and right. I find this notion now back in Hegel (and Kant) as the aporia between deictic and allegorical language; the thing on Hegel in the last *Critical Inquiry* begins this problematic in which I have since progressed a little; elsewhere, I find it again in the tension between truth as name and truth as proposition (in a paper I have just written on Baudelaire by way of Nietzsche). So you are certainly, in my perception, right on target.

"I don't think your text is too dense and have very few suggestions. Irony is a dangerous term, because people think they know what the word means and this forecloses all understanding. 'Reading' is much better; and irony, anyway, is not thematized in *BI*, not even in the section on irony in 'Rhetoric of Temporality.' What Gasché says about it in his recent piece in *Diacritics* with regard to Fichte and Friedrich Schlegel is entirely to the point but applied to *AR* rather than *BI*. As for history, in fact my main and everrecurrent concern, all your hints are in the right direction, including the references to Heidegger and Hegel. I don't see how you could do much more in a limited space.

"My only suggestion is a possible clarification of the term 'the apparent' on pages 10ff., which also leads to the expression 'simulacrity of the simulacrum' to which you seem to take more exception than I do. You very rightly refer to Schiller (lesson 26 of *Ästh. Erziehung*) but this allusion, in my experience, remains cryptic for many readers. I wonder if the most economic way to gloss 'the apparent' (which remains awkward in the oh so pragmatic English language) is not to go through translation and to insert after Schiller, on p. 10, a sentence on 'the apparent' as corresponding to the French 'le paraitre' (in opposition to 'être') and especially to the German Schein or scheinen which, of course, condenses the entire problematic in one single word. Reference could possibly be made to Hegel (das Schöne ist das sinnliche Scheinen der Idee) or, as one instance among many, to the discussion of 'scheint' in a remarkable letter of Heidegger to Emil Staiger à propos of the Mörike poem 'Auf eine Lampe' (in Emil Staiger, *Die Kunst der Interpretation*). 'Simulacrity of the simulacrum' is, of course 'Schein des Scheins' (or des Scheinens) or 'l'apparence de l'apparaitre,' and this may be a help to the readers who know German or French — though it may well compound the confusion of those who don't . . . but tant pis pour eux. The Greek eidos and aletheia or for that matter the Latin videtur could help, but that would lead too far. The merit of the brief Heidegger letter to Staiger is that it also makes the connection with Husserl and the entire project of phenomenology as phainestaia, etc. This rich filiation is all present in your text and the mere mention of the word Schein may help to make it 'erschein' even more clearly. It is only a matter of adding a few words, maybe a dozen. But, also as it now stands, the introduction far sur-passes my best expectations and will be most helpful in orienting the reader in the right direction.

"I was sorry to hear about the untimely death of your father and about your ankle, remembering earlier leg trouble when you were in New Haven—where I wish you still were. I hope you are better and that you and I can fully learn to dismiss illness as 'nur Schein' and a loss of time.

"All my best,
"Cordially yours,
"Paul de Man"

102. Richard Sieburth, "Benjamin the Scavenger," *Assemblage* (forthcoming)

103. Walter Benjamin, *Moscow Diary,* trans. Richard Sieburth and ed. Gary Smith (Cambridge, Mass.: Harvard University Press, 1986), p. 132.

104. I refer here to Frank Kermode, "Dwelling Poetically in New Haven," in Frank Doggett and Robert Buttell (eds.), *Wallace Stevens: A Celebration* (Princeton: Princeton University Press, 1980), pp. 256–73.

105. Quoted by Kermode, "Dwelling Poetically," p. 264.

Critical Writings
1953–1978

# Montaigne and Transcendence (1953)

"Man can be only what he is, and imagine only within his capacity" (II, ch. 12). "These transcendental humors frighten me, like lofty and inaccessible places" (III, ch. 13). On the basis of a great number of similar passages, we are tempted to make rejection of transcendence the axis of Montaigne's thought. He keeps repeating that for him all transcendence is impossible, even harmful: "countless minds are destroyed by their own strength and suppleness" (II, ch. 12). The tone is intensified whenever he asserts man's inability to escape himself; it becomes solemn, very different from his usual ironic grace, when it warns of the dangers we incur when we attempt to overreach ourselves: "I suffered even more vexation than compassion," and so on (II, ch. 12). Although composition was not his concern, it is no accident that these arguments occur at the central points of the work, those we are quite naturally tempted to take as declarations of principle, as summaries of thought—at the very end of the book, at the end of the longest and most elaborate essay (III, ch. 13, and the end of the *Apology*). There is no doubt that the theme is given prominence. From this we conclude that Montaigne is a subjectivist, the chronicler of pure immanence. We invoke him to characterize as extravagant certain spiritual ventures that seek to extend the limits of the human. Our contemporaries who vaunt the proposition that existence precedes essence claim Montaigne as one of their party; he is honored by a (very judicious) study in one of our reviews whose very title seems to indicate a lack of interest in authors of such remote times.[1] The *Essays* become the reflection of an absolute subjectivity—as Hugo Friedrich puts it, *die flüssige Ausdruckslinie der flieszenden Subjektivität* (the fluid line expressing the flow of subjectivity). At last Mon-

3

taigne appears to be summed up in a neat and definitive formula. In a sense this is quite true, but we must take a closer look.

For it is very unlikely that we can enclose Montaigne in a decisive formula, even one that denies him any generality. He has warned us that we must never take him in a normative sense, that he does nothing but *describe;* he never seeks to impose a view on us. When he happens to preach, as in the passages against transcendence, it is not so much the cause preached that matters as the phenomenon of man—Montaigne—preaching. All we can conclude is that there exists, between Montaigne and transcendence, a special link that tends to elicit from him the tone of controversy. But in this incomparably supple mind, every *contra* has a *pro*, and the more vigorous the *contra*, the more powerful the *pro*. Montaigne does not always feel it is necessary to isolate the two poles of the dialectic; to circumscribe them would be to render them static, to confer on them a value as absolutes that would distort them. The aspirations he expresses least are often the most powerful, those that most preoccupy him, those he most risks yielding to, perhaps. We must be careful not to assume that the forces he treats harshly or fails to define are nonexistent for him or even perverse.

There is no doubt the problem of transcendence deeply concerned Montaigne, and that he discussed it from a variety of aspects that we must briefly distinguish. It is also true that one of the dominant motifs of the *Essays* is the refusal to escape oneself. But before drawing exclusive conclusions of any sort from this circumstance, we must follow the course of this thought and see what stages it passes through to reach this point. We must further determine whether this movement tends toward a static equilibrium, like that of the pans of a scale, or if it is a transformation of energy that shifts its dynamics to another realm of the mental world—where it is perpetuated in infinite reflections.

This author, whom we like to regard as purely capricious, has given, as a matter of fact, one of the fullest and profoundest descriptions of the difficult problem of transcendence, the problem of our ambiguous relations with our own being. Montaigne has treated the problem, not in its metaphysical form, but in its experienced or, as we say, its *existential* form. He was quite aware how differently our impatience with our own limits is manifested: by the exercise of reason, by the attraction of an absolute morality, and finally, by the creation of form. His scrutiny is initially epistemological, then ethical, and then—in a diffuse fashion—aesthetic. This enterprise is that of an eminently correct and conscientious mind. Naturally the succession is not indicated systematically; the three types of consideration are for the most part present simultaneously, which is one of the reasons for the extreme density of a mind that always returns to its complex central core, from which it emanates like a spiral, continued to infinity.

We find in the *Apology for Raymond Sebond* (II, ch. 12) the longest and most detailed development, offering a more or less consistent critique of transcendence by the exercise of pure reason: an epistemological critique that is one of the most amply sustained "theses" of the *Essays*. The demonstration is, of course, not rigorous in the sense of formal logic, but it covers a broad area without major digressions and remains—a rare thing in Montaigne—concentrated on the subject for over a hundred pages. Let us recall the general bearing of the essay: that between man and God, the transcendent principle, there is no direct contact, either by mystical communication or rational knowledge. We must be careful not to interpret the religious conclusion that "man will rise by abandoning and renouncing his own means, and letting himself be raised and uplifted by purely celestial means"—as if Montaigne were preaching a natural and in a sense naive transcendence. Altogether conventional, this conclusion actually shifts the problem of grace and salvation outside the realm of consciousness. Montaigne's attitude is, of course, the assertion of the status quo in matters of religion; we shall see the signification of this later on, but for now, it is appropriate to reduce this attitude to the proportion of a secondary passage. It is not here that we shall find the core of his attitude toward transcendence.

Montaigne's epistemological critique is made not in the form of a phenomenology of cognitive consciousness considered in itself but rather in the form of a description of knowledge as experience (*connaissance vécue*); this is not so much an epistemology as an existential psychology of reflective consciousness. Hence he will speak of it from the point of view where we meet knowledge concretely: as a subjective desire to know, and also as the discovery of the totality of knowledge bequeathed us by our intellectual ancestors. He will not deal with the question otherwise, and he cannot approve the detached and pedantic tone of Aristotelian scholasticism: "I do not recognize in Aristotle most of my ordinary actions: they have been covered and dressed up in another robe for the use of the school" (III, ch. 5). Like any other behavior, the action of the *cogito* interests him only as it appears to us, in its most vivid form.

Here is the central intuition of which the entire critique is but an illustration: if we strip knowledge of all its sumptuous trappings, of the entire apparatus in which it decks itself out in order to present itself as an absolute, we find at its heart only a human appetite, frail and arbitrary—like all our appetites. The huge mass of our ancestors' wisdom swarms with contradictions and errors; this would only moderately disturb a rationalist who tries to find some persistent principle in this accumulation of errors and hypotheses. Montaigne, on the contrary, simply declares that no such principle exists. Reason does not function as if it were influenced by a higher principle that drew it as the magnet draws iron filings. It is not directed by successive gropings toward an order that transcends it. Above all, it is not a movement that is achieved in spite of ourselves; our rational faculties do not act passively under the sway of some superhuman power; unlike the tides, they are not subject to gravitational force. Their mainspring is an entirely subjective intentionality; man thinks, not because truth compels him to do so, but because thought affords him human satisfaction. In the last analysis, rational construction does not conceal an objective truth, but is merely the expression of our pleasure in constructing it. "I cannot easily persuade myself that Epicurus, Plato, and Pythagoras gave us their Atoms, their Ideas, and their Numbers as good coin of the realm. . . . Each one of these great men . . . has exercised his mind on such conceptions as had at least a pleasant and subtle appearance. . . . The very search for great and occult things is very pleasant. . . . Study being in itself a pleasant occupation, so pleasant that among other pleasures the Stoics forbid also that which comes from the exercise of the mind" (II, ch. 12).

But what is the source of this satisfaction? The word "desire," or "appetite," is not in itself a closed concept; all desire is *of* something. To say that knowledge rests on an intentionality refers to the problem of describing its mechanism. And the contradictory character of this intentionality is well known to Montaigne, who does not confine himself to the commonplace that all knowledge is impelled by the desire to know. The complication begins once we realize that this desire seeks to destroy itself by dissolving in a world of fixed laws, in which subjectivity is ultimately suspended. Knowledge is not an ordinary desire that seeks out its object and takes possession of it. The object of knowledge is contradictory in essence — in contradiction with the existence of its own intentional structure. In every act of knowledge there is a profound flaw that leads to an insoluble dilemma: its object can be known only at the price of the existence of the knowing agent (cognitive consciousness). Without this sacrifice, there can be no really objective knowledge.

Montaigne is perfectly aware of this, and that is why he speaks of knowledge as a dangerous action. At its origin, as we have seen, the motive for knowledge is "pleasant"; in its consequences, it is the most terrifying impulse imaginable, since it can lead to the very destruction of the thinking being. "Eudoxus longed and prayed the Gods that he might once see the sun at close hand, might understand its form, its grandeur, and its beauty, at the cost of being burnt up by it there and then. He wished, at the price of his life, to acquire a knowledge of which the use and possession was at the same time taken from him, and for this sudden and inconstant knowledge to lose all other knowledge that he had and that he might have acquired subsequently" (II, ch. 12). And we should adduce the passage on Tasso's madness: "Does he not have reason to be grateful to that murderous vivacity of his mind? to that brilliance that has blinded him? to that exact and intent apprehension of his reason which has deprived him of reason? to that rare aptitude for the exercise of the mind, which has left him without exercise and without mind?" (II, ch. 12). Knowledge is impossible: "No, no, we sense nothing, we see nothing; all things are hidden from us, we cannot establish what any one of them is." Yet knowledge persists as a temptation, because it is a source of pleasure, and a dangerous temptation, which leads to madness.

The problem has gained in density; knowledge is complicated by two profound dimensions: that of its essential failure and that of the danger of this failure to being. Many philosophers and poets have come to this—to the despair of *Igitur,* to the silence of Rimbaud, to the first monologue of *Faust;* many have experienced the drama of knowledge with greater rigor than Montaigne and perhaps with greater intensity too (though of course we do not know what impulses may have tormented the young Montaigne, before he began writing the *Essays*). But Montaigne introduced a turn of mind whose originality and validity are forever admirable. Intuitively, without entering into the metaphysical ramifications of this decision, but with the vigor of an intelligence so beguiled by its own exercise that it cannot tolerate for a moment the notion of its own destruction, Montaigne escaped the impasse in which his axiomatic Pyrrhonism might have imprisoned him. If his subjectivity interposes an impenetrable screen between object and mind, then mind will be exercised on the level of this very screen and will find in the acknowledgment of its failure its only positive function. The main object of knowledge becomes the knowledge of its failure. Not of its limits; that would be a banal attitude. The limitation of knowledge is total, in simple as well as in complex problems, for that limitation is inscribed in the very constitution of knowledge, colors its every activity, great or small. But the lucid mind can know its own subjectivity, precisely at the point where subjectivity destroys its functioning. It recognizes that its life consists in an endless series of failures of this order, and it finds that it retains the power to take stock of them all. This power is asserted, thanks to an amazing change of sign, as a positive force; just when the mind falls into the despair of its impotence, it regains all its elasticity in perceiving this very impotence. We see how Montaigne's tone gains in vitality once he can give himself up to this practice. The long, the interminable passage of the *Apology* that never stops listing external reasons why reason cannot be regarded as trustworthy—let us admit that this text becomes quite tiresome. And then suddenly the tone changes: Montaigne is going to tell us how he knows, by his own experience, that his knowledge is impotent. "I who spy on myself more closely, who have my eyes unceasingly intent upon myself . . . I would hardly dare tell of the vanity and weakness that I find in myself" (II, ch. 12). And immediately we find Montaigne in his true and best manner: ironic and playful and eloquent, admirably perceptive and subtle. No one else speaks of himself with such readiness and wit. The ultimate reason for which is that it is the only activity that suits the mind; the mind can justify itself only at the very point where it ceases to be pure.

We are far from total immanence. Subjectivity does not know speech; it laughs, groans, shrieks, or weeps; it never describes. Let there be no mistake: Montaigne speaking of the impossibility of knowing himself is entirely in transcendence. He recounts himself, he knows himself, he observes himself; he is outside himself, he transcends himself. But not altogether, since, quite sincerely, he remains utterly at the mercy of his every shift of mood. Between the living Montaigne, whom a corn on his foot renders inaccessible, and the Montaigne who notes the absurdity of his inconsistence, there is a distinction: the former remains an object for the latter's reflection; he imposes his law on this reflection down to its last details; and he strips it of any force of consistency and absolute truth, but not of its reflecting character. The mind's joys are preserved in a transcendence that exceeds rational transcendence by denying it.

The attitude appears easy only in appearance. The man who has admitted once and for all the impossibility of an abstractly formulable truth deprives himself of all the false security we find in the illusion of governing matter and ourselves. He deprives himself of any possibility of sudden expansion, of any passion in which he commits himself entirely and forgets himself. He strips the mind of that hope of continuity that has inspired so many bold constructions. He compels a withdrawal into the self, ironic, perpetually lucid and curious, and tolerates no cheating: he leaves himself strangely naked and vulnerable to the inevitable powers that assail him and with which he allows himself no identification. Montaigne's gaiety exists, and his wisdom—but they are not those of an ordinary being. This man who claims to be average—*moyen*—is more heroic than many more spectacular souls. His own has none of that skeptical sloth that reposes in the ignorance of its knowledge. On the contrary, this mind nourishes and renews itself on that ignorance, following new and incessant paths while being sustained by nothing but its own energy.

Hugo Friedrich is quite right to locate this posture at the start of a great philosophical tradition that is still very much alive.[2] "Er ist die (literarische) Schöpfung der anderen, von den Naturwissenschaften getrennten groszen Bewegung des modernen Geistes: der moralistischen Phänomenologie" (It is the [literary] creation of the other great movement of modern mind, the movement that is separated from the natural sciences: moral phenomenology). Since Husserl, we have learned to find in this fundamental humility of the mind, which cannot claim to legislate but only to describe, the best source of resistance to the aberrations of our time. If we observe the ethical conclusions to which the premises of Montaigne's very special epistemological transcendence lead us, we find this distinctly confirmed.

The negation of an absolute knowledge implies the negation of a knowable good. "That which our reason counsels us as most prudent, is generally that each man obey the laws of his own country. . . . And thereby what does reason mean, save that our duty has no other rule than what is fortuitous" (I, ch. 23). It is not possible for Montaigne to interpose the Aristotelian concept of happiness as an absolute regulative principle in the world of ethics (*Nicomachean Ethics* I.7), for the very notion of happiness is never pure and distinct; like knowledge, happiness is an arbitrary product of the moment, without consistency and always accompanied by its painful antithesis. And it is not because we may speak of ourselves that we can govern ourselves. Ethical values are entirely relative; we receive them by the accident of birth. They are as individual as the shape of our face, and equally intransmissible.

But just as reason's functioning must be preserved as an integral part of our vitality, the ethical sense cannot dissolve into a pluralistic cynicism that would leave us in an impoverishing stagnation. The ethical gesture must continue, and naturally this gesture will begin in the continuity of an orthodoxy we can learn; there is no reason to leave it behind, since there is no hierarchy of ethical systems. It can validly repeat the rituals it has learned without any real necessity of profound adherence, for it is not *the good* that matters but the formal procedure of ethical exercise. Montaigne's conservatism is essentially ritualistic; he says his prayers and takes absolution like the good Christian he considers himself to be. But above all, he observes and recounts himself practicing these rites, with an eye that is half-humorous and half-serious—exactly as he observed himself thinking without hope of truth. Ritual is what remains of morality when it is drained of absolutes, just as phenomenology is what remains of knowledge when it is drained of objective truth.

Thus history is introduced as a determining force in the present only, as the bearer of a certain ethical system that we accept as our own. This point of view, it is true, seems to offer no account of historical movements and appears to exclude the notion of any invention or rebellion of a moral nature. After all, Christian ritual too was invented; does Montaigne reject all creative action? But we must not decide too hastily. His thought is sufficiently consistent so that, preaching a relativism of history, it has respected that relativism in its own historical judgments. His conservatism is strictly a conservatism of his own age: it presupposes the existence of a solid, ripe, flexible orthodoxy adapted to the demands of subjectivity; an orthodoxy that bears within it a long series of meditations and is responsive to the contradictions of the human condition. The Catholic religion of the sixteenth century had, as Montaigne so admirably puts it, "suffered a long loss of years in ripening this inestimable fruit" (I, ch. 23). To oppose it would require a harsh temerity that Montaigne can understand but to which he will not yield: "For whoever meddles with choosing and changing usurps the authority to judge, and he must be very sure that he sees the weakness of what he is casting out and the goodness of what he is bringing in." His conservatism is, as we say nowadays, entirely "situational." In the perspective of his moment, Catholicism appears as the tested and tolerant doctrine, Protestantism as a fanatical movement. A hundred years later, can we doubt that Montaigne would have sided with Pierre Bayle? If the prevailing orthodoxy hardens, crystallizes into sharp points, becoming massive and opaque, wounding anyone who comes up against it; if it has no concern but to perpetuate itself as an institution and if its ritual becomes a police regulation, Montaigne will be the first to detest it, and it remains for us to imagine what rebellions he is capable of. Listen to him, even now, thundering against the League, in a brief discourse that will apply to so many of Catholicism's subsequent excesses: "But if the inventors [the Protestants] have done more harm, the imitators [the Catholics] are more vicious in that they wholeheartedly follow examples whose horror and evil they have felt and punished. And if there is some degree of honor even in evil-doing, they must concede to the others the glory of invention and the courage of making the first effort" (I, ch. 23).

Let these words be remembered when we would invoke a conservatism like Montaigne's to extenuate some injustice of our own. What orthodoxy, at the present time, can invoke the breadth and comprehension of postmedieval Christianity? The wretched myths that surround us are no sooner born than they degenerate into sclerotic bureaucracies. They must appeal to the most factitious loyalties—those to race and nation—in order to gain any vitality at all. Imagine Montaigne in such surroundings; no doubt he would be on the side of the rebels.

He would be on their side, but without, for all that, taking himself seriously. In the moral realm, his transcendence admits of no protest except against stupidity. Otherwise it is entertained and justified and content to make a patient inventory of the dangerous structures men have produced in hopes of achieving some sort of rule. Montaigne's transcendence describes such structures gently, with a respectful irony and an utter honesty—always asserting their ultimate absurdity, but delighting as a connoisseur in the spectacle of their beauty. This is a phenomenology of the highest order, i.e., in the last analysis, of a formal and aesthetic order. It brings Montaigne much closer to the poets than to systematic minds, whether they be philosophers, scientists, or writers. Friedrich quotes Dilthey, who says quite properly of such minds: "Their eyes remain fixed on the enigma of life, but they despair of solving it by means of a universally valid metaphysics based on a theory of the coherence of the Universe; life must interpret itself—such is the great idea which linked this philosophy of life with worldly experience and literary creation." Nor has Valéry's admirably condensed expression of the same thought escaped Hugo Friedrich's vigilance: "Doubt leads to Form."

This observation wonderfully applies to Montaigne. The paradoxical transcendence that is located beyond failure, that subtle balancing between the serene stability of objects and the fluidity of subjective consciousness, has a name: it is *form,* a gratuitous but rigorous structure that our hands make and unmake without ever completing. This ineffable form is everywhere in Montaigne. It *is,* in the ontological force of the term, the *Essays.* We can never be sufficiently amazed by the extraordinary nature of this enterprise. A man sits down at his desk and writes, without seeking to communicate with anyone in particular, without needing to express any violent sentiment that is tormenting him, without desiring to explain himself to himself or to justify himself morally in his own eyes, without any attempt at fabulation. Proust has been invoked here, but there is a fundamental difference of intention. As in the case of the symbolists (it would be better to say, more restrictively: as in the case of Baudelaire and Mallarmé), what matters for Proust is to give form to the subjective, to transform the chaos of experience into a construction, into a system of relations. His temporal perspective is necessarily that of the past, which has frozen action into the immobility of the irrevocable, and his book is actually written from the point of view of Death—of a man who is already dead. Montaigne has even pierced the illusion of this ultimate transcendence; by the very nature of his work, he has assumed the failure of the aesthetic, with the same good grace with which he has transcended the failure of knowledge and of ethics. His tense is exclusively the present; he moves unceasingly on the narrow ridge where no temporal density can accumulate, where he remains open, so to speak, to every wind that blows. The past collapses straightaway into oblivion, because it works loose from the subjectivity of the immediate; have we sufficiently understood the extraordinary fact that Montaigne never refers to his previous declarations? Quite literally, he has forgotten them. The future, it goes without saying, remains open; no conclusion is definitive, and contradiction is the mind's law. But—a fundamental nuance—this present tense is not the present of Montaigne living through this or that experience; it is the present of Montaigne writing. No separation of the written phenomenon from the moment when he writes, but a formal separation between the action really performed and his observation by means of discourse. The summary image of the *Essays* is that of a man who observes himself in the gratuitous and fundamentally futile act of writing. By the word, Montaigne is detached from himself; he transcends himself, reflects himself with the infinity of his impossible transcendences reflected, including the impossibility of seeing himself as a form, however transitory. It is by the word that he manages, in Merleau-Ponty's phrase, "to be *elsewhere*," but this alterity has destroyed his customary motivation, which is the objectivization of consciousness. For this reason, because all it preserves of aesthetic intentionality is its movement, his attitude will never become a value: Montaigne remains far from the (admirable) symbolist aestheticism. He locates himself beyond aesthetic value; even the very pure beauty of his sentences, the entrancing sinuosity of his thought, constitutes, for him, only a phenomenon he regards with a tranquil irony. It is with the same irony that he must regard our incessant efforts to grasp him.

Translated by Richard Howard

## Notes

1. *Les Temps modernes.*—Trans.
2. Hugo Friedrich, *Montaigne* (Bern: Francke Verlag, 1949).

# The Inward Generation (1955)

There always is a strange fascination about the bad verse that great poets write in their youth. They often seem more receptive than any to the mannerisms and clichés of their age, particularly to those that their later work will reject most forcefully. Their early work, therefore, is often a very good place to discover the conventions of a certain period and to meet its problems from the inside, as they appeared to these writers themselves.

Every generation writes its own kind of bad poetry, but many young poets of today are bad in an intricate and involved way that defies description. Freer and more conscious than any of their predecessors, they seem unable to surmount passivity, which is the very opposite of freedom and awareness. They can be highly formalized, but without any real sense of decorum; extravagantly free, without enjoying their daring; minutely precious, without any true taste for language. At best, they turn around as in a cage, all their myths exploded one by one, and keep making up the inventory of the failures they have inherited. At worst, they strike poses and mistake imitation for mask, talking endlessly and uninterestingly about themselves in elaborately borrowed references. In each case, there is the feeling of being trapped, accompanied by a vague premonition that poetry alone could end the oppression, provided one could find access again to true words. Meanwhile, the flow of language hardly covers up the sterile silence underneath.

I speak of poetry, but I could as well speak of the minds in general, for the same weight paralyzes all human actions and relationships. But is this not a normal phenomenon of youth, the modern expression of *mal du siècle*, the necessary period of negativism that accompanies all spiritual growth? It may seem so, but

12

certain differences suggest a deeper crisis. It is impossible, for instance, for the older generation to look back on the younger with the wisdom and tolerance of those who recognize difficulties that they have overcome. On the contrary, they must feel rather naive if they compare their facile commitments with the withdrawn reserve or the blind violence of their successors. This is, however, the result of a more important change. For well over a century, the sterility alluded to has been itself the central subject of all great poetry. The fact that this could be the case, that it could be spoken about, indicated that one could think of oneself as capable of escaping beyond this condition. Most great poems of this era are about this wasteland, which may turn, avowedly or not, into a renewed country of joy and innocence. The list of examples would be too long: Hölderlin's "Brot und Wein," Keats's "Hyperion," Baudelaire's "Le Voyage," Rimbaud's *Saison en Enfer,* Yeats's "Second Coming," Rilke's *Sonneten an Orpheus.* A parallel line runs through philosophy, most clearly visible in Germany in the evolution from Hegel to Nietzsche and to Heidegger. Whatever the differences between Hegel's absolute spirit, Nietzsche's Zarathustra and what Heidegger merely calls Being, if seen within the historical perspective that these philosophies postulate, all three imply a prophetic vision, a turning away from an erring present to a new beginning.

Regardless of one's judgment of the poetry or systems, this will for a change in them used to be considered a prerequisite for moral and intellectual quality. But this is no longer so. The sharpest break between the last two generations occurs here. For the first time perhaps in over a century, an elite has openly questioned the virtue of historical change and admitted the failure of the imagination to conceive of any change that would be worth the effort. Indignation, hope, rebellion, sheer desire for self-preservation—all forces in which the essentially revolutionary character of nineteenth- and early twentieth-century thought was rooted have lost their power, and the ensuing shift in attitudes is such that all contact between the articulate elements of the last generations has been broken. We must ask ourselves what motives stand behind this retreat, not only because the resulting silence often seems unbearable, but also because one cannot take the risk of giving up such a long and vital effort for the wrong reasons. When are we being deceived: is it when we try to think within a context of death and rebirth, failure and its transcendence, nothingness and being—or is it when we abandon ourselves to a stream of passive permanence? Today, we seem inclined to prefer acceptance; but can we be certain that, in doing so, we are not about to abdicate because we are no longer able to stand the strain of the increasing difficulty of invention? Is not what is sometimes called modern conservatism just another form of nihilism?

From a short-range perspective, the general symptom that, for the sake of convenience we can refer to as "conservatism," now seems to have intellectual rigor and precision on its side. It has this advantage because it established itself partly in reaction against the weaknesses of the prewar era. The twenties and the thirties were primarily the days of political activism and aesthetic formalism; the movements, personalities, and events that gave them their distinctive color and tone always contained this blend of revolutionary spirit and aesthetic refinement. If we confine ourselves to literature, we find this combination in significant movements, for instance, surrealism. This combination distinguishes those near-great writers whose ability to catch the mood of the times always put them in the center of events: André Malraux in France, whose career spans from the surrealist avant-garde to a post as minister of propaganda, Ernst Jünger in Germany and, in a way, both Ezra Pound and Hemingway in the United States. All these men were forcefully committed politically, but their convictions proved so frail that they ended up by writing off this part of their lives altogether, as a momentary aberration, a step toward finding themselves. All were deeply committed to the defense of certain aesthetic values they had inherited from their symbolist ancestors—but, for example, next to Proust, James, and Rilke, their works seem to disappear in banality and imitation. What happened is that the political as well as the aesthetic were being used, not for what they represent in themselves, but as a protection that shielded them from their real problems. Political systems of the left and of the right, and literary experimentations that had originated before them, provided an organized framework within which they could fit and act, without really returning to the questions out of which these systems and experiments had arisen. This may just have been the natural expansion of earlier insight, penetrating through the work of these semipopularizing writers into broader areas of human awareness. The war, however, which here is as much cause as effect, put an end to this illusion. From the moment the political actually became a matter of life and death, not just in a momentary flash of blind action but as a long-drawn-out and tedious threat of extermination, it became a true motive of anxiety and no longer a possible protection against anxiety. And from the moment the poetic was really threatened by a mounting mechanization and automaticism, the defense of form became the defense of being itself, such a fundamental matter that it could no longer take on the benign aspect of a literary movement or an avant-garde magazine.

It is this ambiguity of their motives that makes the political and aesthetic beliefs of the twenties such vulnerable targets for today's conservatism—more vulnerable, in fact, than they deserve to be, because their predicament was not an easy one. Before their successors can claim any superiority, it should be proved that they are not just doing the same thing, in a more vicious and destructive way.

If one extends the historical perspective far enough to include romanticism, the present-day state of mind appears in a much clearer light. This awareness of a deep separation between man's inner consciousness and the totality of what is not himself had certainly existed before 1800, but it becomes predominant around that time. The resulting unbearable tension has to materialize into a form in order to be surmounted. Man is thrown back upon himself, in total inwardness, since any existence within the framework of accepted reality can no longer satisfy him. We know all this; the characteristics of romanticism are now a part of literary history. But we do not generally realize that we are still living under the impact of exactly the same ontological crisis. Never have the truly great minds of romanticism, such as Rousseau, Hölderlin, or Hegel, been more familiar and more directly concerned with our own situation. The specific cluster of ideas that leads from the concept of separation to that of inwardness, and from inwardness to history, is the pattern of that period as it is of ours—with the difference that for us, it is more directly experienced, even to the point where it is often difficult to perceive the motion in which we are caught.

Ever since this inward meditation started, it has always been hampered by a resistance that sometimes tended to decry it as a pathological and morbid development or, more often, suggested concrete systems of organization as substitutes. These systems, whether political, literary, or philosophical, are mainly characterized by the studious avoidance, under a variety of pretexts, of the ontological question. There are many good reasons to avoid this issue, the main one being that we have no language to handle a problem that questions precisely the origin of the logic by which we have lived for so long. This being the case, we must realize that this difficulty prevents us from dealing with the entire realm of problems that result from this awareness of separation, and this includes most matters of contemporary history, literature, and, to a large extent, ethics and theology. When systems claim their ability to solve such problems, they are in fact appealing to a temptation that exists in all of us: a desire for serenity that tries to forget and to repress the original anxiety. We must remember that the inwardness of our age has its origin in what Hegel called the *unhappy* consciousness. Since this consciousness is, per definition, painful and hard to bear, the temptation always exists to give up our awareness of ourselves and to fall back on something that would not be conscious, namely, nothingness. This is the most insidious and persistent form of nihilism. Because our consciousness, at present, is an unhappy one, nihilism appears generally in the misleading shape of a refreshing relief. It seems to contain a promise of serenity, because it keeps us from facing the issues in which our being is at stake.

This type of nihilism preferably takes on the form of antihistoricism. In this, it reveals itself as strategically very acute, for the conceptualization of history has been, together with poetry, the main access kept open to the difficult and necessary question of being. It might seem as if a concern with history were significant of an active and secure period, but the opposite is clearly true. If we feel that our being is threatened, and we want to keep the hope that this threat may subside, then we must admit that even the all-encompassing concept of being is susceptible to change and that it has an existence in time; that, in other words, the ontological itself is historical. The meditation on being will then normally start as a meditation on historical time, the only way to reach a new metaphysical language; this evolution is characteristic of the work of a philosopher such as Heidegger, who begins to consider metaphysics only after having encountered, at the end of his first major work, the concept of time as the "horizon" of all being. An attack on philosophy of history as such, appears, therefore, as the best way to *forget* the ontological. Two widely different and unrelated examples will help to illustrate this point.

In his most sincere, though certainly not his most successful novel, *Les Noyers de l'Altenbourg*, André Malraux meets the problem of historical continuity and permanence, which he has since used as the basis of his studies on the history of art. The passage is well known and quite striking. One of those activist intellectuals, typical of Malraux's earlier ideal, has just taken part in a heated and sterile discussion among fellow intellectuals, patterned on the famous *Entretiens de Pontigny*. The topic of discussion has been the problem of permanence in art, and a German historian who sounds like a hybrid and vulgarized version of Hegel, Spengler, and Jaspers has concluded the debate by offering a choice between a discontinuous, conscious but always fragile and backsliding historical improvisation, and the utter lifelessness of an inanimate thing — as symbolized in a mere log of wood. Between both alternatives, Malraux's hero has the revelation of a balanced synthesis: the old trees that grow on the estate, within view of the cathedral of Strasbourg. They are not death, since they live with the inexorable power of generation, and they are not hyperconscious, like the work of art that is too individual to be transferred from man to man or from age to age. Malraux's studies on the history of art have tried to reveal this dark, permanent current that underlies the life of forms, sturdy and ever-growing like the chestnut trees of the ancestral park. The entire novel is supposed to be penetrated with this feeling of permanence; the fact that, in this particular case, it does not quite get across is a technical matter that does not concern us here. The intent is clear enough.

However seductive the image, what does it in fact amount to? Conscious and self-willed history, by means of which man tries to give form to the tensions of his inner fate, is sacrificed to the unchanging. And the only stability that can be found in man is the animal, the vegetative; no wonder that Malraux's symbol is a tree and his subject, as it appears in the parts of the novel that deal with the two world wars, those semi-herdlike reactions of shapeless impulse, sometimes generous, always gregarious, which make up human behavior in times of collective crisis. In Malraux's case, a masochistic anti-intellectualism causes this abdication of the mind, but it follows the typical pattern from political activism, to an avowed antihistoricism and to a nihilistic conservatism.

Turning to a different field, the German historian of philosophy Karl Löwith, well known for his studies on Nietzsche, recently published a critique of Heidegger's work called *Denker in dürftiger Zeit* (Thinkers in times of want, after the famous line from Hölderlin, often quoted by Heidegger himself: " . . . und wozu Dichter in dürftiger Zeit?" [What's the good of poets in barren times?]). The book was mainly an extension of an article Löwith had published shortly after the war in Jean-Paul Sartre's review *Les Temps modernes,* as his contribution to a polemic on Heidegger's political attitude. Certainly, Heidegger's philosophy, which is full of traps and pitfalls and which has led many a mind to a kind of Lorelei-like perdition, requires a highly alert critical reading. But Löwith's main argument consists in attacking Heidegger's historicism and the eschatological aspect of his thought. This constitutes precisely the most profound impulse that stands behind this philosophy, and it undoubtedly deserves a rigorous examination. Yet, as he starts from a preconceived and reactionary view of history as indifferent and meaningless repetition, Löwith's critique never reaches the level of a dialogue but always remains on that of a rather pointless polemic. The details of this argument are unimportant here; neither Malraux's nor Löwith's book is outstanding, and both might well soon be forgotten. They are merely two instances, chosen among many others, which all have this strategy and this motivation in common: an attack on philosophy of history in the name of permanence (conservatism) as a means to avoid the ontological question. I have taken examples from recent European publications to indicate that the phenomenon is by no means confined to America.

In contrast to nihilistic conservatism, that which poetry "conserves" is altogether different. Poetry is concerned with the rediscovery of whatever makes its existence possible, and it tends to look to the past to reassure itself that there have been times in which it could be. What it keeps and shelters, however, is not the immediate, the stable or the primitive. Instead of seeking protection from painful consciousness, it tries to expose itself completely to a total awareness that can only be the result of the most intense mental concentration. It thinks of truth not as stability and rest but as a balance of extreme tensions that, like a drawn bow, achieves immobility when it is bent to the point of breaking. It needs all the consciousness it can find and shuns whatever tries to dim the vision it has left.

But, in our inward age, this poetry does not get written and only the defensive and the passive find expression. Nihilism attacks even the achievements of the past and tempts us to replace concentration by the comfortable reassurance that whatever has been, will be. Mere admiration of past myths is useless unless we inherit some of the strength that created them.

# Poetic Nothingness: On a Hermetic Sonnet by Mallarmé (1955)

For Mallarmé, poetic nothingness assumes the form of a concrete and specific choice, one that continued to obsess him: "namely, if there is occasion to write."[1] The question remains. Fifty years later, Maurice Blanchot entitles an article on Paulhan's *Fleurs de tarbes,* "How Is Literature Possible?"; these two names — Paulhan and Blanchot — taken together sum up a whole historical period and a present situation. We are in the habit of dating this interrogation back to the work of Stéphane Mallarmé, poet of sterility and the blank page. But is it not all too easy to make the validity of such a question depend on a single poet's integrity and mental equilibrium? Both have been subjected to repeated attacks inspired by the evident but naive concern to eliminate the question by despatching the questioner. As a matter of fact, the same presumption weighs on the whole of the nineteenth century. Two brief quotations from a different poetic and philosophical tradition may widen our perspective. The first is from Hegel: "We have lost the necessity of representing a certain content of consciousness in artistic form. In the sense of its highest destiny, art has become for us a thing of the past."[2] A philosopher can make such a statement with calm assurance, especially since it marks *his* entrance on the stage of history, but for the poet Hölderlin, the same certainty assumes the anguished aspect that has become so familiar to us:

> Indessen dünket mir öfters
> Besser zu schlafen, wie so ohne Genossen zu sein,

So zu harren, und was zu tun indes und zu sagen,
Weisz ich nicht, und wozu Dichter in dürftiger Zeit?

("Brot und Wein," stanza 7, lines 11–14)

[Meanwhile, it often seems to me / it is better to sleep than to
flounder thus / and to be thus friendless. I know not what
to do meanwhile / nor what to say; what use are poets in a time
of dearth?]

Since 1802, when these lines were written, there have been great poets, Mallarmé among them. But his predecessors as well as his successors have achieved greatness by confronting this same obstacle, and not by surmounting it. So we can put the same question more exactly, because we know the various paths that lead to it.

Many sectors of the Mallarméan canon might serve as a point of departure, but the choice of the following sonnet offers certain advantages:

Une dentelle s'abolit
Dans le doute du Jeu suprême
À n'entr'ouvrir comme un blasphème
Qu'absence éternelle de lit.

Cet unanime blanc conflit
D'une guirlande avec la même,
Enfui contre la vitre blême
Flotte plus qu'il n'ensevelit.

Mais, chez qui du rêve se dore
Tristement dort une mandore
Au creux néant musicien

Telle que vers quelque fenêtre
Selon nul ventre que le sien
Filial on aurait pu naître.

[A lace does away with itself
In the doubt of the supreme Game
To half-open like a blasphemy
Only an eternal absence of bed.

This unanimous white conflict
Of a garland with the same,

Fled against the pale pane
Floats more than it buries.

But, in one who gilds himself with dreams
Sadly sleeps a mandora
With music's void in its emptiness

Such that toward some window
Depending on no womb but its own,
Filial one could have been born.]

The poem contains no syntactical difficulties (with one exception, which we shall discuss). It is the last of a series of three sonnets published in 1887 and devoted to the same theme of nothingness (néant).[3]

It must be stressed that all interpretations of Mallarmé are falsified because the discursive language of commentary is limiting and univocal, whereas the pluralism of possible levels of reading is requisite, the reflection it provokes in the reader's mind being an integral part of the poem and constituting one of the forms its subject takes. A visual interpretation of the poems is always necessary and never adequate; criticism that has been deluded into stopping at this point and offering visualization as a complete explanation is a dupe of the worst form of naïveté, the form that derives from the fear of being duped. In a poem like this one, we are concerned with the dramatic representation of a purely mental process, in which certain objects are placed in conditions that make them react on each other. The dramatic fate of these objects corresponds to the unfolding of the intellectual process. Things are complicated insofar as the correspondence between each object and its ideal content cannot of course be perfectly stable or symmetrical. In the same way that the object-symbols exist to permit the drama, the drama serves to reveal the identity of the concepts. We must *see* the scene in order to grasp the meaning of the process, but it is often necessary to know this meaning already in order to isolate the elements constituting the drama. It is as if we saw a play in which the unfolding of the plot served to establish the initially vague identity of the characters taking part in it. This paradox inheres, for Mallarmé, in the very movement of truth, and he attempts to objectivize this movement by deliberately recreating it in his reader's mind.

In the present case, it is easy to *see* the poem; only the ingenuousness of Monsieur Chassé could take this still life (a curtain that parts, shifted by the dawn wind, revealing a musical instrument instead of the bed one might expect) for the totality of the poetic subject. As in so many instances, we may assume that Mallarmé took a quite personal and private perception as his point of departure. We know of his insomnia and the sort of hallucinated contemplation that accompanied it. Several of his poems are written in that half-trance state that follows a sleepless night, impregnated with nervous fatigue and an entirely mental excitement; "Je t'apporte l'enfant d'une nuit d'Idumée" (I bring you the child of an Idumean night) is of course the classic example.

As divergent interpretations show, exegesis turns on the meaning given to the phrase *Jeu suprême*—which most exegetes take to signify sunrise. But in late Mallarmé, *jeu* refers to the most essential action of all; "toute pensée emet un coup de dés" (every thought releases a throw of the dice) implies, among other significations, that all consciousness is a game (a gamble). The word is more particularly applied to poetic consciousness, as in the phrase "l'explication orphique de la Terre, qui est le seul devoir du poète et le jeu littéraire par excellence" (the Orphic explanation of Earth, which is the poet's sole duty and the literary game par excellence). In order to venture a little further into this central intuition, we must repeat an often-quoted passage:

> A quoi bon la merveille te transposer un fait de nature en sa presque disparition vibratoire selon le jeu de la parole, cependant, si ce n'est pour qu'en émane, sans la gêne d'un proche ou concret rappel, la notion pure?
>
> (Foreword to Rene Ghil's *Traité du verbe*)

[What use is the wonder of transposing a phenomenon of nature into its resonant near disappearance, according to the game of speech, unless there emanates from it, without the hindrance of an immediate or concrete prompting, the pure idea?]

By naming an object poetically (as opposed to ordinary speech, merely a means of exchange and communication), this object becomes part of a formal structure. Its material existence as object and as language henceforth participates in a structure that depends only on our free will. The object acquires an ontological ambiguity; it has lost its primary opacity insofar as it is posited for us, but preserves it insofar as it is not a pure instrument. It exists within the fringe of interference between these two modes. The intention that guides this transformation of the given is related to the need of our own consciousness to be grounded in its own being. It is because our consciousness suffers from such an ambiguity that it seeks to transcend it by recognizing itself an analogic material entity, which can be poetic form. Self-consciousness needs to ground itself by this transit into the created object, which then becomes what Mallarmé calls the "pure idea"—in reality, the perfect correspondence between the idea of the object and the object itself. But this gain in consciousness is accompanied by an inevitable dissolution of the object, which explodes, so to speak, in the infinity of its formal possibilities. It is no longer just what it is, for whatever we declare it to be can immediately be replaced by the will to make it otherwise. It then becomes that evanescent movement that flees before the growing consciousness constantly threatening to make it vanish. Mallarmé calls it, very clearly, "its resonant near disappearance."

It is precisely this process that the sonnet's first two lines evoke. The "supreme Game" is the act of (poetic) consciousness, and the "lace" that "does away with itself" is a sort of fringe of the evanescent object in its "resonant near disappearance." The action is "doubt" by its suspension between being and nonbeing. In order to approach the next two lines:

> À n'entr'ouvrir comme un blasphème
> Qu'absence éternelle de lit

> [To half-open like a blasphemy
> Only an eternal absence of bed]

we must resort to another famous passage, which also defines the term *jeu*:

Nous savons, captifs d'une formule absolue que, certes, n'est que ce qui est. . . . Mais, je venère, comment, par une supercherie, on projette, à quelque élevation défendue et de foudre! le conscient manque chez nous de ce qui là-haut éclate.

À quoi sert cela—

À un jeu.

En vue qu'une attirance supérieure comme d'un vide, nous avons droit, le tirant de nous par de l'ennui à l'egard des choses si elles s'établissaient solides et prépondérantes—éperdument les détache jusqu'à s'en remplir et aussi les douer de resplendissements à travers l'espace vacant, en des fêtes à volonté et solitaires.

*(La Musique et les lettres,* p. 647)

[We know, prisoners of an absolute formula, that indeed there is nothing but what exists. . . . Yet I revere how, by a hoax, we project, to some forbidden and thunderstruck height, the conscious lack in ourselves of what explodes on high.

What is this for—

For a game.

Seeing how a higher attraction as though of a void—we are entitled, deriving that void from ourselves by a dissatisfaction with things that were established as solid and preponderant—fanatically detaches them to the point of being filled with them and also endows them with splendors through empty space, festive ad lib and solitary.]

The necessity to transform the given occurs against the background of the fundamental knowledge that immediate being is identical with oneself, that things can be only what they are. Such knowledge, however, cannot satisfy us: we may utter and repeat it, but its expression remains pure "dissatisfaction" [*ennui*]. The mind must move, and every action of consciousness is an effort to escape the monotonous repetition of immediate identity. This does not keep the immediate datum of immediacy from persisting, nor every construction based on this desire to explode it from becoming illusion, snare, hoax, and *game*. Henceforth Mallarmé cannot merely abandon himself to the refinement of destroying the world by means of an intensified consciousness of that world and of himself. Here is one of the aspects of his enterprise to which he tirelessly devotes himself, the only task, in fact, that is worth the trouble of being performed: "I *revere* . . . a hoax," "supreme Game." But such destruction is neither easy nor painless. Since the knowledge of being's immediate identity persists, immediacy also becomes *value*. As opposed to consciousness and to poetry, there exists a world of a spontaneous contact with things, within a single sphere of unity. The more conscious we become, the more desirable and precious this world appears — and the more impossible to achieve. Its presence underlies Mallarmé's entire oeuvre and confers upon that oeuvre its contour and its agonizing depth. That world is represented by a whole chain of images, extending from the very first poems to *Un Coup de dés*. It is sometimes the *Azur* of the poems from *Le Parnasse contemporain:*

> Cher Ennui, pour boucher d'une main jamais lasse
> Les grand drous bleux que font méchamment les oiseaux.

> [Beloved tedium, to plug with a tireless hand
> The great blue holes bored by the spiteful birds.]

It is Hérodiade's hesitation when, having consecrated herself forever to artifice and hyperconsciousness, she admits:

> Vous mentez, ô fleur nue
> De mes lèvres.
> J'attends une chose inconnue . . .

> [You lie, O naked flower
> of my lips. I await a thing unknown. . . . ]

It is the Faun losing his prey for want of renouncing the sensual world and consecrating himself utterly to "the chaster [nymph] . . . with cold eyes blue as a weeping spring." It is consequently a certain type of the eternal feminine (not Méry Laurent) — direct, maternal, spontaneous. Finally, it is the constant presence, beneath the most abstract structures, of the natural, elementary rhythms: day and night, light and darkness, winter and summer, "the symphonic equation proper to the seasons, the practice of sunbeams and clouds."

In our poem, all this is summed up in the one symbol-word *lit* (bed). The evanescent action of dawning consciousness (*une dentelle qui s'abolit* [a lace that does away with itself]) provokes the dissolution and absence of the world of immediacy to which all these values belong, a world that can never exist in consciousness: *absence éternelle de lit* (eternal absence of bed). But this destruction is profoundly tragic, for it signifies a mortal blow to life itself. Moreover it implies the death of God, in the Nietzschean sense, for to Mallarmé the Christian God of his childhood is the God of spontaneous and immediate unity who cannot survive consciousness (see "*Catholicisme,*" one of the *Variations sur un sujet*). Such is the outcome of the concept of poetic nothingness for Mallarmé, a concept condensed here into a brief quatrain.

What are the genesis and structure of this conception in Mallarmé's mind? The next two lines tell us something of their ultimate aspect:

> Cet unanime blanc conflit
> D'une guirlande avec la même

> [This unanimous white conflict
> Of a garland with the same]

This polarity (conflict) within one and the same entity (consciousness becoming object) is the very movement of reflection. The two poles of being (immediacy and self-consciousness) are always present, but the nature of their opposition is constantly refined. Mallarmé begins his poetic career as a *poète maudit:* wearing the mask of Baudelaire, he sees himself as belonging to the race of slaves, oppressed by the vulgar,

> Mordant au citron d'or de l'idéal amer.

> [Biting the golden orange of a bitter ideal.]

But soon he finds in the fulfillment of his craft and in the resources of his technique a new dignity that transforms him from a rebellious slave into a stoic Parnassian. His true enterprise begins with the fanatic and deliberate labor of *Hérodiade,* whose subject owes something to Gautier and which was to be accompanied by the highly Parnassian project of compiling a treatise on precious stones. For several years, Mallarmé struggled, in isolation, to perfect his oeuvre. Then a letter to Cazalis (March 1886) brings testimony of an upheaval:

Unfortunately, by exploring verse this deeply, I came upon two abysses which left me in despair. One is Nothingness, which I reached without any awareness of Buddhism. . . . Yes, I know, we are only vain forms of matter—but how sublime for having invented God and our soul. So sublime, my friend! that I would grant myself the spectacle of matter, conscious as I am of being and yet necessarily venturing into that Dream which matter knows not, changing the Soul and all such divine impressions amassed in us from the earliest ages, and proclaiming, before the Nothing which is the truth, these glorious lies.[4]

The essential thing here, for our purposes, is that this has happened "by exploring verse": by exclusively concentrating on formal creation, poetic consciousness ends by annihilating form, as all pure consciousness destroys its object. Henceforth, form can no longer be taken seriously. The formal experiments Mallarmé continues to engage in with the greatest meticulousness will be essentially frivolous and gratuitous. An ironic skepticism replaces Parnassian stoicism. But the meditation does not stop here. Two years later, while he is working on *Igitur,* Mallarmé writes to the same Cazalis the often-quoted letter:

> This last year has been a terrifying one. My Thought has worked through to a Divine Conception. . . . I write to inform you that I am impersonal now, and no longer the Stéphane you once knew—but an aptitude the spiritual universe has for seeing itself and for developing, through what once was me.

This highest point of self-consciousness, where the mind conceives itself as its own object, is in our poem called "unanimous white conflict," white for its purity, conflict because it represents "the antagonism of that polar dream" that Mallarmé describes in *Igitur.* Once this level is attained, the only poetic "subject" will be Nothingness itself; poetic consciousness will be employed exclusively to evoke the destruction of which it is the cause.

Once this certainty is established in Mallarmé's mind, he is obsessed by the problem of survival, not in the personal sense but in the historical sense of *continuity of mind.* Mallarmé would say with Hegel that mere "life" has no history, since it has neither future nor development. We must take him literally when he says he is now so totally released from personal and psychological concerns that he can speak as a representative of the entire human race and, to a certain degree, as its guardian. This accounts for his being so disturbed by a negating mediation, beyond which any reality of being becomes problematic. The images and symbols of the last period desperately attempt to grasp the visual equivalent of this drama, as if the discovery of such a vision constituted a first step toward the salvation of jeopardized being. Most often, the evocation is that of some disaster, such as a shipwreck from which something seems to survive, floating not entirely engulfed between being and nonbeing. These images obviously constitute the main part of *Un Coup de dés;* they also appear in certain hermetic lines of the last sonnets, such as

> Telle loin se noie une troupe
> De sirènes maintes à l'envers

> [Thus far away drowns a troop
> Of sirens many upside down]

or in "A la nue accablante tu" (Stilled beneath the overwhelming cloud). In the sonnet we are considering, a similar movement appears in the line

Flotte plus qu'il n'ensevelit

[Floats more than it buries]

(which follows a descriptive line

Enfui contre la vitre blême
[Fled against the pale pane]).

While "buries" suggests death and disappearance, "floats" contains a remote promise of survival. *A lace does away with itself,* as a matter of fact, but it floats vaguely, *as if,* perhaps, *something remained.*

Is there something that remains? Does the action of total consciousness reduce everything to nothingness, or does it permit the survival of what for Mallarmé (almost always misunderstood on this point) can only be history? The question had already been raised in *Toast funèbre:*

Est-il de ce destin rien qui demeure, non?

[Then is there nothing of this destiny which remains?]

In our poem, the question receives the hypothetical and ambiguous answer contained in the last two tercets, clearly set in opposition to the quatrains by the *mais* (but) and the comma:

Mais, chez qui du rêve se dore
Tristement dort une mandore
Au creux néant musicien

[But, in one who gilds himself with dreams
Sadly sleeps a mandora
With music's void in its emptiness]

The poet's action (the poet = one who gilds himself with dreams) is the annihilating action of all consciousness, but it might leave a trace, the work's memory suspended in an ideal space and revealing that an action has occurred. "Nothing will have taken place but the place," says *Un Coup de dés,* and here the "place" is the musical instrument, the mandora. It actually *sleeps* rather than *is; sadly,* because it contains the essential tragedy of which it is the formal incarnation. *Au creux néant musicien* (with music's void in its emptiness) should be read, it seems to me, in apposition with *mandore,* as one says *café au lait.* The *creux* (emptiness) then describes the instrument that produces music from its hollow center, like poetry issuing from the consciousness of negation. The symbol is admirable, and whatever level we read it on, evokes ever-new musical, visual, and mental resonances. But these last two strophes also have many frivolous dimensions, in accord with the formal skepticism we evoked above. Emilie Noulet has pointed out the pun on " . . . *ment dore . . . mandore"*, whose sonority she admires—but are not such devices ironic rather than musical, looking forward to Queneau rather than harking back to Verlaine? The whole visual image, moreover, has something a bit suspect about it: that protuberant abdomen of the mandora that will give birth is perhaps an overrealistic analogue. Yet we must be careful here, for such jokes, in the Mallarmé of the last manner, often counterpoise the gravest declarations, at the furthest reaches of thought. This final strophe expresses the central concern of Mallarméan poetics: the conception of the poetic as a privileged action, the only one by which the possibility of a new innocence and of a possible future, beyond negation, can still be conceived. The word *naître* (to be born) is set in opposition to the *absence éternelle de lit* (eternal absence of bed) that it transcends. The survival of the immediate existence of things is established, but without value, for it has neither consciousness nor history—it might just as well not be at all. But a certain conscious, i.e., poetic, action indicates a possible future birth, because it perpetuates *something* that transcends the antithetical notions of mediation and immediacy. Such an action contains the revelation of the new, but at the same time the consistency and the solidity of truth. We are reminded of Hölderlin's line, so elaborately discussed by Heidegger:

Was bleibet aber stiften die Dichter

[What remains, that the poets establish]

This *something* Mallarmé cannot name of course; short of rediscovering the true meaning of the verb "to name," that would be to destroy the hope that remains. He says as much in this fine passage from *Catholicisme:*

> . . . ni rien dorénavant, neuf, ne naîtra que de source. . . .
> Une magnificence se déploiera, quelconque, analogue à l'Ombre de jadis. . . .
> . . . Le nuage autour, exprès: que préciser. . . . Plus, serait entonner le rituel et trahir, avec rutilance, le lever de soleil d'une chape d'officiant, en place que le desservant enguirlande d'encens, pour la masquer, une nudité du lieu. (p. 395)

> [ . . . and henceforth nothing new will be born unless it be from the source. . . .
> A magnificence will appear, ordinary enough, analogous to the bygone Shade. . . .
> . . . The particular cloud around it: what is to be said. . . .
> More, would be to intone the ritual and betray, glaringly, the sunrise of

an officiant's robe, whereas ministering to it might wreathe with
incense—to mask it—a nakedness of place.]

In September 1866, Villiers de l'Isle-Adam wrote a letter to Mallarmé in which
he advised him on his reading: "Let me recommend the Dogmas and Ritual Magic
of Eliphas Levi. . . . They are astonishment itself. As for Hegel, I am really
delighted you have given some attention to this miraculous genius, this unrivaled
procreator, this reconstructor of the universe." The document is a precious one
for locating Mallarmé in the general development of the nineteenth century. The
experience of poetic nothingness that he apprehended so intensely and that he conceived as the inevitable correlative of consciousness itself, is a specifically
"romantic" experience; it is Hegel's "unhappy consciousness," Hölderlin's "separation" (*Trennung*), the alienation experienced by all the century's great minds.
There are two ways of meeting the challenge this experience presents to the mind:
one is defensive, the other confronts the problem. This second way attempts to
save both life and consciousness in a new synthesis that Hegel had the audacity
to name but that less imprudent minds limited themselves to foreseeing. The
defensive way, on the other hand, is anchored in the occult tradition, which is
chiefly a Neoplatonist development: it organizes rites, techniques, and disciplines
aiming at the organization of immediate life, at the maintenance of the ineffable
moment in all its plenitude, and it thereby seeks to prevent the negative consciousness from being established.

Given this option, there can be no doubt about Mallarmé's choice: he inclined
toward Hegel rather than toward Eliphas Levi. I have studied elsewhere[5] the
historical question of Hegel's possible influence on Mallarmé, but that is a largely
academic matter. In 1866 Mallarmé did not need to read Hegel to encounter certain shared problems and to confront them in an analogous fashion. All the elements necessary to this orientation were already present in the early work. If I
had to sum up his entire enterprise, I would say that it is the nostalgic but categorical rejection of the temptation of the occult.

Translated by Richard Howard

## Notes

1. Stéphane Mallarmé, *La Musique et les lettres,* p. 645. All references are to the Pléiade edition.
2. G. W. F. Hegel, *Vorlesungen über die Aesthetik,* vols. X and XI. In *Sämtliche Werke* (Leipzig
and Hamburg: Felix Meiner, 1905–). This reference, vol. X, p. 16.
3. In *Mallarmé, l'Homme et l'Oeuvre* (Paris, 1953), Guy Michaud offers a hypothesis, which
seems impossible to verify, that these three sonnets date back to 1866 and that their present form is
a later, reworked version. This is not unlikely. But all of Mallarmé's themes crystallize at this period
and, to a certain degree, it might be said that all his subsequent work is a repetition of the certainty
acquired at this time—in the sense that *Un Coup de dés* is a new version of *Igitur.*

4. It is interesting to compare this text with the passage quoted above from *La Musique et les lettres,* of which, twenty-five years previously, it constitutes an equivalent.

5. "Mallarmé, Yeats, and the Post-Romantic Predicament" ( Ph.D. diss. Harvard University, 1959).–Trans.

# The Temptation of Permanence (1955)

In a well-known letter of Rilke, the disquiet of our age in the face of the menacing development of the technological world finds expression in a personal and intimate form: "for our grandparents a house, a well, a tower were still infinitely more than these things themselves, infinitely more intimate.[1] Almost everything presented itself as a vessel where they discovered and into which they poured the human. From America have come to us now empty, indifferent things, artificial things that deceive us by simulating life. . . . In the American sense, a house or an apple tree or a grapevine has nothing in common with the house, the fruit, or the grape in which our ancestors have invested their hopes and cares."[2] One should not be surprised to find this text cited by Heidegger, whose thought was so profoundly inspired by the horror he felt for any enslavement to technology.[3]

And nevertheless . . . When one lives in this land of inhumane technology, is it indeed the annihilation of man that one finds there? Under the immense skies of America stretches earth essentially unmarked as yet by technology, earth and sky that swallow the monstrous cities of industry. External life, certainly, is caught in the automatism of production, but that life remains so poor and rude that all quality soon becomes interior and leaves nothing of the world remaining but this vast, empty horizon in the center of which man finds himself deprived of all support save that of thought. If it is necessary to find a virtue in technology, it would be that it is too rude to offer even a simulacrum of appeasement. The security of Rilke's melancholy dreams, the security of our ancestors in their houses and vestments — was this real or is it merely a product of our imagination? And the peace we feel ourselves in thinking that they possessed this security — a

30

thought that satisfies the mind and lulls it to sleep at the same time—can we rely on this? Perhaps in the degree to which technology is impoverishment and burns history without leaving material residue, technology forces us to rid ourselves of what is only after all a false serenity. Man in the center of space, man whom nothing protects from the sky and the earth is no doubt closer to the essential than the European, who searches for a shelter among beautiful houses polished by history and among fields marked by ancestral labor. For he is in the midst of his own struggle: the elaboration of his history with this physical entity that is given to him and that, with Heidegger, one could name the Earth. This earth resists him by its opacity and passivity; from this point, it is not surprising that he finds in the transparency of the sky the model of total liberty for which he searches, and which is a perfect approximation of his action to his being. It is the eternal conflict

Of the hostile earth and cloud, oh grief!

in which consciousness is founded, the conflict the experience of which, according to Hegel, is the movement of the dialectic. Often, in the unrolling of this conflict, one believes in the triumph of one of these opposed forces. In the moments of vigor and zest, it is to the sky that man believes himself equal, and he escapes far from all heaviness, rises toward pure transparency. But in moments of fatigue, he hides himself in earth and believes he finds repose there. Our age seems certainly to be an age of fatigue. One sees so many examples of this prostration of the spirit seeking refuge in the earth. Nevertheless as signs do not often present themselves as what they are, and as we suffer all this fatigue, our enfeeblement appears to us in the contrary form of a promise, of an alleviation. If one wants to escape being duped, one must try to recognize this alleviation for what it is. We want to try to show an example of this sort of thing in two thoughts that affect the present world and that are susceptible to leading to the death of the mind by the way of the temptation of permanence.

In *Man's Hope* (1937) by André Malraux, one finds a scene, admired by Sartre, where a dead woman is described as pressing on the earth with all her weight as if to encrust herself there and to transform herself into earth. The passage has the intensity by which an author shows his most profound intentions. It is necessary to place the passage in relationship to pages of similar intensity in the later work of Malraux. There is, for example, this central scene of *The Walnut Trees of Altenburg* (1943), where the principal character receives the revelation of the permanence of man by seeing the ancient trees of the ancestral manor. One remembers that this revelation takes place after a discussion with a philosopher of history in which a choice is imposed between a historical invention— conscious, but discontinuous and perilous—and the death of things.[4] It is certain that the image of the tree opposes itself in its essence to the problem proposed by the historian, and which, to simplify things, is surely that of the Hegelian historicism of the nineteenth century. The opposition resides in the nature of the two movements confronting each other. The historical movement is that of be-coming: *being* consciously created, whether as the work of art or historical deed in general, is unstable in its essence, and it denies itself to be reborn in another *being*. The two are separated by the abyss of a negation (in organic language: a death), and the passage from one to the other is essentially discontinuous. The movement of the ancient tree, on the other hand, is a growth: its being remains immediately identical with itself, and its movement is only the extension of what already is and always will be. One sees how, in a later text (*The Voices of Silence*, pp. 633ff.) Malraux can oppose becoming to being and pretend that the first sub-stitutes itself for the second in what we call the historical consciousness.[5] But as he considers historical consciousness always under an organic form, discon-tinuity is for him death in the biological sense of the term — civilizations know that they are, literally, mortal — and as death is in essence the destiny of man, histori-cal consciousness becomes the acceptance of destiny, acceptance that is passivity. To this passivity is opposed the quintessential free act that is the act of artistic creation. Art so conceived, in opposing itself to destiny (or to death), opposes it-self in fact to becoming and to history. Art as antidestiny is antihistorical; its movement will certainly no longer be a discontinuous vibration, but it will be like the slow and certain growth of a tree. The mind at once complies in this affirma-tion, where it finds repose. To reflect on art thus conceived would be to espouse the unassailable and solid security of the walnut tree, and, as time is eliminated by a grounded future, to rise splendidly toward a sky that one will not be long in reaching. We would no longer need to trouble ourselves with this space be-tween the sky and earth that Heidegger names the world, since we would be simi-lar to the earth that ends by confusing itself with the sky, to a horizon the distance of which troubles us no longer, since we do not cease to grow. In becoming trees, we have lost the precarious situation of being *on* the earth to become creatures *of* the earth. This is to yield to the temptation of permanence, for art so consid-ered is in reality only a sediment without life, which integrates itself with the soil instead of opposing it. Pretending to think being, Malraux thinks in reality earth, which he desires.

In this particular case, it is possible to designate the precise spot where the mind capitulates: in refusing to think the negation and in assimilating it to death pure and simple, in refusing the effort and the pain of interiorizing the exterior negation that is organic death. It is to pretend that one thinks against Hegel when actually one is thinking at the most against Spengler. In a dialectical movement of the mind, the idea of continuity is no longer essential, for the discontinuity has lost its character of mortal destiny in becoming an integral part of the life of the mind. While the moment of discontinuity is certainly that of a death, it is nevertheless also that of a renewal, difficult and uncertain, but possible. From this perspective, history is neither passive destiny nor a growth. The only permanence is that intention of the absolute that creates history, and the lesson of the past consists in the repetition of this intention, recognized beyond its successive defeats, the remnants of which cover the surface of our earth. The new produces itself by the confrontation of becoming in process with anterior movements, a confrontation through which a unity of intention reveals itself. The poets seem to have known this more often than historians, and it is a poet (supposed furthermore to be antihistorical) who repeated this with force and clarity: "All interrupts itself, is self-contained, in history, little transfusion: or the connection consists in this, that the two states shall have existed, separately, for a confrontation by the mind. The eternal, that which appeared such, does not rejuvenate, plunges in caverns and piles itself up: nor shall henceforth anything new be born except in the source."[6] What the Renaissance drew from the Roman world, or romantic neo-Hellenism from Greece, is not the immediate identity of a permanence, a common root in which being finds itself stabilized in its diverse manifestations, but the intention of taking up a prior struggle, with methods that cannot be the same since they have previously failed. The Renaissance nourished itself in meditating, perhaps without knowing it, on the Latin decadence, and it is in thinking, very consciously this time, the death of Greece that neo-Hellenism produced its major works. Far from being antihistorical, the poetical act (in the general sense that includes all the arts) is the quintessential historical act: that through which we become conscious of the divided character of our being, and consequently, of the necessity of fulfilling it, of accomplishing it in time, instead of undergoing it in eternity.

The attitude of Malraux is one in which the great fatigue of the century justifies itself, one that has encountered negation in history and for whom history has thus become painful. This fatigue has found its political doctrine in a nationalistic conservatism, which it can seem curious to see establishing itself most solidly in the Western country that has the least to conserve, the United States of America. Because the protective sediment, which is the residue of the past, is there so thin, and since consequently man is more exposed in his profound division, conservatism there is proclaimed almost desperately — to the point of importing what has to be conserved. But what constitutes the value of this sediment? And however much it merits being conserved, it is conserved as ruin and not as house; it is as witness of a defeat that exhorts us to invention and to the maintenance of this tension that is thought. To conserve it by leaving it as it is, in the hope of establishing a suprahistorical continuity in transmitting it from age to age, is to watch over a dead thing, to conserve the earth. Such conservation is an easy task, for the earth is precisely what is always present and conserves itself by itself. To conserve being in its truth is to conserve the incessant struggle that constitutes it, and it is consequently to think in a necessarily insurrectionary mode.

The connections of history and destiny have been described by Heidegger in a manner that seems certainly in opposition to that of Malraux. It is perhaps one of the principal merits of his influence to have led the problem of history back onto the ontological level where Hegel had situated it, and to detach it thus from naive forms it had taken in the interior of activisms and political determinisms. Relying on the relation, in the German language, between the word "destiny" *(Geschick)* and the word "history" *(Geschichte)*, he affirmed in various ways that history is the concrete manifestation of the very movement of being, movement whose fundamental ambiguity is the origin of the historicity of our destiny. This conviction is found from *Being and Time* to the most recent texts, as in fact this passage testifies: "If we authorize ourselves to speak of a history of being, we must first remember that being designates the presence of the present, that is to say, division *(Zwiefalt)*. It is only by beginning with this thought that we can ask ourselves the significance of the term 'history.' It designates the destiny of the division. It is the revelatory process by which unveiled presence persists and in which present things appear."[7] Fittingly, it is especially on this point that Heidegger has been attacked by those who, like Malraux, see history only as a shapeless fatality.

The idea of being as division is located throughout the work of Martin Heidegger; one of the ways to follow his thought is to trace there this idea's evolution. For our very limited purposes here one could refer to the passage in the essay on the origin of the work of art in *Holzwege* (1950), where the division is clearly described: "The world is the opening-up of wide paths created by the simple and fundamental decisions of a people from the interior of its historical destiny. The earth is the appearance of what always hides itself and thus protects. The world and the earth are essentially different from each other but without ever being separated. . . . The opposition of the world and the earth is a struggle."[8] The manner in which Heidegger describes this struggle, as one in which "the adversaries raise each other into the mutual affirmation of their authentic being, respectively," defines it certainly as becoming in the Hegelian sense; the apparent stability of the work, if it is produced, envelops a dialectical movement: "In this struggle, it is the unity of the world and the earth which is at stake. By this opening-up of a world are decided the victory and defeat, the happiness and distress, the domination and enslavement of a historical people. In revealing what remains indecisive and unmeasured, the world just coming to birth reveals the hidden necessity for decision and measure. But by the opening-up of a world, the earth surges forth. Earth reveals itself as the support of all things, as that which hides itself in its own law and refuses persistently to be unveiled. The world demands decision and measure, and it situates beings in the opening-up of their own paths. As foundation surging up, earth strives to remain hidden and to submit everything to its law."[9] There is nothing here that could not be translated into Hegelian terms. Nor even in the phrase that follows: "The struggle is not a tearing like the opening of a crevice, but it is the interior fervor *(Innigkeit)* with which the two adversaries belong to each other." That is to say, there have to be two for there to be a struggle; it is true that in the struggle opponents belong to each other (even with fervor, with love) in the measure, appropriately, to which they are forced to struggle. One does not have this belonging in a unity of being, but only in a duality that is the structure of the dialectic. It was in this sense that Hölderlin had to say that "reconciliation was only the testimony itself of struggle."[10] There will not be reconciliation if there was unity. One understands less well the sequence of this passage of Heidegger: "This tearing *(Riss)* carries *(reisst)* the adversaries into the unity of their origin, which has a common ground. The tearing becomes thus a tracing-out, a ground-plan *(Grundriss)*. It is the design *(Aufriss)*, the sketching-out of the ground of the opening by which beings will be illuminated. The tearing does not allow the adversaries to struggle to the point of breaking apart; it resembles rather an opposition within a common outline *(Umriss)*."[11] In a passage of this order, carried by verbal analogies, one leaps over in a few moments vertiginous distances, passing from the idea of struggle to that of unifying contour. Since it is a question here of the work of art, the mind attaches itself nevertheless to this image of contour, of form, which belongs to the essence of the work and which makes appear possible the passage from "struggle" to "contour." But what is the contour? Judging from the point of view of the being who finds himself on the earth, one would say it is surely the limit by which a world is established, in separating itself from the earth. In keeping with the image of the engraver (Dürer) to which Heidegger refers a bit later, one could say that in hollowing out the contour in the earth, the engraver introduces the sky: that he denies the earth in order to transform it, by the force of his hands, into its contrary. Always from this same point of view, the contour does not separate the work from the sky; that is not necessary, for, in the measure to which it participates in the essence of the thing, it is already only too far distant. The work of the engraver operates in an inverse sense: the contour tries to imitate the sky in separating the world from the earth. This is surely why Hölderlin (cited in a later context by Heidegger) in one of his letters defines "fable" as "the architectonics of the sky."[12] The emphasis should fall on the word "sky" and not on "architectonics." The work is architecture even in spite of itself, because it can be made only *with* the earth *against* the earth. The intention of architecture is to deny the earth, not in uniting it to the sky but in making it sky. The world of the work of art, seen from the earth, is the negation of the earth in the desire for the sky; by contrast, in fixing oneself a point of view of the being who is under the sky, one could make an inverse description equally valuable, the contour appearing thus as an intention of forms and dense structures, as the negation of the sky in the desire for the earth. The work remains fluid and shapeless, because it can be made only in the sky, against the sky. The possibility of such an inversion is the characteristic of all dialectic, and it excludes all permanent unity.

How then can Heidegger say that the work, insofar as it is contour, gathers opposition in its unity, and that in a manner apparently permanent? Is *being* this unique foundation of their unity? But if two *beings* are defined in their being as opposed, the common fact of being could not constitute in itself a unifying principle, since their division extends precisely to the foundation. The tearing apart is thus not *Grundriss* (ground plan), that is, a groove in the foundation with a view to construction, but *Riss des Grundes,* a tearing open of the foundation itself that prevents all true construction.

If this turn in the thought of Heidegger remains obscure, at least in this particular essay, one could always understand the motif that determines it with the help of his more recent publications on the same subject. The essay of the *Vorträge* which continues that on the origin of the work of art is called, after a verse of Hölderlin, " . . . Dichterisch wohnet der Mensch . . . " ( . . . Poetically man dwells . . . ).[13] It takes up and develops the idea of the poetic act as "gathering contour." The term "ground plan" *(Grundriss)* is found there, but in a new association: "The measure of the human by the dimension which is delegated to him brings with it dwelling *(das Wohnen)* in its ground-plan."[14] It is this association between the plan (which provides the tearing apart, the struggle) and the inhabiting that it is necessary for us to try to grasp. Heidegger directs us here by the idea of architecture, of construction *(bauen)* — an idea prepared for by the word "plan" — and finally by the idea of measure, both of the world and of metrics, which leads us directly to poetry. But measure, even conceived in a purely qualificative sense, supposes, he says, an entity against which one measures, and which should be different from the entity measured; and the entity that is not the world is the sky, or God, pure and absolute transparency. Thus God is the invisible, the unknown; poetry is thus the measure of the invisible, and that is why it speaks in "images . . . which are imagined as the visible inclusions of the unknown, of the strange, in the aspect of the familiar."[15] One rediscovers, by way of an ontological path, a conclusion to which Sartre came with the help of a phenomenological description when he defined, in *The Psychology of the Imagination* (1940), the work of art as an unreality. The passage of Heidegger is remarkable by its profound justification of poetic metrics — one thinks of perspectives that he opens on the quasi-obsessional metrics of a poet like Hölderlin, whose works the classical metrical analyses seem powerless to evaluate. But one will notice that this passage is in fact not only a new way of naming the struggle. Metrics, as a measure of what is unknown, is, properly speaking, a constant challenge to the impossible, and as such, it is struggle through and through and forever. It is what is expressed by the verse of Hölderlin that gives this essay its title:

> Voll Verdienst, doch dichterisch, wohnet
> Der Mensch auf dieser Erde.[16]

> [Full of merit, but poetically, man
> Dwells on this earth.]

In his commentary, Heidegger accentuates "dwells," which he puts on the same level as "poetically," establishing thus the unity of the two: from "measure" in the ordinary sense, an obvious association leads to the idea of construction, of house, of dwelling, of abiding. But if one accentuates the word "poetically" by opposition to the word "dwells," as an apposition in paradox suggested moreover by the word "but," the opposite idea appears. The simple and pious declaration, "full of merit . . . man dwells on this earth," is thus destroyed by the opposition "but poetically"; since the poetic, in the sense of the metrification of the unknown, is defiance and struggle, it opposes itself to the serene idea of dwelling. To the extent that he is a poet, man can no longer dwell, for his inquietude and suffering are thus, as is said by a later verse of the same text, a "struggle with God." This finds itself repeated in another verse in the poem, when Hölderlin asks

Is there measure on earth?

and responds

There is none.

On this passage Heidegger comments: "What we name in saying 'on the earth' exists only inasmuch as man dwells on the earth and in his dwelling lets the earth be earth."[17] Why can one say "to dwell" in place of "to be," utilizing a serene term that contains the idea of residence in place of saying "being in time," an expression that contains division? Or is it necessary to identify dwelling and the history of being, which, for Heidegger too, is nevertheless the destiny of division and struggle? Is it necessary to eliminate the promise of repose and peace contained in the word "dwell," a promise that is surely what one wants to gain in trying to think beyond the metaphysical, and in thinking the tension of Being with beings in place of thinking, as does Hegel, the tension of the object and of the idea?

It certainly does *not* seem necessary. In the essay entitled "Bauen Wohnen Denken" ("Building Dwelling Thinking"),[18] which is rather more a hymn than an exposition, Heidegger promises explicitly the transcendence of division and speaks more overtly than in his earlier work of the necessity to learn to think the simplicity of the earth (*Einfalt,* by opposition to *Zwiefalt*): the earth, the sky, mortal man, and God thought in their unity. This unity is *thought* as an act: to take care of things and in raising them, to approximate building *(bauen),* which approximates in its turn dwelling *(wohnen).* Heidegger uses the same term "dwelling" to indicate this action and to indicate poetic action; he thus invites the mind to make with him this leap that identifies the two kinds of act. To build is to build the object, and the object is thought, as a bridge, to be "the gathering to itself in its own way of the earth and sky, of the divine and the mortal."[19] But the bridge exists precisely as the junction between two entities separated by a distance, by an abyss. Such a division is exclusively characteristic of the earth, and not of the sky, which lets itself be divided by nothing. Heidegger has said to us that the division of the sky and the earth was of the order of difference and not of separation. How to conceive then this junction of the two entities by a bridge, thought of not as a mediation, which would be contact in struggle, but as a true gathering? The bridge is only an extension of earth fabricated by man, and it does not seem that the architecture and metrics that would construct it could have anything whatever in common with poetic metrics.

If therefore one agreed to make the identification that Heidegger suggests — that is not to say he makes it himself — and if one agreed to think the construction of the thing as similar in its being to poetic construction, one would have in fact succumbed to the temptation of permanence. Insofar as the *building* of the essay "Building Dwelling Thinking" is the building of the earth, it is certain that that is eternal and that it abides. But it passes to the side of history, for it does not establish a transcendence of the division of being. Perhaps the ambiguity is conserved in the enigmatic reservation: "the bridge gathers in its way the earth and the sky." Does "in its way" signify that its manner is that of a struggle? But then can one speak of dwelling when, as Heidegger has told us, dwelling signifies "being satisfied, being at peace"?[20] This interrogation seems to reopen its circle to infinity.

One attains thus one of these points of thought that it is necessary to try to transcend in order to arrive at the truth. One of the ends of the method of exposition of Heidegger is to lead us to such knots of resistance. But in this case, here one genuine temptation risks masking the heightened tension that should issue from this cessation in development. For in this last essay, at least, Heidegger speaks more and more in the name of the earth. Malraux could allow to subsist from human existence only the passive gestures in which the biological part of our nature reveals itself at moments of supreme crisis; these are the gestures that rule in the place of the historical decision. In thinking the "building" in the sense of "abiding," "dwelling," Heidegger ends in a similar climate of thought. It is a question of a vegetative "building," and one rediscovers more and more, in these essays, examples and metaphors borrowed from the life of the earth: the forest, labor, the land, etc. The fixed idea seems to be the necessity of protecting the earth, of watching over it as a peasant watches over his fields; technology takes on diabolical proportions insofar as it is the enemy of the earth. But the function of protecting is precisely that of the earth itself and not that of being; a thought that only protects is not the thought of being. It is more dangerous than technical thought since instead of attacking an earth that is quite capable of defending itself, it betrays the movement of being.

One would do well not to see in these notes the general sketch of a critical commentary on the work of Heidegger. They detach fragments from a much more complex whole in the attempt to clarify a particular point of view that Heidegger does not treat as such. In the work as a whole, this problem participates in a fundamental tension, the very one that makes the originality of Heidegger's contribution and that constitutes the center of the possible critical dialogue. One of the ways of approaching this problem would be to consider the effort of Heidegger as an attempt to sublate *(aufheben)* the antinomy between Hegelian historicism and Kantian eternalism by conserving what is essential in each. The critique of the work would then be the examination of the validity of this attempt. But here at the very most it is a question of putting one on guard against the possibility of letting oneself be seduced by promises of permanence that these texts suggest, and which can support the mind in a state of beatitude that properly speaking is a lethargy. For a thinker who calls himself *dürftig* — poor, bare — the language of Heidegger has a movement so captivating that it carries one along and tends to hide its discontinuities. To what extent is this seduction willed? One would need a study far more extended to decide this question. The seduction is effective inasmuch as it requires a great vigilance finally to resist it. Perhaps that is its end, for vigilance is the very weapon of the struggle of being.

Translated by Dan Latimer

## Notes

1. As originally published, "Tentation de la permanence," *Monde Nouveau,* 93 (October 1955), pp. 49–61. The French version of this paper incorporated its footnotes within the body of the paper. To increase the number and amplitude of the references, I have moved them to the end of the article. — Trans.

2. Rainer Maria Rilke, *Briefe* (Wiesbaden: Insel Verlag, 1950), pp. 898–99.

3. Martin Heidegger, *Holzwege* (Frankfurt am Main: Klostermann, 1972), p. 268. See "What Are Poets For?" In Martin Heidegger, *Poetry, Language, and Thought,* trans. Albert Hofstader (New York, 1971), p. 113.

4. André Malraux, *The Walnut Trees of Altenburg,* trans. A. W. Fielding (London: Lehmann 1952), pp. 62–116. Mollberg says: "If the world has any meaning, death should find its place in it, as it did in the Christian world; if humanity's fate is a story with a point, then death is a part of life: but if not, then life is a part of death. Whether it's called history or given some other name, we must have a world that we can understand. Whether we know it or not, that, and that alone, can gratify our yearning for survival. If mental structures disappear forever like the plesiosaurus, if civilisations succeed one another only in order to cast man into the bottomless pit of nothingness, if the human adventure only subsists at the price of a merciless metamorphosis, it's of little consequence that men communicate their ideas and their methods to each other for a few centuries; for man is a chance element, and, fundamentally speaking, the world consists of oblivion" (p. 107).

5. André Malraux, *The Voices of Silence,* trans. Stuart Gilbert (Garden City, N.Y.: Doubleday, 1953), pp. 630–42. Malraux writes: "It is art as an organic whole . . . that our culture for the first time is arraying against destiny. . . . It is we, the men of today, who are wresting from the dead past the living past of the museum. . . . Pitiful indeed may seem the lot of Man whose little day ends in a black night of nothingness. . . . Yet surely no less impotent is that nothingness of which he seems to be the prey, if all the thousands of years piled above his dust are unable to stifle the voice of a great artist once he is in his coffin. Survival is not measurable by duration, and death is not assured of its victory, when challenged by a dialogue echoing down the ages" (p. 641).

6. From "Catholicism," in *Stéphane Mallarmé 1842–1898,* trans. Grange Woolley (Madison, N.J.; Drew University Press, 1942), p. 130. From Mallarmé's *Divagations* (1897). This is the second

time de Man has quoted Mallarmé in this essay. The line appearing earlier, "Du sol et de la nue hostiles, o grief!" is from "Le Tombeau d'Edgar Poe" (1876) from *Hommages et Tombeaux*.

7. Martin Heidegger, "Moira," in *Vorträge und Aufsätze*, vol. III (Pfullingen: Neske Verlag, 1967), p. 48. For another translation see Martin Heidegger, *Early Greek Thinking*, trans. D. Krell and F. Capuzzi (New York: Harper & Row, 1975), p. 97–98.

8. *Holzwege*, p. 37. For Hofstadter's translation, see *Poetry, Language, and Thought*, p. 48.

9. *Holzwege*, p. 51. In Hofstadter, p. 63.

10. Friedrich Hölderlin, *Sämtliche Werke, Historisch-Kritische Ausgabe*, 2nd edition begun by Norbert von Hellingrath, continued by Friedrich Seebass and Ludgwig von Pigenot, 6 volumes (Berlin: Prophyläen Verlag, 1923ff.). See volume III, p. 321.

11. *Holzwege*, p. 51. In Hofstadter, p. 63.

12. Hölderlin, vol. 2, p. 333. Cited by Heidegger, *Vorträge und Aufsätze*, II, p. 76.

13. Heidegger, *Vorträge und Aufsätze*, II, pp. 61–78.

14. *Vorträge und Aufsätze*, II, p. 70. In Hofstadter, p. 221.

15. *Vorträge und Aufsätze*, II, p. 75. In Hofstadter, p. 226.

16. Hölderlin, VI, pp. 24ff. De Man's note: "We are dealing here with a poem probably apocryphal, at least in part, one which perhaps owes its strange power of suggestion to chance. One might do well to mention that Hölderlin himself did not publish it and is not its subject." See also Hölderlin, edited and translated by Michael Hamburger (Baltimore, 1961), pp. 245ff. Hamburger adds the poem at the end of his collection under the heading of "Poems of his Madness." It seems that the poem is taken from a novel by Wilhelm Waiblinger, *Phaeton* (1823), the central character of which is based on Hölderlin, whom Waiblinger knew and on whose last writings he drew to put together this poem.

17. *Vorträge und Aufsätze*, II, p. 75; Hofstadter, p. 227.

18. *Vorträge und Aufsätze*, II, pp. 19–36; Hofstadter, pp. 145–61.

19. *Vorträge und Aufsätze*, II, p. 27; Hofstadter, p. 153.

20. *Vorträge und Aufsätze*, II, p. 23; Hofstadter, p. 149.

# Keats and Hölderlin (1956)

The parallel between Keats and Hölderlin has often been suggested – so often that it tends to be taken for granted. Mr. Hamburger, in his introduction to translations of some of Hölderlin's poems, refers to it as a matter of course,[1] and it has found its way even into such semipopularizing works as Gilbert Highet's *The Classical Tradition*.[2] The fact is, however, that the only published work on record entirely devoted to this comparison was written by an obscure German Oberlehrer in 1896,[3] when the major part of Hölderlin's poetry was still entirely unknown, even in Germany.[4]

As the understanding and interpretation of Hölderlin have developed, his stature has steadily grown, to the point where he appears as one of the central figures in modern literature. Evaluation of Keats has shown a similar – though, of course, less dramatic – upward trend. A comparison may thus find a basis in the conviction of their common greatness, but it must necessarily remain confined to an enumeration of thematic analogies. The two contemporary poets were, of course, unaware of each other's existence and have no specific literary or philosophical sources in common; certainly, their respective Hellenisms are all too individual to serve as a starting point for comparison. And the language differences make any comparison of texture a highly hazardous undertaking, which would have to be preceded by extensive comparative theories concerning English and German poetical techniques.

The most immediate value of a Keats-Hölderlin parallel is a clarification of Keats's major themes, which, as divergent opinions in recent Keats criticism well show, are far from being unambiguously defined. For this purpose Hölderlin's almost blinding clarity can be of great assistance. After a period of searching growth and experimentation, his later work succeeds in saying what he had to say with a directness and simplicity on which no discursive paraphrase can ever hope to improve. As Martin Heidegger's studies show,[5] this part of Hölderlin's work, from 1800 up to his insanity in 1806, allows for entirely internal exegesis. The burden of comprehension lies in the reader's capacity to relive the spiritual experience, which is stated with the greatest possible clarity. Keats, on the other hand, never had the opportunity to reach a degree of control over his poetic and spiritual impulses that allowed him to speak with full assurance.

His work, seen as a whole, tends to divide itself into two parts: the poems in which he accepts a limited theme and occasionally achieves a high degree of formal perfection, and those in which he tries to say everything but generally fails to maintain control of the overall texture. "The Eve of St. Agnes" and the ode "To Autumn" are clear examples of the first category, while *Endymion* and both versions of *Hyperion* undoubtedly belong to the second. Very little remains to be said about the former works, but the latter remain — and are bound to remain forever — objects of endless speculation. Whenever Keats criticism has gone astray, it has been in trying to force a thematic unity on the entire work. Some have tried to annex the entire "obscure" zone of Keats's mind by making it appear as mere sensation, on the most superficial level of the term; Mr. Newell Ford's reading of *Endymion*[6] is the most recent example of this trend. Others have searched for metaphysical complexity in purely narrative poems like "The Eve of St. Agnes"; Mr. Wasserman's book is the latest product of this school of thought.[7] Would it not be preferable to allow for the existence of a major and a minor Keats and to classify and evaluate the works accordingly? One would, of course, have to argue at some length as to where to locate such border cases as *Lamia* or even the odes.

In this study I shall undertake a close examination of the complex themes of Keats's two most ambitious works, *Endymion* and *Hyperion*, in the light of Hölderlin's treatment of similar themes. The similarity in title between Hölderlin's and Keats's *Hyperion* is misleading. In the general development of their respective work, Hölderlin's novel, *Hyperion*, corresponds to Keats's *Endymion*. After an examination of these products of the two poets' preparatory periods, we shall proceed to their maturation, to a comparison of the two versions of Keats's *Hyperion* with the three fragments of Hölderlin's *Empedokles*. Beyond *Empedokles*, the comparison would be both meaningless and somehow unfair to Keats.

Hölderlin was more fortunate than Keats in the choice of his first master; as an example of literary excellence, Schiller is certainly preferable to Leigh Hunt. His well-known influence on Hölderlin appears very clearly in the early *Hyperion* fragment, generally referred to as the *Thaliafragment*. It was written in 1793 and appeared in Schiller's *Neue Thalia*, IV (last volume). The theoretical statement that introduces the text is very similar in tone to Hölderlin's later philosophical fragments.

> Es gibt zwei Ideale unseres Daseins: einen Zustand der höchsten Einfalt, wo unsre Bedürfnisse mit sich selbst, und mit unsren Kräften, und mit allem, womit wir in Verbindung stehen, *durch die bloße Organisation der Natur,* ohne unser Zuthun, gegenseitig zusammenstimmen, und einen Zustand der höchsten Bildung, wo dasselbe statt finden würde bei unendlich vervielfältigten und verstärkten Bedürfnissen und Kräften, *durch die Organisation, die wir uns selbst zu gebin im Stande sind.* Die exzentrische Bahn, die der Mensch, im Allgemeinen und Einzelnen, von einem Punkte (der mehr oder weniger reinen Einfalt) zum andern (der mehr oder weniger vollendeten Bildung) durchläuft, scheint sich, *nach ihren wesentlichen Richtungen,* immer gleich zu sein. (*Fragment von Hyperion,* II. p. 53)[8]

[There are two ideals of our existence: a condition of the highest simplicity, in which our requirements with themselves, and with our powers, and with everything, with which we are connected, *by way of the simple organization of nature* without our assistance, reciprocally agree; and a condition of the highest consciousness, in which the same thing would take place in endlessly multiplied and strengthened requirements and powers, *by way of the organization which we are in a position to give to ourselves.* The eccentric road, which man, in general and in particular, from one point (of more or less pure simplicity) to others (of more or less completed consciousness) follows, seems always, *in its essential direction,* to be the same.]

That Hölderlin should have put this key passage at the very beginning of his first important work is an impressive example, even at this early date, of the self-exegesis to which we have alluded. For it is indeed an accurate and complete summary of the novel that follows—not just the *Thaliafragment* but the final *Hyperion,* written in 1796—and contains several of the themes that will remain central through *Empedokles* and the later work. The two terms *Einfalt* (simplicity) and *Bildung* (consciousness) correspond to Schiller's *naiv* and *sentimental.* In Hölderlin, the literary concepts become live experience. Simplicity is the supreme value, the state of complete innocence where a spontaneous friendship exists between man and the world that surrounds him, associated, in individual life, with the condition of childhood:

> Da ich ein Knabe war,
> Rettet' ein Gott mich oft
> Vom Geschrei und der Ruthe der Menschen,
> Da spielt' ich sicher und gut
> Mit den Blumen des Hains,

Und die Lüftchen des Himmels
Spielten mit mir.
(II, p. 47)

[In my boyhood days
A god often saved me
From the noise and rod of mankind;
Then I played, secure and good,
With the flowers of the field,
And the breezes of heaven
Played with me.]

Simplicity, *Einfalt,* then, is the starting point of all existence, an entirely self-sufficient and complete state in itself: "Ja! ein göttlich Wesen ist das Kind. . . . Es ist ganz, was es ist, und darum ist es so schön" (*Hyperion,* II, p. 93). (Yes! The child is a divine being. . . . It is entirely what it is, and precisely for that reason it is so beautiful.) However, it does not prevail: " . . . ein göttlich Wesen, so lang es nicht in die Chamäleonsfarbe der Menschen getaucht ist." "Da ich noch ein stilles Kind war und von dem allen, was uns umgiebt, nichts wußte" (ibid.). ( . . . a divine being, as long as it is not dipped in the chameleon colors of mankind. Then I was still a quiet child and did not know of all this that surrounds us.) With the development of consciousness the unity is destroyed:

Freundlichen Götter! . . .
Zwar damals rieff ich noch nicht
Euch mit Nahmen, auch
Nanntet mich nie, wie die Menschen sich nennen,
Als kennten sie sich.
(II. p. 47)

Friendly gods! . . .
Of course, in those days I did not yet
Call you by names,
Nor did you ever
Name me, as people name each other
As if they knew each other.

The "naming" of the world and the claim of knowing disturb the original unity and start the long "eccentric road" that Hölderlin names *Bildung. Bildung,* consciousness by initiation, is thus directly associated with *Trennung* (separation, the first negative key term) — the initial act of consciousness destroys the given fellowship of being. At this point in Hölderlin's work this is merely stated as an awareness existing within himself, as an expression of his own reality; the general philosophical and poetic motivation will come later. But he already knows that the separation is a free, self-willed human act of which we, as humans, carry the burden and the responsibility:

> Aber sage nur niemand, daß uns das Schiksaal trenne! Wir sind's, wir! wir haben unsere Lüst daran, uns in die Nacht des Unbekannten, in die kalte Fremde irgend einer Welt zu stürzen, und war' es möglich, wir verließen der Sonne Gebiet und stürmten über des Irrsterns Gränzen hinaus. (*Hyperion,* II, pp. 101–2.)

> [But don't let anyone say that it is fate that separates us! We do it, *we*! We have our joy in it, this plunging into the night of the unknown, into the coldly alien space of *any* other world, and if it were possible, we'd leave the territory of the sun and dash beyond the boundaries of the comets.]

The language of Hölderlin's central subject is still vague and almost conventional, but the theme is there; controlled consciousness *(Bildung)* is the beginning of dissonance *(Trennung)* between man and nature.

The unfolding of consciousness, the "organization which we are able to give ourselves," consists of the series of means by which the original unity tries to restore itself. "Alles Getrennte findet sich wider" (Everything that is separated is joined again), says Hyperion at the end of the novel (II, p. 291), and the desire for unity is the prime mover of man's life, the supreme moral goal. The different stages of the initiation lead closer and closer to the final value of unity:

> Eines zu seyn mit allem, was lebt, in seeliger Selbstvergessenheit wiederzukehren in's All der Natur, das ist der Gipfel der Gedanken und Freuden, das ist die heilige Bergeshöhe, der Ort der ewigen Ruhe, wo der Mittag seine Schwüle und der Donner seine Stimme verliert und das kochende Meer der Wooge des Kornfelds gleicht. (*Hyperion,* II, p. 91)

> [To be at one with everything that lives, in blessed self-oblivion to return to the unity of nature, that is the summit of thoughts and joys, that is the holy mountain peak, the place of eternal rest, where noon's heat and the thunder's voice are lost and grainfields are like a foaming sea of waves.]

Such is the final destination of the "eccentric road" that, through consciousness, leads from simplicity to recovered unity. Part of this idea is familiar enough from many similar statements in the Sturm und Drang writers, in Rousseau, or in Wordsworth's "The Child is father of the Man . . . " But, in Hölderlin, childhood is not just a state to be remembered nostalgically in the elegiac mood of the pastoral; the necessity to get beyond this mood is inscribed in reality. By means of a deliberate and totally responsible series of acts, man takes himself toward the recovery of this unity. *Bildung* is entirely aimed toward the future and takes on the urgency of a moral imperative.

Hölderlin's own thought continues to emerge in the statement that concludes the passage: "The eccentric road which takes man, individually and collectively, from one point (more or less pure simplicity) to the other (more or less complete consciousness) seems, in its essential directions, to be always the same." The idea is taking shape that this movement is not erratic or a result of individual caprice, but that its development is itself a law that the mind can seize. The *Bildungsroman* thus takes on a new significance; not only is the initiation determined by its two extreme points (from simplicity through separation to recovered unity), but the intermediate cycles are determined in kind and in order. The succession of events, instead of being mere accidents of destiny, is a first approximation to this law of gradual growth.

In *Hyperion,* the succession is clearly marked; if the sequence may seem blurred at first reading, this is due to the monotony of the amorphous texture; we are still far removed from Hölderlin's later economy. But the mere statement of events shows the hierarchy of the repeated cycles. All of them have the same inherent structure; a certain degree of unity is achieved, then destroyed, in a manner that is similar to the initial destruction of the unity of childhood. The underlying seasonal rhythm forms the natural background on which the human struggle for harmony takes place.

The first cycle is that of instruction, in which the figure of Adamas, presumably representing Schiller, accomplishes the first of a series of initiations. He introduces the hero to the existing body of human wisdom and reveals to him the greatness of the Hellenic world. The ease with which Hyperion outgrows this stage is characteristic of Hölderlin's assurance in freeing himself from influences, but the relationship between master and disciple remains an essential and growing theme to the very last poems.

The second cycle is that of friendship, exemplified in the relationship with Alabanda. The immensely exalted tone and the fact that Alabanda returns in later episodes are indications of the gravity that this experience assumes in Hyperion's quest. Friendship is one of Hölderlin's holy words; it is the specific mood of innocent man to be a "friend" of nature, not in the sophisticated manner of Theocritus's shepherds, but in a powerfully spontaneous way. In the friendship between men, this feeling prevails perhaps in its purest form. Friendship is unity and, beyond that, it is conversation *(Gespräch)* within the sphere of unity, the worldly equivalence of the conversation between the gods and the child that was at the beginning of things. More than the ambiguous Alabanda, the invisible Bellarmin is perhaps the true incarnation of the friendship theme in *Hyperion,*[9] and the letter form is partly justified on that basis. In one of the later poems, the theme is still remembered:

> Wo aber sind die Freunde? Bellarmin
> Mit dem Gefährten? . . .
> ("Andenken," IV, p. 62)

> (But where are the friends? Bellarmin
> With his companions? . . . )

The next cycle of initiation is of course love, as it appears in the Diotima episode. Taken in itself, this is probably the most traditionally "romantic" passage in Hölderlin — the lifting of earthly love to the level of experienced unity of being: "Zart, wie der Aether, umwand mich Diotima. Thörichter, was ist die Trennung? flüsterte sie geheimnisvoll mir zu, mit dem Lächeln einer Unsterblichen" (*Hyperion*, II, p. 215). (Tenderly, like the aether, Diotima held me. "Fool, what is parting?" she whispered mysteriously to me, with the smile of an immortal.) More characteristic of Hölderlin is the place this experience occupies within the general plan of *Bildung*. It is definitely only a step within a development, a necessary stage to be transcended. Diotima's solitary death is altogether different from the Tristan love-death, and her divinization is merely the divinization of the idea of unity and not the religous-erotic complex of Novalis's *Geistliche Lieder*. Her death marks the end of the directly lyrical love theme in Hölderlin's work. In the first version of *Empedokles,* Delia is merely a disciple, and in the subsequent fragments she disappears altogether. In "Andenken" women exist as highly stylized and remote figures, and only such women are present at the moment of divine revelation:

> An Feiertagen gehn
> Die braunen Frauen daselbst
> Auf seidnen Boden,
> Zur Märzenzeit . . .
> (IV, p. 61)

> [On holidays brown women
> In that very place walk
> On silken earth
> When March has come . . . ]

After the cycle of love follows the cycle of action, Hyperion's disappointing participation in the struggle of his oppressed countrymen. Of all the major experiences, this one is perhaps at its most fragmentary in *Hyperion,* particularly if compared to its later development. Its importance is clear from its position as the central episode of the novel, but the motivation of events remains arbitrary and disconnected.

Following a series of episodes that are mostly necessities of plot or side themes—Alabanda's departure, Diotima's death, the beautiful "Schiksaalslied" (Song of Fate), the violent diatribe against Germany—come the concluding pages, which need interpretation. The last step in Hyperion's initiation, which permits the hopeful though suspended ending ("alles Getrennte findet sich wieder" [Everything that is separated is joined again]), is mysterious; all possible experiences seem to have failed or been transcended. The explanation may be found in the vision of Diotima's return and in the change of tone in the last passage. The apparition of Diotima is the only episode in the novel that has a supernatural dimension. And the tone of the final page changes from the elegiac memories of a defeated hero to a hymnal tone of lyrical praise. Does it not represent the inward movement of a soul that, up till then, has conducted its search for unity in a world that lies outside of itself? In the world of friendship, love, and action, the soul forgets itself in the hope of discovering a new unity. When it has failed, it turns inward and starts the same road over again, but this time with the additional dimension of inwardness. This is Hyperion's discovery, after he has run the complete course of his outward cycle. He has joined Diotima "bei den Deinen," (among his own) in the life of the spirit. "Wir lieben den Äther doch all' und innigst im Innersten gleichen wir uns" (*Hyperion,* II, p. 291). (We love the aether, all of us, and in the most inward part of our inwardness, we are one.) The revelation occurs in the spring; it marks a new beginning, a new cycle is going to develop; "Nächstens mehr" (More very soon) are the last words of the novel. The road from simplicity to harmony in consciousness leads through our inner self. The theoretical essay that connects most directly with *Hyperion* starts with the study of "der reine Geist, die reine Innigkeit" ("Grund zum Empedokles," III, p. 316) (The pure spirit, the pure inwardness).

Keats's *Endymion* can be, and has been, read in a great variety of ways. A recent article by Mr. Wigod[10] gives a comprehensive survey of the different schools of thought; they cover a wide range of conflicting opinions. But the main issue always seems to come down to the same point—how to relate the serious and coherent statement in Book I, the passage starting with "Wherein lies happiness?" (I, lines 777ff.), with the desultory and apparently disconnected passages that follow. Is there any unity of theme or does the poem go entirely astray? In his most ambitious works, with which *Endymion* belongs, there are good reasons to give Keats at least the benefit of doubt as far as both seriousness and unity are concerned—the most important reason being the undeniable organic growth of a work that, not unlike Hölderlin's, keeps restating its essential problems with increasing depth and lucidity. The assumption of an underlying poetic—or even metaphysical—unity of purpose is perfectly compatible with as apparently nonphilosophical a mind as Keats's. True philosophers deal with the issues common to all men. The difference between their expression and that of poets (or artists, in general) is one of terminological exactness, and not of matter or intent. It is therefore possible that a deep analogy exists between a philosophically aware poet like Hölderlin and an intuitive poet like Keats, and that it is legitimate to apply as it were, the philosophical conclusions of the first to the poetic utterances of the second. If there is indeed a definitely determined road along which human unity attempts to restore itself, the discovery of such a road in Keats's poem would substantiate the seriousness of the main theme and reveal at least some unity in the general conception.

On the basis of the "Wherein lies happiness?" passage and Book I as a whole, *Endymion* can well be described, in Hölderin's terms, as a quest to bring "our needs into a state of harmony with themselves, with the forces within us, and with everything we enter into contact with." We know of such a state by the revelation of an initial "situation of utter simplicity" in which this harmony was achieved "by means of the mere organization of nature." The pastoral opening seems to be the literary representation of this pervasive mood of natural unity that, quite fittingly, finds its symbol in the great God Pan, the god of ripening and of the dark rhythms of nature. He stands at the beginning of the mystery of original oneness. He is the "Dread opener of the mysterious doors / Leading to universal knowledge" (I, lines 288–89). He is asked to "be still the leaven / That spreading in this dull and clodded earth / Gives it a touch ethereal—" (I, lines 296–98). Awareness of natural unity is the beginning of our earthly undertaking. The theme is a persistent one in Keats; in its most implicit form, it becomes the freshness of his sensation, which always maintains a kind of childlike openness.

In this situation of ideal simplicity, the torn hero appears, suffering because of his mortal condition, which has destroyed his initial perfection. No longer a child, he has lost his happy innocence; Hölderlin's division has reached him. At the same time, he has attained the conviction that he must set out to restore this unity, which is no longer given him but must now be achieved "by the organization which [he] is able to give [himself]." His task becomes a quest for unity. He must feel again "A fellowship with essence" (I, line 779) and step "into a sort of oneness" (I, line 796). This aim is strikingly similar to Hyperion's ideal, "Eines zu sein mit Allem, was lebt, in seeliger Selbstvergessenheit wiederzukehren . . . " (to be at one with everything that lives, in blessed self-oblivion to return . . . ) (*Hyperion,* II, p. 91). It is the main theme of both works.

*Endymion,* then, is a poem about unity, not about love, as Mr. Newell Ford would have it, not just about "ideal beauty that is ideal love," as Mr. Wigod argues. Neither is it about the ideal in general, in the Neoplatonic sense, but specifically about the ideal of unity—which, if need is felt for a philosophical antecedent, is a pre-Socratic concept rather than a Platonic one. The line on fellowship with essence, in which the language, to some extent, is metaphysical, should be emphasized more than the introduction of Cynthia as "a love immortal" (I, line 849); the latter line can be read as a metaphorical restatement of the former. The main reason for the confusion of the poem lies in the fact that the concept of unity is consistently expressed in a symbolic language borrowed from the experience of erotic love. Love is not a metaphysical category here, like the Platonic Eros, but a metaphor. This image is natural enough, particularly in a poet whose very concrete imagination always tends to see abstractions in terms of physical sensations – to which can be added the sensual obsession that, during the period when *Endymion* was written, seems to have made it difficult for Keats to talk about any experience in nonerotic terms. Further confusion arises from the presence, within the poem, of an actual love experience, in a literal, nonsymbolic sense. In the passages that deal with it, the language is descriptive instead of metaphorical. The actual love episode is given undue emphasis, for the very same and obvious reason that prompted the symbolization of unity as a sexual embrace. The introductory enumeration of themes generously gives "an orbed drop / Of light, and that is love . . . " (I, lines 806–7) thirty-five lines of development while none of the other themes receive more than five. This lopsided balance receives still further disequilibrium through the climaxes that, at the end of each experience, are supposed to convey the blending of achieved unity and that, in accordance with the prevalent imagery, are mostly stated in terms of "naked waists" and "fondling and kissing." No wonder it becomes difficult to keep apart the passages in which love is an actual experience, among others, from those in which it is a symbol for something else. But only at the expense of this effort can *Endymion* be given a thematic coherence that Keats's *Hyperion* amply substantiates.

Like Hölderlin's *Hyperion, Endymion* should be seen as a *Bildungsroman* in which we follow the different repetitive stages of the hero's initiation to the point where he becomes ready to recover the unity of being, lost at the start. Like Hölderlin, Keats feels this initiation as a series of experiences ordered in a general and deliberate pattern of growth. Even two such divergent critics as Mr. Newell Ford and Mr. Wasserman have emphasized the repetitive pattern in Keats's work, which they refer to respectively as "prefigurative imagination" and "the finer tone." The movement is constant in Keats, and he is himself aware of it. When it is first stated, in "Sleep and Poetry," it may seem borrowed from Wordsworth. But Keats keeps coming back to it, in moments of greatest seriousness, in the most important letters – to Reynolds on May 3, 1818, to George and Georgiana Keats on February 14, 1819, etc. – and in both versions of *Hyperion*. There can be no doubt that this is Keats's deepest and most personal conviction; he sees life as a task of ever-growing consciousness, which has to encompass a wider and wider range of knowledge and experience, harmonized by the repeated awareness that moments of unity between the self and the world are the supreme ideal, around which the entire act of living has to be organized. This feeling is much closer to the forward-looking and deliberate *Bildung* (consciousness) of Hölderlin than to the elegiac recollections of Wordsworth's "Tintern Abbey" or the "Intimations of Immortality."

The succession of the different stages is very close to that in Hölderlin's

*Hyperion.* Book I announces the progression that is more or less adequately represented in the succeeding events. Starting from the spontaneous enjoyment of nature, we come to the "old songs waken from enclouded tombs" (I, lines 787ff.). This passage refers to the discovery and study of the world of art and learning; it is of some importance that it does not refer to practice of art as a creative poet. Neither in Hölderlin nor in Keats is there a suggestion, at this point in their work, that their heroes will reach their aim by the practice of poetry. They are solicited by a wide variety of experiences, and their final choice is still much more general than the poetic act in itself. Endymion's delight in art is Keats discovering Shakespeare, Homer, and the Elgin marbles. These are the formative years of study, the discovery of the masters and of the past: "old songs," "old ditties," "ghosts of melodious prophecying." The theme corresponds to the Adamas passage of Hyperion's education, and it receives its allegorical representation in Book II, in the voyage "through the hollow, / The silent mysteries of earth" (II, lines 213–14). We can suppose the "dusky empire . . . with all its lines abrupt and angular" (II, line 228) to be the severe world of science (of which Keats had some experience). Out of this world, Endymion moves into the more congenial world of art, mythology, and poetry, to reach the climactic ecstacy of the final scene—all in all one of the worst in *Endymion.*

It does not require much argument to present Book III as the development of "enthralments far / More self-destroying" (I, lines 798–99); the Glaucus episode has generally been read to express sympathy with human suffering and friendship, which then leads to humanitarian action. Perhaps the character of Peona can be added as another example of Keats's theme of friendship. Book III would then correspond to Hölderlin's Alabanda episode and to Hyperion's battle for the liberation of Greece, though the order of the two last cycles (love, action) is inverted, since Keats obviously wants to save his love theme for the end. The love symbolism, more or less incongruous in Book II, becomes more confusing here; the liberation of suffering humanity is rather bizarrely represented by the freed lovers. Significantly, it is this theme, which is at its most fragmentary in both poems, that will become eternal in the later work.

In *Endymion,* Diotima's equivalent has become an Indian maiden, a nice illustration of Keats's lack of actual experience. He is completely stifled here by the inevitable clash between earthly love and unity represented in terms of love; this leads to the awkward complications of plot at the end. The only advantage, to Keats's credit, of the scenes of jealousy between Cynthia and her earthly rival is that the final statement, which remains rather vague in Hölderlin, stands out somewhat better here. Even Mr. Ford refers to the final decision of Endymion as an "eremitic resolution." Endymion's preference of Cynthia over the maiden is clearly a movement from the material to the spiritual, from exteriority to inwardness. If the union with Cynthia represents recovered unity, then the final statement of both works is remarkably similar; unity has to be conquered first within our inner self.

The unity of *Endymion* is thus the unity of the "eccentric road which seems in its essential directions, to be always the same." The fact that the road actually turns out to be the same in both works is in itself an argument for Hölderlin's assumption, a more convincing one than either work could contain within itself. And it is a strong argument in favor of the true seriousness of *Endymion*. But both poems are preliminary statements of essential themes rather than their full poetical expression.

Their defects, too, are strikingly similar: oversentimentality and overintensity of tone; incoherence of structural design, despite the underlying unity of theme; overworked texture, which hides the real profundity of the idea under a superficial gloss of decorative diffuseness—with, in both cases, sudden moments of clarity that prophesy what is to come. These defects are closely linked to the actual statement of both works, which, in fact, is a negative one. Unity of being cannot be achieved in the series of concrete experiences that the outer world normally offers. The coherence of existence, which Hölderlin boldly postulates and of which Keats has an ardent and groping premonition, cannot be perceived without going through the experience of inwardness. Neither Hyperion nor Endymion is capable of this, since they are incarnations of the self, which both poets have only just sufficiently outgrown to be able to objectify it. Neither Hyperion nor Endymion could see what their authors are only beginning to ponder in necessary solitude. And neither of their messages in final. The problems of the concrete lie on the other side of inwardness and will reappear within this new perspective. This will be the subject of Hölderlin's *Empedokles*.

Unlike Hölderlin's *Hyperion,* which is diffuse but perhaps all too simple, the three fragments of *Empedokles* are very difficult texts. They were written over a period of two years, between 1798 and 1800,[11] and their difficulty is due to Hölderlin's constant growth and development during this time.[12] They form the connecting link between the early period, well exemplified in *Hyperion,* and the greatness of the later hymns. Keats's *Hyperion* occupies a similar position in his work; it accomplishes the same deepening of his original themes, in a movement that can be followed in passing from *Endymion* to the first fragment, *Hyperion* (April 1819), and then to the second, *The Fall of Hyperion* (December 1819). For no good reason *Hyperion* seems to have been neglected in recent Keats criticism, which has apparently devoted most of its attention to the odes.[13] Like Hölderlin's *Empedokles,* Keats's *Hyperion* suffers from being a work of transition toward summits that Keats, however, was never to reach. An examination of this parallel may help to bring out the considerable importance of a fragment that remains almost necessarily inadequate to the inexhaustible richness of its theme.

Hölderlin's development from *Hyperion* to *Empedokles* can be seen in the change that occurs in the central theme when, after turning inward, it rises to a new power. The ideal of unity, postulated in *Hyperion* as the final goal of a series of unconnected though necessary steps, becomes now a causally coherent and defined inner process.[14] Instead of being a static condition that can be reached as one reaches a certain point in space, unity is seen as a dialectical motion between two antithetical poles.[15] Unity *(Versöhnung)* is no longer a solution, but only an infinitesimal moment in a process. Hölderlin calls this process *Übermaß der Innigkeit* (Excess of inwardness), the movement by which a man rises to a new level of synthesis by going to the extreme of the opposites among which he lives.

Empedokles is the man who has lived through this process. He has transcended the dialectic of *Trennung* on the level of inward life, and has emerged with a new synthesis; in him the self stands out as never before, and through his word nature shines with an unseen splendor. Seen historically, he is the first man of the New Age, and, as such, he is bound to stand in complete opposition to his contemporaries. But, since his essential intent is precisely the reconciliation (however temporary) of opposites, he will feel his task to be the leading and instructing of his people, just as he has been led and instructed by his insight into the transcendental principle (here called nature) that stood beyond and outside of him. His situation, then, is that of a man whose inner greatness has grown in solitary but restless meditation, pledged to reestablish contact between the self and what seems to oppose and to ignore this self. The immediate consequence of this achieved greatness, however, is to involve him completely in the historical destiny of his nation. The totally inward man has to open up to the movement of history and, since he must be defining himself in opposition to the order that surrounds him, this involvement will take on the appearance of a struggle. The energy that carried him through the effort of reaching a new synthesis was fed by the knowledge that the existing order—the existing condition of opposition between self and nature—was no longer tolerable. It is clear, from *Hyperion,* that the reality offered to him could not have satisfied his need for conscious harmony. He has to seek and to fight his opposite, in the form of the static, stratified, and artificial order of the age. Seen from the point of view of his contemporaries, he appears both immensely attractive, since he holds all the promise of the new, and extremely dangerous, since he requires the destruction of all existing institutions. He will be loved by some (Delia, Pausanius) as no one ever was, but hated by others (Hermokrates) who thrive on institutional stability, while the masses of the people keep wavering between love and fear.

This is the situation at the beginning of *Empedokles;* and it is the same scene as that on which Apollo enters at the beginning of Book III of Keats's *Hyperion,* after an exposition that Keats has made more explicit than that of Hölderlin's drama. All we know about Empedokles' fellow citizens stems from the conversations between Hermokrates and Kritias *(Emp. I)* and Hermokrates and Mekades *(Emp. II)*; the main focus is always on Empedokles. On the other hand, the first version of Keats's *Hyperion* devotes two entire books to the fallen Titans, the equivalent of Hölderlin's "hyperpolitischen, immer rechtenden und berechnenden Agrigentern" (hyperpolitical, always adjudicating and calculating) ("Grund," III, 329). Their relationship to Apollo is similar to the relationship between Empedokles and the leaders of Sicily. They are characterized by their strictly hierarchical, hyperconservative stratifications; they sound as would Shakespeare's Greeks, in *Troilus and Cressida,* after centuries of passive obedience to Ulysses' law of degree. Even at the brink of disaster, the undefeated Hyperion cannot freely break the rules of hierarchy ("Fain would he have commanded, fain took throne / And bid the day begin, if but for change," I, 290–91); and the speech of Oceanus, which is the opposite of Ulysses' speech in another famous council scene, is bound to be heresy to the Titans' ears. In total opposition to them, Apollo appears as the new man, the force of youth and future growing beyond the existing order.[16] Like Empedokles the self-achieved harmony of pastoral unity leaves him dissatisfied:

> O Why should I
> Feel curs'd and thwarted, when the liegeless air
> Yields to my step aspirant? why should I
> Spurn the green turf as hateful to my feet?
>
> *(Hyperion,* III, lines 91–94)

and he grows out of his dissatisfaction by opening up to history, by becoming intellectually conscious of the dialectic of being that occurs in the world, as he knew it to occur within himself:

> Knowledge enormous makes a God of me.
> Names, deeds, grey legends, dire events, rebellions,
> Majesties, sovran voices, agonies,
> Creations and destroyings, all at once
> Pour into the wide hollows of my brain,
> And deify me . . .
>
> (ibid., lines 113–18)

The distinctive originality of this passage and, at the same time, the deeper analogy between *Hyperion* and *Empedokles* appear in this résumé of Keats's historical awareness. History is no longer the static example of certain high achievements, as antiquity was to the neoclassic age, but a movement that includes destruction and chaos ("creations and destroyings, all at once . . . ") as well as achievements. True historical awareness seems to be consciousness of the congruence between the curve of inner growth of an individual man and the outer real growth of the life of nations. And as nations rise and fall, live and die, so man's thought and development become a succession of agonies and rebirths, instead of the gradual and determined growth of Hölderlin's *Hyperion* or of Keats's

*Endymion.* The growth of Apollo is stated in an imagery that suggests a constant interplay between life and death, culminating in the final paradox: "Die into life":

> Soon wild commotions shook him, and made flush
> All the immortal fairness of his limbs;
> Most like the struggle at the gate of death;
> Or liker still to one who should take leave
> Of pale immortal death, and with a pang
> As hot as death's is chill, with fierce convulse
> Die into life . . .
>
> (ibid., lines 124–30)

Similarly, the climax of *Empedokles,* his descent into the crater of Mount Aetna, is to be an act of life-giving death. Seen from a point of view that transcends the individual, the point of view of the sage—Oceanus in Keats, Empedokles himself and Manes *(Emp. III)* in Hölderlin—the vision of history becomes the alternating movement of rise and fall of the often-quoted passage:

> And first, as thou wast not the first of powers,
> So art thou not the last; it cannot be:
> Thou art not the beginning nor the end . . . [17]
>
> (*Hyperion,* II, lines 188ff.)

These lines have their equivalent in Hölderlin:

> Es scheun
> Die Erdenkinder meist das Neu und Fremde;
> Daheim in sich zu bleiben, strebet nur
> Der Pflanze Leben und das frohe Tier.
> . . . Menschen ist die große Lust
> Gegeben, daß sie sellber sich verjüngen.
> Und aus dem reinigenden Tode, den
> Sie selber sich zu rechter Zeit gewählt
> Erstehn, wie aus dem Styx Achill,
> Unüberwindlich—die Völker.
> So wagts! was ihr geerbt, was ihr erworben,
> Was euch der Vater Mund erzählt, gelehrt.
> Gesez und Brauch, der alten Götter Nahmen,
> Vergeßt es kühn, und hebt, wie Neugeborne,
> Die Augen auf zur göttlichen Natur.[18]
>
> (*Empedokles, I,* III, 146–47)

> [Children of earth are mostly frightened
> By the new and strange;
> Only the happy beasts and plants strive

To stay at home in themselves.
. . . To mankind is given the great joy
Of self-rejuvenation.
And out of purifying deaths,
Which they themselves choose
At the proper moment,
Arise, like Achilles from the Styx,
Unconquerable—the people.
So dare it! What you have inherited,
What you acquired,
What you have heard and learned from your
Fathers' mouths
Law and custom, names of the old gods,
Boldly forget and raise, as if newly born,
Your eyes to divine nature.]

The new hero who has awakened to this historical awareness—Apollo after his initiation by Mnemosyne—starts his task of leadership and instruction with a knowledge his predecessors did not possess—the knowledge that his achievements are ephemeral. By accepting and requiring the destruction of what exists, he also accepts the transitory nature of his own undertaking and realizes that his birth contains within itself his own death. Since he takes within himself the total destiny of his people, he also assumes their failure and downfall as an inherent part of his personal destiny:

Denn wo ein Land ersterben soll, da wählt
Der Geist noch Einen sich am End, durch den
Sein Schwanensang, das letzte Leben tönet.
(*Empedokles III,* III, 223)

[For when a country is to die, the Spirit chooses
one more man at the end, through whom
his swan song, the last life, sounds.]

Thus, what first appears as an act of intellectual growth and insight gradually takes on an ethical dimension of supreme sacrifice, of suicide in the highest possible sense. Both poets become increasingly aware of this as their meditation progresses, and their works shift from the theme of historical rejuvenation to the theme of sacrifice. The scene of the third *Empedokles* fragment is the slopes of Mount Aetna, and the fragment deals exclusively with Empedokles' state of mind and vision immediately before his voluntary death; whereas the birth and death imagery of Keats's *Hyperion* is replaced, in *The Fall of Hyperion,* by the imagery of suffering and sacrifice that finds its supreme symbol in the Christlike face of

Moneta. The theme of love, which was so prominent in the early work, thus reappears in an altogether new light, as the sacrificial act of historical commitment by which a superior individual becomes the example that serves to regenerate his people. "Das Schiksaal seiner Zeit erforderte auch nicht eigentliche That; . . . es erforderte ein *Opfer,* wo der ganze Mensch das wirklich und sichtbar wird, worinn das Schiksaal seiner Zeit sich aufzulösen scheint, wo die Extreme sich in Einem wirklich und sichtbar zu vereinigen scheinen" (Nor does the fate of his time require actual deeds; . . . it requires a sacrifice, in which the whole man becomes true and visible, in which the fate of his time seems to dissolve, in which the extremes seem truly and visibly to unite themselves in one person) ("Grund," III, p. 327). Before he realized this, Empedokles could rightly say that he had "Die Menschen menschlich nie geliebt, gedient" (Never humanly loved or served humanity) (*Emp. III,* III, 204); but, once he has seen his true role, he can die in tranquil serenity.[19]

The figures of Empedokles and Apollo thus grow from poet ("Er scheint nach allem zum Dichter geboren" [He seems after all to be born a poet], "Grund," III, p. 326) to leader. But, by his act of supreme sacrifice, Empedokles takes on the dimension of the Savior. Both poets could identify themselves with their hero in the first two stages, but not in the last; there is no trace of *hubris* in Hölderlin or in Keats. Keats's allegory is clearer here than Hölderlin's. The identification Keats-Appollo is obvious enough, and Apollo, like Empedokles, grows to understand the necessity of love for "soul making." He becomes one of "those to whom the miseries of the world / Are misery, and will not let them rest" (*Fall,* I, lines 148–49). But the actual act of sacrifice is not within his power, and the poet is merely the one who has *seen* the sacrifice, with the mind's eye, as Moneta reveals it to him:

> The sacrifice is done, but not the less
> Will I be kind to thee for thy good will.
> My power, which to me is still a curse,
> Shall be to thee a wonder; for the scenes
> Still swooning vivid through my globed brain,
> With an electral changing misery,
> Thou shalt with these dull mortal eyes behold
> Free from all pain, if wonder pain thee not.
>
> (*Fall,* I, 241–48)

In *Empedokles,* the disciple Pausanius, who stays with Empedokles to the very last, fulfills the same function; but Pausanius is not identified with the poet as clearly as is Keats's Apollo. A later hymn of Hölderlin, "Wie wenn am Feiertage" [As on a holiday], defines the role of the poet as necessarily distinct from that of the Savior. Before His arrival, the poet is the one who kept the minds of the people open for the perception of the sacrifice; during the crisis he is the one who has stood by Christ and understood His suffering ("eines Gottes Leiden mittleidend" [suffering a god's suffering with him]), and, when all has been accomplished, he transmits the power of the supreme example:

> Doch uns gebührt es, unter Gottes Gewittern,
> Ihr Dichter! mit entblößtem Haupte zu stehen,
> Des Vaters Strahl, ihn selbst, mit eigner Hand
> Zu fassen und dem Volk ins Lied
> Gehüllt die himmlische Gaabe zu reichen.

(IV, 153)

> Truly it is fitting for us, beneath God's storms,
> Ye poets! to stand with bared heads
> To grasp the very lightening of the fathers with our own hands,
> And to extend to the people the heavenly gift,
> Enveloped in the song.

The thematic analogy between *Empedokles* and *Hyperion* is more profound than a quick survey of two very complex fragments can suggest. The kinship between the poets is partly ontological; both being total and very pure poets, they share elements that pertain to the being of the poetic as such. It is partly temperamental, in that both poets are, to some extent, metaphysically inclined—Keats certainly not in a technical sense but, undeniably, in his constant concern with ultimate problems, as appears in *Endymion, Hyperion,* and the letters.[20] But the kinship is also, to no small degree, historical—that is, typical of how a poetic consciousness was bound to react to the intellectual and political atmosphere of the early nineteenth century.

The Keats-Hölderlin parallel acquires a clearer relief if it is seen within the general perspective of contemporary European poetry. This cluster of problems, this specific relationship between the poetic, the historical, and the divine, has not ceased to haunt our modern consciousness. In more recent poets, the attitude toward this set of problems may have changed, but the continuity of their presence still forms the substratum of the present-day poetic mind. To explore the significance of Keats and Hölderlin as standing at the beginning of this development goes far beyond the framework of an introductory essay, but it would be a fruitful way to formulate the spiritual crisis that forms the background of twentieth-century literature.

Translation of all quotations from German by Dan Latimer

## Notes

1. Michael Hamburger, *Hölderlin: His Poems* (New York: Pantheon, 1952), p. 89.

2. Gilbert Highet, *The Classical Tradition* (New York and London: Oxford University Press, 1949), p. 378.

3. G. Wenzel, *Hölderlin und Keats als geistesverwandte Dichter* (Magdepurg: Prog. d. Realgym., 1896, no. 270). There exists an Edinburgh dissertation, G. Guder, "A Comparison of Hölderlin and Keats in Their Respective Backgrounds as Romantic Poets" (1938), to which I have not had access.

4. The first reliable complete and critical edition of Hölderlin was begun by Norbert von Hellingrath, who died in 1916, and completed in 1923 by Ludwig von Pigenot and Friedrich Seebass. This edition, as well as the later one by Frank Zinkernagel (Insel Verlag), is now superseded by the definitive Grosse Stuttgarter Ausgabe, edited under the direction of Friedrich Beissner, of which five volumes have been published since 1946. Interest in Hölderlin has only just begun in the United States, as is clear enough from the article by P. M. Mitchell, "Hölderlin in England und Amerika," *Hölderlin Jahrbuch* (1950), pp. 131-146. Probably the most noteworthy addition since is by R. L. Beare, "Patmos, dem Landgrafen von Hombarg," *Germanic Review,* 28 (1953), pp. 5-22.

5. Martin Heidegger, *Erläuterungen zu Hölderlins Dichtung* (Frankfurt: Klostermann, 1951).

6. Newell Ford, "The Meaning of Fellowship with Essence in *Endymion,*" *PMLA,* 62 (1947), pp. 1061-76; "*Endymion* – A Neo-Platonic Allegory?" *ELH,* 14 (1947), pp. 67-76; *The Prefigurative Imagination of John Keats* (Stanford: Stanford University Press, 1951).

7. Earl Wasserman, *The Finer Tone* (Baltimore: Johns Hopkins University Press, 1952).

8. All quotations from Hölderlin are from the six-volume edition begun by Norbert von Hellingrath and finished by Seebass and Pigenot: *Hölderlins Sämtliche Werke* (Berlin: Prophyläen Verlag, 1923). Italics are Hölderlin's.

9. One of the complexities and probably of the weaknesses of the Alabanda episode is that the friendship is strangely interwoven with its antithesis. Aside from being the friend, Alabanda is a sort of anti-self, the symbol of another "eccentric road" Hyperion has rejected. We have a foreshadowing here of the relationship between Empedokles and his brother opponent ("der Gegner") that was to be part of *Empedokles auf dem Aetna.*

10. Jacob K. Wigod, "The Meaning of *Endymion,*" *PMLA,* 68 (1953), pp. 779-90.

11. The original idea had first been stated in a preliminary sketch from 1797, the so-called *Frankfurter Plan,* which uses elements from Diogenes Bios (see Gisela Wagner, *Hölderlin und die Vorsokratiker* [Würzburg, 1937], pp. 97ff.) Some of these elements remain in the first and longest version of *Der Tod des Empedokles (Emp. I,* III, 75-171); the second version, under the same title, is much more fragmentary (*Emp. II,* III, 172-95); and the third *Empedokles auf dem Aetna (Emp. III,* III, 199-227) differs entirely from the two preceding ones. There has been some question as to the order in which the three fragments were written. The Hölderlinian equivalence of Mr. Finney's thesis on Keats – putting *The Fall of Hyperion* before *Hyperion* – is represented by the dissertation of W. Böhm, *Studien zu Hölderlins Empedokles* (Weimar, 1902). Böhm considered *Empedokles auf dem Aetna* as the first text. In his later work, however, he took a different view; see W. Böhm, *Hölderlin* (Halle-Saale, 1928).

12. This growth is reflected in the *Philosophische Fragmenten,* which date from the same period. Exegesis of *Empedokles* is difficult without reference to these all-important texts, particularly the two essays, "Das Werden im Vergehen" (III, 309-15) and "Grund zum Espedokles" (III, 316-335). Some critics, however, prefer to deal with *Empodkles* without using this theoretical framework; see, for instance, Romano Guardini, *Hölderlin. Weltbild und Frömmigkeit* (Leipzig, 1939) or E. Tonnelat, *L'oeuvre poétique et la pensée de Hölderlin* (Paris, 1950).

13. Among recent commentaries on the odes see F. R. Leavis in *Revaluation* (London: Chatto & Windus, 1936); J. Middleton Murry in *Katherine Mansfield and Other Literary Portraits* (London:

Neill, 1949); Allen Tate, "A Reading of Keats," *American Scholar*, 15 (1946), pp. 55–63, 189–97; Kenneth Burke, *A Grammar of Motives* (New York: Prentice-Hall, 1945), pp. 447ff.; R. H. Fogle, "Keats's Ode to a Nightingale," *PMLA*, 68 (1953), pp. 211–22; Earl R. Wasserman in *The Finer Tone*. In contrast, the only recent article on *Hyperion* is by Kenneth Muir, "The Meaning of *Hyperion*," *Essays in Criticism*, 2 (1952), pp. 54–75.

14. This process is explained in the *Philosophical Fragments* that accompany *Empedokles* rather than in the drama itself. The lack of this needed theoretical background accounts to a large extent for the obscurity of the text, which also labors under the impossibility of expressing in a dramatic medium the lyrical development that precedes the concrete situation at the beginning of the action — Empedokles' inner crisis before his fellow citizens decide to reject him.

15. The metaphysical definition of these poles is an important part of Hölderlin's thought, more essential to him than the dialectic itself, which, unlike his friend and school companion Hegel, he sees as an ontological *donnée* rather than as an intellectual act. At this stage in his development, the two poles are generally called *Natur* and *Kunst*. *Natur* is whatever is universal, infinite, undifferentiated supratemporal — a concept that goes far beyond the idea of nature in a pastoral sense. Hölderlin summarizes these properties in the term *aorgisch*, as distinct from *anorganisch*, which would simply mean: not alive. Hölderlin's nature is intensely alive, but it is a life which has not particularized itself in an individual consciousness. (On this point, see Gisela Wagner, *Hölderlin* p. 168.) *Kunst*, on the other hand, coincides with the human self, that being which, by an act of consciousness recognizes itself as individual, particular, finite, distinct from the totality of being — summarized in this misleading term *organisch*. In the later work of Holderlin, this polarity changes and the two poles are simply referred to as man and the gods, while nature becomes an all-encompassing, suprapolar entity. See, e.g., M. Heidegger's comment on the hymn, "Wie wenn am Feiertage," in *Erläuterungen*, pp. 72ff.

16. A similar argument, with a different terminology, is made by Mr. Muir ("The Meaning of *Hyperion*," pp. 59ff.) in his contention that *Hyperion* describes the victory of "men of achievement" over "men of power." Men of achievement are characterized by "negative capability," which, seen historically is the ability to conceive of the new. And the ethical problem raised by the apparent detachment of the poet gifted with negative capability is solved in *The Fall of Hyperion*, where this very ability takes on a tragic dimension that gives it great moral dignity. See particularly *Fall*, I, 161–76.

17. Oceanus's speech has traditionally been interpreted as a speech on progress. But it is a very unusual idea of progress, since it states the necessity of decadence as well as that of improvement and emphasizes the discontinuity of all historical development. The new generation's main attribute is not so much any intrinsic superiority over the older, but primarily the greater strength of its youth, a transitory value as the following lines explicitly state: "Yea, by that law, another race may drive / Our conquerors to mourn as we do now" (*Hyp.*, II, 230–231).

18. For a complete statement of Hölderlin's theory of history, see the essay, "Das Werden im Vergehen" (III, pp. 309ff.), of which the thought is actually ahead of the Empedokles tragedy and finds its poetic fulfillment in the later hymns.

19. The analogy, in spite of important differences, of this theme with Hegel's *Der Geist des Christentums und sein Schicksal* has been pointed out by several commentators.

20. "[Keats's] unceasing endeavor to solve the problem of sense and knowledge, art and humanity, is in itself an index of his stature." Douglas Bush, *Mythology and the Romantic Tradition in English Poetry* (Cambridge, Mass.: Harvard University Press, 1937), p. 182.

# Situation of the Novel (1956)

The four essays on the novel Nathalie Sarraute has collected in *L'Ere du soupçon* (The age of suspicion) (Paris: Gallimard, 1956) constitute a coherent and attractive study. They are written from inside the present situation of the French novel, by a novelist who has offered her hostages and taken up a position with regard to tendencies identified here in order to justify her own way of writing. The book therefore offers a twofold interest: it proposes a diagnosis of the present state of a literary genre that has become problematic, and it suggests a solution, an approach the author believes to be still accessible and productive.

Sarraute defines her aesthetic in opposition to three other types of novel that she regards as pernicious or outmoded: the novel of analysis, the novel of the absurd, and the "realist" novel. There is not much to say about the last save that it is difficult to understand why Sarraute devotes so much space to condemning a genre that, as she describes it, scarcely seems to deserve serious critical attention. Since she cites no names, her attack can apply to the general run of contemporary fiction. Of course we shall have no difficulty accepting Sarraute's negative judgment, though the disparity between the critical level of the first three essays, which deal with such writers as Dostoevsky and Proust, and that of the fourth, which takes to task future unknowns, is regrettable.

Let us proceed, therefore, to the novel of analysis. "The works of Joyce and Proust," Sarraute informs us, "already loom like distant witnesses of a bygone age." It would seem that the Americans (and especially Hemingway) have relegated them permanently to the museum, where they can only be contemplated as exhibits of academic tedium; if by chance they are still admired, it is for very

61

bad reasons. This notion appears here only fleetingly, and it is immediately qualified. But we must continue to protest against the historical concoction that has turned up in a certain kind of literary criticism, and whose chief culprits are the Sartre of *Situations I* and the Claude-Edmonde Magny of *L'Âge du roman américain*. Reasons that have nothing to do with literature have encouraged the error of putting very great writers on the same level as an author like Hemingway, who belongs precisely among those "realists" Sarraute treats so harshly. Yet she is right on one point: Proust and Joyce certainly question the novel's *possibility of being;* their work implies the failure of the fictive, in the same way that Mallarmé's implies the failure of the poetic. With Hemingway, Steinbeck, or Dos Passos, the novel runs no risk, and with reason: we do not expect to see a good producer declare the merchandise he manufactures to be useless or dangerous.

Moreover it is a mistake to apply the well-worn epithet "psychological analysis" to Proust or to Joyce, as Sarraute does in reference to an unimportant text by Virginia Woolf. When she speaks of interiority as a technique, Sarraute distorts the intention of authors who in fact signify the transcendence of the psychological in favor of *being*. This permits her to produce a formula whose impossibility has been proved by these very authors: the depths of being are attained by a certain form of dialogue that enables the work to escape the stifling embrace of pure interiority. The novels of Proust and Joyce are born of a desperate effort to establish a dialogue that has become increasingly difficult—and the word "dialogue" must here be understood in the broadest possible sense, covering all aspects of intersubjective language, and not only realistic dialogue. The central moment of *Ulysses,* the long-prepared meeting of Bloom and Stephen Dedalus (written with far-reaching irony in the form of the Catechism's questions and answers), certainly indicates the total impossibility of any contact, of any human communication, even in the most disinterested form of love. As for Proust, it is difficult not to see in *Á la recherche du temps perdu* the implacable erosion of intersubjectivity by a temporality that replaces it, because it is closer to being, because it is that reality to which, as Sarraute rightly says, the novelist must sacrifice everything—including dialogue.

Had Sarraute sought to be complete (though this is not her intention) she would have had to add the name of Henry James to those of Proust and Joyce. We note this only because she makes so much of Ivy Compton-Burnett. In James's late works—*The Wings of the Dove,* for example, and *The Golden Bowl*—he shows the irreversible dissolution of dialogue into interiority. He shows this, not thematically, like Joyce or Proust, but in the novel's very substance. The prefaces James wrote for the New York edition of his works constitute a commentary on this movement, one all the more precious for being entirely technical.

This arguable view of the novel of analysis necessarily weakens what Sarraute tells us about the novel of the absurd. As a matter of fact, she denies the latter's existence, since it amounts, for her, to a hidden form of the novel of psychological analysis. The observation applies nicely to Camus's *The Stranger* or even to Kafka, insofar as these writers remain on this side of the self-consciousness Proust or Joyce had achieved. It will no doubt be granted in the case of Camus, but we may wonder if Kafka has not been overvalued, precisely for certain antiliterary reasons of "psychological" identification. Things are seen quite differently in the case of those who make the ever more considerable and ever more urgent effort to invent a language that would still be "novelistic" but must transcend dialogue. Perhaps we should no longer call them novelists of the absurd, a term with an overpsychological resonance, but designate their works as antinovels or counterfictions. They continue, moreover, a great line, for it cannot be denied that some of the greatest novelists of the nineteenth century were in fact novelists of the absurd: one thinks, for instance, of *Moby-Dick* or of Dostoevsky, no matter what Sarraute says of him. For when the human relation, as in Dostoevsky's work at essential moments, is located on the level of sacrifice, there can no longer be any question of intersubjectivity — rather we enter a world that is also that of the absurd.

The image Nathalie Sarraute furnishes of the novel's situation touches upon essential problems, but she seems at once too negative and too affirmative — too negative in that she blithely elides works whose direct influence is far from being exhausted; too affirmative in that she seems to regard this elision as a simple technical renewal, one that remains in the continuity of the genre's development. We may suppose that the crisis of the novel is so fundamental that it cannot find a solution that is not absolutely radical.

Translated by Richard Howard

# Process and Poetry (1956)

When contemporary thought, in its most legitimate forms, concerns itself with poetry, it is generally by conferring on it a power of eternity that makes it either distinct from or superior to a process of becoming.[1] Those writers who try to move beyond the historical concept of becoming that preoccupied nineteenth-century consciousness approach poetry as anticipating, in Heidegger's terms, "that which *remains* in the process of becoming." Poetry thus acquires a value analogous to that which childhood held for certain romantics: that of an ideal state from which we have freely separated ourselves, but one that acts in memory as a redemptive power. It is a world of irresistible charm, even though its remoteness makes it magical, strange, and totally unknown. However, by overcoming the dread felt in the face of something unknown only because it is in reality the one thing that is truly familiar, we would somehow be able to move back into the light, and finally "to dwell poetically on the earth."

This view remains historical in appearance, since it situates poetry with respect to a certain temporal destiny of being. But this temporal movement is always one of error and forgetting, whereas poetry, inasmuch as it is a recollection of original being, remains superior to it. Here the historical destiny of the created object that poetry becomes, and which generations of readers will use for various purposes, has therefore strictly speaking nothing in common with the poetic act itself. In this history, says Maurice Blanchot, "neither the work of art, nor the reading is present."[2] This kind of metatemporality coincides at bottom with a belief that poetry founds Being immediately, without having to work its way toward it by a risky process of successive mediations and stages of consciousness.

In the long run, every metatemporal poetics is reassuring with respect to the fate of poetry, whatever negative or even terrifying dimensions it may attribute to it. For such a poetics knows that no matter how strong the pull exercised by a historical process that would assimilate poetry to its own movement, it is always possible for poetry to elude this pull since it is not bound to it essentially, and to return to the immediate self-presence that is also an immediate presence to Being. "Why is it," asks Blanchot, "that at the point where history contests and subordinates it, art becomes essential presence?" (p. 229). Such a question contains its own answer since it is obvious that, if art (or poetry) can be essential presence, that is, grounded and preserved, then history can have no hold on it. Its permanence and power remain secure despite the hollows and chasms it contains. Moreover, this is what explains how it then becomes possible to speak of these chasms in an even and balanced tone that changes what are often terms of terror into an atmosphere of serenity that leaves open the question of whether it has been *earned.*

There is reason to question the validity of this assurance to the precise extent that it is possible to see poetry as indeed being threatened, not by a historical process of becoming that acts on it from without, but from within the very process of becoming. At a particular moment of its development, for example, poetry is threatened by reason of the increasing difficulty of accomplishing the movement it assigns itself. Were it in fact possible to invest the poetic act with a redemptive power of such magnitude, this would reduce to the level of error every tradition of thought that conceives consciousness as a movement in which poetry has an integral part. But some of the most authentic and greatest poets have put into question precisely this redemptive possibility. Their testimony is not in itself decisive, but failing to take it into account leaves us open to the aberrant forms of thought that result from an unwarranted simplification of the task of poetic consciousness.

It is in its protest against the present historical reality, in a categorical refusal of participation, that poetic eternalism draws its most powerful forces. It assimilates the idea of becoming to that of historical efficacy, and by setting itself up as a kind of superior truth, it opposes itself to the illusory character of every thinking that believes it can know history in the same way that a science knows its object. Such, in fact, is the origin of the oversimplifications history is subject to when it is characterized as a *labor* governed solely by the principle of utility, and on the basis of which it becomes possible to remove in a radical way both art and poetry from the sphere of its action. The direct ancestor of this kind of thinking is of course Nietzsche, who, in a text that is nothing if not brutally clear, writes: "With the word 'the unhistorical' I designate the art and power of *forgetting* and of enclosing oneself within a bounded *horizon;* I call 'suprahistorical' the powers which lead the eye away from becoming towards that which bestows upon existence the character of the eternal and stable, towards *art* and *religion. Science*

. . . which sees everywhere things that have been, things historical, and nowhere things that are, things eternal, lives in a profound antagonism towards the eternalizing powers of art and religion, for it hates forgetting, which is the death of knowledge, and seeks to abolish all limitations of horizon and launch mankind upon an infinite and unbounded sea of light whose light is knowledge of all becoming."[3]

This assimilation of becoming and history to a positive science is entirely justified within the polemical context of an attack against a certain ossification of the mind with which every living form of thought violently grapples. Nonetheless, this can constitute only a secondary concern for it. Such an assimilation can also be justified from a historical point of view as characteristic of a moment in a larger process, since every thinking, at least at its inception, tends to view itself as absolutely and eternally true, whereas the previous form of thought appears to it as a merely passing error. But in this case, the justification itself presupposes the existence of a process of becoming, and in so doing it disappears in an internal contradiction. Such a justification is natural enough without for all that being true. In any case, when the simplification turns out, as in the present case, to be a desire to oppose a valid form of thought, not to a dead and degraded one, but to a different though equally valid one, it is neither true nor legitimate. Under the pretext of attacking Strauss or Eduard von Hartmann, Nietzsche is in fact venting himself on Hegel and the entire tradition behind him. Something similar occurs among our own contemporaries when they identify a process of becoming with technology or a certain political activism. They distort the idea of becoming for strategic reasons, and make a caricature out of it that is then all too easy to scorn or ignore.

For the idea of becoming as it is affirmed in modern thought since the romantics is the exact opposite of an overpositive and confident idea. In the philosophical commentary that accompanies the tragedy *Empedocles,* the archetypal tragedy of historical process, Hölderlin takes care to oppose his hero to "the hyperpolitical citizens of Sicily who are constantly engaged in judging and plotting," and he defines the action of Empedocles as entirely outside the institutions of a national community.

However, even though Empedocles is a wholly subordinate being, a poet infinitely removed from the public stage, it is in him that the spirit of his time is incarnated and accomplished, and it is Empedocles rather than his fellow citizens whose action is essentially historical, that is, productive of a future. And he owes this power to his knowledge of the noneternal character of poetic language, a language that, for him, coincides with that of truth. It is by meditating on the paradox of human existence (*Dasein*), which is a desire for eternity but which can take shape only in the finitude of the moment, that Hölderlin arrives at an essentially tragic conception of the literary work. Poetry becomes the putting into language of the failure of the true to found itself. And since the process of becoming is what constitutes the very experience of this failure, poetry appears as the *logos* of this becoming. As such, far from being what Nietzsche calls an eternalizing power, poetry is the constant negation of the eternal. But it is a negation that transforms the eternal aspect of what is immediately given into an intention, and it does so to the precise extent that it recognizes the necessity of *naming* the eternal by means of an entity—language—that is immediately adequate to neither eternal nor temporal being.

The real force of such a conception lies in the way it is able to transpose the experience of nonunity into being itself and thus allow for a certain form of thought and its language to continue beyond the failure to found itself as eternal truth. What we call the process of becoming, then, becomes equivalent to a consciousness of the eternal as intention and not as existent (*étant*). Far from being a knowledge with a positive and determinate content, the process of becoming is thus essentially the knowledge of a nonknowledge, the knowledge of the persistent indetermination that is historical temporality. Hölderlin's Empedocles, for instance, knows that his thought gives form to the decline of his own truth (and the truth by which his people have lived), and that by becoming conscious of this decline in poetic language, by thinking and living it unreservedly, he reopens a future that, precisely because it is not uniform, could still not be called eternal. Not far from the end of the last fragment of the tragedy, he says:

> For where a land must die, there the spirit
> elects in the end the One and only
> through whom its swan song, the last life, shall resound.
> I knew it well, still I served him willingly.
> It's done. To mortals I now belong no more.
> O end of my time!

And a few verses later the chorus emphasizes his death with just one word: Future (*Zukunft*)—which we should be careful not to take in the optimistic sense of modern political tracts, but which in the context would be better rendered by such negative terms as "indetermination" or, thinking of Mallarmé, by "chance." Through the experience of a voluntary death—that of Empedocles or that of Igitur—these poets were not necessarily attempting to transform negation into determination, as Maurice Blanchot thinks. On the contrary, they resigned themselves to the transformation of the eternal into the temporal and recognized the necessarily temporal character of poetry. It is by starting with *this* notion of becoming that the problem of process and poetry is posed, and not in relation to the deformed version offered to us by Nietzsche and his successors.

If the eternal is an intention, and poetic language the sign of this intention's failure, will it then be possible to rest content with such knowledge, that is, to equate poetry with a universal process of becoming satisfied in the certitude of its own accomplishment, even if such accomplishment be apocalyptic? To judge from the unfolding of those poetic oeuvres that have gone furthest in reflecting on the process of becoming, this is by no means the case. On the contrary, the poetry of Hölderlin, Keats, or Mallarmé remains exceedingly tormented and uncertain, constantly experimental and unsatisfied with itself. There are, however, in addition to them, poets who categorically reject the idea of process, without for all that leaving any doubt about the authenticity of their poetic vocation. The question of process and poetry seems, then, to leave suspended certain essential tensions.

To illustrate this problem, I will make use of two parallel texts: the fragment of Mallarmé's *Igitur* entitled "Midnight" and Baudelaire's prose poem, "The Double Room," in *Spleen de Paris*. The parallelism is far-reaching enough to extend all the way to symbolical detail, and it would be tempting to place Baudelaire's poem among the sources of *Igitur,* were it not that the posthumous date of its publication makes it almost certain that Mallarmé could not have known it at the time he was writing *Igitur*. Both texts evoke the fate of a reflection that succeeds in reaching its truth. Here is how Baudelaire describes this experience:

> Une chambre qui ressemble à une rêverie, une chambre véritablement spirituelle, où l'atmosphère stagnante est légèrement teintée de rose et de bleu . . .
>
> Les meubles ont des formes allongées, prostrées, alanguies. Les meubles ont l'air de rêver; on les dirait doués d'une vie somnambulique, comme le végétal et le minéral. Les étoffes parlent une langue muette, comme les fleurs, comme les ciels, comme les soleils couchants.
>
> Sur les murs, nulle abomination artistique. Relativement au rêve pur, à l'impression non analysée, l'art défini, l'art positif est un blasphème. Ici, tout a la suffisante clarté et la délicieuse obscurité de l'harmonie.
>
> . . . O Béatitude! ce que nous nommons généralement la vie, même dans son expression la plus heureuse, n'a rien de commun avec cette vie suprême dont j'ai maintenant connaissance et que je savoure minute par minute, seconde par seconde!
>
> Non! il n'est plus de minutes, il n'est plus de secondes! Le temps a disparu; c'est l'Eternité qui règne, une éternité de délices!

> [A room that is like a dream, a truly spiritual room where the stagnant atmosphere is lightly colored with blue and rose . . .
>
> The furniture has contours that stretch, curl, and languish. It seems to be dreaming, as though it had been endowed with a kind of vegetal or mineral somnambulous life. The hangings speak the mute language of flowers, skies, and setting suns.
>
> On the walls, none of art's abominations. In comparison to pure dream and unanalyzed impression, a clearly defined and positive art is blasphemous. Here, everything is bathed in the adequate clarity and delicious obscurity of harmony.

. . . O beatitude! What we generally call life, even in its happiest moments, has nothing in common with this supreme life which I now know and savor minute by minute, second by second!

No! There are no more minutes, no more seconds! Time has disappeared and eternity reigns, an eternity of delight!]

In contrast to this absolute negation of time, the temporal content of the same experience in *Igitur* is obvious:

Et du Minuit demeure la présence en la vision d'une chambre de temps où le mystérieux ameublement arrête un vague frémissement de pensée, lumineuse brisure du retour de ses ondes et de leur élargissement premier, cependant que s'immobilise (dans une mouvante limite) la place antérieure de la chute de l'heure en un calme narcotique de moi pur longtemps rêvé; mais dont le temps est résolu en des tentures sur lesquelles s'est arrêté . . . . le frémissement. . . . de l'hôte, dénué de toute signification que de présence.    C'est le rêve pur d'un Minuit en soi disparu, et dont la Clarté reconnue, qui seule demeure au sein de son accomplissement plongé dans l'ombre, résume sa stérilité sur la pâleur d'un livre ouvert.

[And the presence of Midnight remains in the vision of a room of time whose mysterious furnishing puts a stop to a vague shudder of thought, a luminous breaking of the return of its waves and their initial extension, while the previous site of the hour's fall is immobilized (through a moving limit) into a narcotic calm of pure self long dreamed; but whose time has dissolved into the drapes on which has lighted the shudder of the host, stripped of all meaning other than presence.

Pure dream of a Midnight disappeared in itself, and whose Clarity recognized, which alone remains in the depths of its accomplishment plunged into shadow, concentrates its sterility in the paleness of an open book.]

Whereas for Baudelaire truth is a triumph over time, albeit a momentary one, a space from which time has been eliminated, and a purification of a space inside which time appears as a negative and destructive element, Mallarmé, on the contrary, finds the essence of truth in the synthesis of the double significance, both spatial and temporal, of the term "presence." Destruction of truth in Baudelaire consists in the overwhelming return of time, which destroys everything without leaving the slightest trace:

"Oh! oui! le Temps a reparu; le Temps règne en souverain maintenant, et avec le hideux vieillard est revenu tout son démoniaque cortège de Souvenirs, de Regrets, de Spasmes, de Peurs, d'Angoisses, de Cauchemars, de Colères et de Névroses . . .

Oui! le Temps règne; il a repris sa brutale dictature. Et il me pousse comme si j'étais un boeuf, avec son double aiguillon.

[Oh yes! Time has reappeared, Time reigns supreme now, and along with the hideous old man has returned the whole fiendish troop of Memories, Regrets, Spasms, Tears, Anxieties, Nightmares, Wraths, and Neuroses . . .
Yes! Time reigns. It has reassumed its brutal dictatorship, and prods me with its two-pronged goad as though I were an ox.]

In *Igitur* something subsists even after the failure of truth to maintain itself: "Certainly remains a presence of midnight." It is not the objective content of the moment of supreme unity, since Mallarmé tells us elsewhere that Midnight has "disappeared in itself." What the future holds is rather the possibility and necessity of repeating the moment of truth and, even more important, of recognizing it as such: "clarity recognized, which alone remains." By itself, repetition preserves nothing, since it would amount only to a gloomy procession of similar failures. But from the moment we become aware of this repetition, it becomes possible to identify the intention hidden behind it. In the final analysis, what is preserved of the language of truth or of the work is nothing but the statement of this intention, "the silence of an ancient saying spoken by him, in which, come back again, this Midnight evokes its finite and null shadow in these words: I was the hour that must make me pure." This consciousness of a repetition that can be recognized, but which by the very fact that it has to be recognized is never the same, is indeed the consciousness of a process of becoming, not, as in Nietzsche, an eternal return of the same, but an infinite becoming of consciousness.

The poetic consciousness of becoming, then, maintains itself as self-consciousness. Such poetry knows itself fully and is able to account for its own existence. Mallarmé's text justifies its existence by the truth it states; since it establishes a poetic language that is able to state an intention that persists beyond its failure, this text itself, along with the entire work, would be "that language, the ancient saying spoken by him." The truth of Baudelaire's poem, on the other hand, is in direct contradiction to the existence of the work, since the poet tells us that art has no place in moments of genuine self-presence of which, moreover, nothing subsists. We know, however, that a work does subsist, not as a transparent consciousness that would know itself in every respect, but as an opaque thing that is established in spite of itself, established in fact *against* the affirmation of what it knows about itself.

But if, on the one hand, the concept of becoming allows for an extremely acute form of self-consciousness, this clarity, on the other hand, is made possible only by a necessary sacrifice of the sensuous object. Rather than establishing correspondences that would make the movements of consciousness look like the sensuous phenomena of the natural world, the Mallarmean metaphor transforms the

physical world into operations of the mind. By making use of the total interiorization of the world as a base on which to found its reflection, such a metaphor succeeds in maintaining itself by in fact transferring the negation to the inside of the
object and then annihilating it. More than anyone else, Mallarmé constantly described this dialectic thanks to which an object is transformed into "its vibrating
near disappearance." And in this respect, one has only to think of the translucid
climate of his last poems, where a supremely acute inward vision perceives nothing but the spectacle of a disappearance of objects that are already disembodied.
Such is the necessary result of a poetry of process. Starting from an experience
of alienation or separation that is universal, it tries to suspend it by safeguarding
the movement of consciousness at the expense of the object, to save consciousness
by killing the object. On the other hand, an eternalistic poetry, such as Baudelaire's, sacrifices consciousness to a certain extent, since it gives up trying to account for its own necessity to be and, in agreement with Nietzsche, succeeds in
partly forgetting what it is. But it does preserve a sensuous materiality, for it is
beyond doubt that Baudelaire's poem exhibits a material texture that is infinitely
richer than Mallarmé's (though it should be obvious that there is no question of
value judgments here).

Thus, we are led to distinguish two kinds of poetic attitude: the first would be
that of a poetry of process, maintaining itself as consciousness at the expense of
the sensuous object, whereas the other would be a poetry of substance, maintaining the sensuous object at the expense of consciousness.

Quite clearly, though, this schema is oversimplistic. The problem of poetry
and process does not present itself in the form of a choice between two equally
possible directions. A genuine poetics has to be able to include this oscillation in
a vision of the whole that would account for its passionate, and sometimes even
tragic, character. Now among the poets already mentioned, there is one who has
expressed himself, poetically and philosophically, on this question; it is the Hölderlin of the last poems and the theoretical texts that accompany his translations
of *Oedipus Rex* and *Antigone,* texts that are among the last poetic works he was
to work on before the onset of his madness.

These commentaries express the distinction between a poetry of process and
a poetry of the sensuous as a dialectic of intentions and desires. For the poet capable of self-consciousness, the enthusiasm for process soon transforms itself into
a nostalgia for the object, and his language, more and more animated by the desire
to recapture a lost plenitude, becomes almost haunted by a preoccupation with
the sensuous. For the poet capable of attaining the object, on the contrary, it is
the power of spirit that appears as the most desirable goal, and his language becomes the language of self-consciousness. Hölderlin makes use, as Hegel often
does, of a historical symbolism to illustrate his thought. He defines the Hellenic
world as one in which language is capable of reaching the sensuous object immediately, whereas in the occidental world, it grasps itself only insofar as it is

spirit, that is, as distinction and mediation. The Greeks are able to attain something (*etwas treffen*) whereas we can grasp ourselves reflexively (*sich fassen*). Because the poet does not generally say what he already possesses but much rather what remains foreign to him, Greek art will appear capable of an exemplary lucidity of structure, which nonetheless is in no way characteristic of its actual properties (Hölderlin is thinking especially of Homer here). On the other hand, occidental art, which is naturally self-conscious, easily succeeds in producing the pathetic accents of a love of sensuous substance, of which in fact it is incapable — and here he is thinking particularly of the romantic poetry of his time.

Here we come face to face with an attempt to go beyond the idea of process without at the same time falling back into its antithesis, which is the eternal. For Hölderlin, the ultimate truth of poetry resides neither in the eternal nor in the temporal, but in the turning back through which a poetry of the sensuous tears itself away from its need to become self-consciousness, or a poetry of process tears itself away from its desire to get back to the object.

The power of this vision has its source in the renunciation that is at its center, and is expressed in the profoundly original idea that what is inborn appears to us as what is most difficult, whereas spirit finds it easy to thrive in what is most foreign to it. Although we should be careful not to apply this notion in an overliteral historical sense, we should nonetheless ask about its significance for Western poetry.

To do this, though, we have to resituate it in the context in which it was conceived. We know that these meditations accompany the translations of Sophocles' tragedies. And thanks to a letter to his editor, Wilmans, on September 20, 1803, we also know that Hölderlin wanted not only to translate Sophocles, but as he says quite frankly, to correct him by making him accessible to a modern readership. It is a question, then, of transposing Greek poetry, which, as we recall, expresses what is foreign to Greek spirit (that is, consciousness and clarity) into Western poetry, which expresses what is foreign to Western spirit (that is, immediate pathos and sensuousness). The most significant example of this transposition is also one that Hölderlin himself analyzed. In *Antigone,* Zeus's name appears in the narration of the myth of Danaë (act 4, scene 1), where it is said that she "watches over the seed of Zeus, born of the shower of gold." Hölderlin translates Zeus by "the father of time," and Danaë thus becomes the one who watches over the growth of time (the son of Zeus) or over the process of becoming. Such would be the poet of process, whose language preserves and concentrates the movement of becoming. But for Western man, for whom becoming is just as natural as the sensuous was for the Greeks, this term does not have a positive value, since the task of watching over what he already possesses appears to him as neither desirable nor necessary. On the contrary, he prefers to count out the time that separates him from what he no longer has. Therefore, in order to make himself understood by his Western readers (who do not understand or rather who immediately corrupt the word "becoming"), Hölderlin translates the passage by saying not that Danaë "watches over the process of becoming" but that she "counts out the hours." "It is always so," he adds in his commentary. "Time becomes calculable when it is experienced in suffering, for then the heart follows the movement of time by taking part in it, and thus comprehends the simple passing of the hours, rather than the mind's inferring the future on the basis of the present."

The occidental poet who celebrates the sensuous (in a necessarily pathetic tone since he is already separated from it) is therefore the one who in fact "counts out the hours" that still separate him from the long-awaited moment when he will be able to regain access to what he has lost. Here we have the archetypal modern poet—Baudelaire, for example. He is haunted by the past and exotic places, and he vigorously denies what he is. Time, which separates him from what he would like to be, appears to him as his foremost enemy. In the modern world, he is the exact antithesis of what Homer was in the Greek world, for we have to imagine in the "naive" Homer a preoccupation with self-consciousness every bit as power-ful as the preoccupation with lost sensuousness and concrete beauty that is found in the "conscious" Baudelaire. The nature of their suffering, though, is different. To a certain degree, we are able to imagine Greek virtues and happiness since we know about them through the nostalgia we have for them, but we cannot know the extent of their desire for the clarity that we possess. In our own torment there is always a flavor of the lack of object, while the lack of temporal conciousness, the eternal, appears to us as a godsend. Our pain comes from our knowledge that we are temporal creatures, for whom Zeus is the progenitor of a time that keeps us separated from what we are no longer. This results in a satanic revolt against the divine, which is by no means a negation, and it also results in the fact that poetry becomes a mask, a constant dissimulating through which we attempt to hide from ourselves. This is a form neither of weakness nor of hypocrisy in West-ern poetry, but rather its profoundest necessity. Such poetry must go out of its way in trying to imprint, on its true face, the mask of the eternal, precisely in the sense that Nietzsche defines the highest will to power as the attempt "to im-print on the process of becoming the character of being," where being is con-ceived as the eternal.[4]

However, this undoubtedly goes counter to the process of becoming. For be-coming is oriented not toward what we no longer have but toward what we do not yet have. By "counting out" the hours that separate us from what we have lost, we draw no closer to it, nor do we advance in the direction of what we are in real-ity. Becoming is of the order of being other and not of having been; the occidental poet who is haunted by the sensuous constantly and desperately hardens himself against what he is. In other words, and still according to Hölderlin, Western po-etry has not yet found itself, has not yet dared to be itself, has not yet attained its summit. For the highest point of any thought is the point at which it dares to face what is truly proper to it. Antigone reaches her most elevated language when she identifies with Niobe, whose myth, in turn, represents the fullest incarnation of Greek spirit. According to the myth, Niobe is the one who allows herself to be changed into rock, so that Antigone's supreme act, through which she accomplishes a turning back to her true nature, is therefore the act by which she accepts, in her death, a metamorphosis into stone. In this way, she remains completely faithful to herself, for she allows herself to be what in fact actually lies open to her, that is, the eternal object. The greatest Greek poetry is that which dares to reflect on this turning back, which Hölderlin describes as "native" (*vaterländisch*) in order to mark it as a return toward what is inborn and not acquired by practice or imitation.

Turning back, then, is not necessarily becoming, and for the Greeks turning back was a return not to the temporal but rather to the eternity of things. This is why they consider the truly divine to be that which draws one out of oneself toward the beyond, while for us turning back is a more acute self-consciousness in the form of temporal being. It is in this sense that Hölderlin can say of the occidental God that he acts from the beyond toward being-in-the-world, that Spirit penetrates us instead of entering into objects.

This seems paradoxical to us since we hear it affirmed so often that by giving in too much to the ease of becoming poetry is distorted and thus strays from its authentic vocation. Hölderlin tells us precisely the opposite: what is easiest is to give in to the call of the object and the eternal, whereas what is required for us to be ourselves is to accept the death of things and to turn back toward the process of becoming, which we have in fact not yet begun to think.

To turn back to a thought of becoming—such a formula remains obscure because, as Hölderlin himself well knew, we have corrupted the sense of this word. We can start to shed light on it negatively, by reaffirming yet again that this turning back in no way implies a return to what we consider our present historical and political reality, a world of utility and technology. This world is much sooner the expression of our basic ineptitude and incapacity to handle objects, the expression of our preoccupation with reaching what we cannot know at any cost. As such, it is the material sign of our resistance to thinking the process of becoming. The native turning back (which Hölderlin, using a term that became ambiguous only later on, called a national turning back—*vaterländische Umkehr*), this turning back, despite what certain commentators who are hardly occidental have thought, is situated at the furthest remove from an ideal of political supremacy.

But by the same token it is also necessary to guard against the temptation to think the turning back toward becoming in eschatological terms, as an end to the time of distress, *die dürftige Zeit,* "the tunnel, the epoch," as Mallarmé calls it. The work of its accomplishment can begin only with a loss of hope, for we have to give up, as though it were something foreign, whatever it is we are striving toward. It isn't even prophetic: since it is in the essence of becoming not to posit itself as eternal, we cannot count on a poetry of becoming as though it would necessarily find accomplishment. An act of consciousness and an asceticism of thought, the process of becoming appears as a task whose law is that of an incessantly heightened concentration and rigor, but which finds in the past no guarantee that it will be possible for it to come into being.

Why, then, does this task belong in particular to poetry? To judge from the privileged place contemporary thought accords poetry, we seem to have a vague premonition of why this should be so. It is because poetry is the most disembodied of all the arts, the furthest removed from the object, the only one that is able to construct that "architectonics of the sky" mentioned by Hölderlin and which is in fact the opposite of the marmoreal architecture of Greece. Epic and dramatic poetry was the art of what the Greeks were not, while their true nature was expressed most naturally in sculpture. It is in this sense that we saw Antigone become the incarnation of Greek spirit by choosing to be a statue carved in stone. The inverse takes place in Western art; only when poetry is willing to give up its desire to be concrete and eternal will it be able to find accomplishment.

It seems, then, that no matter how we view the turning back that Hölderlin demands, all that it promises is aridity, barrenness, and deprivation. Perhaps this is because, at least in its beginnings, such is the climate of our truth.

Translated by Kevin Newmark and Andrzej Warminski

## Notes

1. The original title of the essay is "Le Devenir, la poésie." We have translated *le devenir* variously as "process," "process of becoming," and "becoming" according to context. Aside from the fact that the English present participle "becoming" never quite conveys the full range of the French substantive *le devenir* (or the German *das Werden*), there are philosophical reasons that make it necessary to introduce a term like "process." That is, the essay works with (and ultimately *un*works) a Hegelian conception of becoming, i.e., a process of consciousness's coming to itself, to self-consciousness, in and *as* a dialectically mediated history of "becoming."—Trans.

2. Blanchot, *L'Espace littéraire* (Paris: Gallimard, 1955), p. 216.

3. *Untimely Meditations*, trans. R. J. Hollingdale (Cambridge: Cambridge University Press, 1983), p.. 120.

4. *Der Wille zur Macht* (Stuttgart: Kröner, 1959), p. 617.

# Thematic Criticism and the Theme of Faust (1957)

If there is one work that contemporary criticism should be able to explicate and provide commentary for, it is certainly Goethe's *Faust,* which is generally considered to be the paradigmatic poem of modern consciousness. Nevertheless, in spite of a great number of critical studies in all languages, the commentators are far from agreeing, even in general terms, on questions as fundamental as the structural unity of the poem, its place in the history of European thought, or even its value in relation to other versions of the same theme. Can one speak of the two parts of the poem as constituting an organic whole, or have the peculiar conditions of its often interrupted composition made unity impossible?[1] Will one say that since Goethe had declined with age, the end of the second part of *Faust* betrays the spiritual attitude of the first;[2] or that, on the contrary, a progressive movement with profound inner coherence unites the diverse parts? Should one consider *Faust* as a manifestation of the Age of Enlightenment or as a rejection of the rationalist eighteenth-century in the name of traditions belonging to the Renaissance?[3] Or must one see there the beginning of a problematic that considers the modern era for the first time as the historical moment of technological productivity?[4] To take only the best-known episode of the poem, does one read the death of Margaret as being simply a moral drama leading by way of repentance to redemption;[5] or as marking, on the contrary, the overcoming of individualist morality for a metapersonal, collective, and historical morality;[6] or as an archetype with transcendental, religious connotations?[7] None of the commentators has returned to the question of the relative value of the two principal works based on the theme of *Faust*, namely, Marlowe's and Goethe's.[8] This is a legitimate question and one that indicates that the critical placement of Goethe's *Faust* in world literature is not established once and for all. These variations and indecisions of criticism, as it grapples with a complex, ambiguous work, are not in the least surprising. They are instructive to the degree that they reflect different methodologies, and therefore permit, with Faust as touchstone, the bringing to light of their own respective virtues and insufficiencies.

Those studies to be considered here, studies that bear more or less directly on the criticism and history of the Faust story, have in common the fact that they are thematic studies, that is (to define this term for the moment only negatively), they do not concern themselves, or only very secondarily, with problems of form. Still, there are profound differences between them. For Charles Dédéyan, "thematic" signifies the historical element in the Faust legend, the description of narrative variations that are produced in this legend as the legend changes according to country and period. For the American historians of ideas (as we shall see) the Faust theme plays an important, though often implicit, role; but in their eyes, "theme" signifies the general figure, the continuous and completed development of a certain problematic expressed in rational language. And when Maud Bodkin includes Margaret in a series of symbolic incarnations of the eternal feminine, and Mephistopheles in a typology of masculine heroes,[9] the word "theme" begins to signify "myth," both as a recurrent narrative structure (or archetype) and as a movement oriented toward contact with the divine. Current thematic criticism, then, appears sometimes as a history of themes, sometimes as a history of ideas, and sometimes as a mythology.

Of these three forms of thematic criticism, the first seems by far the least speculative, the one that lends itself the most to scientific caution. Moreover, the case of *Faust* is for this kind of criticism a propitious one, because the Faust story is of relatively recent origin and because it has been possible to study its fortunes in detail, from the original historical personage to the network of popular and literary traditions that have preserved this figure until our day. Even if the historical Faust remains rather obscure, one still has, less than fifty years after his death, the perfectly established text of the *Volksbuch* (1587), from which point the literary tradition develops without inordinate difficulties. In his general study of the theme of Faust, Dédéyan gives evidence of two major virtues of historical criticism by being at once exhaustive and cautious. The usefulness of his book, well constructed but a little slow, consists in gathering in one work research found dispersed in many. He gives thus an overview that includes works not strictly Faustian but nevertheless closely related. The most important example is that of the *Mágico Prodigioso* of Calderón. This extension necessitates a somewhat problematic distinction between "legend" and "theme," but surely such an expansion accounts for the work's originality and prevents it from being merely a compilation. The appearance of editions and recent translations has permitted Dédéyan to include *Vathek* by William Beckford, *The Monk* by Matthew Gregory Lewis, and *Melmoth* by C. R. Mathurin, interesting migrations of the Faustian thematic into the English domain. This effort to be complete will be especially valuable in Dédéyan's third volume, still to appear, which will treat the period between romanticism and the present—a period in which Dédéyan obviously has far fewer predecessors.[10] As for scientific caution, that virtue manifests itself in the rejection of any comparison not "inscribed" in the composition of the story, in the refusal to consider as a source anything not demonstrably borrowed, and even in the hesitation to accept historical conjectures that are elsewhere generally accepted.[11] One can consider this work as representative of a proven historical discipline, the rules of which will not cease to constitute the minimum that one can ask of any work of literary history.

But are these rules enough to create a true thematic? Certainly such studies would have little interest if they did not lead to a better critical understanding of great texts, in this case those of Marlowe and Goethe; and if they do not lead to such an understanding, what is the point in poring endlessly over a succession of clearly minor works? Meanwhile, when Dédéyan feels moved to formulate evaluations or to make literary interpretations, he makes very little use of comparisons of different versions of the theme. More often, he makes use of criteria unrelated to thematics, criteria that depend on internal criticism. There are psychological analyses of characters, references to other works, or even an employment of commonsense principles that do not shrink from repeating the obvious. None of this is a matter of authorial deficiency at all; it is a deficiency of the method itself. The purely historical study of the legend is just not likely to shed much light on questions of essential interpretation. The causes of this incapacity must be considered now.

Because at its very basis the historical thematic gives high priority to the existence of continuity, it has the invaluable advantage of a definite point of view. The continuity is the story itself, the primitive anecdote—those certain names and adventures that obstinately refuse to disappear into oblivion. One is tempted to assume that the story is the crystallization of a particularly important problematic, and that the succession of the different versions represents different ways of treating that problematic, the variations of which are so significant because they constitute, properly speaking, the history of the theme. But it would be wrong to believe that this thematic is defined by the content of the legend alone, or especially that the continuity of the anecdote's existence necessarily implies a continuity of the underlying problematic. The connections between the deep intentions of an author and his manner of choosing and treating a subject are much more complicated than that. One can see this fact clearly when one considers the history of the Faust story in its entirety.

From its beginnings up through Marlowe, inclusively, one encounters a genuine identification between the content of the story and the inner problem of the writer who makes use of it. With Marlowe one can still speak of a profound consciousness of evil (obvious in the terror of the final scene) leading back to the clearly Lutheran origins of the theme. Still, already at this point, the elements belonging to pagan humanism superimpose themselves on the Lutheran elements of the *Volksbuch* (most notably in the famous apostrophe to Helen), thus modifying the equilibrium and overflowing the narrative frame to the point of reducing it to a secondary and conventional structure.[12] Moreover, we know that after Marlowe the theme of Faust virtually disappears from the literary scene for more than a century and a half, and that no one would have troubled himself over it any more had Lessing not rescued it from oblivion. It is obviously because of Goethe that one later studied the German marionette theater of the seventeenth century with such zeal. And it is certainly probable that Goethe would never have written *Faust* if Lessing had not brought the topic back to the surface.[13] Now Lessing's motives in reviving Faust are well known, and they have little in common with the content of the legend itself. For Lessing it was a question of returning to a national German tradition—in reaction to Gottsched, for whom the classical French theater was the only possible model. Besides, Lessing the Man of Reason, who had no use for medieval skeletons, took pains to purge the Faust tradition precisely of those irrational elements that abound in it. In creating a Faust now saved for the very reason that had damned him before—the thirst for knowledge—Lessing accomplished two things at once: he restored a national theme by purifying it, and he separated the theme from its primitive significance. It is obvious that similar motives can be found in Goethe, who was certainly drawn to Faust in part because it was a traditional theme; tradition becomes a literary value independently of the content.

Even if we suppose that the *Volksbuch* contains a problematic that can be described and interpreted, numerous alien elements have managed to attach themselves to and superimpose themselves on this initial basis. These elements—humanism, rationalism, literary nationalism, tradition, and so on—are extremely complex, and each one requires attentive study to determine the manner in which it was used in each particular case. The narrative motifs, if they were preserved, have taken on such a different significance that a simple comparison no longer does much good. Such comparison can only serve to demonstrate the absence of all continuity. The *Faust* of Goethe does not simply treat in its own way the same moral or theological problem as the *Volksbuch;* it treats an altogether different problem, and the narrative similarities are for the most part purely formal. One cannot have recourse to thematic comparison in order to pass from the level of narration to the level of ideas because the thought refracts itself in the structure of the story along paths it is first necessary to try to retrace. The story itself is not a point of departure, a kind of mold into which the author pours his material. The story is, on the contrary, the end product of poetic invention, the final sign of a number of multiple intentions that criticism cannot unravel simply by observing their final result. Ideas explain the structure, not the other way around. The history of themes (*Stoffgeschichte*) is an end, and not the preamble to a history of ideas (*Geistesgeschichte*). The history of themes is a necessary end because it is only at this level that criticism and history rediscover the structural dimensions that properly belong to literary language. But this end demands considerable preparatory work—so much work that very few studies can pretend to have come so far. Some do manage to indicate the proper direction to follow. If one thinks of the work of authors of such diverse tendencies as Curtius, Cassirer, Auerbach, Lukács, Hazard, Beguin, or Praz, one sees that all in their way try to define various problematics whose narrative themes are formal emanations, and that they bring us back, therefore, from the history of themes to the history of ideas.

No one among the "historians of ideas" has approached the theme of Faust in its entirety. Some have produced studies of Goethe, a fact all the more natural in that Goethe, in a rather spontaneous way, was one of the initiators of what later became the history of ideas. Cassirer has commented on one of his maxims, "to unite the creative impulse to history" (*das Produktive mit dem historischen zu verbinden*): Goethe "rejects history when history is imposed on him as mere matter [*Stoff*]; but he reclaims it as a necessary way finally to understand form in itself and in its own creativity."[14] The remark can serve as a definition of the entire history of ideas.

In France, where formalist criticism (in the American sense) still exists only in its nascent state, the history of ideas is struggling to gain some status beside traditional literary history. That a considerable number of recent theses are, strictly speaking, theses in the history of ideas seems to indicate that a methodological expansion is in progress.[15] In the United States, where conflicts of method are more obvious—because of the absence of a uniform university tradition—the history of ideas, after having exercised a considerable influence, finds itself now on the defensive against formalist methods. This situation, due in part to the very virtues of formalist criticism (which we do not need to consider here), results equally from certain inherent weaknesses in the history of ideas, as it is generally practiced. Unless one thinks, with the formalists, that history should be avoided entirely, these weaknesses deserve to be examined. And it seems difficult to accept the extreme argument that holds that formalist criticism has until now produced only detailed exegeses of lyric poetry, an argument that alone would suffice to indicate that the study of a work of such magnitude as *Faust* could not entirely dispense with the historical method.

By definition, the history of ideas finds itself tied to a philosophy of history. So it is understandable that it is a philosopher, Arthur Lovejoy, who, in the United States, has been the most important theoretician of the discipline. His influence could be compared, if one makes allowances for changes of context, to that of Brunetière in France or Dilthey in Germany. When we turn to his best-known work, *The Great Chain of Being*,[16] we again find ourselves face to face with the problem central both to the structure of *Faust* and to the history of ideas in general: the problem of historical continuity.

Lovejoy approaches this problem in a rather indirect manner. He makes a horizontal incision in the history of philosophy, isolating what he calls a "unit-idea," the development of which he then follows through the entire history of the Western world. Although the process of isolating these units is not without its arbitrary side, Lovejoy correctly prefers it to the study of *movements* like classicism, romanticism, or even Christianity, conglomerates much too unstable and diverse to be described. *The Great Chain of Being* begins with an ambiguity in the conception of the divine in Plato in order to oppose two notions of the relationship between the real and the transcendent. The first such notion, found in the *Republic,* reduces the real to the status of appearance without any contact with the transcendent Being of the Good, which is entirely sufficient unto itself. The second notion, found in the *Timaeus,* maintains the absolute anteriority of transcendent Being, but assumes that this Being, in its intrinsic generosity, somehow overflows into the creation of particular beings, which fill the world by exhausting all potentialities of existence in their infinitely varied incarnations. The idea of plenitude will ultimately combine with that of the continuity of the species (in Aristotle) to end in the vision of the Neoplatonic universe, hierarchical and diverse, but continuous and full. Lovejoy thus sees the history of Western thought as an immense effort to reconcile these two apparently contradictory notions of Being, conceived either as pure transcendence or as total, immanent plenitude. After having passed in review the great moments of this problematic, he ascertains in the nineteenth century, in romantic thought, a definitive break. This moment is like an explosion of a coherent unity that had been supposed to contain Being and the real at the same time. Being finds itself thrust into a beyond situated outside earthly experience and dismissed, temporally speaking, to a past or to an infinitely distant future. Meanwhile the real, because of this departure, becomes as if inhabited by a void destructive of all possibility of continuity. And Lovejoy, thinking here exactly as a sort of romanticism does, concludes that

> the history of the idea of the Chain of Being—in so far as that idea presupposed . . . complete rational intelligibility of the world—is the history of a failure. . . . A world of time and change . . . is a world which can neither be deduced from nor reconciled with the postulate that existence is the expression and the consequence of a system of "eternal" and "necessary" truths inherent in the very logic of being. . . . Yet this is only half of the . . . moral which our history suggests. The other half is that rationality, when conceived as complete, as excluding all arbitrariness, becomes itself a kind of irrationality. . . . The world of concrete existence . . . is no impartial tran-

script of the realm of essence. . . . It is, in short, a contingent world.[17]

It is significant that Lovejoy, in order to demonstrate that this essentially negative conclusion is inscribed in romanticism, should make reference to Schelling,
whom he uses as a *deus ex machina* to give the quietus, once and for all, to a persistent aberration of the mind. For Schelling, at least as Lovejoy presents him to
us, the idea of growth and development takes on a purely voluntaristic, irrational
aspect that, after having animated preromanticism, led to Schopenhauer and
brought to light certain elements that are still to be found in Nietzsche. Lovejoy
thus condemns himself to a curious paradox: the philosophical conclusions of his
book destroy its methodological conception. Inasmuch as *The Great Chain of Being* wants to be an example, or even a model, of what ought to be the history of
an idea, the book remains very narrowly tied to a successive notion of continuity:
the "ideas" that Lovejoy treats develop like a dramatic story, and their coherence
is entirely founded on the presupposition of a logical, chronological continuity.
But since ultimately its argument ends in the impossibility of conceiving the real
as continuous, Lovejoy's entire analysis becomes an arbitrary hypothesis, and the
history of ideas becomes the enumerations of reasons for which this history cannot exist.

The publication of this work in 1936 marked the high point of Lovejoy's influence in the United States—and the history of ideas, as a critical method, never
recovered from the book's internal contradiction. Its initiates remained hypno-
tized by the problem of romanticism, of which they were—more than they
realized—the rather belated perpetuators. Articles by Lovejoy (some of which are
of considerable interest) and a special issue of the journal published by his
followers[18] were dedicated to romanticism, without any of this material, however, ever managing a coherent point of view. Lovejoy, who, in a fine example
of excessive continuity, had meanwhile attacked romanticism as an unconscious
precursor of Nazism, finally suggested that the term could be abandoned as devoid of any precise meaning[19]—one of his more generally convincing responses—
in the name of a frankly formalist organicism and in the name of historical common sense.[20] The pluralism inherent in the conclusion of *The Great Chain of Being* is concretely obvious in certain suggestions of Lovejoy, such as the rather extravagant idea of having Milton's *Paradise Lost* studied by a group of specialists
whose collaborative labors would end in an ideal exegesis. The *Journal of the
History of Ideas* remains one of the best university organs published in the United
States. But its methodological unity makes room for a certain eclecticism: the articles it publishes are meritorious if the writers who write them are. None of the
available merit derives from a preestablished method.

Is there another way of looking at all this? The answer lies in the absence, in
*The Great Chain of Being*, of two figures whom simple historical precision should

have placed alongside Schelling, namely, Goethe and Hegel. Goethe is mentioned only indirectly when the famous phrase of *Faust,* "Wer immer strebend sich bemüht . . . [He who always makes an effort to strive . . . ]," is cited as characterizing romantic voluntarism (p. 307). Now the problem that Lovejoy, by invoking Schelling, has claimed to vanquish, is precisely the one that Goethe asks at the beginning of his drama. Here we find Faust able, but not inclined, to accede to the understanding of the Neoplatonic world (the macrocosm) that for Goethe is the world in its reality. This world cannot suffice for Faust because he himself does not possess the self-presence that belongs only to Being. Faust has to remain outside, contemplating it as a pure spectacle of alterity: "Welch Schauspiel! Aber ach! ein Schauspiel nur! [What a spectacle! But alas! Nothing but a spectacle!]."

His desire, on the contrary, is for Being as eternal omnipresence, to which Goethe gives the name of Earth Spirit, an image of fire and sun, which is his way of conceiving of transcendence properly speaking. This spirit is not immediately perceptible because it blinds, literally, those who try to contemplate it. Neither the visionary mode nor lucidity of mind can directly attain it. This is the torment of Faust, inordinate and insatiable at the beginning of the drama, an irrational, essentially dispersed character, whom only a chaotic will prevents from sinking into nonbeing.

If Faust had remained in this condition, he would be the perfect example of the romantic dispersion as Lovejoy describes it. But what Lovejoy considers the end of the line is only a point of departure for Goethe, who situates his drama entirely on the opposite slope of this problematic. The depth and novelty of *Faust* are not in the initial anguish of its central character but in the way he conquers that anguish, namely, in the recognition of the necessary copresence of Mephistopheles, in the conviction that Being is accessible only in the repeated negation of that through which Being reveals itself to him. When, through the experience of love, Faust finds that he has yielded to Being, he knows also that his path will be littered with parts of himself that his development has had to abandon along the way, will be marked by a series of cruel, degrading sacrifices that Mephistopheles will always be delighted to carry out on his account.

> O dass dem Menschen nichts Volkommnes wird,
> Empfind' ich nun. Du gabst zu dieser Wonne,
> Die mich den Göttern nah und näher bringt,
> Mir den Gefährten, den ich schon nicht mehr
> Entbehren kann, wenn er gleich, kalt und frech,
> Mich vor mir selbst erniedrigt, und zu Nichts,
> Mit einem Worthauch, deine Gaben wandelt.
>
> [O that nothing complete is granted to man
> I sense now. You gave me with this bliss,

Which brings me so near the gods,
This companion which I no longer
Can do without, even though, cold and insolent,
He degrades me in my own eyes, and to nothingness,
With a breath, transforms your gifts.][21]

This dialectic can be found in the whole drama, up through the last scene of the death of Faust, when negation appears under the still more revealing name of Care (*Sorge*). But the separation from the real and the transcendent does not prevent formation of a path toward Being, which will be the one Faust follows in his diverse experiences, each one catastrophic in itself, but which as a whole will be harmonized by their uniform direction.

The vision of a human experience that continues and expands by passage through the necessary sorrow of negation evokes, of course, the work of Hegel exactly contemporaneous with *Faust I—The Phenomenology of Mind*. Moreover there exists a profound analogy between the most salient structural characteristic of the two works—the bipartite division, the first part of which presents the history of a singular and individual consciousness (Goethe's *kleine Welt*) while the second presents the history of an intersubjective, universal consciousness, preoccupied with the *grosse Welt*. In the development of the consciousness of self, as in the example of Faust's life, the passage from one stage to the next constitutes the central moment. Beyond their considerable differences, Hegel and Goethe do have this idea in common.

Only dialectical thought, like that of Georg Lukács, who has demonstrated this analogy better than anyone else, can give an account of this essential dimension, in the absence of which the work would be deprived of any unity. Because he has an accurate conception of Goethean historicism, Lukács is able to give a convincing interpretation of the necessity for the Margaret episode, of the relationship between Faust and Mephistopheles, and of the technological symbols in the final scene. But dialectical historicism does not exhaust the wholeness of the work and leaves, as we will see, even subtler movements unexplained; nevertheless its importance is such that, in its absence, *Faust* would remain incomprehensible.

This conclusion underlines the impossibility that a history of ideas, conceived according to the general directives of Lovejoy, could give an account either of *Faust* or by extension of a great number of earlier and later works that reflect similar preoccupations. Many poets and thinkers find themselves faced with the paradox that Lovejoy describes at the end of his book, but more than one have found ways beyond it without having abandoned quite so completely all pretensions to continuity or all prerogatives of rational consciousness. One of these ways, that of Goethe, is the dialectic. It is difficult to conceive how a historical method could avoid giving considerable space to the dialectic.

Dialectic accounts for the two rhythms according to which *Faust* is organized — the binary rhythm that divides the poem into two complementary parts, and its progression by repetition. Faust grows by passing through a series of adventures whose general structure is always similar: he ceaselessly desires more and obtains what he desires, but at the price of destroying the object desired. Beside these two readily observable rhythms, there are others that extend from the beginning to the end of the poem, rhythms it is considerably more arduous to reveal. The dialectics of Lukács is too rudimentary to account for these movements that, rather than belonging to the massive oppositions of *Faust I* (oppositions of plentitude and negation, of real and ideal, individual and collective), participate in the interior dialectic of imaginary life. None of the episodes of the second part is "real" in the sense that the episode of Margaret is or the scenes at the beginning are. In Part II everything happens as in a dream. Still there is in that part something like a continuous variation of oneiric density. Dreams embed themselves within dreams as do the "plays within the play" of Elizabethan theater, and the distance of the episodes from the real is never constant. Enchanted by the luminosity of Goethean verse, one runs the risk of not noticing the uniquely fantastic character of *Faust II,* in which zones of the imaginary, degrees of surreality, and multiple temporalities are superimposed on one another to make a tangle of indescribable complexity. These variations are not arbitrary but obey their own rhythm.

Max Kommerell, a critic who is not always clear but who has his moments of great penetration, has at times managed to describe this rhythm in pages that in their way are as faithful to the interior forces of the work as the pages of Lukács are to the work's exterior dimensions.[22] He has noted, for example, the pulsation from exteriority to interiority that, even when the action of *Faust* takes place in the sphere of the universal, leads the hero, in those decisive moments of transformation, to the interiority of imaginary life.

The "possession of the world" [*Weltaufnahme*] shows only one of the faces of the activity proper to the principle of the person (that is, to Faust). The other face would be rather a concentration around a central nucleus, a withdrawal to oneself, and an interiorization. The two states alternate rhythmically, and in *Faust II,* this cosmic vision of the life of the person replaces the biographical order that (following the model of the *Bildungsroman*) is perceived as leading to a development. How is this concentration represented? By catastrophes, or even better, by the metamorphoses of Faust: the agitated sleeper of the first scene of Part II, the unconscious man at the beginning of the second act, the essentially petrified Faust of the end of the third act, the Faust who contemplates the cloud formations at the beginning of the fourth act, and the blind, dying man of the end of the play.[23]

Parallel to the broadening of the world of action, there is a deepening of interior exploration. The further one moves into the drama, the more this deepening gains in importance, to the point of relegating the action to the background. To be complete, an exegesis should describe these two movements and define just to what extent they condition each other.

One sees, therefore, the necessity of establishing a thematic of the imaginary, which should be of equal importance to the thematic of ideas. It is necessary to distinguish between a work, or part of a work, that imitates the real, and another that imitates the imaginary. The secondary characters of *Faust I* (Margaret, Wagner, Martha, etc.) are modeled on people of flesh and blood, while beings like Helen, Homunculus, or Euphorion are chiefly, as Maud Bodkin says,[24] daimons in the Platonic sense. As for the Mothers and the entelechy of Margaret in the last scene, they all belong to a zone of being still closer to an origin and can be called "archetypes," a term already charged with equivocation.

This is a term that marks the passage to another kind of thematic criticism – the mythological variety. Although it is the most experimental form of literary criticism, it already occupies an important place, especially in English-language universities. There it is a most curious phenomenon indeed: necessarily subjective research, deriving often from confession, has chosen to express itself in a didactic, even proselytizing tone. In some cases the fervor of this research has made it into a secular religion. There is in this research the more obvious danger that it falsifies the mythopoetic function of literary language by assimilating it to the certitude of the revealed word.

The mechanism of this deformation is clearly visible in a representative book, that of Maud Bodkin, in which some chapters are dedicated to *Faust*. Taking her point of departure from Carl Jung, Bodkin sees poetry as a way of access to experiences of the collective unconscious. Certain dramatic, symbolic structures can be found in a great number of works and permit the description of typical experiences, the repetition of which constitutes the true continuity of literary experience. Maud Bodkin in this way ends in a universal poetic pattern, a single theme, in relation to which individual works are like so many variations, or like episodes that adumbrate this or that passage of the cosmic fable. This fable is not difficult to recognize. It is the story of the redemption of man by his return to originary unity. In the symbolism of this book, it is clear that all symbols are only preparations for the final symbol, that of the rebirth of man through a new divine presence. The feminine archetype Margaret, for example, is interpreted as the sublimation of the erotic and instinctive love of the young Faust, a love that thus becomes a premonition of transcendent rapture. The interpretation is correct, although incomplete, and in any case is badly placed: one must not forget that the final scene is not the representation of Faust's redemption – this redemption was never really in question and consists precisely in the dynamic activity of his life – but that it describes, exactly, his death. The end of Faust is not a return to the divine (which, moreover, for Goethe, has never been absent), but is rather the evocation of the absolute interiorization that is death.

Maud Bodkin would have trouble admitting this, since for her, poetry is the language in which the divine is preserved and to which, therefore, one never returns to die; one returns to language to be reborn. She takes her critical enthusiasm from the particular satisfaction she feels in discovering an archetype, that is, from the assurance that the experience of being that is hers is in fact the *repetition* of a previous experience.[25] She assumes then that the particular feeling of this assurance is also that of the poet, a very common kind of projection and especially tempting here. Because if in fact the poetic is repetition, it presupposes the existence of an originary experience to be repeated; and in this case, the poetic language will be, in fact, the preeminent originary (or divine) language. One would have only, in some way, to wash away the temporal impurities that have accumulated during one's earthly sojourn in order to return to Being—and it is to this quasi-sacred task that one kind of mythological criticism devotes itself.

But is it true that poetry is the repetition of the originary? The reader has an easy job of it: he listens to a voice that speaks to him, and if this voice repeats to him his own desire, he is forthwith reassured of the universality of his experience. Nevertheless, the poet, for his part, hears only silence. It is indeed in the hope of breaking the silence that he invents words. But inasmuch as the words are only his own, they repeat *themselves;* they do not repeat *anything else.* If that were not so, Orpheus would not have addressed himself to creatures; he would only have listened to them. Art is not an imitation (or a repetition) but an endless longing for imitation, which by virtue of imitating itself, hopes finally to find a model. In other words, poetic language is not an originary language, but is derived from an originary language it does not know; consequently, as a language, it is mediate and temporal.

So mythological criticism cannot claim, as it has the tendency to do, the totalitarian position of absolute authority. The imitation of myths, in fact self-engendered, becomes one literary strategy among others, more or less profound depending on the particular case. The description of archetypes, as important as it is, does not possess an intrinsic precedence over the description of ideas, forms, and historical imitations. The special attraction of myth study is tied to the impatience of a period whose predominant quality consists in the acuity of its self-consciousness. It is to the degree that myth, in its naive and spontaneous form, is a challenge to us that it is called on to play so central a role in poetry and in contemporary thought. As long as that qualification is not forgotten, myth criticism has a considerable contribution to make, though in a somewhat different sense than certain myth specialists assume. In transferring to the domain of reflection what belongs to the domain of naive imagination, its function is essentially to demythologize and to become in fact a critique *of* the mythic—just as so much poetry, since Symbolism, is not symbolist poetry but a poetry *of* the symbol. This critique of the mythic constitutes the first step in a true thematic criticism, which, contrary to what one generally assumes, should pass from myth to idea, and from idea to formal theme, before being able to become history.

Translated by Dan Latimer

## Notes

1. Benedetto Croce, *Goethe* (Bari: Laterza, 1921).

2. Friedrich Gundolf, *Goethe* (Berlin: Bondi, 1920), pp. 778ff.

3. Harold S. Jantz, *Goethe's Faust as a Renaissance Man* (Princeton, N.J.: Princeton University Press, 1951).

4. Georg Lukács, *Goethe und seine Zeit* (Bern: A. Francke, 1947).

5. Charles Dédéyan, *Le Thème de Faust dans la littérature européenne,* 4 vols. (Paris: Lettres modernes, 1955–1956). See vol. II, p. 171.

6. Lukács, *Goethe und seine Zeit.*

7. Maud Bodkin, *Archetypal Patterns in Poetry* (Oxford: Oxford University Press, 1934).

8. Harry Levin, *The Overreacher: A Study of Marlowe* (Cambridge, Mass.: Harvard University Press, 1952), pp. 133ff.

9. Bodkin, *Archetypal Patterns in Poetry,* pp. 205ff; pp. 224ff.

10. E. M. Butler, in *The Fortunes of Faust* (Cambridge: Cambridge University Press, 1952), includes Thomas Mann and Paul Valéry but, not trying to be complete, does leave some gaps. Moreover Butler confines himself strictly to works dedicated to Faust. The fine book of Geneviève Bianquis, *Faust à travers quatre siècles* (Paris: Droz, 1935), is limited to the major texts and was published before the work of Mann and Valéry.

11. Thus Dédéyan (see I, p. 46 note), with regard to Marlowe, refuses to accept as proved the notion that the immediate source of Marlowe was not the German *Volksbuch* but the first edition of the English version, which was the work of a certain P.F., whom Dédéyan, following Butler, justly praises. Since the edition of Henri Logeman, *The English Faust-Book of 1592* (Ghent: University of Ghent, 1900), this filiation seems well established, and the most recent Marlowe specialists (C. F. Tucker Brooke, Harry Levin, and M. Poirier) have not taken up the question again. Here, then, Dédéyan's prudence seems almost excessive. Let it be said in passing that Dédéyan earns a reproach for not giving the original English in his citations from Marlowe (though luckily he gives the German original in those from Goethe); he relies on the translation of F. C. Danchin, which is frankly mediocre.

12. Influenced by the later development of the theme, critics have exaggerated the importance of the character of Helen in the *Volksbuch,* where her appearance is a secondary episode. For the same reason they have exaggerated the trace of Faust's possible redemption from the first text (see Butler, *Fortunes of Faust,* p. 11; Dédéyan, *Thème de Faust,* I, p. 30). Thomas Mann, who based his *Doktor Faustus* on the *Volksbuch,* understood that the point of the story is Faust's damnation.

13. On this subject see Bianquis, *Faust,* p. 77, also cited by Dédéyan, *Thème de Faust,* I, p. 264.

14. Ernst Cassirer, *Goethe und die Geschichtliche Welt* (Berlin: Bruno Cassirer, 1932), p. 26.

15. See, for example, such different theses as those of Lucien Goldmann, *Le Dieu caché* (Paris: Gallimard, 1956); Marcel A. Ruff, *L'Esprit du mal et l'esthétique baudelairienne* (Paris: A. Colin, 1955); Robert Champigny, *Berkeley et le romantisme anglais* (in typescript).

16. Cambridge, Mass.: Harvard University Press, 1936. This work is the product of a lecture series (The William James Lectures) given at Harvard in 1933.

17. Lovejoy, *Great Chain of Being,* pp. 329, 331, 332.

18. A. O. Lovejoy, *Essays in the History of Ideas* (Baltimore: Johns Hopkins University Press, 1948); *Journal of the History of Ideas (JHI),* 2 (1941).

19. "On the Discrimination of Romanticisms," *PMLA*, 29 (1924), pp. 229–53, reprinted in *Essays*. "The Meaning of Romanticism for the Historian of Ideas," *JHI*, 2 (1941).

20. Leo Spitzer, "*Geistesgeschichte* vs. History of Ideas as applied to Hitlerism," *JHI*, 5 (1944), with a reply from Lovejoy in the first issue; René Wellek, "The Concept of Romanticism in Literary History," *Comparative Literature*, I, 1 and 2 (1949).

21. It seems certain that the Spirit (*Erhabener Geist*) to whom these words are addressed is the Earth Spirit of the first scene, since it is specifically described as having appeared in flame (I.3219). On this subject also see Lukács, *Goethe und seine Zeit*, p. 165.

22. Max Kommerell, *Geist und Buchstabe der Dichtung* (Frankfurt am Main: Klostermann, 1944). Kommerell was one of the favorite disciples of Stefan George before separating from the Circle. One needs to exercise some restraint not to judge him solely by the somewhat disturbing title of his first important work, *Der Dichter als Führer in der Deutschen Klassik* (Berlin: Bondi 1928).

23. Kommerell, *Geist und Buchstabe der Dichtung*, page uncited.

24. Maud Bodkin, *Archetypal Patterns in Poetry*, page uncited.

25. This tendency becomes very explicit in a later work of the same author, *Studies of Type Images* (Oxford: Oxford University Press, 1951).

# A New Vitalism: Harold Bloom (1962)

Harold Bloom's new book on English romanticism, *The Visionary Company: A Reading of English Romantic Poetry* (New York: Doubleday, 1961), coming after his *Shelley's Mythmaking* and preceding an announced study of Blake, testifies to an upsurge of active interest in romanticism among a new generation of critics. Not very long ago, someone of Bloom's talent and temperament would in all likelihood have centered his attention on early twentieth-century poets such as Yeats, Eliot, or Stevens, while his historical interest would probably have been directed toward the metaphysical poets; this was the predominant pattern under the influence of leading New Critics. Romantic studies were certainly never in decline, but the most important contributions in that domain — such as Meyer Abrams's *The Mirror and the Lamp* and W. J. Bate's *From Classic to Romantic* — took on the form of intellectual history rather than pure literary criticism. Bloom's book is dedicated and greatly indebted to his former teacher Meyer Abrams, but he is not writing as a historian: his purpose (though not always his tone) is that of a militant critic motivated by far-reaching commitments, willing to upset established hierarchies and evaluations. Though obviously schooled in modern poetry, he is fully aware that no real discontinuity exists between romantic and contemporary poetry. The romantics are being reinterpreted as very close and immediate ancestors, a trend all the more significant since it is by no means confined to English-speaking critics; some aspects of German romanticism are for the moment livelier topics than George or Rilke, whereas a French critical avant-garde is actively discovering that Lamartine and Hugo are perhaps even more interesting than Mallarmé or Rimbaud.

This critical revival of romanticism is accompanied, oddly enough, by a return to a more traditional picture of English literary history than that proposed by the New Critics. It reestablishes the romantics' own dependence on Milton and Spenser, rather than Donne and the Metaphysical poets, as the main creators of English poetic diction. Hence Bloom's frequent references to Milton, and under the influence of Northrop Frye, to a debatable version of Spenser as an archetypal poet. This perspective too is a familiar one among writers for whom New Critics have become old-fashioned; one thinks, for instance, of Frank Kermode's passionate plea for Milton and his rejection of Eliot's "dissociation of sensibility" as a historical category, in the last chapter of *The Romantic Image*. As is so often the case, the exponents of a relatively radical critical position thus find themselves defending a more traditional outline of literary history than the highly conservative New Critics—although they could argue with some justice that *their* Milton and *their* Spenser are not the traditional ones.

In its subject matter and historical orientation *The Visionary Company* thus is typical of a general trend in contemporary criticism. But it is an unusual book in that it goes well beyond most others in upsetting established values and opinions. This is not immediately apparent. Especially after Bloom's rather aggressive study on Shelley, it seems, at first sight, tame and conventional enough: a running commentary on the well-established main texts of English romanticism, loosely organized along chronological lines, casually written in the tone of lecture notes for an undergraduate survey course, aimed at the general public rather than the specialist, and eager to provide readers with as inclusive a picture as possible; no major figure and very few major poems are omitted, regardless of their length or difficulty. The result is a guided trip at breathtaking pace through vast expanses of poetry, including texts of the size of *The Four Zoas, The Prelude, Don Juan, Prometheus Bound,* and *Endymion*. There are many cross-references from author to author within the body of English romantic poetry, treated as one homogeneous whole, while various suggestive allusions to Yeats, Stevens, Hart Crane, and others are embedded in the commentaries and establish the unbroken link between romantic and modern poetry. Bloom seems to be going out of his way to present his material as clearly and objectively as possible; he abounds in gentle praise for all his authors and politeness toward his readers, using a minimum of technical terminology and confining his critical references to the writings of his own friends. This apparent eclecticism leads at times to odd discrepancies in the texture of the writing; one ranges from such indisputable information as, for instance, "Kronos means 'Time' in Greek" to rather more intricate (and debatable) assertions of the following kind: "like Blake, Shelley is always alert to the combative possibilities of interweaving an antinomian rhetoric with a dialectic that exposes the inadequacies of both the orthodox in morality and religion and any position that seeks merely to negate orthodoxy by an inversion of categories" (p. 276).

Because his medium is that of an expository commentary on a series of anthology pieces, Bloom is forced to give a great deal of space to the summarizing of dramatic action—something bound to lead to pretty awkward writing in a case like *Endymion*—as well as to straightforward paraphrase on the most elementary level. This is hardly avoidable, since he chooses to present his book as an authoritative reading within the framework of an established position rather than as an argument for this position. Such slight drawbacks are altogether minor; if I find myself regretting that this study of romanticism is not presented as a theoretical argument rather than in its pseudodidactic form, it is because the commentaries fail to do justice to the power of the thesis. For this is not, appearances to the contrary, a series of close readings leading up to a general opinion about romanticism, but an a priori belief about romanticism illustrated by far too wide a choice of texts. The readings of specific poems are always hasty and fragmentary, even when they are perceptive; they seem quite unaware of any expressive value other than explicit statement. Time and again, one is tempted to take issue with local points of exegesis, but one soon realizes that this would not touch on the core of the main assertion. The thesis of *The Visionary Company* does not depend for its demonstration on the details of the analytical commentary; one has to come to grips with it as it stands in itself. For Bloom's criticism has a much deeper virtue than the polite tone of his latest work suggests. It is the product of a genuine intellectual passion that actually has little patience with balanced judgments and strikes out for absolute positions. The outward moderation is only a concession to urbanity, or perhaps a device to lure the reader into the author's camp. What counts in this book is the general thesis, as a brief discussion of what seems to be its most original and controversial aspect should indicate.

The unifying theme that permits Harold Bloom to treat Blake, Wordsworth, Shelley, and Keats as one single "company" of poets (Byron and Coleridge being included for the sake of historical completeness, not as essential parts of the argument) is not in itself strikingly new: he stresses above all their common belief in the powers of the imagination. The concept of the poetic imagination, however, is no longer derived from Wordsworth or Coleridge; in their stead, Blake has become the only complete poet of the imagination and all others are measured by reference to his achievement. The value emphasis thus becomes very clear. Bloom openly and candidly affirms Blake's superiority over Wordsworth while in the next generation Shelley surpasses Keats to the exact extent that he resembles Blake more closely. Such ratings, however arbitrary, are not meaningless here since it is obviously the author's avowed intention to express this kind of evaluative judgment. Whether one will be convinced by it will depend entirely on the assent one can give to Bloom's theory of the imagination.

This theory, itself an interpretation of Blake, emerges most clearly in the analysis of the earlier Blake poems, prior to the *Book of Urizen;* after that, the bulk of the material is too vast to allow for tight exposition. Blake's imagination is described as the power by means of which man can rise above a given state of nature (which Blake calls Beulah) to the superior state of Eden. Consciousness of "nature" in Beulah is that of an identity between human and natural processes, both experienced as recurrent, eternally repetitive cycles. As such, it is a happy or innocent relationship between subject and object, in which the senses of the subject passively espouse the forces that inhabit natural things; Bloom suggestively (though not responsibly) equates Beulah with Milton's Garden before the Fall and with Spenser's Garden of Adonis. But because this state is ultimately a static one (cyclical but not dialectical), man cannot remain there; by alienating himself from this pastoral bliss (the act of experience) he may be able to ascend to a higher realm. Blake's main originality resides in the way in which he experiences this progression as a gradual humanization of the natural world. The subject, by means of a power called imagination, can transform the natural world into its own mode of being, and thus substitute for a subject-object antithesis an intersubjective relationship between two entities that are no longer estranged from each other. The contact between man and nature, which was originally pure sensation, thus becomes the dialogue (the I-Thou relationship of Martin Buber) between man and "the human form divine" of a transfigured nature; the *Garden* of Eden becomes the *City* of Jerusalem in which all relationships are humanized, including the relationship between man and God.

One could argue whether this is indeed an accurate description of Blake's vision of things, but such a discussion is better postponed until Bloom's planned full-length study of Blake becomes available. From what appears of it in this book, it is likely to be a coherent but monolithic reading, allowing for no changes or contradictions in Blake's own insight, nor any discontinuities in his development. For our present purpose, it matters only that Bloom accepts this theory of the imagination uncritically. He does not question, for instance, the continuity postulated in passing from an objective to a humanized nature—although, if the continuity remains problematic, humanization might lead to the destruction of an essential element in nature and to a much worse predicament than the self-reflective, narcissistic paralysis of Blake's Ulro. Neither does Bloom question the origin of the power by which the transformation is to be achieved. In the lower regions of the natural state, it is very clearly sexual desire, yet sexuality is a composite force, as much a subject-object sensation as it is an intersubjective relation. If it is to grow from the former into the latter, there has to be a discontinuity somewhere, a renunciation, or a sacrifice, at any rate a delicate and obscure point in the development that cannot be merely crossed by means of the sheer stamina of a blind *élan vital*. The problem remains whether, in Bloom's version, Blake's extraordinary visionary power is not earned at the expense of the richness of his objective perception, if he is not all "vision" and very little "sight." His original sense of nature may well be incomplete, thus making it easy for him to transcend what he has in fact never fully known; certainly the passage that Bloom singles out (on p. 102) to indicate that Blake's sense of nature is second to none is not very convincing. Blake emerges from this interpretation as a vitalist, not as a dialectical mind, and one may wonder if his "vitalism of the imagination," as Bloom very aptly calls it, is not a form of perpetual desire. In other words, one may wonder if Blake ever fully reached beyond the state of innocence into the state of experience, if his greatness is not due to the fact that he belongs with what Yeats calls the "saints" rather than the "poets." Perhaps the late Yeats is truly the place to look for a sardonically ironic treatment of Blake's literalism of the imagination.

Bloom almost forces one to raise such questions, since he uses his image of Blake as an absolute norm by means of which all other romantic poets are to be understood and measured. Wordsworth's highly complex attitude toward nature, for instance, which Bloom refers to as "naturalism," thus becomes a quest "to find the unfallen Eden in nature, to read in her a more human face" (p. 437). The "unfallen Eden" is seen as equivalent to Blake's Beulah, the state of remembered childhood of the *Immortality Ode*. According to Bloom, Wordsworth strives to recapture this state by apocalyptic experiences of unity between mind and nature, patterned on the "sexual analogy" (p. 123). His failure—illustrated biographically in the waning of his creative powers as he grows older—stems from his unwillingness to relinquish his nostalgia for this lost paradise, to transcend innocent desire by the humanizing ordeal of experience.

This reading seems to be a distortion of Wordsworth's feeling for nature as well as of his theory of recollection. Nature in Wordsworth is never like Blake's Beulah, not even in childhood; it always contains an element that can be called divine precisely to the extent that it entirely escapes the possibility of being humanized. No dialogue could ever be possible between man and the profound otherness, the "it-ness" that is always a part of Wordsworth's nature. In childhood, this element impresses the mind with sheer terror; in later life, the more tranquil eye of imaginative perception can behold it with increased serenity. But no vitalized *relation* can ever bring human consciousness into contact with the fully perceived natural world. It is a serious misreading to represent Wordsworth's mind and the external world as "fitted, each to the other, even as man and wife . . . and accomplish[ing] a creation the meaning of which is fully dependent on the sexual analogy" (p. 122). This kind of "adjustment" exists for Wordsworth only in the totally asexual realm of pure consciousness in "a vision in which the mind knows itself almost without exterior cause or else as no less real, here, no less indestructible than the object of its perception"—an admirable definition of Wordsworth's imagination quoted by Bloom (p. 155) but due to Geoffrey Hartman. The passages on a masculine Wordsworth trying to conquer a feminine nature (coupled with suggestions that his virility was not quite up to the task) are not to the point. Far from being Blake's pure energy, Wordsworth's imagination is an extended mode of seeing, originating in the act of visual perception and not in sexuality. Instead of humanizing nature, Wordsworth creates increasingly dehumanized entities, a world in which it is hard to tell men and women from rocks and stones. He may be indeed "a man talking to men," but he is talking to them about nonhuman beings. And the "face" that his memory tries to recapture is not the innocent Adam in Beulah, nor the "human form divine," but more closely akin to Yeats's "looking for the face I had / Before the world was made." In short, Blakean categories do not apply here; they lead to an inaccurate description and an irrelevant evaluation.

The same is true, to a lesser degree, of Keats (and even, I suspect, of Shelley — though this point would better be discussed in regard to Bloom's first book). The Keats chapter of *The Visionary Company* (in which a reference to Earl Wasserman's *The Finer Tone* would have been in order) probably contains the best analyses of individual poems, and the analogy between the pastoral dream-world of *Endymion* and Blake's Beulah is undeniable. Yet, the dialectical way in which Keats opposes the world of sensation to that of poetic consciousness is not Blakean. Keats time and again emphasizes the discontinuity between the two worlds and, consequently, the total sacrifice involved in passing from one to the other — a sacrifice so absolute that it would be hybris for the poet to take it upon himself; hence that, even in *The Fall of Hyperion,* Keats remains the witness rather than the subject of sacrificial initiation. This is not due, as Bloom suggests, to Keats's deliberate choice of "the lower paradise" (p. 426), but to a richer aware-ness of the natural world than Blake's. None knows better than Keats the cost resulting from the necessary transcendence of the merely natural. This remains the central theme of his poetry, not the capitulation to the vegetative forms of a sexualized nature — as Bloom would have us believe, by giving to the final sestet of the sonnet "Bright Star" an unwarranted authority, misleadingly based on the fact that it is the last thing Keats wrote. Here again, Bloom's allegiance to his ver-sion of Blake interferes with his reading of other romantic poets.

Another way of putting my disagreement with Bloom's thesis is by stressing his systematic avoidance of the neo-Hellenic element as a constitutive component of the romantic sensibility. Not only do the romantics, including Blake, inherit from Renaissance poetry a rhetoric and a large amount of *topoi* that stem directly from the Greco-Roman tradition, but they derive from the same source an aware-ness of the richness and complexity of the natural world, which makes it ex-tremely difficult for them to remove the source of divine presence from natural entities. It is true that their attitude toward the world of nature is estranged and nostalgic in a non-Hellenic way, but it does not follow that the Hellenic element can simply be eliminated. It has to be overcome if the threat of paralysis inherent in romanticism is to be broken, but this can only occur by means of a true dialec-tic. Other poets of the same tradition have gone far toward a full awareness of the complexities involved in an encounter between a Hellenic conception of na-ture and a modern conception of consciousness. Such widely different figures as Rousseau, Goethe, Hölderlin, or Baudelaire have experienced this antinomy in a manner that makes them the true representatives of the Western tradition. In English romanticism, Wordsworth and Keats resemble them most, whereas Blake—and especially Blake as Bloom describes him—remains an admirable but somewhat eccentric figure. Bloom shows a true kinship with Blake by defending a similarly admirable but somewhat eccentric conception of English romanticism.

# Giraudoux (1963)

It is a nostalgic experience to encounter Giraudoux dressed in the dignity of a foreign translation that, coming several years after his death, consecrates him as an "immortal" figure (*Three Plays: Judith, Tiger at the Gates, and Duel of Angels,* trans. Christopher Fry [Oxford: Oxford University Press, 1963]). His works — the now too neglected novels as well as the works of the theater — had something deliberately ephemeral about them, a self-ironic lightness that made little claim to future fame and mocked any monumental pose. When they came out during the thirties, they blended so easily with the flow of literary life that one took them for granted; it was in the order of things that Louis Jouvet would offer as an almost yearly rite a new Giraudoux play at the Théatre de l'Athénée. Those plays almost always lived up to expectations. They provided a marvelous medium for actors so well known and liked that they seemed to matter even more than what they performed, and they made one enter a world as distinctive and familiar as the presence of a well-liked person. The nostalgia, then, stems partly from making a literary interpretation of something that used to be directly accessible as live experience. Not that these plays offer a particularly faithful reflection of their period; they never aimed at anything that lofty or inclusive. But precisely because they never assumed a point of view beyond or above that of their period, they easily became a part of its intimate mood. The same is true of various other good minor French writers around the same time — Colette or Jean Cocteau — all of whom, by the way, have been taken almost too seriously in the United States. They nowise could be counted among the architects of that complex edifice

97

known as the *entre deux guerres,* but they provided the furniture for some of its smaller, more comfortable rooms.

Nowadays, in this edition of three plays translated by Christopher Fry, Giraudoux looks very different: much weightier, more problematic, at times almost oracular. This is no doubt partly due to the particular selection of plays contained in this volume, of which only one, *Tiger at the Gates (La guerre de Troie n'aura pas lieu),* is truly characteristic. The two others, the earlier *Judith* as well as the late *Duel of Angels,* depart in tone rather than in theme from Giraudoux's customary manner; a mixture of elegance and banter that skillfully creates an illusion of profundity. It is again typical of our time (these translations were presented in London between 1955 and 1962) that one should choose the profundity over the elegance. We are all in favor of humor and gracefulness, but only if we are sure of darker depths underneath. Here is the case of a writer who chose to be brilliant, almost glossy, and witty, except on two or three occasions when he tried a degree of high seriousness. And it is precisely these two or three occasions that, to judge by this book, are considered most worthy of interest. In a sense this is legitimate. *Duel of Angels* and *Judith* reveal a great deal about Giraudoux. They, better than *Amphitrion 38,* or *Electre* or *Ondine,* place him within the thematic continuity of the modern theater—a task rather remote, however, from these pleasant prewar evenings at Jouvet's theater. We then can see how these plays contain implicitly much that has since become explicit in Anouilh, in Sartre, even in Ionesco and Beckett. Harold Clurman, who writes the introduction to this edition, reassures us that we can enjoy Giraudoux without bad conscience since, for all his frivolity, he is nevertheless a precursor of the "theater of the absurd." And so he is, without doubt, as are many of his contemporaries.

The self-conscious, almost tragic Giraudoux that meets us in these pages illustrates one of the attempts to master a recurrent problem of modern literature: how to produce drama without real heroes or, at least, without a recognized system of values powerful enough to inspire heroic action. Outwardly, the plays remain faithful to the traditional structure of drama organized around a central figure of heroic dimensions; Judith, Helen, and Lucille in the three plays here presented. But the nature of their heroism is altogether different from that traditionally associated with the term. As a matter of fact, their first dramatic function is to destroy whatever traces of conventional heroic values may remain in the audience's mind. Hence the ironic use of figures from the great Western myths: Judith, Helen of Troy, Lucrecia, Eve herself. The purpose is certainly not to show the archetypal permanence of the mythological situation, nor is it (as in Joyce) to show the degradation of the archetype in the contemporary setting. Instead, Giraudoux wants to humanize the myth radically, by stripping it of all universal significance, by reducing it to a strictly individual, particular and, as such, necessarily banal and trivial event. All the large and masculine categories that make up the heroic mood—love and war, courage, history—disappear. There is no room at all for

Achilles in this version of the war of Troy, and even Hector, for whom war is an absurd butchery when it loses universal purpose, does not have the slightest grip of human destiny in spite of all his goodwill. With their tendency to generalize, men are the first great victims of Giraudoux's humanized mythologies. They are steadily being cuckolded by a destiny that has chosen to mate with their women, and they are as ungracious about it is as the cuckolds of comedy are traditionally supposed to be. When they are trying to cast Judith in the role of a national martyr, she tells them in reply: "I believe God is only concerned with *me,* not with Holofernes or the Jews. . . . There is no history of nations. There is only the history of Judith driven to her knees." In more ironic versions, this feminine sense of individual reality keeps reducing the most pathetic myths to everyday comedy.

But this is only the negative aspect of Giraudoux's heroines. The very similar feminine protagonists that reappear in play after play achieve a kind of positive heroic status of their own, a status so compelling that even the gods are completely seduced by it, let alone helpless mortal males. It comes from the heroine's ability to stave off evil by refusing to recognize it as such. Imagine Eve, after her encounter with Satan, simply refusing to fall and continuing life as if nothing had happened. Such are Giraudoux's women: they manage to forget the past, which is the source of guilt, and refuse to have anything to do with the future, which is the source of anxiety; no common meeting ground can exist between Helen and Cassandra. The plays abound in talk about innocence and purity, but of a very peculiar kind. There are few virgins on Giraudoux's stage, nor does virginity seem to be particularly valued there. Whether real or imaginary, rapes turn into rather cheerful affairs. Whoever interprets this "purity" as a prelapsarian, childlike innocence, misses the point. Much rather, it is the ability to sin gracefully and elegantly, a feat symbolized by a love night so successful that all other considerations are blotted out for the moment. This seems to be the only genuine candor left in a world where all forms of virtue have become hollow.

Helen in *Tiger at the Gates* is, of course, the prototype of this paradoxical angel who knows neither pity nor repentance. Since the dramatic interest is provided here by a caricature of the antics of contemporary international politics, Giraudoux can keep his female figure whole and pure. In the two other plays, where a not altogether successful attempt is made to present a more rounded, more true-to-life human being, the dramatic structure is more complicated. It rests on a surprise effect: after having been led to believe that some form of conventional morality will have the last word, the spectator suddenly discovers the Giraudoux heroine is in all her triumphant charm "beyond good and evil." Thus the pseudo-Lucrecian Lucille from *Duel of Angels* appears as a crusader for staunch morality until she suddenly shifts sides in the last scene of the play; instead of dying to avenge her honor, she dies to avoid pomposity, gladly assuming a sin that in fact she has not committed. We understand then that the "virtue" that drove her to fight against ugly forms of vice has nothing to do with the heavy-handed morality of the masculine world; it is in fact much more akin to the sense of style, of detachment, of bright-colored beauty that animates Helen in the Trojan play. And Judith is an even clearer case, although here the apparent conflict is not so much moral as religious, between a transcendental world of divine order and a world of immanent, sensuous pleasure. Up till the end, we are being told that Judith has achieved a transcendental grandeur in spite of herself and that, regardless of what her own feelings may be, she has been an instrument of divine purposes. Appearing in the guise of a drunken guard, a supernatural angel pronounces her a martyr—until, in the very last lines, the truth comes out: Judith has in fact brought down the gods to the level of human pleasures. Such is the power of feminine seductiveness when it casts off the weight of sin that, instead of raising humans to the level of the immortals, it humanizes the gods to the point where they forget their station.

This triumph of beauty, however, is by no means the triumph of elemental, animal forces of sensation; nothing could be more remote from the spirit of Giraudoux's aesthetic. Some of the men, and the gods themselves, partake of the natural, but women are creatures of refinement and artifice. Their struggle against the paralyzing power of moral fear is conducted with aesthetic weapons. In this, they are very close to true poets. "You should imitate me a little," says Lucille in *Duel of Angels*. "Trust less to your thoughts and more to language. . . . A flight of pure words lifts me into the sunshine." Like those statesmen in *Tiger at the Gates* who can meet at the eve of war and exchange polished statements, the poet maintains the miracle of an elegant language among the many vulgarities of the present. When he does not actually put himself on the stage as a choral voice, Giraudoux makes his poetic presence constantly felt by claiming our steady attention to feats of language that mirror exactly the stylistic qualities of his feminine heroines. The conflicts unfold through a series of verbal contests, with the author's sympathy always belonging to the one who has spoken best.

Today, we may have some difficulty in responding with equal enthusiasm to the charm of these ladies, and to the slightly mechanical elegance of the style. They look a little too much like fashion models. Next to writers like Valéry and Gide, who also, at times, upheld deliberately "frivolous" conceptions of style as a defense against the temptations of profundity, Giraudoux is both shallow and facile. Yet the feminine type he invented, the most original achievement of his theater, becomes part of the literary gallery of the eternal feminine. He owes this to the bold determination with which his heroines leap across the conventional boundaries separating good from evil. In this, Giraudoux is a precursor of many later playwrights: his plays reduce established morality to absurdity, not by rebellion or indignation, but simply in the name of an urbane good taste. And a genuine element of poignancy is added by the fact that these shining women and their limpid language do not have the slightest chance of resisting the rising tide. They always go under, their only achievement being that they maintain or even fulfill their style in defeat. Giraudoux's Helen may seem brittle enough next to Valéry's Jeune Parque or Proust's Albertine, but if one compares her to the sultry, sulking heroines of the *nouvelle vague,* she rather gains in stature. One of the actresses who used to excel in Giraudoux's feminine roles was Madeleine Ozeray, and when I compare her to, let us say, Jeanne Moreau, it becomes clear that little progress has been made since the thirties in the invention of an irresistible feminine type.

Much of the charm of Giraudoux's theater comes across in this translation by Christopher Fry, though a certain amount of the verbal ironies and virtuosities is lost and little effort is made, I must say, to retrieve them. The disappearance of many good jokes increases the slightly misleading impression of solemnity left by the English text. But Fry shows a professional's skill in preserving the brisk tempo of Giraudoux's dialogue, and I can imagine that this version would do very well on the stage. It is an excellent introduction to the work of an author whose influence has been altogether salutary.

# Heidegger Reconsidered (1964)

The main interest of William Barrett's *What Is Existentialism?* (New York: Grove Press, 1964) stems from the contrast between the two parts in which it is divided. They deal with the same topic — the work of the contemporary philosopher Martin Heidegger — but were written twelve years apart. The first essay originated shortly after the war, at a time when American intellectuals were discovering existentialism, a movement that by then had practically become a part of French popular culture; the second essay is dated 1963. Among the many attempts to write on a nontechnical level about this subject, I find this book more useful and informative than most of its predecessors, mainly because it does not pretend to carry out the dangerous assumption of its title: that "existentialism" could be neatly defined and described, conveniently summarized in a few formulas, thus sparing everyone a lot of tiresome reading and the hard task of learning a foreign terminology. Precisely because Professor Barrett writes for the general public, but from a philosophical point of view (and not as a member of the general public trying to philosophize), he spares us the usual hasty résumés of Kierkegaard, Nietzsche, Sartre, and even Heidegger that, in the past, have purported to tell us what existentialism is all about. Instead, by the juxtaposition of the two essays, he allows us to follow the development of his own attitude toward a certain mode of thought. This provides us with a glimpse into a significant occurrence: the reaction of a mind brought into contact with a particularly powerful source of philosophical insight. In the process, we may not learn very much about the source itself, but we are at least told something important about the mental attitude with which it should be approached. And that, after all, is the best a nontechnical book on a philosophical subject can accomplish: not to pretend to offer a shortcut, but to put the reader in a receptive frame of mind to embark on his own search.

Although the author tells us that he is "more surprised by the continuity [of the two essays] than by their divergences," it is certainly the latter that call for comment. In one respect, Mr. Barrett's philosophical intuition did not betray him, even when he was writing on existentialism in the late forties. He realized then as now that any treatment of the subject had to start from the work of Heidegger, and that any treatment of Heidegger had to start from his early and most important work, *Being and Time* (*Sein und Zeit,* 1926). This was not obvious at the time: the success of Sartre's and Merleau-Ponty's literary and theoretical work had pushed the influence of Heidegger into the background; one was altogether willing to see him replaced and bypassed by the younger French existentialists whose politics were much more appealing. Moreover, Heidegger's work seemed to be stalled since the publication of *Sein und Zeit*; he purported to dismiss the unfinished treatise as a false start, without, however, replacing it with another work of similar proportions. There was thus a great deal of merit and discernment in Mr. Barrett's insistence, from the start, on the determining importance of *Being and Time.*

But, granting this, the first part of the book certainly presents an inadequate and distorted view of Heidegger, not because of any deliberate prejudice, but clearly because Barrett came to him with certain false expectations, which naturally had been shaped by his philosophical and ideological background. Barrett was an American student of philosophy before the advent of logical positivism and linguistic analysis, with strong progressive leanings and a vivid interest in the more literary aspects of French existentialism. The atmosphere is pleasantly familiar to those who lived on the subway circuit between uptown Columbia and downtown Astor Place in the New York of the forties; one can find it curiously stylized and reflected back to one of its sources in the special issue on the United States that Sartre edited for *Les Temps modernes* around that time. Such a background (in contrast perhaps to the one existing today) was open and eclectic enough to allow for an initial curiosity and sympathy in approaching Heidegger, but it was bound to stand in the way of a correct first reading. Especially under the French influence, it would tend to focus on the aspects of *Sein und Zeit* that may, at first sight, appear to have to do with the realm of immediate experience rather than with a rigorous philosophical discourse on this experience.

To some degree, *Zein und Zeit* may lend itself to this kind of confusion. It contains, after all, such phrases as "being towards death," talks at times (though much less often than is generally assumed) about such familiar-sounding experiences as care, guilt, anxiety, etc., devotes a footnote to Tolstoy's *The Death of Ivan Ilyitch* (though this is the only literary reference in the book), and mentions, albeit with strong philosophical reservations, Kierkegaard. A reader may therefore assume that this is a "subjective" book that, like Sartre's essays, somehow tries to *cope,* in terms of actions, values, and beliefs, with such matters as our anxieties, our historical predicament, or our mortality. In addition, *Sein und Zeit* is written in a harsh, polemical, somewhat arrogant tone that was characteristic of Heidegger's temperament and can be mistaken for the pathos of ideology or belief. In fact, it is nothing of the sort. At best, it expresses the genuine passion for truth and animates all major philosophical inquiries, at worst the frustration of a junior professor chafing under the tyranny of seniority in the German academic system.

For nothing is more remote from Heidegger than this confusion between the pathos of direct experience and the knowing of this experience – a confusion that, ironically, has become associated with so-called existential thought, mainly because of Sartre's famous and unfortunate phrase about the precedence of existence over essences. One could rather describe *Being and Time* as the most thoroughgoing attempt to cleanse our thought from that confusion not only in language, but in the philosophical project as a whole. Heidegger begins his argument by insisting that the very act by which man, instead of abandoning himself to the immediacy of experience, always interprets this experience in the direction of a cognition, is constitutive for the human way of being as such. To put this very crudely, it means that we are human to the extent that we are able to understand our own subjectivity by transforming it into language and, ultimately, by seeing it exactly as it is, in the pure language of true philosophy. Therefore Heidegger does not in any way wish to plunge one into the undifferentiated and opaque mass of direct actions, feelings, or emotions; his entire enterprise strives in the opposite direction. When he talks about death, for instance, it is not to awaken within us the kind of visceral response, the immediate pathos associated with the experience. Instead he speaks of death in order to establish a crucial distinction between two ways of knowing: the inauthentic, evasive manner in which we generally "know" of our mortality as something that happens only *now* to others and *not yet* to ourselves, and the authentic knowledge of ourselves as finite and therefore essentially temporal creatures. Death, then, is mentioned primarily for epistemological reasons and not, as the much abused term would appear in its popularized version, for "existential" reasons. The word "existential" Heidegger uses to mean exactly the opposite: philosophically conscious knowledge as opposed to immediate, intuitive, experienced knowledge.

On his first reading of *Being and Time,* the author of *What Is Existentialism?* was obviously not aware of this, hence his summary of the book puts all the emphases in the wrong places. The historical antecedents of Heidegger are not correctly stated and the all-important neo-Kantian background ignored. By again and again stressing "existential pathos" as being Heidegger's real concern, Barrett obscures the main argument of the book. Heidegger's aim in this book is primarily to show how the possibility of an inauthentic and partial relationship toward things inheres in the very nature of the human makeup, along with the intent to overcome it. The entire organization of *Being and Time* is determined by this theme, which Barrett only mentions as a topic among others. The very notion of temporality, which originally has nothing to do with our everyday use of past, present, and future, depends on this passage from a "fallen" to an "authentic" consciousness. Since this is not clearly brought out, Mr. Barrett's summarizing paraphrase necessarily goes astray, and his critical remarks do not apply to Heidegger's actual statement.

But in the later chapters of *What Is Existentialism?* a considerable change has taken place and the author is now a great deal closer to the movement of Heidegger's thought. His analysis of the distinction between Sartre's basically unphilosophical undertaking and Heidegger's is one of the real contributions of the book. In this section, my only reservations have to do with the end of the chapter, "Historical Prophecy" (pp. 213–16), in which Barrett, taking his cue from some of Heidegger's pronouncements on technology, indulges in some consideration on the future state of our historical world that, despite a reassuring ironical tone, might be misleading. I know that Heidegger himself, in his later essays, has occasionally adopted an oracular tone—but this is perhaps an understandable human weakness in someone who may well feel he is not correctly understood. Utopian prophecy in any form is alien to him, a dangerous misconception of time as a determined, particularized entity, the very opposite of the open and free time of man's historical project. It is a classic case of confusion between—to use Heidegger's vocabulary so well explained by Mr. Barrett himself—an "ontic" and an "ontological" view of history, all the more dangerous since the unprepared reader is likely to focus on such passages; they seem concrete and revealing precisely to the extent that they are fantastic. And they breed another kind of confusion in that they are often linked with Heidegger's avowed interest in poetry in later life.

It is well known that although *Sein und Zeit* contained an almost striking lack of literary allusions, Heidegger's subsequent work devotes a great deal of attention to poetical exegesis. Are we to assume that this is a turning away from the rigorous language of philosophy to a freer, vaguer mode of discourse? Or is this similar to Sartre's easy moving back and forth between theory and fiction? It is likely, rather, that poetic language interests Heidegger because it is not less but more rigorous than the philosopher's, having a clearer consciousness of its own interpretative function. Since man is defined as the philosophical animal, the being that interprets itself by means of language, true poets can often go further in man's essential project than the philosophers, not because (as Mr. Barrett says) they are closer to nature, but because they are closer to language. Heidegger's own poetical exegeses are of particular interest to students of literature because they provide a philosophical basis for the act of exegesis itself.

Mr. Barrett's second essay contains many valuable suggestions. His considerations on Heidegger's interpretation of Kant and Plato, on the change (or lack of change) between the early and the late Heidegger, on his conception of history, on his notion of man as a creature of possibilities, on his place in the development of Western philosophy, are all most useful. It is not that Mr. Barrett has been, as it were, "converted" by Heidegger during that twelve-year period, for no truly philosophical work ever demands that kind of response. But we are now precisely at the point where his criticism is of great interest, and one can only hope that he will choose to pursue his dialogue with Heidegger further. What has happened is simply that he now reads him on his actual terms instead of looking for his own problems and constructs—and this is by no means so easy as it may seem.

A new period seems to have started in this country's attitude toward Heidegger. A painstakingly accurate (though not altogether felicitous) English translation of *Sein and Zeit,* by John Macquarrie and Edward Robinson, has recently appeared (New York: Harper & Row, 1962), making Heidegger available for serious study here for the first time. Coupled with Mr. Barrett's eminently sensible essay, it will do much to further a correct understanding of an intellectual movement that has been much maligned, as well as much admired, for the wrong reasons.

# Spacecritics:
# J. Hillis Miller and Joseph Frank (1964)

Ever since the war, American criticism has remained relatively stagnant. This does not mean that no outstanding individual works have been produced, or that no gifted and original newcomers have appeared on the scene. It is from a methodological point of view that no striking innovations have taken place; the assumptions on which literary criticism has been living, in the universities and in the journals, have not been fundamentally challenged. This in itself is not necessarily distressing; it may well be that the developments that occurred earlier, in the thirties, were so rich and varied that it took more than twenty years to refine and exploit them to the full. Yet, a certain paralysis seems to have set in, especially in comparison with recent European effervescence. New Criticism has turned into the fruitful and didactically effective discipline of close reading, replacing philology and conventional literary history as a propaedeutic, but unable itself to lead to larger undertakings. Marxist and psychoanalytic criticism have shown little vitality; although their existence has been known for quite a while, the impact of writers such as Lukács, Benjamin, and more lately Adorno has hardly been felt here. Even works that appear on first reading to open up new perspectives, such as Northrop Frye's *Anatomy of Criticism,* turn out at closer examination to be merely a somewhat artificial synthesis of well-established earlier approaches, a combination of archetypal and formalist criticism less interesting than were, in their days, the essays of T. S. Eliot. The newcomer who tries to find stimulation and guidance in the work of his elders may well be overcome by a feeling of weariness that drives him to other shores or, if he is timid, to an even more remote return to traditional literary history.

To this somewhat gloomy picture, one should not oppose an image of brilliant liveliness and enthusiasm in Europe. That certain recent developments in France and Germany seem endowed with a kind of revolutionary freshness is due, to no small degree, to the incredible inertia that surrounds them; if one speaks of a twenty-year-long stagnation in the United States, one should speak of a century-old stagnation in most European academic institutions. And if one can regret that American criticism has not been sufficiently aware of certain theoretical specula-tions on the Continent, and has shown a somewhat provincial reticence in wanting to remain almost dogmatically empirical, this shortcoming is more than counter-balanced by the profound ignorance and distrust with which Europeans consider what is soundest and most valuable in American approaches to literature.

In fact, it is not true that the main currents of European criticism have not penetrated into this country. Good phenomenological and existential criticism is being taught and written on American campuses; the suppler, highly enlightened historical methods of Curtius and Auerbach have made considerable inroads; Cassirer has curtailed the somewhat fantastic subjectivism that surrounded many American concerns with myth and symbol; Leo Spitzer's influence is felt in more erudite and rigorous attempts at stylistic analysis. But much of this goes on behind the often opaque walls that, in most universities, keep the various departments hermetically sealed off from each other, at least as far as critical methods are con-cerned. In an eloquent passage from his preface to *European Literature and the Latin Middle Ages,* Ernst Robert Curtius complained bitterly about "the special-ized departmentalization of our [German] universities . . . which expresses the intellectual assumptions of the 1850's and which, in 1950, seem as antiquated as the railroad system of a century ago." Things are by no means as rigid in the United States today, but the fact remains that American scholars and critics have often remained oblivious to methods carried out, sometimes very successfully, by their French or German counterparts across the hall—the same being just as true, I hasten to add, in the other direction. As a result, even the closest academic coexistence has not succeeded in breaking down the barriers that separate Ameri-can and European criticism.

It is therefore particularly satisfying to record the publication of two recent es-says that seem to mark a new departure. Both undeniably belong to the field of English and American studies, but in one of them—Hillis Miller's *The Disappear-ance of God* (Cambridge, Mass.: Harvard University Press, 1963)—the filiation with certain contemporary European trends is overt; in the other—Joseph Frank's *The Widening Gyre* (New Brunswick, N.J.: Rutgers University Press, 1963)—the same filiation is more intuitive and, for that reason, all the more striking. This conscious or unconscious resemblance to European models is, in itself, totally unimportant. Nothing could be falser than to suggest that American critics should go to school in European criticism. Something much more fundamental is at stake: each approach, in its own way, has worked toward an understanding of the literary process as such. In so doing, they are now both confronted with problems that have appeared as the result of the increased awareness they have brought about; to the extent that, in both cases, this awareness has brought them closer to the true center of their subject, they are bound to encounter similar questions (though, at first, the similarity may remain hidden by radical differences in terminology and tradition). A more active exchange of ideas—for which perhaps no real need was felt until now—will then inevitably take place. These two books are symptoms of such a tendency, and one can only hope for European equivalents to follow soon.

The methodological novelty of Hillis Miller's and Joseph Frank's books is perhaps best illustrated by trying to define what, for all their differences, they have in common. The differences are clear enough. Mr. Miller's book deals with a group of writers belonging to a well-defined period of English literature and is based on an exhaustive knowledge of their entire literary production, not merely the main texts but also such collateral material as journals, letters, etc. It succeeds in its avowed purpose of being a major contribution, not only offering integrated images of complex figures but placing them within the relevant period. And Mr. Miller doesn't stop there. He attempts a general diagnosis of the spiritual crisis that characterizes the English nineteenth century and relates it to the fundamental movements of Western thought. Joseph Frank's collection of articles offers instead an almost random collection of shorter pieces on twentieth-century authors from Proust and Malraux to Blackmur and John Peale Bishop, rather loosely connected by some of the theoretical points made in the first essay. The methods of analysis are also very different. Miller's approach derives directly from that of his erstwhile senior colleague at Johns Hopkins, Georges Poulet; his book indicates how much of an impact this critic had during the very few years he spent in this country. To point to this influence in no way detracts from Miller's originality, for if Poulet's approach assumes considerable erudition and a "total" knowledge of a work as a whole, it also assumes an irrevocable subjectivity in the relationship between critic and poet and thus postulates the singularity of criticism. One can copy Curtius or Spitzer or even Bachelard, but to copy Poulet is to betray him. Miller never does so; yet the presence of some of Poulet's frames of reference and structural devices, as well as, on the negative side, the avoidance of certain historical and formalist techniques, gives to Miller's book a very distinctive character. Although his manner never becomes mechanical or systematic in the bad sense of the term, it points to its own method with obvious and legitimate pride and wears it, so to speak, for all to behold. As a result, the similarity in approach with European critics of the same generation who have also been influenced by Poulet is very apparent. Nothing in method or in quality sets aside Hillis Miller's book from those of Jean-Pierre Richard, for instance, or Jean Starobinski, or Jean Rousset, except for the irreducible originality that this way of dealing with literature demands. Joseph Frank, on the other hand, remains eclectic and varied, reminiscent at times of Ransom and Tate in a relaxed mood, frequently resorting to straightforward exposition, without even seeming to apply in practice the very interesting speculations on spatial form that are indicated in his first essay.[1] And yet, something similar is taking place in both essays that sets them apart from other current American criticism.

It is best put negatively: neither of these studies is historical or New Critical, and both—each in its own way—deal with the rejection of the concepts of form and of history that have been at the basis of much contemporary work. The great contribution of New Criticism had been to retrieve the autonomy of the literary work and to preserve the delicate equilibrium of its structure from the onslaughts of crudely deterministic systems. This allowed its practitioners to acquire a flexible and subtle exegetic skill, still without equivalence in Europe. But it also had grave drawbacks: by setting up works of literature as if they were a priori given entities susceptible of being described and analyzed in themselves, it made false assumptions about the nature of poetic language. Much was gained by separating the temporal and spatial organization of literary language, as it crystallizes in rhythm and imagery, from the experience of time and space. But even more was lost by ignoring the highly problematic and intentional nature of these entities. Since they are made of invented space and invented time, they cannot possibly be described as if they were natural objects—i.e., objects whose spatial and temporal nature are given and not posited, let alone invented. The hopeless confusion that surrounds the notion of intentionality in Wimsatt and that is carried over in Frye's discussions of the problem, indicate the shortcomings of the underlying ontology. The practical consequence is that New Criticism was never able to rise above the essential but merely preparatory task of local exegesis, and never offered a convincing interpretation of entire works or historical periods.

Seen as reactions to this, Mr. Frank and Mr. Miller's books can indeed be heralded as a renewal. They break out of the impasse of American formalism by rediscovering the constitutive and intentional nature of poetic language, and they both do so, albeit in very different ways, by growing conscious of the true nature of literary space. Instead of the frozen, static space of the New Critical form (or, for that matter, of Northrop Frye's system of archetypes), Joseph Frank sees aesthetic space as the fundamental project of the writer who transforms random experience into the order of a spatial structure. It matters little that Mr. Frank's historical exposition of this process is highly debatable; his references to Lessing and Worringer are very sketchy intellectual history, and his way of equating "spatial form" with twentieth-century literature would demand so many qualifications as to become practically meaningless; the problem goes back at least as far as the early Renaissance. But his basic insight is nonetheless valid. A novelist like Proust—far from imitating or preserving empirical time—modulates, by a system of complex reflective juxtapositions, from a temporal into a spatial realm.[2]

Proust's entire novel can be understood only in terms of this aesthetic project. "Proust's 'pure time,' " says Mr. Frank, "obviously is not time at all—it is perception in a moment of time, that is to say, space." One should add that this space is essentially different from actual space in that it has the richness as well as the frailty of an intentional act.

Mr. Frank develops this insight with great clarity in his essay, and illustrates it effectively in his study of Malraux's books on art history. But the purely literary essays that conclude the work make little use of the methodological possibilities inherent in the concept of spatial form. The fact that they make some prominent New Critics look themselves like part of history, by treating them with proper distance, is the only evidence of Mr. Frank's further critical evolution. Hillis Miller on the other hand, without going into theory, has made similar convictions an integral part of his method.

This method proceeds by the organization of a complete literary work in terms of the underlying intent, though not in the narrow psychological sense that the author somehow expresses or objectifies certain private obsessions. Though individual with each writer, this intent marks all literary creation and thus is susceptible of universal understanding. The development of this intent will not necessarily follow the chronological order in which the works have been written, and the critic has to rearrange the material in terms of his understanding of the whole. It is therefore not true (as is so often claimed), that the rearrangement suggested by critics of this school is arbitrary; like all exegesis, it assumes a prior understanding, but it stands or falls with the quality of that understanding. Such a procedure is altogether sound from a hermeneutic point of view. There is nothing different here from what happens when, in an interpretation of a short poem, we feel entitled to progress not simply line by line but by establishing relationships backward and forward. (Whether the critic has the right, as Miller, J. P. Richard, and others do, to sever without further ado passages from the contexts in which they appear, is a vital matter, but one with which I cannot deal here.) At any rate, as a result of this ordered *découpage,* to use a term recently suggested by Roland Barthes, we are no longer left with a chaotic succession, but with a figure, a trajectory, a network, from which emerges (if the critic is a good critic) the accurate image of the author's undertaking. Image, network, figure, trajectory—all these terms are spatial metaphors, and it should by now be clear that the universal character of the literary intent resides, for Hillis Miller, in its "spatial" nature, exactly in the sense defined by Mr. Frank. Hence the importance of geometrical figures (circles, spirals, triangles, gyres) in this terminology, hence also a frequent interest in parallels with the plastic arts. What Mr. Miller offers us, in his frequently masterful condensations of complete lifeworks, is like a projection on one plane of intricate entities that exist in multiple dimensions. But such a projection is possibly only because this tendency is present in and determined the original work itself. The "existential project" (to quote Barthes again) of the poet or novelist is not just any project, but the specifically aesthetic one of converting time into space. Hillis Miller does not explicitly speak of space; he uses instead a semitheological vocabulary and, as his title indicates, sees Victorian poetry as a dialectic of proximity and distance (which are, of course, spatial terms) in relation to the divine. But this is clearly because, in his view, the Victorian effort to reconquer God becomes for the Victorian writer the aesthetic effort to reconquer space in the closed circularity of the poetic form. Failure (as in the case of Matthew Arnold) or success (as in the case of Emily Brontë) to reconquer this space, coincides with failure or success to reach God—and Hillis Miller is very careful and rigorous in not making this failure or success into an evaluative criterion. One can say that, for Miller, the artist's God is space. The entire method proceeds from there.

Before taking this question a bit further, I want to stress that Hillis Miller's insight allows him to extend our understanding of these writers well beyond the point reached until now. *The Disappearance of God* is without doubt one of the most penetrating and original works of criticism to appear in this country for quite a while. There is much to take issue with, in detail as well as in the general considerations to which I must here confine myself. But in general conception as well as in specific contributions, this is an impressive achievement. Mr. Miller has a sly way of making his argument rebound; at the very moment that one suspects him of going astray, he turns about in his last paragraphs and forces one to reconsider one's judgment. The entire book is organized in that way; after working through an amusing de Quincey, a somewhat lengthy Browning, and a somewhat sketchy Emily Brontë, one is suddenly stirred up by an extremely convincing Arnold, to end up with truly outstanding pages on Hopkins. But when all this is said, I still must confess that I find Mr. Miller's concluding sentence and his introduction (which is in fact a summarizing conclusion and was written last) disappointing, not because of any real slackening in his thought, but because they reveal a flaw in the method.

Both Mr. Frank and Mr. Miller write very disparagingly about history. "By this [spatial] juxtaposition," says Mr. Frank, "history becomes a-historical. . . . What has occurred . . . may be described as the transformation of the historical imagination into myth—an imagination for which historical time does not exist" And in his introduction Mr. Miller argues against historicism with an ardor reminiscent of Nietzsche's second *Unzeitgemäze Betrachtung,* "Of the Use and Misuse of History for Life." This aversion to history seems consistent enough; history being, by definition, temporal, it is bound to appear as the very chaos that the aesthetic consciousness is obliged to put into shape. And historicism, which implies a certain priority of temporal over spatial events, thus naturally becomes the main enemy of the literary sensibility.

Is this not the point where the assumption of spatial forms begins to reveal its

inadequacy, in that it dangerously oversimplifies the dialectical relationship between space and time in the work of art? What is called "time" here is the inauthentic, degraded, evasive temporality of everyday experience. To this is opposed the
cycle of myth and nature beyond time, which can indeed be called spatial. According to Mr. Frank and Mr. Miller, the nineteenth- and twentieth-century
writer strives to be reunited with this kind of space, driven at times by such strong
nostalgia as to call it God. Mr. Miller refers to this as the "heroic attempts to recover immanence in a world of transcendence" and he can go very far in showing
how and why these heroic attempts fail. What he does not see (though he comes
tantalizingly close) is that Arnold certainly, and most likely Hopkins, is ahead of
him in having discovered that, by presumably transcending time toward aesthetic
space, the realm one reaches is no longer spatial at all. Instead, they rediscover
time, although on an altogether different, more fundamental, and, one might say
with some caution, "purer" level—although this purity is not Proust's "pure time,
which is but space." Mr. Miller's flawless essay on Arnold shows very well how
the spatial dialectic of proximity and distance becomes superseded, not just
metaphorically but in actual fact, by a radically different temporal dialectic—but
from which Mr. Miller fails to draw the conclusions that would impair his
method.[3] The matter is even more involved and more instructive in the case of
Hopkins. With admirable consistency, Hillis Miller shows us how Hopkins devised strategies of infinite refinement and delicacy to detect or create an analogy
between the self (which is temporal) and a natural God which he still experiences,
probably under strong Hellenic influence, as spatial; we owe Miller's outstanding
reading of "Pied Beauty" to such an analysis—the only example, by the way, of
a poem read as a whole in the entire book. When these attempts fail, Hopkins
recognizes that the failure is due to his too narrow conception of God as a natural,
spatial entity and, finding support in pre-Socratic thought as well as in non-
Thomist Christian theology, he expands his conception of the divine to include
a mode of being that is no longer natural or analogically related to nature. Mr.
Miller describes this very well, with a perfect awareness of the philosophical and
theological background of this "conversion," and with an equally sensitive ear for
the changes it brings about in Hopkins's poetic language. But the critic's own language is less rigorous at this point, for spatial metaphors such as "interlocking
harmony of nature in Christ" or the naturalistically spatial reading of the word
"pitch" in Poem 65 (at the expense of the much richer "throw-ness" merely indicated in a footnote) contradict Hopkins's own conviction at this stage of his
spiritual growth. By now, the poet no longer locates man's project in relation to
Being, but in his will, consciousness, or, as he calls it *arbitrium*. But this kind
of will no longer exists as the will-toward-space of Joseph Frank's Proustian artist. It has finally separated itself, perhaps with infinite pain, from that illusion.
It now exists in the difficult, unresolved realm of time, where everything is always
still ahead of us, at once threateningly imminent and elusively beyond our grasp.

Mr. Miller rightly puts the exclamation of the dying nun in "The Wreck of the Deutschland," "O Christ, Christ, come quickly," at the center of Hopkins's doctrine of grace, but he fails to stress that this is essentially a temporal outcry. Throughout his crucial last pages on Hopkins, I find Hillis Miller's distinctions between "nature" and "God," "correspondence" and *arbitrium,* "freedom" and "grace" insufficiently thought through; it is quite possible that these distinctions remained blurred in Hopkins himself, but it would have been Mr. Miller's task to unravel them instead of maintaining the ambivalence. His reading of Arnold would have been an excellent model.

Of course, had he done so, his method would have been affected, and he could not have written the same introduction. For if poetic language is not really oriented toward space, but ultimately toward time, then its description can never be as plastically "closed" as Mr. Miller would have it, nor can it be so loftily disengaged from actual exegesis or history. A text that exists in time cannot be projected in a definitive and well-rounded shape. It has to be integrated into a continuous interpretation, for it is itself a fragment in the incessant interpretation of Being that makes up our history. Those so-called spatial and metahistorical visions of literature are in fact still imprisoned in the fallen time from which they try to free themselves. This is all too apparent in the conventional view of literary history to which both authors remain committed; I have already mentioned Mr. Frank's rather useless excursion into eighteenth-century aesthetics. But in Hillis Miller's book, the error is more insidious, for he seems to hold to the naive fiction of a past "where being and value lie in *this* world," and he seems to think of romanticism as the last period in which man set out "to create through his own efforts a marvelous harmony of words which will integrate man, nature and God." Romanticism is precisely the period during which the illusory character of spatial analogies was being revealed, often in a much more radical and consistent manner than in postromantic symbolism and Victorian poetry. I can think of no better challenge for the critical method so competently represented by these two writers, than to apply it to the main figures of the romantic period.

## Notes

1. An interesting encounter with Poulet's work nevertheless occurs in Joseph Frank's case also. In his recently published essay on Proust, *L'Espace proustien* (Paris: Gallimard, 1963), Georges Poulet refers to Mr. Frank's early article on Proust which dates from 1945, and indicates the similarity of their views on Proust.

2. Mr. Frank's description coincides with the most perceptive analyses by French critics, especially Ramon Fernandez, *Messages* (Paris: Gallimard, 1926; translated into English by Montgomery Belgion, New York: Harcourt Brace, 1927), pp. 160 and 210, respectively, quoted by both Frank and Poulet, and G. Poulet, *L'Espace proustien.*

3. I do not think that, in spite of many appearances to the contrary, the same spatial priority can be found in the thought of Georges Poulet, if one considers it in its evolving totality. The determining

aesthetic event, for Poulet, is always the impulse of originating consciousness in what he calls the *cogito,* and the *cogito* is for him entirely temporal. It is significant in that respect that, after the above-mentioned essay on Proust, which seems to coincide so entirely with Joseph Frank's view, he inserts an essay on Bergson that moves in precisely the opposite direction and in which Proust is referred to as a *penseur intermittent.*

# Sartre's Confessions (1964)

Last year, when Jean-Paul Sartre's autobiography began to appear in his review *Les Temps modernes,* it stirred up great expectations among its readers. One had the impression of rediscovering a voice that had spoken with great authority in the past but that had lost some of its power in more recent years. Sartre's influence reached its peak during the occupation, when it was by necessity confined to France, and in the years immediately following the war, when it spread rapidly over the entire world, giving him an international reputation almost unprecedented in French literature; one would perhaps have to go back as far as Voltaire to find a comparable case of a writer whose influence extended well beyond literature, into the realm of philosophical, historical, and political thought. At that time, Sartre was known primarily for his first novel *La Nausée,* two philosophical works (the book on imagination and the treatise *Being and Nothingness),* and the essays of literary criticism now collected in *Situations I.* Somehow, during the years that followed, Sartre lost much of his influence; when one remembers, for instance, the hopes that accompanied the launching of *Les Temps modernes* and compares them with the present day reputation of the review, it becomes obvious that something must have gone wrong along the way. The causes for this relative decline are complex and by no means all in Sartre's disfavor; the rise and fall of his influence constitutes an important and still unfinished episode in the intellectual history of our century. But with the publication of *The Words,* now translated into English by Bernard Frechtman (New York: Braziller, 1964), one had hopes of finding the original Sartre, enriched by new dimensions of maturity and experience. After so many novels, plays, and essays in which he had put his talent in the service of causes and ideologies, he seemed to have found the way back to his own self, recovered the sense of subjectivity that made *La Nausée,* for all its stylistic awkwardness, one of the significant books of the century. Writing directly about himself, apparently unhampered by any considerations beyond those of enlightened self-insight, with a control of language that allows him to be lucid, elegant, constantly interesting, and frequently entertaining, *Les Mots* seemed destined to take its place among the great autobiographies in which French literature, from Montaigne to Proust, has been particularly rich.

In truth, *The Words* as a finished product gives a somewhat different impression. In Bernard Frechtman's competent translation,[1] it is a remarkable book, bound to have a considerable influence on many readers. But it differs much less from Sartre's other postwar work than may seem the case at first sight and, like all his work, it raises controversial issues in a way that no truly autobiographical book can ever do. One can dislike the Montaigne of the *Essays* or the Rousseau of the *Confessions,* but one is not inclined to argue with their views. The quality of intimacy of these books is integral to them, and has nothing to do with rational argument; the seduction emanates from the immediacy of the language itself. In the case of Sartre's memoirs, the main part of the book fails to arouse empathy of this sort, but it does propose a thesis. *The Words* is thus not the kind of book it pretends to be.

Contrary to what the brisk narrative pace would lead one to assume, *The Words* has had a rather complex history. It is a combination of two not altogether compatible texts, written several years apart: the main part, as Sartre himself confirmed in an interview with *Le Monde,* was written in 1954, but he modified and completed his first version for publication in 1964. The first text was a stern self-examining essay that radically rejected literature in the name of political action. Numerous traces of this earlier view remain in the present volume, to such an extent that no reader can be blamed for still interpreting *The Words* along those lines. Since 1954, however, Sartre's concept of political action became a great deal less one-sided, and especially in "Writing," the second part of the book, a much more ambivalent position begins to emerge. The result is rather puzzling, reflecting more bewilderment than assurance and proposing an attitude in which the author himself no longer believes. *The Words* is also a moving document about human inconstancy and the search for self-knowledge—a search carried out, in the best French tradition, in a very public manner. For better or worse, the inner crises of French writers have been the main link with actual experience for many European intellectuals, and Sartre has become Gide's successor, involving a whole generation in the mutations of his inner life.

As far as the earlier part of *The Words* is concerned, it can be called an autobiography in name only. It constitutes in fact another pamphlet among the many pamphlets and studies—the book on Baudelaire, the essay *What Is Literature?* *Saint Genet,* large fragments of the recent essay on method in *Critique de la rai-*

*son dialectique* — in which Sartre has launched a systematic attack on what he assumes to be a bygone, romantic conception of literature. Whether, despite Sartre's repeated but ambiguous assertions to the contrary, this amounts to an attack on literature itself, is a question that cannot be answered quickly. But many passages in *The Words* will provide ammunition for those who think of Sartre as fundamentally an unliterary man, engaged in destroying something of which he understands little, and all the more dangerous since he seems able, at least in this book, to use literary skill as a weapon against the very act of writing.

What strikes one, especially in the first part of the book, is the extraordinary tightness and rigor of composition, qualities that seem oddly incompatible with the autobiographical genre. For whether the successful autobiography is aimed at self-discovery only (as in Montaigne's *Essays*), or whether it is a confession and an apologia in the Augustinian tradition (as in Rousseau's *Confessions*), the narrative always remains open and seemingly erratic. The people, events, and details that occur in an autobiography may well be reported inaccurately, distorted by lapses of memory, or by the passions involved whenever a man speaks about himself, but they occur without plan or interpretation, the way things happen in actual experience. Interpretation follows the event, whereas in fiction the opposite is true.

When Rousseau, in the *Confessions*, describes one of his earliest memories of unspoiled happiness, he feels compelled to mention a series of altogether irrelevant details: a swallow entering the window, a fly on his hand, minute details that have no meaning beyond themselves. They serve no symbolic, psychological, or narrative function whatsoever but force themselves on the author's consciousness and demand to be named because they possess the quality of authenticity: it seems to Rousseau that, at the moment at which they were perceived, he was not separated from them. Their evocation is poignant because this immediacy is lost for the Rousseau who later writes about them; what writing brings back to him is not the thing itself, in all its original authenticity, but an inner echo.

In the opening pages of *The Words*, the description of Charles Schweitzer, Sartre's grandfather, plays a comparable part and offers a revealing contrast to Rousseau's genuinely autobiographical manner. The character is introduced by two anecdotes that, like all family lore, are so neat and stylized as to be totally stilted: in the first, Grandfather Schweitzer is mistaken for God himself, and in the second, he dramatically announces the victory of the Marne in an Arcachon movie house. None of these events is narrated as it might have appeared to the child who witnessed them; we are instead plunged directly into a highly developed social and ideological world. In the paragraphs that follow, Sartre's bearded patriarch incarnates a certain picture of virtue, patriotism, religion, and literature that we recognize all too quickly: Sartre, conscientious teacher that he is, hastens to point out that Schweitzer represents the very image of nineteenth-century bourgeois idealism. The portrait is well composed and subtle; it is conveyed with great economy of means, every detail significant—entirely different from Rousseau's random and subjective impressions. We are shown how, beneath the surface of Schweitzer's virtues, lies in fact the nihilistic terror of a man who has deliberately removed himself from reality. His intellectual achievements and acts of love are in fact a sinister comedy, corrupted at the core by the falseness of his convictions. Sartre's purpose, in composing this picture, is clear enough; he is attacking a form of bourgeois idealism. In order to do so, he creates a type, exactly in the sense in which the Marxist critic Lukács describes Balzac as having created types, composite characters who summarize a sociological and ideological reality. The description of the type seems valid enough, the indictment quite convincing. What is misleading, however (and misleading in a very bourgeois, idealistic way), is to present such a type as if it were an actual experience, to present a composite, organized, symbolic entity as if it were part of one's own childhood. Balzac would never do such a thing; indeed, when he adopts a more intimate form of narration, in *Louis Lambert,* for example, he does so precisely because he wants to stress that his hero is *not* typical. Even if the point of Sartre's description—and this is by no means clear—were to show how the alienation of the bourgeois tends to turn him into a type, it would still be unfair to the person of Charles Schweitzer to rob him to such an extent of his individuality. Nor is Sartre being philosophically sound in thus short-circuiting, by a formal literary trick, the whole complex dialectic that leads from the particular to the typical.

Grouped around the central figure of the grandfather, the other members of the family are shadowy, subdued figures. The death of Sartre's father, which occurred before he had a chance to know him, is treated as the symbolic act that severs the child forever from normal life. The death of one's mother at one's birth (as in Rousseau's case) still leaves, in a sense, the normal cycle of nature intact, but the death of one's father represents the irrevocable break with all established order, a radical alienation from society, from the self, and from reality.

Sartre's brisk narrative, which artfully mixes reminiscence with reflection, contains in fact a full-fledged clinical essay on the experience of alienation. His relationship with his family is based on entirely false premises: cast from his earliest years in the role of a child prodigy, he is never allowed to behave naturally, except at the rare moments when his relatives drop their masks; at such times, grimacing before the mirror, young Sartre cruelly experiences the gap between what he actually is and what he is supposed to be. The apparent solicitude of his family (except perhaps for the mother, who remains a scarcely real figure throughout the book) is never directed at him, but at an idea that suits its fancy. The same is true of his relationships in society: his teachers, friends of his family, and especially other children exist in this book only as opaque, negative forces whose only function is to reject him the moment he stops playing his assigned part. Even the streets of Paris and the gardens of the Luxembourg join in this hostility, and Sartre feels safe only when he hides out on the sixth floor of the apartment building where he lives, high above a world that rejects him. Nor does he find compensation in self-love: he is not so blinded that he does not realize his own ugliness. The image he sees reflected in the look of others is the one he has always been trying to avoid.

The remedy for his predicament can come only from the world of fantasy: from books and, later, from the act of writing. The imagination, then, is here a compensatory faculty that helps to make his alienation bearable. At first, after he has taught himself to read, he merely pretends to enjoy books far beyond his years in order to strengthen the myth of his precocious genius. But he is soon caught at his own game; from the day his mother gives him children's books to read, literature becomes for him an interminable daydream from which it will take him more than forty years to awake. And when his grandfather urges him to write, for reasons that are not more imperative than those that attracted him to reading, he discovers the added satisfaction of inventing his own heroes instead of identifying with those invented by others. Some of the best passages in *The Words* retell the heroic romances in which Jean-Paul is allowed to master all the situations with which he is unable to cope in reality. Later on he discovers that, in the very act of writing, he rises above all human predicaments and becomes the perfect aesthetic entity toward which all literature presumably strives: "Chance has made me a man, generosity would make me a book. I could cast my missive, my mind, in letters of bronze; I could replace the rumblings of my life by irreplaceable inscriptions, my flesh by style, the faint spirals of time by eternity." But as soon as he enters the lycée and at long last makes friends with his contemporaries, the long process of recovery begins; his gradual weaning away from his youthful aberrations will be the subject of the announced sequel to *The Words*.

The case history is so neat that the conclusion forces itself on the reader: Sartre chose the autobiographical form for a book that is, to a large extent, an ideological essay. He did so in part, no doubt, to put the weight of personal experience behind his assertions. But a deeper issue is involved: beyond the ideological attack on late nineteenth-century misconceptions about literature, Sartre obliquely gives expression to his own uncertainties about a more far-reaching problem: the assumption that literature is one of the means by which the lost feeling of authenticity can be recaptured.

On this point, *The Words* is unquestionably ambivalent. A man never feels as negatively about his first love as when he is about to betray it, and when, in 1954, Sartre was discovering real political action (the resistance having been a privileged way of reconciling ideology and action), he was very hard on literature. As it turned out, his marriage to political action soon ended in a separation, if not a divorce, but the first version of *The Words* was clearly written during the brief honeymoon. Literature is called an imposture, a neurosis. He thinks of it as an activity by means of which a man hardens and perpetuates his alienation from society, yet the only possible authenticity left seems to lie in social action;

hence the stress on the isolation of the young Sartre at the time when he was entirely taken up by his literary daydreams. But in the later additions to *The Words,* a considerable shift in tone occurs and Sartre speaks about writing in the voice of a sobered middle-aged man who realizes that he owes everything, including whatever sense of himself he has acquired, to literature, "I write and will keep writing books," he tells us at the end of *The Words.* "Culture doesn't justify, but it's a product of man: he projects himself into it, he recognizes himself in it; that critical mirror alone offers him his image."

This may sound very different from the pompous statements about eternal truth and beauty with which old Schweitzer poisoned little Jean-Paul's vivid imagination. But it remains very close to the assertion made by many great writers in the past when called on to justify their function. Rousseau, Baudelaire, Proust, even Flaubert and Mallarmé—all these "bourgeois" writers could claim this sentence for themselves with much more justification than Sartre can. Something of the same naive pose that inspired the dreams of Sartre's childhood still lingers on in the bold gesture with which he tries to sweep away, once and forever, the problems inherited from our postromantic situation. He uses the very medium preferred by the romantics—the autobiography—to explode their myths. The traditional romantic treatment of childhood presents it as an age of harmony and happiness; hence Sartre's insistence on the contrary aspects of his own experience. The traditional romantic autobiography devotes much attention to nature and setting; both are almost entirely absent from Sartre's memoirs, although he grew up in one of the most beautiful sections of Paris. Isolation and solitude, for the romantics, are often signs of superiority or, at least, have the virtue of increasing the writer's awareness of himself; Sartre emphasizes how his own solitude increased his sense of unreality and distorted his view of life. The romantic attitude toward poetry and literature is, on the whole, a positive one: in Proust, the possibility of literary creation justifies the futility of existence. Sartre is almost fanatically opposed to any form of aestheticism. Even the imagination, the faculty held most sacred by the romantics, is ridiculed in Sartre's descriptions of his juvenile identifications with the heroes of Jules Verne and comic strips. Music, Germany, the confusion between art and religion, sexuality (curiously subdued in *The Words*)—all of the major romantic themes are present here, in order to be debunked.

Is it fair to object to this book merely because the author is tendentious about his own recollections? Yet, by treating so intimate a subject in so abstract a way, Sartre's result is very different from what he intended. Rousseau's *Confessions* support Montaigne's claim that "all men carry within themselves the entire human condition," yet the final impression left by *The Words* is strangely narrow. In the last analysis, we remain with an awareness of a psychological case: a man who now has recourse to ideology (as he formerly did to literature) to cure his own neurosis—and not too successfully at that. True, *The Words* is an ideological essay, but it is also an act of self-therapy that, as such, does not belong to literature. Every reader can make his own diagnosis of what Sartre's psychological difficulties may be; what matters, however, is that every reader will feel compelled, after reading *The Words,* to ask that kind of question. After reading Rousseau, or Proust, or even Flaubert's letters, one may well feel that one knows more about oneself, but has, to some extent, forgotten about the author. This is because these writers have been concerned with interpreting, and not with curing, their own predicament. They have never left the proper domain of literature. Long before Sartre, the romantics discovered that writing was primarily a way to self-knowledge, the "critical mirror" that reflects the writer's true image—although they would probably not have used the analogy of the mirror since the entity to be reflected was as immaterial as the human consciousness. They realized that literature, in spite of its inherent distortions, remains a privileged way of access to reality, not because it reflects this reality, but because it reveals degrees of authenticity that no other activity is able to reach. For them, too, political action and social reform were part of this process of self-knowledge, and they found it far less difficult than we do now to reconcile the demands of history with those of the self. This ability seems to have been lost in the course of the nineteenth century. The romantic historical consciousness declined on the one hand, into the kind of parody of idealism which Sartre's grandfather represents and, on the other hand, into the materialism (dialectical or otherwise) that made many historically oriented minds forget their own idealist origins. Sartre's waverings can be traced back to this misconceived antiromanticism.

The result is an inconclusive book, partly ideological, partly psychological in a narrow sense, antiliterary at times but inconsistently so. Many autobiographies have been written in which the author narrates a conversion, a change of mind that makes him change his ways. But *The Words,* for all its semireligious overtones, does not quite fit this pattern. No effort is made to recapture the quality of an inner crisis. If the Sartre who considers literature to be a "critical mirror" of the self were to write his autobiography, it would be a very different kind of book. *The Words* is not yet the work that gives us back the man who, for a moment, came close to speaking for an entire generation.

## Notes

1. The mixture of colloquialisms with rather self-consciously "poetic" phrasings, already somewhat unsettling in French, becomes rather ludicrous in the English translation. There is no excuse for the fact that the publisher, presumably to magnify the size of the book, has divided the text into separate paragraphs, thus making the continuous narrative look like a collection of aphorisms, while the places where Sartre actually had made divisions are now concealed.

# A Modern Master:
# Jorge Luís Borges (1964)

*Empty eyeballs knew*
*That knowledge increases unreality, that*
*Mirror on mirror mirrored is all the Show.*

—W. B. Yeats

Although he has been writing poems, stories, and critical essays of the highest quality since 1923, the Argentinian writer Jorge Luís Borges is still much better known in Latin America than in the United States. For the translator of John Peale Bishop, Hart Crane, e. e. cummings, William Faulkner, Edgar Lee Masters, Robert Penn Warren, and Wallace Stevens, this neglect is somewhat unfair. There are signs, however, that he is being discovered in this country with some of the same enthusiasm that greeted him in France, where he received major critical attention, and has been very well translated. Several volumes of translations in English have recently appeared, including a fine edition of his most recent book *El hacedor (Dreamtigers*[1], trans. Mildred Bayer and Harold Morland [Austin: University of Texas Press, 1964]) and a new edition of *Labyrinths* (trans. Donald Yates and James E. Irby [New York: New Directions, 1962]), which first appeared in 1962. American and English critics have called him one of the greatest writers alive today, but have not as yet (so far as I know) made substantial contributions to the interpretation of his work. There are good reasons for this delay. Borges is a complex writer, particularly difficult to place. Commentators cast around in vain for suitable points of comparison, and his own avowed literary admirations add to the confusion. Like Kafka and contemporary French existential writers, he is often seen as a moralist, in rebellion against the times. But such an approach is misleading.

It is true that, especially in his earlier works, Borges writes about villains: the collection *History of Infamy* (*Historia universal de la infamia*, 1935) contains an engaging gallery of scoundrels. But Borges does not consider infamy primarily as a moral theme; the stories in no way suggest an indictment of society or of human nature or of destiny. Nor do they suggest the lighthearted view of Gide's Nietzschean hero Lafcadio. Instead, infamy functions here as an aesthetic, formal principle. The fictions literally could not have taken shape but for the presence of villainy at their very heart. Many different worlds are conjured up — cotton plantations along the Mississippi, pirate-infested South Seas, the Wild West, the slums of New York, Japanese courts, the Arabian desert, etc. — all of which would be shapeless without the ordering presence of a villain at the center.

A good illustration can be taken from the imaginary essays on literary subjects that Borges was writing at the same time as the *History of Infamy*. Borrowing the stylistic conventions of scholarly critical writing, the essays read like a combination of Empson, Paulhan, and *PMLA*, except that they are a great deal more succinct and devious. In an essay on the translations of *The Thousand and One Nights*, Borges quotes an impressive list of examples showing how translator after translator mercilessly cut, expanded, distorted, and falsified the original in order to make it conform to his own and his audience's artistic and moral standards. The list, which amounts in fact to a full catalogue of human sins, culminates in the sterling character of Enna Littmann, whose 1923–28 edition is scrupulously exact: "Incapable, like George Washington, of telling a lie, his work reveals nothing but German candor." This translation is vastly inferior, in Borges's eyes, to all others. It lacks the wealth of literary associations that allows the other, villainous translators to give their language depth, suggestiveness, ambiguity — in a word, style. The artist has to wear the mask of the villain in order to create a style.

So far, so good. All of us know that the poet is of the devil's party and that sin makes for better stories than virtue. It takes some effort to prefer *La Nouvelle Héloïse* to *Les Liaisons dangereuses* or, for that matter, to prefer the second part of *La Nouvelle Héloïse* to the first. Borges's theme of infamy could be just another form of *fin de siècle* aestheticism, a late gasp of romantic agony. Or, perhaps worse, he might be writing out of moral despair as an escape from the trappings of style. But such assumptions go against the grain of a writer whose commitment to style remains unshakable; whatever Borges's existential anxieties may be, they have little in common with Sartre's robustly prosaic view of literature, with the earnestness of Camus's moralism, or with the weighty profundity of German existential thought. Rather, they are the consistent expansion of a purely poetic consciousness to its furthest limits.

The stories that make up the bulk of Borges's literary work are not moral fables or parables like Kafka's, to which they are often misleadingly compared, even less attempts at psychological analysis. The least inadequate literary analogy would be with the eighteenth-century *conte philosophique:* their world is the representation, not of an actual experience, but of an intellectual proposition. One does not expect the same kind of psychological insight or the same immediacy of personal experience from *Candide* as from *Madame Bovary,* and Borges should be read with expectations closer to those one brings to Voltaire's tale than to a nineteenth-century novel. He differs, however, from his eighteenth-century antecedents in that the subject of the stories is the creation of style itself; in this Borges is very definitely postromantic and even postsymbolist. His main characters are prototypes for the writer, and his worlds are prototypes for a highly stylized kind of poetry or fiction. For all their variety of tone and setting, the different stories all have a similar point of departure, a similar structure, a similar climax, and a similar outcome; the inner cogency that links these four moments together constitutes Borges's distinctive style, as well as his comment on this style. His stories are about the style in which they are written.

At their center, as I have said, always stands an act of infamy. The first story in *Labyrinths,* "Tlön, Uqbar, Orbis Tertius," describes the totally imaginary world of a fictitious planet; this world is first glimpsed in an encyclopedia that is itself a delinquent reprint of the *Britannica.* In "The Shape of the Sword," an ignominious Irishman who, as it turns out, betrayed the man who saved his life, passes himself off for his own victim in order to tell his story in a more interesting way. In "The Garden of the Forking Paths," the hero is a Chinese who, during World War I, spies on the British mostly for the satisfaction of refined labyrinthine dissimulation. All these crimes are misdeeds like plagiarism, impersonation, espionage, in which someone pretends to be what he is not, substitutes a misleading appearance for his actual being. One of the best of his early stories describes the exploits of the religious impostor Hakim, who hides his face behind a mask of gold. Here the symbolic function of the villainous acts stands out very clearly: Hakim was at first a dyer, that is, someone who presents in bright and beautiful colors what was originally drab and gray. In this, he resembles the artist who confers irresistibly attractive qualities on something that does not necessarily possess them.

The creation of beauty thus begins as an act of duplicity. The writer engenders another self that is his mirrorlike reversal. In this anti-self, the virtues and the vices of the original are curiously distorted and reversed. Borges describes the process poignantly in a later text called "Borges and I" (it appears in *Labyrinths* and also, in a somewhat better translation, in *Dreamtigers*). Although he is aware of the other Borges's "perverse habit of falsifying and exaggerating," he yields more and more to this poetic mask "who shares [his] preferences, but in a vain way that converts them into the attributes of an actor." This act, by which a man loses himself in the image he has created, is to Borges inseparable from poetic greatness. Cervantes achieved it when he invented and became Don Quixote;

Valéry achieved it when he conceived and became Monsieur Teste. The duplicity of the artist, the grandeur as well as the misery of his calling, is a recurrent theme closely linked with the theme of infamy. Perhaps its fullest treatment appears in the story "Pierre Ménard, Author of the Quixote" in *Labyrinths*. The work and life of an imaginary writer are described by a devoted biographer. As the story unfolds, some of the details begin to have a familiar ring; even the phony, mercantile, snobbish Mediterranean atmosphere seems to recall to us an actual person, and when we are told that Ménard published an early sonnet in a magazine called *La Conque*, a reader of Valéry will identify the model without fail. (Several of Valéry's early poems in fact appeared in *La Conque*, which was edited by Pierre Louys, though at a somewhat earlier date than the one given by Borges for Ménard's first publication.) When, a little later, we find out that Ménard is the author of an invective against Paul Valéry, as well as the perpetrator of the shocking stylistic crime of transposing *Le Cimetière marin* into alexandrines (Valéry has always insisted that the very essence of this famous poem resides in the decasyllabic meter), we can no longer doubt that we are dealing with Valéry's anti-self, in other words, Monsieur Teste. Things get a lot more complicated a few paragraphs later, when Ménard embarks on the curious project of reinventing Don Quixote word for word, and by the time Borges treats us to a "close reading" of two identical passages from Don Quixote, one written by Cervantes, the other by Pierre Ménard (who is also Monsieur Teste, who is also Valéry) such a complex set of ironies, parodies, reflections, and issues is at play that no brief commentary can begin to do them justice.

Poetic intervention begins in duplicity, but it does not stop there. For the writer's particular duplicity (the dyer's image in "Hakim") stems from the fact that he presents the invented form as if it possessed the attributes of reality, thus allowing it to be mimetically reproduced, in its turn, in another mirror image that takes the preceding pseudoreality for *its* starting point. He is prompted "by the blasphemous intention of attributing the divine category of *being* to some mere [entities]." Consequently, the duplication grows into a proliferation of successive mirror images. In "Tlön, Uqbar, Orbis Tertius," for example, the plagiarized encyclopedia is itself falsified by someone who adds an entry on the imaginary region Uqbar, presenting it as if it were part of an imaginary country as *his* starting point, another falsifier (who, by the way, is a Southern segregationist millionaire) conjures up, with the assistance of a team of shady experts, a complete encyclopedia of a fictional planet called Tlön—a pseudoreality equal in size to our own real world. This edition will be followed in turn by a revised and even more detailed edition written not in English but in one of the languages of Tlön and entitled *Orbis Tertius*.

All the stories have a similar mirrorlike structure, although the devices vary with diabolical ingenuity. Sometimes, there is only one mirror effect, as when at the end of "The Shape of the Sword," Vincent Moon reveals his true identity as the villain, not the hero, of his own story. But in most of Borges's stories, there are several layers of reflection. In "Theme of the Traitor and the Hero" from *Labyrinths* we have: (1) an actual historic event—a revolutionary leader betrays his confederates and has to be executed: (2) a fictional story about such an occurrence (though in reversed form)—Shakespeare's *Julius Caesar;* (3) an actual historic event that copies the fiction: the execution is carried out according to Shakespeare's plot, to make sure that it will be a good show; (4) the puzzled historian reflecting on the odd alternation of identical fictional and historical events, and deriving a false theory of historical archetypes from them; (5) the smarter historian, Borges (or, rather, his duplicitous antiself), reflecting on the credulous historian and reconstructing the true course of events. In other stories from *Labyrinths,* "The Immortal," "The Zahir," or "Death and the Compass," the complication is pushed so far that it is virtually impossible to describe.

This mirrorlike proliferation constitutes, for Borges, an indication of poetic success. The works of literature he most admires contain this element; he is fascinated by such mirror effects in literature as the Elizabethan play within the play, the character Don Quixote reading *Don Quixote,* Scheherazade beginning one night to retell verbatim the story of *The Thousand and One Nights.* For each mirrored image is stylistically superior to the preceding one, as the dyed cloth is more beautiful than the plain, the distorted translation richer than the original, Ménard's Quixote aesthetically more complex than Cervantes's. By carrying this process to its limits, the poet can achieve ultimate success—an ordered picture of reality that contains the totality of all things, subtly transformed and enriched by the imaginative process that engendered them. The imaginary world of Tlön is only one example of this poetic achievement; it recurs throughout Borges's work and constitutes, in fact, the central, climactic image around which each of the stories is organized. It can be the philosophically coherent set of laws that makes up the mental universe of Tlön, or it can be the fantastic world of a man blessed (as well as doomed) with the frightening gift of total recall, a man "who knows by heart the forms of the southern clouds at dawn on the 30th of April 1882" as well as "the stormy mane of a pony, the changing fire and its innumerable ashes" ("Fumes the Memorious," in *Labyrinths*). It can be vastly expanded, like the infinitely complex labyrinth that is also an endless book in "The Garden of the Forking Paths," or highly compressed, like a certain spot in a certain house from which one can observe the entire universe ("The Aleph"), or a single coin that, however insignificant by itself, contains "universal history and the infinite concatenation of cause and effect" ("The Zahir"). All these points or domains of total vision symbolize the entirely successful and deceiving outcome of the poet's irrepressible urge for order.

The success of these poetic worlds is expressed by their all-inclusive and ordered wholeness. Their deceitful nature is harder to define, but essential to an understanding of Borges. Mirror images are indeed duplications of reality, but they change the temporal nature of this reality in an insidious fashion, even—one might say especially—when the imitation is altogether successful (as in Ménard's Quixote). In actual experience, time appears to us continuous but infinite; this continuity may seem reassuring, since it gives us some feeling of identity, but it is also terrifying, since it drags us irrevocably toward an unknowable future. Our "real" universe is like space: stable but chaotic. If, by an act of the mind comparable to Borges's will to style, we order this chaos, we may well succeed in achieving an order of sorts, but we dissolve the binding, spatial substance that held our chaotic universe together. Instead of an infinite mass of substance, we have a finite number of isolated events incapable of establishing relations among one another. The inhabitants of Borges's totally poetic world of Uqbar "do not conceive that the spatial persists in time. The perception of a cloud of smoke on the horizon and then of the burning field and then of the half-extinguished cigarette that produced the blaze is considered an example of association of ideas." This style in Borges becomes the ordering but dissolving act that transforms the unity of experience into the enumeration of its discontinous parts. Hence his rejection of *style lié* and his preference for what grammarians call parataxis, the mere placing of events side by side, without conjunctions; hence also his definition of his own style as baroque, "the style that deliberately exhausts (or tries to exhaust) all its possibilities."[2] The style is a mirror, but unlike the mirror of the realists that never lets us forget for a moment that it creates what it mimics.

Probably because Borges is such a brilliant writer, his mirror-world is also profoundly, though always ironically, sinister. The shades of terror vary from the criminal gusto of the *History of Infamy* to the darker and shabbier world of the later *Ficciones,* and in *Dreamtigers* the violence is even starker and more somber, closer, I suppose, to the atmosphere of Borges's native Argentina. In the 1935 story, Hakim the impostor proclaimed: "The earth we live on is a mistake, a parody devoid of authority. Mirrors and paternity are abominable things, for they multiply this earth." This statement keeps recurring throughout the later work, but it becomes much more comprehensible there. Without ceasing to be the main metaphor for style, the mirror acquires deadly powers—a motif that runs throughout Western literature but of which Borges's version is particularly rich and complex. In his early work, the mirror of art represented the intention to keep the flow of time from losing itself forever in the shapeless void of infinity. Like the speculations of philosophers, style is an attempt at immortality. But this attempt is bound to fail. To quote one of Borges's favorite books, Sir Thomas Browne's *Hydrothapia, Urne-Buriall* (1658): "There is no antidote against the *Opium* of time, which temporally considereth all things." This is not, as has been said, because Borges's God plays the same trick on the poet that the poet plays on reality; God does not turn out to be the archvillain set to deceive man into an illusion of eternity. The poetic impulse in all its perverse duplicity, belongs to man alone, marks him as essentially human. But God appears on the scene as the power of reality itself, in the form of a death that demonstrates the failure of poetry. This is the deeper reason for the violence that pervades all Borges's stories. God is on the side of chaotic reality and style is powerless to conquer him. His appearance is like the hideous face of Hakim when he loses the shining mask he has been wearing and reveals a face worn away by leprosy. The proliferation of mirrors is all the more terrifying because each new image brings us a step closer to this face.

As Borges grows older and his eyesight gets steadily weaker, this final confrontation throws its darkening shadow over his entire work, without, however, extinguishing the lucidity of his language. For although the last reflection may be the face of God himself, with his appearance the life of poetry comes to an end. The situation is very similar to that of Kierkegaard's aesthetic man, with the difference that Borges refuses to give up his poetic predicament for a leap into faith. This confers a somber glory on the pages of *Dreamtigers,* so different from the shining brillance of the stories in *Labyrinths.* To understand the full complexity of this later mood, one must have followed Borges's enterprise from the start and see it as the unfolding of a poetic destiny. This would require not only the translation into English of Borges's earlier work but also serious critical studies worthy of this great writer.

## Notes

1. Other translations, aside from stories in anthologies or reviews, are to be found in *Ficciones,* ed. Anthony Kerrigan (New York: Grove Press, 1960). Bibliographical indications on the work of Borges, including mention of some critical studies, can be found in the New Directions volume *Labyrinths.* A much more extensive bibliography has just appeared in Paris, in the latest issue of *L'Herne,* which is entirely devoted to Borges (Paris: Lettres modernes).

2. Prologue to the 1954 edition of *Universal History of Infamy,* trans. Norman Thomas di Giovanni (New York: Dutton, 1972).

# Whatever Happened to André Gide? (1965)

It has almost become a commonplace of today's criticism to state that André Gide's work had begun to fade away even before the author's death in 1951. Compared to Proust, to Valéry, to Claudel, and outside France, to Henry James, Joyce, and Thomas Mann, he seems hardly to be part of the contemporary literary consciousness. An easy contrast can be drawn between the relative indifference that now surrounds his work and the passionate intensity with which the generation of Europeans born before 1920 used to follow his every word, considering his private opinions a matter of general concern. During the thirties, he was without doubt the most public literary figure in France, much more so than Malraux, Camus, and Sartre, for all their overt political activity, ever were. Yet his political attitudes were highly inconsistent: they ranged from his adhesion to the ultraright-wing *Action Française* during the First World War to his brief but full commitment to communism in the thirties, ending with a rather withdrawn position of nonparticipation during the Second World War. None of these changes was ever justified objectively: his *Return from the USSR* (a book that sold well over 100,000 copies at the time) certainly failed to show any striking insight into political realities. Gide's authority rested entirely on the power of his personality as it was revealed in a literary work almost exclusively concerned with psychological and aesthetic matters. Why then was the extraliterary, political influence of so socially irresponsible a figure so strong?

Wallace Fowlie's sympathetic and delicate general study of Gide (*André Gide: His Life and Work* [New York: Macmillan, 1965]) does not give us much assistance in confronting this question. It is written with a slightly defensive affection for its subject that is not typical of the feeling toward Gide prevalent today. The surprising mildness in Mr. Fowlie's bland essay is characteristic of several books in which some of the most unsettling figures of the recent literary past — such as Nietzsche or Yeats or Stefan George — have been reduced to a reassuring common denominator. In this view, Gide is interpreted as "the man who won out over guilt and neurosis through the discipline of art." And the historical scheme suggested by Mr. Fowlie also recurs frequently in interpreters of the same temper: Gide was strongly influenced, in his early years, by the more extreme forms of *fin de siècle* nihilism — in his case, by Mallarmé, Wilde, and Nietzsche — but he triumphed over the negative forces of his predecessors by a gradual humanization of his aestheticism. He retained his absolute commitment to art but overcame the violence inherent in an extreme aesthetic position by restoring to it the human dimensions lacking in his masters. The resulting picture may be a comforting one, but it bears little relation to the realities of twentieth-century thought and its antecedents.

Jean-Paul Sartre showed a much shrewder understanding of Gide's role when, on the occasion of his death, he spoke of the general relief that greeted the departure from this earth of someone who had managed to remain a constant irritant. Sartre's remark was made in praise of Gide and goes a long way toward explaining the relative neglect in which he has fallen. The lives of certain writers become mythologized because they can be easily turned into examples behind which we hide our own shortcomings. Rimbaud's decision to stop writing, for example, provides a fine pretext to those who were never able even to begin; Mallarmé's heroic renunciation of a certain form of personal happiness excuses those unable to achieve it; Proust's introspective refinement provides an incentive for self-indulgent alienation, the introverted Byronism of the twentieth century. But Gide offers little opportunity for such self-deceptions. Whenever he was tempted to make uncritical assertions, he pulled the rug out from under them. On the one occasion, in *Corydon,* where he rationalizes his personal aberrations into self-justifying generalities, his bad faith is so blatant that he can hardly be taken seriously. Most of the time, his irony and self-criticism remain fully operative. The constant self-analysis that underlies the autobiographical works, the *Journal,* and most of the novels, is always aimed at dispelling false constructs of the self that would allow him to strike seductive but artificial poses. It is perhaps not a very good sign for our own time that he now receives so little attention. To a period presumably so concerned with authenticity, so eager to root out what it considers false in its nineteenth-century, idealistic heritage, it would seem that Gide's work could be particularly valuable. Difficult and diffuse it certainly is, for it is not easy to group the diverse elements of his literary production into a coherent structure. It is also, for all its diversity, a curiously narrow work. Yet within the limited area it stakes out for itself, it is genuinely revealing.

Mr. Fowlie may be guilty, albeit with the best of intentions, of taking the sting out of Gide's subversiveness. Nevertheless, especially toward the end of the book, he shows a fine understanding of his subject. The following statement, for instance, is extremely perceptive about the main characteristic of Gide's personality. Speaking of the journal that Gide kept throughout his lifetime, Mr. Fowlie writes:

> The *Journal* is not a mirror. Gide was not Narcissus as he wrote it. He looks at himself in order to be seen by others. . . . The motivation of Gide's writing is to make a place for himself in the society of mankind.

One could not put it more accurately or more succinctly. Mr. Fowlie's book proves how difficult it is to keep literary and social concerns apart in this case; in a study primarily aimed at the work, he has had to include chapters that deal with Gide's attitudes toward his family, institutionalized religion, and politics. Indeed, perhaps the most enlightening study of André Gide is not a literary study at all, but an account of Gide's involvements with his father, his mother, and his wife during the first part of his life; the author, Jean Delay,[1] is a clinical psychologist. Gide elicits this kind of approach because of his natural bent toward other human beings and society.

In the long tradition of introverted, self-reflective meditation that is so prevalent in romantic and postromantic writing, the withdrawal into the self has always been a moment in which the writer moves away from others, toward a contemplation of his own consciousness as it confronts entities that are precisely not other human beings: the activity of the mind in relation to nature (sensation), in relation to time (memory), and to space (imagination). Even in realistic writers such as Flaubert or Proust or Thomas Mann, the deepening and generalizing power of the novels is always founded on the inwardness, the self-contemplation of the character; hence the importance of "poetic," i.e., metaphorical and symbolical modes of language more or less harmoniously combined with realistic detail. With few exceptions (the early *Nourritures terrestres* being the most striking one) nothing similar happens in Gide. He is not concerned with the moment of complete inner self-realization, but rather with the moment at which he reaches out for other people, in a gesture prompted by a combination of curiosity and interest. Drama in his life as well as in his work originates in conflicts between the incompatible responses awakened by his involvements with other people. He has himself interpreted his entire destiny as determined by his relationship with his wife, not however in the sense that an authentic relationship would have determined his outlook, but in the very different sense that this relationship, by its very inadequacy, always drew him outside of himself, oriented him forever toward other people and society and made his entire experience an interpersonal one.

From the point of view of the writer, this all-consuming curiosity directed toward other human beings is by no means a weakness. It stands the novelist in good stead by giving him the kind of energy that propels him through a variety of social worlds without getting mired down in the heavy boredom that tormented Flaubert—a boredom reflecting his boredom at having to concern himself with human beings so much less rewarding than his own inner self. Some of Stendhal's gaiety is certainly present in *The Counterfeiters* and *Lafcadio's Adventures,* the sheer buoyancy with which the novelist discovers the unpredictable variety of human personality. Moreover, the same inclination endows the writer with a particularly acute moral sense. Moral problems are best dramatized by conflicts between people. Gide's writing illustrate this very clearly: from *Strait Is the Gate* and *The Pastoral Symphony* to *Thésée,* they always describe the turmoils created in a society by a certain moral stance or moral crisis. Gide has often been classified with the traditional French moralists; his ancestors are La Bruyère, La Rouchefoucauld, and Chamfort, critics of man in society, rather than Montaigne, whose self-examination was not primarily a moral one, precisely because his interest lay in his subjective self rather than in the self in relation to others.

It is in these terms that one should understand Gide's political impact; although his novels, unlike Stendhal's, are acted out on a very narrow social stage, they nevertheless are, in a very real sense, politically oriented, concerned as they are with individuals grouped according to their relations with others. It matters little how sizable or representative the group happens to be; it can be a family as in the *Pastoral Symphony* or even a couple as in *The Immoralist:* so long as the relationship is governed by the desire "to make a place for oneself in the society of mankind" it potentially has a political significance. Sociological details, matters of money, property, or class distinction, are always as carefully documented in Gide's novels as they are in Henry James's, though less obtrusively. Gide did not have to contradict any fundamental part of himself when he moved into the political sphere, a move for which his particular bent of mind predestined him. Already in his earliest letters to his mother, we find him instinctively explaining his behavior in terms of social morality.

Neither did he have to betray his aesthetic commitments when transposing them into social attitudes. The early satire of aestheticism, *Marshlands,* of which the English translation has just been reissued (*Marshlands and Prometheus Misbound,* trans. George D. Painter [New York: McGraw-Hill, 1953]), illustrates this in a rewarding way, for the book is more amusing and cuts deeper than some of Gide's later satires. The hero, who bears the Virgilian name of Tityre, is a totally committed aesthete whose only purpose in life is the writing of a rather unpromising but rarefied literary text entitled "Marshlands." The work is to express his very determination to pursue his artistic calling in all its barren rigor. The project itself is never undermined or ridiculed from the inside; the passages from the book in progress that are being quoted are not in themselves ludicrous or inept. The satire is carried out in a different way, by showing how Tityre behaves in his natural social milieu. We see him being outdone by a more virile rival, watch him getting entangled in the amenities of literary parties and weekend escapades.

The portrait that emerges resembles Monsieur Hulot rather than Mallarmé. Transposed into a social setting, the aesthete reveals a ludicrous aspect that remains hidden as long as he remains confined to his own self. Here again, Gide transfers an inward experience to a social level and thus allows us to judge from a moral (and potentially political) point of view. For the early Gide—and this remained true throughout his career—no real conflict exists between an aesthetic and a moral commitment. Both are united by the same overriding attraction toward other people or society. In one of his earliest works, the *Treatise of Narcissus* dedicated to Paul Valéry, he writes:

> The rules of morality and of aesthetics are the same: works that do not express themselves are useless and, by the same token, bad. Men who do not express themselves are useless and evil. . . . All things must be made manifest, be brought into the open, even the most harmful.

In this text, as always in Gide, "to make manifest" means: to bring into the open "in order," to use again Mr. Fowlie's words, "to be seen by others."

Such a unified treatment of art, society, and morality would be an admirable achievement, even if it had to occur at the expense of a certain poetic inwardness. But unfortunately things are not that simple. In trying to expose a certain form of bad faith, one frequently gets trapped into an even more insidious duplicity; the path of "sincerity" is full of pitfalls. Gide's moral attack on aestheticism is most effective: Tityre is worthy of taking his place next to Valéry's Monsieur Teste, Mann's Aschenbach, and Stefan George's Algabal, among the more sinister embodiments of aestheticism. But, after this, Gide's evolution was much less clear: his later heroes, the Ménalque of *The Immoralist,* the Edouard of *The Counterfeiters,* the Thésée that appears in his last book, are a great deal more ambiguous.

The ambiguity stems from a hidden confusion, in Gide's mind, between the other human being considered as a conscious, moral person and as an object for erotic gratification. A predominantly erotic theme runs throughout the work, but the treatment of this theme is double-faced, certainly not because Gide is secretive about his own sexuality, but for much more fundamental reasons. The duplicity is best revealed in what remains Gide's most important work: *Les Nourritures terrestres.*

*Les Nourritures* sounds at first like a book of social revolt, a rejection of the authority vested in families and institutions. Written as a pseudojournal, with a very planned absence of plan, in a lyrical and fervent language reminiscent of Zarathustra's quieter moods, *Les Nourritures terrestres* seeks to liberate the self from all confinements, including those of society. "Families, I hate you"; this Rimbaud-like battle cry sends the writer out on voyages, some actual, some imaginary, recorded in moments of inner fulfilment. The theme of liberating rebellion, the exaltation of restlessness—"the only rest I long for is that of sleep or of death"—the choice of the moment over duration, of ever-reawakening desire over wisdom, all this clearly ranks *Les Nourritures terrestres* with other manifestations of a similar revolt, like André Breton's surrealist manifestos. As such, the book contains a potentially explosive political power. For this rebellion was, of course, a historically dated rebellion against a historically dated society and it constituted a threat against this society. For the young bourgeois at the beginning of the century, Gide's call often sounded like a call to political subversion; it is no surprise to find that the heroes of the novels written by Gide's close friend Roger Marin du Gard carry in their pockets. *Les Nourritures terrestres* next to leaflets exhorting soldiers of the First World War to fraternize with the enemy.

But Gide's *Nourritures* also has another dimension. Within a well-established tradition, his appeal to a liberation of the self from society is stated in erotic language; Montaigne and Diderot had used sexuality in the same manner as a socially subversive symbol. Sexuality can well be experienced as a bridge toward another, as a way to reenter the social world from which one has retreated in moral indignation. But this is not what happens in *Les Nourritures terrestres*. Sexuality is present on every page, to the point of making the book a treatise on paneroticism. Gide constantly lets his language linger over sensations that are a mixture of ardor and satiation, of oasis and desert, containing the very pattern of sexual desire. The descriptions of landscapes, of places, of impressions that make up this poeticized journal always fall in an erotic rhythm. The sexuality, however, is never oriented toward other human beings. It is a return toward the inwardness of the self, a way of using the outside world—including others—to explore and refine the awareness Gide has of his own selfhood.

Gide's autoeroticism thus reintroduces, somewhat surreptitiously, the antisocial, inhumane element present in aestheticism, the negative side of a coin whose positive side is Mallarmé's self-reflection. Under the guise of rebellion, Gide in fact urges us to rediscover our authentic inner self in an erotic fervor even more intensely inward than Mallarmé's concentration on the poetic resources of language. "Be faithful only to what you feel to be present in yourself and nowhere else": in this exhortation, one hears the sound of the eternal voice calling man back to his personal center, to the inner world of his private thoughts and sensations. Bourgeois society is being rejected here not because it is morally wrong, but because it is restrictively moral. The rebellious forces of the absolute self triumph in the myth of Eros, the same forces in fact that had helped shape the aestheticism of which the Gide of the *Nourritures terrestres* was showing himself to be a late disciple after all.

*Les Nourritures terrestres* is not, however, altogether typical of Gide's work, although one cannot begin to understand him without it. In Gide's insistence, in the concluding section, that the reader should throw the book away, there is a revealing sense of discomfort, just as there is a strong element of disavowal in the later preface to the second edition (1927). Just as *Marshlands* transferred the early aestheticism to a social setting, Gide's subsequent work becomes a transposition of the values expressed in *Les Nourritures terrestres* to the setting of moral conflict of *The Immoralist, Strait Is the Gate,* and the later work. Faithful to Gide's all-determining need to make himself "manifest" to others, he reintroduces moral and potentially political elements. But whereas, in the case of *Marshlands,* the result was a rejection of aestheticism, no such criticism of the *Nourritures* is implied in the later work. Except for the ambiguous reservations just alluded to the protagonist of the *Nourritures* remains an exemplary figure.

The result is very powerfully and dangerously subversive, in a much more insidious way than the straightforward rebellion of *Fruits of the Earth.* In tone and texture, the work seems to possess all the attributes of moral and social responsibility, yet it is founded on the asserted priority of the self as Eros, which amounts in fact to a radical rejection of others as a moral anti-self. One could very well conceive of a literary work that would remain faithful to such a priority of the self as Eros: Rilke and, in an ironic mode, Valéry, are examples of such an attitude. But they remain removed from concrete social concerns and return to moral issues only at the end of long explorations that have to do with the nature of poetic language rather than with interpersonal relations. Or one could conceive of works that are frankly nonpoetic in their emphasis on political morality, as in the novels of Malraux and Sartre. Gide's combination of both attitudes, however, is not a synthesis but a disguise: a political statement in literary clothing, or, perhaps more accurately, a somewhat hesitant poetic message that tries to gain a good conscience by becoming socially oriented. Before condemning Gide for this, one should remember how characteristic this ambivalence is for our time: the attempts to reconcile Marx and Freud are most significant in this respect. Gide's work remains so important for us just because it reveals some of the difficulties involved in thus trying to reconcile the needs of the self with those of society.

## Notes

1. Jean Delay, *La Jeunesse d'André Gide* (Paris: Gallimard, 1957). Two volumes exist in an abridged English edition.

# What Is Modern? (1965)

The full title of the substantial and ambitious anthology, *The Modern Tradition: Backgrounds of Modern Literature,* edited by Richard Ellman and Charles Feidelson, Jr. (New York: Oxford University Press, 1965), twice uses the word "modern," thus stressing modernity as the key concept that binds together a miscellaneous collection of literary and philosophical essays dating from the second half of the eighteenth century up to 1960. On the other hand, the title also contains two words that, at first sight, seem to contradict this claim: "tradition" and "backgrounds." The various appeals for modernity recurrent throughout the nineteenth and the twentieth century very deliberately set out to demolish tradition and to replace the literary past by actual experience; when Rimbaud, for instance, speaks of the need to be "absolutely modern," he means that we should free ourselves precisely from those ideas that are likely to be found in anthologies and strike out instead on our own. That such new departures are often short-lived or illusory should not blind us to the fact that they do nevertheless occur. It is all too easy to point to apparent repetitions in the history of the human mind for proof that there is nothing new under the sun, but this can only be done by confusing tradition with the commonplace and by mistaking the stagnation of one's own mind for the stagnation of history.

The editors of this anthology certainly cannot be accused of slackening the élan of modernity by a stifling approach to tradition. In their preface, they make it very clear that they are perfectly aware of the paradox involved in the phrase "modern tradition." Although it is in the nature of modernity to be without precedent, the phenomenon of modernity itself is by no means unique: "modern" movements,

137

each with a distinctive content of their own, occur again and again, and become the very articulations of history. It is characteristic of periods that live off the capital accumulated by their predecessors, so to speak, that they would think of their era as the only one worthy of being called truly modern. The thirties and the forties undoubtedly were such a modernistic period: following a generation of considerable inventive power, the writers of the period were bound to mythologize the preceding generation into the absolute embodiment of modernity and to scorn whatever preceded it as hopelessly out-of-date. Not so long ago one could still find considerable intellectual satisfaction in dismissing Victorian and romantic ideas as old-fashioned. Things have changed over the last ten years; none of the younger literary critics would consider himself the least bit disgraced by writing about, say, Wordsworth or Matthew Arnold (or even Gray and Pope) rather than about Stevens or Valéry—nor would he feel that he is doing something essentially different, or dealing with altogether different problems, when he is interpreting a late eighteenth-century rather than a contemporary poet. This probably indicates that our own period—unlike the thirties and the forties—is in the process of developing its own modernity, since it is again able to interpret the previous "moderns" as part of a historical process—an undertaking that is entirely different from denying them genuine modernity in the name of a conservative theory of tradition. Any attempt to expand our historical awareness in this manner is itself both modern and useful, and in this respect, this anthology is an admirable undertaking. Nor could one have wished for more competent and informed editors than Professor Ellmann and Professor Feidelson, both in their own right distinguished interpreters of important sections of modern literature.

Begun under such favorable auspices, it is somewhat disappointing to find the anthology representing so little of the emerging modernity that it strives to define. This may be due, in part, to the fact that the editors themselves are still partly laboring under the fallacious prewar illusion of modernism. It is not altogether clear, on the basis of the principles that command the selection and organization of the texts, whether the term modern still refers to the literature of Yeats, Joyce, Eliot, Lawrence, Proust, Valéry, Gide, Mann, Rilke, and Kafka, or whether it refers to a later period for which these authors are already part of history. More than half of the anthology seems to conform to the first definition. It offers theoretical background material useful for a study of early twentieth-century literature; some of the main documents of nineteenth-century aestheticism (Wilde, Pater, etc.); a few selections on realism, rounded off by some representative texts from Schopenhauer, Nietzsche, Bergson, and Croce. Little attempt is made to depart from the obvious in presenting a period that has been so abundantly studied and documented elsewhere. But some other selections, as well as the emphasis on certain themes (such as existential theories of consciousness, neorealist and neo-Marxist writing, negative theologies, etc.) seem to point toward later and different developments of Western thought and literature. This tends to suggest that the modernism of the first quarter of the twentieth century should be seen in a wider perspective, starting, for instance, not with the aestheticism of 1880 but earlier, with romanticism, and ending, not with Yeats-Valéry-Rilke or Proust-Joyce-Mann, but with writing that does not belong to the heritage of symbolism. The editors obviously made a serious effort in that direction, since they included passages from Kant, Vico, Rousseau, Blake, and Wordsworth as well as from Robbe-Grillet, Dubuffet, and Sartre. Nevertheless, they fail to convey a convincing picture of the larger movement that contains the modernism of the early twentieth century as a moment in its growth, and not as its ultimate outcome. They missed the opportunity of clarifying the relationship between the rather specialized aesthetics of symbolism and realism, and the broader intellectual current that gives unity to the two-hundred-year time span covered in the anthology. If "modern literature" is to be defined as romantic and postromantic rather than as symbolist and postsymbolist—and this seems to be the challenging assumption on which this book is based—then the best texts of the period should be linked by a coherent itinerary, a meaningful network of themes. That the editors suggest such a network is indicated by the headings under which they group their selections, and by their preference for a thematic rather than a chronological organization of the material. Yet it is by no means certain that their scheme succeeds in capturing the originality and inventiveness of the modern mind.

Precisely because they have an appearance of impersonality about them, encyclopedias or anthologies can be among the most subjective of documents. In this case, a careful effort was made to present a balanced picture and to offer a wide range of ideological trends (reaching from Marx and Engels to T. E. Hulme) that would allow the reader to draw his own conclusions. Nevertheless, a general pattern of interpretation soon becomes apparent, not only because the editors reflect a definite point of view—that of an enlightened American liberalism—but as a result of the ideological weight of the texts themselves. This pattern is somewhat misleading: it overstresses certain aspects of contemporary thought at the expense of other, perhaps more decisive ones. I am referring, for instance, to the deliberate bias against all analytic modes of thought, to the tendency to overrate currents of irrationalism, and to the somewhat confusing mood of pseudoexistential nihilism combined with a messianic desire for redemption that characterizes many of the selections. When one meets a similar emphasis in such writers as Erich Heller or Karl Löwith, then this appears to be the altogether legitimate and interesting expression of a certain point of view. But when it is applied to some of the greatest names of modern literature and philosophy, the impression can be dangerously misleading. Not only in their choice of the main currents, but in the manner in which these trends are presented, the editors' judgment is often open to question.

This may well be the result of the natural tendency of anthologists to prefer very general, programmatic texts that sound like manifestos to more detailed or methodologically oriented passages. If one were compiling an anthology of the eighteenth century, it would not be too difficult to find essays that combine a wide programmatic interest with concreteness of particular detail; that century still possessed a sense of the unity between the universal and the specific that enabled it to be of general interest even about the most specialized of topics. But in the nineteenth and twentieth centuries, the relationship between part and whole, between text and context, became a great deal more complex. The tendency to generalize has not, of course, disappeared, but it has become increasingly dependent on the minutiae of highly detailed, technical, and rigorous analyses that cannot be separated from the general statements. Read by themselves, the generalities are often vague and pompous, and they take on meaning only within contexts that are often ambiguous or ironic, and always very closely particularized. This is true of philosophers as well as of poets and novelists. No philosopher, for instance, can make a greater claim for generality than Hegel; yet the philosophical power of Hegel's thought can never be extracted from isolated, summarizing statements, but rather from the careful examination of very tightly articulated dialectical movements. Nietzsche tends toward aphoristic formulations, but as every reader who has tried to make sense of his entire work has found, these assertions are qualified by a network of contradictory counterstatements that demand close contextual study on the part of the intepreter. Poets like Mallarmé or Valéry seem to offer us, in their prose essays, a running commentary that clarifies what may remain hidden in the refined diction of their poems — but, on closer examination, the relationship between the critical essays and the poetry turns out to be so involved that it becomes impossible to consider one part of the work independently of the other. The same is true of a poet like Yeats, whose prose works simply cannot be taken at face value, since they are part of an intricate creative process directed primarily toward the elaboration of the poems. One can very well read Voltaire's historical works in their own right, without having to concern oneself with his tragedies or poems, but anyone who reads Yeats's historical speculations in *A Vision* out of the contexts of Yeats's poetic work will fail to do justice to world history as well as to W. B. Yeats. Professors Ellmann and Feidelson would certainly grant this about particular writers, yet in their selections they have inevitably reached for the most sweeping, oracular statement possible, and often presented it in excerpts so truncated and fragmentary that the uninitiated reader, unassisted by notes or comments, is likely to be led astray.

Let us take the case of so well known a writer as Jean-Paul Sartre, who is represented by no less than five selections. Whatever opinion one may have of Sartre's thought, his importance in the shaping of the modern temper certainly more than justifies his presence here. His influence stems from his ability to combine the technical treatment of specific philosophical problems, in such books as *Being and Nothingness,* the *Critique of Dialectical Reason,* and the early work on imagination, with the very accessible version of related problems in drama and fiction. This has made him into something more than a powerful popularizer of ideas that did not always originate with him; he also gives the impression that he is able to put these ideas into practice, and although this impression is in part an illusion, the effectiveness of his action nevertheless stems from an unusual combination of theory and praxis. At his best Sartre, therefore, is either purely theoretical or altogether literary: in the philosophical work or in novels like *Nausea, The Wall,* or the recent autobiography *The Words.* In between lies the generalizing, preaching, boring Sartre who freezes himself into static formulations that his nimble mind fortunately will not allow him to maintain. A text such as *Existentialism and Humanism,* a kind of campaign speech that used to be read in many European cities after the war, is all too typical in this respect—and this is precisely the text from which the editors have taken all the extracts for their anthology. In this manner, they help to spread the mistaken conception of existentialism as a dogmatic but irrational stance, a dramatic stoicism invented to help cope with situations of crisis and derived from the darker insights of Dostoevsky or Kafka. In fact, the sources of existential thought, including Sartre's, are not literary; the relationship of existentialism to literature is problematic and varies considerably from writer to writer; the importance of the movement is primarily methodological and heuristic, far removed from general definitions or value theories, and tied to a specialized and not very felicitous terminology. One is not likely to discover these facts from the chapter on existentialism in *The Modern Tradition.* Not a single excerpt illustrates the phenomenological rigor or the critical acumen of good existential writing; the two short excerpts from Heidegger, almost completely meaningless out of context, and also taken from the least suitable of texts, do not remedy this situation in the least. We are offered some vague talk about authenticity but very little authentic language, in an area of modern thought that has at least some to offer.

Or one could take the excerpt from Lukács on realism as another example. It showed initiative on the part of the editors to include a writer who is still little known in the United States and who has exercised a strong influence on recent European criticism of fiction. Again, Lukács's writing, especially during his Marxist phase, is frequently stilted and doctrinaire when he indulges in generalities, but he can show penetrating insight in matters of detail. I remember Etiemble's remark that what first impressed him about Lukács was not some general theory but the manner in which the critic compared the horse-race scenes in *Anna Karenina* and *Nana.* Ellmann and Feidelson (alas!) offer us very few horse races, but the dreariest of introductions to Lukács's rather gray book on realism that is not likely to fire any student's curiosity. Yet, if one wanted to include some sociologically oriented writings on literature, it would not have been difficult to find more exciting passages, in Lukács himself, or in Walter Benjamin's so truly "modern" essay "The Work of Art in the Era of Technical Reproduction," or in Herbert Marcuse or Adorno. In general, one regrets that the editors have included so few samples of literary criticism or specific writings about literature. We hear a lot about art as ethics, as mission, as religion, as mysticism; a lot about history, the unconscious, Being, dread, guilt, God, and faith. But we lose sight of the all-important point that nineteenth- and twentieth-century literature is primarily a reflection on literature itself that can provide a great deal of lucid insight into the nature of literary language. Furthermore the reports of writers on their own work are not always or necessarily the most illuminating. Keats's or Flaubert's letters, Baudelaire's *Salons* or Mallarmé's *Divagations,* may well reveal a degree of consciousness close to that found in their purely literary work, but this is certainly less so for Stevens, Yeats, Eliot, or Rilke, while the critical essays of a writer like Valéry lag far behind his poetry in reflective penetration. Granted that there was perhaps little point in reprinting some of the better-known and easily available essays by American critics, nevertheless a text like the last chapter of Auerbach's *Mimesis,* or an essay by E. R. Curtius on European literature, would perhaps have done more to illuminate the modern literary consciousness than theoretical prose written by the poets themselves. The editors, after all, did include some actual critics, such as I. A. Richards and Lukács, but why did they stop there? With their method of selection, only those writers who have expressed themselves discursively about their art are represented, and this is bound to result in an incomplete and lopsided picture. Here again, one has the feeling that a great deal of repetition and dispersion could have been avoided by resorting to more particularized statements. And a more accurate picture of the modern mind would certainly have emerged.

For it is the persistent attempt of a consciousness to reach an understanding of itself that characterizes modern thought at its best, whether it be literary or not. The very tension resulting from this effort leads to certain aberrations that the editors do not entirely avoid. As a consciousness develops and progresses, it is bound to encounter an increasing resistance to its own growth. The more it understands its own progression, the more difficult or even painful this progression becomes. Naturally enough, this increased resistance leads to a nostalgic regret for earlier, less advanced stages of self-awareness that may seem surrounded by an aura of innocent simplicity. Hence the tendency, in periods of acute self-consciousness, to regress toward more primitive levels of experience and to idealize them into something very different from what they actually are. All modern writers and thinkers have moments during which they give in to such regressive tendencies, especially when they feel tempted to undertake vast, general syntheses. The editors of this anthology seem to have a marked preference for moments of this kind. Why for instance, as one example among many, include without warning the highly untypical and juvenile essay of Mallarmé here entitled "Art as Aristocratic Mastery" (*L'Art pour tous*), written when Mallarmé was less than twenty years old, and likely to strengthen the worst oversimplifications about the moral irresponsibility of aestheticism? Each section (as well as the book as a whole) suggests that although the ideas of the "modern" period were first articulated by rational means, this attempt was soon stifled and fell back into primitivism: from the philosophy of history one regresses to the crudeness of the nearly inarticulate (the section on history begins with Hegel and ends with Henry Miller!); from history one moves on to the unconscious, and from the unconscious to myth. In the most important section of the work, entitled "Self-Consciousness," we reach the truly central insight of modernity, for here the selections are intended to show how self-understanding can lay bare the divided structures of consciousness: irony, alienation, conflict of appearance and being, etc. The choice of texts, at this point, is altogether sound (despite the inadequacy of Baillie's translation of Hegel's famous passage on the unhappy consciousness, where the twenty-four paragraphs of this tightly organized argument are arbitrarily truncated to the first four). But when one moves on to Dostoevsky's *Notes from Underground* and to the pages on overcoming the self in Zarathustra, one is inevitably led to believe that the attempt at self-understanding begun in the eighteenth century and pursued into the first half of the nineteenth ended in a hopeless impasse and that violent, apocalyptic modes of thought had to take over. The liberating effect of Nietzsche's and Dostoevsky's rebellion is thus placed in the wrong light. And when this section leads into the chapter on existence, presented as an irrational cult of the absurd, and then concludes with a section on faith, one has indeed been well prepared to accept Maritain's denunciation of "The Errors of Modern Rationalism," which falsely presents Descartes and Rousseau as the initiators of an anthropocentric naturalism. Indeed, instead of *The Modern Tradition*, the title for this work could well have been taken from one of Lukács's bleakest and most doctrinaire works about the same historical period, *The Destruction of Reason* (*Die Zerstörung der Vernunft*, 1962).

The same bias leads to a mistaken emphasis on the privileged role of literature in modern thought. Literature is the unchallenged hero of the anthology, an emphasis to which one can subscribe for many reasons: the ideological and philosophical importance of literary thought since the eighteenth century is overpowering. However, one gains the impression from this anthology that literature achieves this prominence because it is the repository of the irrational forces in man, forces that lie beyond the reach of consciousness. Literature therefore becomes the activity of the mind on which to fall back once the "destruction of reason" has taken place: it is the language in which our darker powers find expression. One may well believe the opposite to be true, that the oppositions between rational thought and irrational poetry, between existential and analytic philosophy, between faith and consciousness are false and misleading polarities. The best modern writers and philosophers have made human consciousness the center of their concern and language the medium of their exploration; perhaps the only genuine opposition is between them and the positions of extreme objective positivism or equally extreme subjective primitivism that have surrendered the autonomy of the conscious mind to the unquestioned hegemony of the physical world. It is clear, from their own books, that the views of Professors Ellmann and Feidelson on these matters are enlightened; all the more reason to warn readers of this challenging anthology that it needs to be counterbalanced by a great deal of complementary reading.

# The Mask of Albert Camus (1965)

The subtle but radical change that separates the intellectual atmosphere of the fifties from that of the sixties could well be measured by one's attitude toward the work and the person of Albert Camus. During his lifetime he was for many an exemplary figure; his work bears many traces of the doubts and agonies that such an exalted position inevitably carries with it. He has not ceased to be so: in several recent literary essays, written by men whose formative years coincided with the period of Camus's strongest influence, the impact of his presence can still be strongly felt. On the other hand, one can well imagine how he might prove disappointing to a new generation, not because this generation lacks the experience that shaped Camus's world, but because the interpretation he gave of his own experience lacks clarity and insight. That Sartre and Merleau-Ponty, different from each other as they are, seem more closely attuned to the modern temper is by itself no proof of their superiority. Nor indeed does this make Camus necessarily the defender of permanent values. Before we can blame our times for moving away from him, we must clarify our notion of what he represents.

The publication of the *Notebooks* is a useful addition to the understanding of a writer who, in his fiction, always chose to hide behind the mask of a deliberate, controlled style or behind a pseudoconfessional tone that serves to obscure, rather than to reveal, his true self. The "I" that addresses the reader in *The Stranger* and in *The Fall,* and the collective "we" of *The Plague,* are never to be directly identified with the voice of Camus; in accordance with the tradition of the novel, the author reserves the right to keep his interpretations of characters and events implicit and ambivalent. The genre of the novel is, by definition, oblique, and no one thinks of blaming Cervantes for the fact that, up to this very day, critics cannot agree whether he was for or against Don Quixote. More contemporary figures, however, are not allowed the same immunity especially if, like Camus, they openly intervene in public and political matters and claim to experience personal conflicts that are typical of the historical situation in general. In such cases, one is certainly entitled to look for utterances in which the true commitment (or the true uncertainty) of the writer is revealed.

Camus's *Notebooks* do not offer an easy key to the understanding of an irresolute man. In this second volume (trans. Justin O'Brien [New York: Knopf, 1965]) of his private notes—the first volume of the *Notebooks,* covering the period from May 1935 to February 1942, has also been published in English (trans. Philip Thody [New York: Knopf, 1963])—Camus's personal reserve has increased rather than diminished, and the lack of intimacy or of self-display is both admirable and unusual. There is nothing here of the abandon, the indiscretion of many intimate journals, very little self-justification or, for that matter, self-analysis. The second volume of the *Notebooks* deals with the period from January 1942 till March 1951, during which the main events in Camus's personal, public, and literary life took place: his forced stay in occupied France after the Allied landing in North Africa, his participation in the resistance and subsequent political activity as editor of *Combat,* the considerable success of his novels and plays, which made him one of the most influential writers of the postwar era. It is during this period that he wrote *The Plague* and the ambitious essay *Man in Revolt* (*The Rebel* in its American edition), which interprets the modern predicament as a historical conflict of values. It was also during this period that Camus's inner conflicts and hesitations gained in intensity, leading to a growing retreat from public action, the eventual break with Sartre, and the combination of bitterness and lucidity that one finds in *The Fall*.

Obviously it was a very rich and complex period—but only the remotest echoes filter through to the pages of these notebooks. Readers who expect revelations, strong opinions, anecdotes, and the like will be disappointed. Even the most unsettling personal episodes in Camus's life appear in remote and indirect perspectives. For instance, when he suffered an unexpected recurrence of his early tuberculosis in 1949, his reaction to the event appears in the *Notebooks* only in the form of a poignant note quoted from one of Keats's last letters, written while he was dying in Rome of the same disease. The example, one among many, shows how remote the notebooks are from a personal journal. They are essentially workbooks, comparable to the sketchpads that certain painters carry with them, in which reactions to the outside world are recorded only insofar as they are relevant to the work in progress.

The *Notebooks* consist primarily of outlines for future plays or novels, notes on current reading, early versions of passages, records of situations or remarks observed at the time and stored away for later reference. Camus made considerable use of these notes: many key passages from later books first appear here, frequently as brief notations without further comment or reflections. For a student of Camus's work, the *Notebooks* thus contain much important information. The present collection will prove indispensable, especially to interpreting *The Plague* and *The Rebel*. Together with the notes and variants established by Roger Quilliot for the *Pléiade* edition of the novels and plays, the *Notebooks* give us the kind of information about the genesis of Camus's writing that is ordinarily made available only many decades after an author's death.

But the *Notebooks* can also serve a less specialized function, and help toward a general consideration of Camus's development. No matter how rigorous the reserve, how decorous the self-restraint, a fuller image nevertheless shines through these pages, though more by what they leave unsaid than by what they bring to light. One is struck, for instance, by the considerable difference in tone between the later pages of the *Notebooks* and those contained in the previous volume. The earlier remarks frequently had the spontaneous, lyrical quality of ideas and impressions revealed for their own sake. No deep gulf separates the actual person from the writer, and what is of interest to the one also serves the other. When, in 1940, Camus describes his reactions to the city of Oran he does so with a vivacity of perception that brings the city to life even more effectively than in the opening pages of *The Plague*. The pages on Oran in the 1940 notebook are felicitous in themselves and useful to his later work as well. As the notebooks progress, and especially after the war, such happy conjunctions between the writer's experience and his literary work become less and less frequent: Camus deliberately tore himself away from his natural inclinations and forced on himself a number of alien concerns. As a result, the *Notebooks* reflect an increasing feeling of estrangement and solitude. One feels an almost obsessive commitment to work, a rejection of any moment of private experience as self-indulgence. The man and the writer have less and less in common, and the writer owed it to his avocation to keep repressing his personal life:

> Only by a continual effort can I create. My tendency is to drift toward immobility. My deepest, surest inclination lies in silence and the daily routine. . . . But I know that I stand erect through that very effort and that if I ceased to believe in it for a single moment I should roll over the precipice. This is how I avoid illness and renunciation, raising my head with all my strength to breathe and to conquer. This is my way of despairing and this is my way of curing myself.

The resolution undoubtedly has moral grandeur, but it requires the constant rejection of a personal quality that is, in fact, not just oriented toward silence and mechanical routine. Outcries of rebellion against solitude punctuate the notebooks and give them a more somber tone than is found in any of Camus's dramatic or fictional works. Optimistic assertions about the necessity of dialogue and the ultimate value of the individual are interspersed with notations of despair: "Unbearable solitude—I cannot believe it or resign myself to it"; "Utter solitude. In the urinal of a major railway station at 1 a.m." The spontaneous elation that inspires the pages on Algiers, Oran, and the cities of Italy in the early notebooks has been replaced by this note of despair and alienation: for the solitude that torments Camus is most of all an estrangement from what he considers his authentic former self. The more he gets involved with others, with social issues and public forms of thought and action, the more he feels a loss of contact with his true being.

This evolution is so frequent in modern literature that it certainly does not, by itself, warp Camus's interpretation of his times. His loneliness is genuine, not a pose; the scruples that haunted him while he was being increasingly rewarded by a society in which he participated so little are apparent in many passages of the *Notebooks*. It cannot be said of him, as of the hero of *The Fall*—who is an amalgamation of several contemporaries with certain personal traits of Camus himself—that he lived in bad faith, buying a good conscience by substituting for genuine abnegation the stance and the rhetoric of sacrifice. If one suspects that Camus was thriving on his exposure of contemporary nihilism, enjoying an intellectual position that claimed to suffer from the absurdity of the age while making this absurdity fashionable—then the note of real disarray sounded throughout the *Notebooks* should dispel such doubts. The paradox in which Camus was caught is both more interesting and more intricate: it is not his good faith but the quality of his insight that is to be questioned.

Camus very rightly made his own isolation the basis of his negative diagnosis of the present course of history. He then interpreted this isolation as a conflict between the individual and history. There never is any doubt in his mind that the source of all values resides in the individual, in his ability to resist the monstrous encroachments that history makes upon his integrity. And for Camus this integrity, which he strove to shelter from totalitarian and deterministic forms of thought, is founded in man's capacity for personal happiness. Camus's concern for others is always protective: he wants to keep intact a potential happiness, a possible fulfillment that every individual carries within him. Socialism is for him an organization of society that safeguards this potentiality: hence his enthusiasm for Belinski's "individualistic socialism" against Hegel's claims for totality and universality. The source of this conviction, however, is to be found in Camus's own experience, and the quality of his thought depends, finally, on the intrinsic quality of his inner experience.

On this point, early works such as *Noces* and especially the earlier *Notebooks* dating from before *The Stranger,* are highly instructive. Camus's sense of personal fulfillment is perhaps most clearly revealed in the exalted pages he wrote in September 1937 during a visit to the cities of Tuscany:

We lead a difficult life. We don't always succeed in adjusting our actions to our vision of things. . . . We have to labor and to struggle to reconquer solitude. But then, one day, the earth shows its primitive and naive smile. Then it is as if struggles and life itself were suddenly erased. Millions of eyes have contemplated this landscape before, but for me it is like the smile of the world. In the deepest sense of the term, it takes me outside myself. . . . The world is beautiful, and nothing else matters. The great truth the world patiently teaches us is that heart and mind are nothing. And that the stone warmed by the sun, or the cypress magnified by the blue of heaven are the limits of the only world in which being right has meaning: nature without man. . . . It is in that sense that I understand the word "nakedness" [dénuement]. "To be naked" always contains a suggestion of physical freedom and I would eagerly convert myself to this harmony between hand and flower, to this sensuous alliance between the earth and man freed of humanity if it were not already my religion.

These passages have the intensity of a writer's most personal vision. They stand behind Camus's entire work and reappear at the surface at those moments when he speaks in his own voice: when Rieux and Tarrou free themselves of the historical curse of the plague in a regenerative plunge into the sea; when the snow falls on Amsterdam at the end of Clamence's confession in *The Fall.* We can see from these passages that what Camus calls solitude in the later notebooks is not, in fact, solitude at all but the intolerable intrusion of others on the sacred moment when man's only bond with reality is his bond with nature. In Camus's mythology, the historical parallel to this moment is Greece and he laments at length the disappearance from our own world of Hellenic simplicity—as he laments the disappearance of landscapes from his own books. He quotes Hegel: "Only the modern city offers the mind the terrain in which it can be conscious of itself" and comments: "Significant. This is the time of big cities. The world has been amputated of a part of its truth, of what makes its permanence and its equilibrium: nature, the sea, etc. There is consciousness only in city streets!" And yet cities play an important part in Camus's novels: *The Plague* and *The Fall* are intensely urban in spirit; Amsterdam and Oran are far more than a mere backdrop; they play as central a part as any of the characters. But in Camus's cities a man does not come to know himself by contact with others even by experiencing the impossibility of such contact. In their inhuman anonymity, they are the nostalgic equivalent of the unspoiled nature that has departed from this earth. They have become the haven of our solitude, the link with a lost Arcadia. When city and nature unite in a landscape of nostalgia at the end of *The Fall,* his hero's outcry seems natural enough: "Oh sun, beaches and the isles under the seawind, memories of youth that cause one to despair!" Baudelaire knew a similar nostalgia in the midst of the modern city, but he set himself sharply apart from those who gave in to it, extending to them only pity. The *Notebooks* make it clear that, on this point, there is no distance between Camus and his fictional characters. And whereas the nostalgic figures in Baudelaire feel the attraction of a homeland that has really been theirs, Camus feels nostalgia for a moment that is ambivalent from the outset.

For if one considers this moment, to use his own words, as an instant of "physical freedom" when the body fits within the balance of the elements, then it would be a legitimate assertion of natural beauty on a rather primitive level. "The world is beautiful and nothing else matters." The sentence expresses an idyllic state that does not involve other people and stands outside time—Adam not only before the Fall but before the birth of Eve. In this condition "love is innocent and knows no object." Solitude is no burden since so little consciousness is present; on the contrary, it protects us from alien intrusions. One could compare the feeling with passages in D. H. Lawrence or understand in its terms Camus's affinity with certain aspects of the early Gide. It could be the basis for an amoral and asocial anarchism: Camus explicitly stresses that this encounter can only take place between nature "without man" and man "freed of humanity." This "nakedness" is an athletic freedom of the body, an Arcadian myth that the romantic neo-Hellenists could only have treated in an ironic mode. Camus's use of irony and ironic narrative devices never put this fundamental vision in doubt; in the privacy of his *Notebooks*, it asserts itself even more powerfully as an act of indestructible faith. Camus protests against history as a destroyer of nature and a threat to the body. History is a diabolical invention of German philosophers, a modern curse: "The whole effort of German thought has been to substitute for the notion of human nature that of human situation and hence to substitute history for God and modern tragedy for ancient equilibrium. . . . But like the Greeks I believe in nature." In this respect, Camus is indeed as remote as possible from existential modes of thought, and one can understand his irritation at being so frequently associated in people's minds with Sartre. In a remark that anticipates their future quarrel, Camus accuses Sartre of wanting to believe in a "universal idyll"—apparently unaware that he is himself the prisoner of an idyllic dream that differs from the one he attributes to Sartre only in the respect that it is personal rather than universal. There is no evidence that he ever woke up from this dream.

Camus's work, however, does not display a consistent development of this single vision. Even in the quoted passage from his earlier notebooks, when his naive Hellenism asserts itself in its purest form, a word play on the term *dénuement* introduces the other aspect of his thought. The "nakedness" implied by the *nu* in *dénuement* suggests the barrenness of a human condition that is essentially unsheltered and fragile—not man's "physical freedom" but his subservience to the laws of time and morality. Camus has a sense of human contingency. The *Note-*

*books* record many brief episodes, imagined or observed, in which the frailty of the human condition is suddenly revealed when everyday routine is interrupted by an unexpected confrontation with death or suffering—as when he records his mother's horror at the thought of having to face the war years in the dark because of the blackout, or notes the expression on people's faces in a doctor's office, or tells of the death of an old actor. On a larger scale, the nightmarish aspects of the last war have the same effect, but several notebook entries reveal Camus's sensitivity to this kind of experience well before the war.

His best essay, *The Myth of Sisyphus,* develops from observations of this kind. His particular moral sense, one of protectiveness, is rooted in this awareness of man's "nakedness." But this nakedness has nothing in common with "physical freedom." A reconciliation of the two notions is not easily achieved; it comes about only in the highest manifestations of art or thought. And the first step in such a reconciliation always involves the renunciation of the naive belief in a harmony at the beginning of things. When Camus characterizes Greek art as a "benign barrenness" (*un dénuement souriant*), he does not seem to realize that this equilibrium is the final outcome and not the starting point, of a development that is anything but "natural." Rooted in a literal and physical notion of unity, his own thought falls apart, on the one hand, in a seductive but irresponsible dream of physical well-being and, on the other, in a protective moralism that fails to understand the nature of evil. Camus never ceased to believe that he could shelter mankind from its own contingency merely by asserting the beauty of his own memories. He made this assertion first with proud defiance in *The Stranger,* and later, with more humility but no essential change, in *The Fall.* He always considered himself exemplary, the privileged possessor of a happiness the intrinsic quality of which he overestimated. Others, whose sense of happiness was deeper and clearer than his own, had long since understood that this gave them no increased power over their own destiny, let alone over that of others. His work contains some beautiful flights of lyrical elation along with some astute observations on the incongruity of the human condition. It is lacking, however, in ethical profundity despite its recurrent claims to high moral seriousness. And it is entirely lacking in historical insight: ten years after its publication, *The Rebel* now seems a very dated book. The *Notebooks* make the reasons for this failure clearer. Without the unifying surface of a controlled style to hide them, the contradictions are much more apparent than in the novels or the essays. The figure that emerges is attractive in its candor, but not authoritative in its thought.

When Camus was a young man, he used to be a goalkeeper for a student soccer team and he wrote articles, in the club paper, extolling the joys of victory or, even more eloquently, the melancholy of defeat. The goalkeeper of a soccer team is, to some extent, a favored figure: the color of his shirt differs from that of his team mates, he enjoys the privilege of touching the ball with his hands, etc. All this sets him apart from the others. But he has to pay for this by accepting severe restrictions: his function is purely defensive and protective, and his greatest glory to avoid defeat. He can never be the agent of real victory and, although he can display style and elegance, he is rarely in the thick of things. He is a man of flashy moments, not of sustained effort. And there is no sadder sight than that of a defeated goalkeeper stretched out on the field or rising to retrieve the ball from the nets, while the opposing attackers celebrate their triumph. The melancholy that reigns in the *Notebooks* reminds one of Camus's youthful sadness on the soccer field: too solitary to join the others up front, but not solitary enough to forego being a member of the team, he chose to be the goalkeeper of a society that was in the process of suffering a particularly painful historical defeat. One could hardly expect someone in that difficult position to give a lucid account of the game.

# Modern Poetics in France and Germany (1965)

Continental poetics remain remarkably autonomous and isolated within their national traditions. A few major figures extend their influence beyond the national borders and there are instances of fruitful cooperation between writers from different nationalities. But on the whole there is less contact between, for instance, French, German, and Italian poetical theorists than there is between the actual poets of these countries.

In France, up to a recent date, literary theory was overshadowed by the techniques of *explication de texte,* a discipline that is not primarily concerned with poetics. It aims at the correct reading of literary texts and is pedagogical rather than critical in purpose. To the extent that it contains an implicit theory of poetry, this theory is positivistic. From Taine, it inherits a considerable interest in the extrinsic forces that act on literature: social, intellectual, and political history play a large part in the works of the most eminent representative, Gustave Lanson. Its methods are highly analytic and are characterized by the virtues of precision and caution inherited from the natural sciences. Because of the particular structure of French literary history, with its high period in the classical seventeenth and eighteenth centuries, the method was primarily devised to deal with authors of that period, hence the emphasis on rhetoric. Orthodox explication is much less at home with nineteenth-century romantic and especially symbolist literature, avowedly antirhetorical in purpose. The gap between live poetry, which continued to develop in the wake of symbolism, and the methods taught in the schools kept widening and a reaction was bound to occur.

One should mention Bergson and Valéry among the main initiators of this reaction, because both translated the heritage of symbolism into poetic theory. In Valéry's case, this continues the tradition of a poetry that, ever since Baudelaire and Mallarmé, had been acutely aware of the problems created by its own existence, and had often expressed itself on matters of a theoretical nature. Valéry's main contribution may well have been his help in reawakening interest in theoretical poetics as such, by the numerous and widely read essays in which he advocates a direct study of poetic creation, independently of historical and critical considerations. His efforts culminated in the establishment of a chair in poetics at the Collège de France, where Valéry himself, from 1937 to 1945, delivered a series of lectures that, unfortunately, have not been recorded. The actual content of his theory has been less influential, possibly because it did not mark such a sharp departure from the premises of the natural sciences. It was primarily the self-reflective, hyperconscious aspect of symbolism (especially in Mallarmé) that interested Valéry; his thought aims at a rational description of the poetic act, often using his own creative experience as a starting point toward "reducing poetry to a scientific operation of feeling" (Jean Hytier). Devoid, as Valéry deliberately was, of Mallarmé's dedication to the poetic work as an absolute expression of the human spirit, his theories lead to valid insights but remain, on the whole, the isolated display of his own intellectual idiosyncrasies. Nevertheless, his writings on poetics contain suggestions of great value on the relationship between the workings of the poetic and the rational mind, such as his critique of naive conceptions of "inspiration" and his emphasis on the deliberate, calculated aspects of poetic composition.

Although he was not primarily concerned with poetics and did not write systematically on the subject, Bergson exercised a profound influence on French poetic theory. His constant emphasis on the presence, in human consciousness, of subjective elements pertaining to memory, imagination, intuition, next to—though sharply separated from—elements that possess objective reality, amounts in fact to a poetization of human experience. The entire area of man's contact with the outside world (perception, sensation, etc.) becomes similar to the experience found in works of art and literature. The poetic image, for instance, becomes a close verbal approximation to what perception and sensation are actually like, much closer, at any rate, than the purely intellectual representation of reality found in the scientific concept. Poetics thus becomes a vital source for theoretical psychology, rather than a minor part of it. It has been shown (among others by Fiser) that Bergson's conception is a close equivalent, in philosophical language, of the kind of imagery used by symbolist writers, from Baudelaire to Proust. The unity of a symbolist work always resides in the inner coherence between its images, a coherence similar, in Proust's words, "to the single relationship which, in the world of science, is called the law of cause and effect." Bergson's work is concerned with this same process as the unifying theme of human consciousness.

Later thinkers such as Jean Wahl or Gaston Bachelard are not to be considered

Bergson's disciples in the usual sense of the term, but their independent speculations pursue a direction that Bergson had initiated. By his writings on poetry, by
the considerable place he allots to poetics in the field of metaphysics and by his
influence as a teacher, Jean Wahl has contributed to a renewal that by now has
reached down into the field of practical literary criticism. By means of poetry,
as Wahl puts it in a very Bergsonian formula, man will again be able "to communicate substantially with what is substantial in things"; genuine metaphysical
thought can also achieve this, but poetry and thought are so closely related as to
be almost one and the same thing. A similar insight more systematically developed, appears in the series of studies that Gaston Bachelard, a philosopher of
science, has devoted to what he calls "material imagination." He shows the imagination as acting in a manner that differs from rational cognition by being a direct,
unmediated apprehension of matter, a "dreaming about" matter rather than an act
of knowledge (one notices the similarity with Bergson's critique of the scientific
"symbol" as the sole mode of cognition). In a series of four books, Bachelard attempts a typology of the poetic imagination, cataloguing images according to
their dominant material element (fire, water, earth, air). The resulting method
does not cover the entirety of the literary work: it describes only the imagery and,
it could be argued, only a certain kind of imagery; when used without the inner
sympathy with the poet's imagination that Bachelard constantly demands, it could
easily become mechanical. The impact of these studies on current French literary
criticism is considerable. They allow for a return to the poetic experience as an
experience of *concrete* reality, a return that is implicit in Bergson's philosophy.

Although often critical of Bergson, Jean-Paul Sartre is close to him in his contributions on poetic theory. His study of the imagination insists on the radical distinction between perception and imagination, a thesis that figures prominently in
Bergson's early *Matière et mémoire* (1900). The method of existential psychoanalysis that he advocates in *L'Être et le néant* (1943) involves an interpenetra-
tion between matter and consciousness that, despite important differences of emphasis, remains Bergsonian; its similarity to Bachelard's theory of material
imagination would suffice to indicate this. Sartre's own literary criticism contains
examples of such analyses, but in younger critics it is often difficult to separate
Sartre's influence from that of Bachelard. In later writings, such as the essay *What
Is Literature?* (1949), Sartre has abandoned the pursuit of theoretical poetics that
was at least potentially present in his earlier work. By drawing a sharp distinction
between literary prose and poetry, he reintroduces interpersonal, ethical considerations in his evaluation of literature and, for the time being at least, puts aside
problems of theoretical poetics.

Bachelard's and Sartre's poetics are attempts at a phenomenology of the poetic
consciousness. They differ from each other by the original situation that is taken
as a starting point: in Bachelard it is man's relationship to the texture and the spatial dimensions of matter, in Sartre it is the existential situation. Another writer

who belongs in the same group, Georges Poulet, starts from the poet's sense of temporality, and shows how the structure of the style expresses his specific experience of time; aside from its philosophical implications, the interest of this approach stems from its concern with style and from the possible link it suggests between phenomenological analysis and stylistics. The manner, however, in which Poulet establishes this link remains problematic and in need of a theoretical foundation.

Such a foundation can only be discovered in an exhaustive study of the poetic act; French literary theory has more and more felt the need for an ontology of the poetic as preliminary to a study on such a highly integrated level as that of style. The writer who has perhaps gone furthest in the formulation of such an ontology is Maurice Blanchot. If Valéry and Bergson can be considered as the theorizers of symbolism, Blanchot appears in a somewhat similar relationship to the surrealist movement. Already in the oblique and subtle essays of Jean Paulhan and in the tormented meditations of Georges Bataille, some of the surrealist themes had continued to find expression. Blanchot shows how the works of poets gravitate around the ontological question, how they try and fail always again to define human existence by means of poetic language. His writings are unsystematic and highly subjective, but if the necessity for a fundamental questioning of the poetic act is granted, it is bound to begin as a tentative, difficult exploration, and not as a self-assured doctrine.

Practical applications of these and related theories to criticism and history have multiplied in later years. As could be expected, they are centered in the area of the nineteenth century, and they have modified the traditional picture of French literary history as dominated by seventeenth-century classicism. The success of historical studies founded on a symbolist poetics, such as Albert Béguin's book on romanticism (*L'Âme romantique et le rêve,* 1937) or Marcel Raymond's study of symbolism (*De Baudelaire au surréalisme,* rev. ed., 1952), illustrates this trend. The study of the sixteenth and seventeenth centuries has also been influenced by the new trends, and the new emphasis on sixteenth-century baroque can undoubtedly be traced back to the same shift in orientation. Among typical examples of books that make use of phenomenological poetics, one should mention Jean Pierre Richard's essays on the nineteenth-century novel and symbolist poetry (*Littérature et sensation,* with an important preface by G. Poulet, 1955), *Poésie et profondeur* (1956), as well as his recent study of Mallarmé (*L'Univers imaginaire de Mallarmé,* 1962), which give a clear picture of the possibilities and the limits of the method. Roland Barthes's *Le Degré zéro de l'écriture,* 1956) is noteworthy because it suggests connections between phenomenological analysis and the structure, history, and sociology of style. The very brief essay merely indicates the problem, but if further studies could help to bring these various disciplines closer together, French poetics would move on to a stage where synthesis becomes possible.

While French *explication de textes* derived its methods primarily from the natural sciences, German literary studies of the same era seem to have been especially eager to emulate the social sciences, as they were practiced in Germany at the turn of the century. Various forms of organic historicism appear as the dominant characteristic of several works. Sometimes, as in H. A. Korff's *Geist der Goethezeit* (5 vols., 1925–57), the concept of history is triadic and Hegelian; in others, such as Walzel or Richter, it is derived from the visual arts—in this case Wölfflin's theories of vision and of "open" and "closed" form. Others still search for historical continuity in specific literary traditions and *topoi* (Curtius), in recurrent themes and attitudes (Unger, Rehm), in archetypal patterns (Kerenyi), in philosophical or aesthetic attitudes (Cassirer, Auerbach). In all these instances, the problem is essentially one of historical continuity: a certain theory of history is shown to bring order and coherence in the apparently erratic development of literature. Some of the authors mentioned have produced works of lasting value that often go far in revealing the inner workings of the poetic mind. But since they all start from the literary work as an unquestionable empirical fact, they do not claim to be writing on poetics, in either sense of the term. It is partly in reaction against the considerable authority of much philological and historical literary science that a new concern with poetics developed, not unlike that in France, although the issue is much less clearly defined.

As one significant example of such reactions, the disciples of the poet Stefan George set themselves up as deliberate opponents of the prevalent methods of literary study. Although George claimed that "from him, no road led to science," most of his later followers taught in universities. Since several among them were men of considerable learning, they exercised a great deal of influence. Their approach was antiphilological in the extreme (no footnotes, sources, or bibliographies), but their merit lies rather in their respect for the autonomy of the poetic mind than in their attacks on traditional methods. The writer on literature must come as close as possible to the creative experience itself, helped in this by admiration and love for his subject rather than by scruples of accuracy and objectivity. There is great emphasis, also, on the messianic role of the poet as an almost superhuman figure, to be dealt with in a language closer to that of myth or religion than that of science. That such an approach is not always incompatible with true learning is clear from Gundolf's books on Shakespeare and Goethe. Only a few of George's disciples are still alive, and a vigorous reaction has, in turn, set in against the arbitrary elements in their works. This reaction, however, should not blind one to their contribution. It was certainly necessary, around 1910, to bring German philology into closer contact with live poetry; George's disciples renewed the established image of Goethe, they were instrumental in the discovery of Hölderlin and contributed to the emphasis on the neo-Hellenic tradition that runs as a continuous strand through German literature, from Winckelmann to the present. But if the George Circle was militantly aware of the need for poetic autonomy, the contribution of its members to poetics remains diffuse, mostly because their insistence on the messianic element tends to overshadow the formal element of poetry altogether. In their master, George himself, the tangible expression of the transcendental value of poetry was to be found in the perfection of the form; it was by the act of extreme formal discipline, a kind of ascesis of the form, that the poet earned the right to statements of prophetic weight. If this formal discipline is taken away, the entire messianic attitude becomes dangerously arbitrary. Significantly, it is after he had left the George Circle that one of the most gifted among its members, Max Kommerell, wrote studies on the drama, on Faust, and on Hölderlin that show real insight in poetic motivation and its relation to formal structure.

More recently, another challenge has been offered to German philology, emanating this time from a philosopher, Martin Heidegger. In 1937, Heidegger began the publication of commentaries on the poetry of Hölderlin, and in subsequent works he has given an increased importance to the poetic as a prominent part of his philosophy, with occasional excursions in the practical field of exegesis. Heidegger's conception of the poetic is part of his attempt to reach beyond what he considers the limits of the Western metaphysical tradition. Because of their greater proximity to language, poets reflect the fundamental tensions of human existence more faithfully than even the greatest among the metaphysicians. And the purest of them all, the poet who, according to Heidegger, has been able to name the very essence of poetry, Hölderlin, offers therefore an insight into Being that is without antecedent in the history of human thought. Whoever is able, with the assistance of the commentary, to listen to Hölderlin, will stand in the presence of the poetic itself and discover that it is the unmediated language of Being. For Heidegger, the poet's language has eschatological power and is to be interpreted, not by means of a critical analysis that assumes a common frame of reference, but as a kind of revelation that, at best, we can hope to perceive but never to grasp critically, as one can grasp a concept. The methodological consequences of this attitude go against the very foundation of philological science. The implication is that traditional philological methods, based on the assumedly objective status of the work, are themselves imprisoned within Western rationalism, and therefore unable to gain true poetic insight. This inability extends to the era where the authority of philology reigns undisputed, that of the correct establishment of texts—and Heidegger has participated, directly and indirectly, in the controversies that surround the critical edition of Hölderlin's complete works. He has often been accused of stretching and distorting texts to make them conform to his own views; these controversial readings, however, are always consistent with his own philosophical assumptions, and they can only be discarded or criticized within the context of this philosophy.

If Heidegger's commentaries are an extreme example of a poetics founded on "creation," German scholars have also made important contributions to the poetics of style. Stylistic research (*Stilforschung*) is probably the most international among the trends we have mentioned. It originated out of an encounter between German philology and the philosophy of the Italian aesthetician Croce. One would expect Croce's main influence to be in the field of history of literature, since this is the area with which his massive philosophical work is primarily concerned; the orientation of his numerous Italian disciples has generally been in this direction. But it seems now as if his impact is perhaps most strongly felt in stylistic studies, although he was himself somewhat reticent toward *Stilforschung*. The close friendship between Croce and the German philologist Karl Vossler, leader of the Munich school of stylistic criticism to which Leo Spitzer also belongs, is an important personal factor in this influence. Croce and Vossler's intellectual kinship has for its common root the revolt against the scientific positivism of the nineteenth century which it criticized in the name of Hegelian idealism; the revealing title of Vossler's first work is *Positivismus und Idealismus in der Sprachwissenschaft* (1904). Vossler's later work is mainly a study of the dominant stylistic traits of literary language, as a key not only to the personality of an author but even, as in his book on France (*Frankreichs Kultur und Sprache,* 1929), to the spirit of a nation. Leo Spitzer, using more intricate and more refined techniques, pursues a similar aim: he selects a distinctive feature of the style to penetrate into the work and reach the distinctive quality of a poetic personality: the study of one crucial passage in *Phèdre,* for instance, allows for a general interpretation of Racine. Such attempts may seem purely technical, but they are in fact a practical application of the monistic assumptions that dominate Croce's poetics. The writers of the Munich school derived from Croce the precept that, since poetic style is not to be separated from poetic experience and personality, it is legitimate to reach an exhaustive interpretation on the basis of the aspect of the work that is most readily and objectively available, namely, the style. This kind of stylistic analysis differs sharply from positivistic stylistics in that it assumes the work to be an autonomous aesthetic unit. It restored to the systematic study of poetry values of taste and sensitivity, without falling back on impressionistic subjectivism, and it refined the tools of analysis and interpretation to a considerable extent. Vossler enjoyed a high reputation in Spain and thus established a link between German, Italian, and Spanish literary studies; Dámaso Alonso's book on Góngora was perhaps the most accomplished work to come out of this school.

Partly in reaction against the psychological aspects of Vossler's method, a new trend in stylistic study has recently originated in Zurich around Emil Staiger and the review *Trivium* (now no longer published). Staiger's techniques are still those of stylistic analysis, based on close reading, study of syntactical, rhythmical, and metaphorical structure, but his ultimate purpose is to reveal the metapersonal attitude of the poet toward the fundamental categories of existence, especially temporality. One is reminded of similar trends in France; Staiger, however, is backed by the highly developed methods of stylistic research established by his German predecessors. His most theoretical work, *Grundbegriffe der Poetik* (1946), is based on the classical distinction between the three genres, lyrical, epic, and dramatic. It is especially noteworthy for its description of the lyrical as the fundamental poetic genre, the ideal from which all poetry springs forth and to which it tends to return. In this assertion, Staiger makes explicit a preference that is found in most of the tendencies that have been mentioned. Because it draws on a variety of doctrines, Staiger's school offers a balanced method of descriptive poetics. It is avowedly better suited to deal with the details of relatively brief lyrical poems, rather than with larger dramatic units. This reveals once more what has been apparent throughout this survey: the recent trends in French and German poetics (and in European poetics in general) are the theoretical expression of the poetics implicitly contained in nineteenth-century romantic and symbolist poetry.

# The Literature of Nihilism (1966)

Two recent books on the German literary tradition—Erich Heller's *The Artist's Journey into the Interior and Other Essays* (New York: Random House, 1965) and Ronald Gray's *The German Tradition in Literature 1871–1945* (Cambridge: Cambridge University Press, 1965)—serve to show that highly competent treatment of detail can be warped by a misleading general view. Both works deal with the same topic: the development in the history of German thought and literature that took place during the nineteenth century and at the beginning of the twentieth. Erich Heller, who now teaches in the United States after having spent several years in England, is particularly known for his collection of essays, *The Disinherited Mind*. The book under review has a similar subject: it contains studies of Faust and Schiller, of Nietzsche and Wittgenstein, as well as the title essay, an interpretation of the "romantic mind." It interprets the period from Goethe to Wittgenstein as the developing expression of a unified central experience vast enough to contain aspects of Weimar classicism, of romanticism, and of the post-symbolist poetry and philosophy of such writers as Nietzsche and Rilke. References to other national literatures widen the book's scope still further, suggesting Heller's comprehensive understanding of contemporary literature and its background in the nineteenth century. The book is not historical in the academic sense, but essayistic, as lively and polemical in thought as it is felicitous in expression. It seems to be Heller's aim to cast light on the present human predicament by means of a critical examination of its intellectual antecedents. *The Artist's Journey into the Interior* is "committed" criticism in the best sense of the phrase.

Ronald Gray, lecturer on German literature at Cambridge, is no less "committed" than Heller, although his tone is more academic and his book more special-ized. *The German Tradition in Literature* consists mainly of two substantial studies of Mann and Rilke, and there are two additional sections that attempt to relate the detailed analysis of both writers to politics and intellectual history generally. The period covered is a limited one: from the Wilhelminian era (1871) to the defeat of Hitler (1945), with only scant references to the earlier classical and romantic periods in German literature. At first sight, there seems to be some discordance between Gray's detailed study of Mann and Rilke and his sweeping survey of political and intellectual history. But this discordance is only apparent. Gray considers Mann and Rilke to be typical of the German "mind" in general and it is the quality of this mind that he attempts to define. No less than Heller's book, *The German Tradition in Literature* has as its theme a fundamental crisis in nineteenth-century thought. Nor does Gray refrain from taking sides. More thematic than Heller's, his book is even more openly polemical; he has no qualms about passing from literature and philosophy to political questions.

Both books, Gray's openly, Heller's more obliquely, assume that German philos-ophy and literature, from the late eighteenth century on, have to be called to ac-count for having provided the intellectual basis for Nazism. With the easy hind-sight of the naive historian, Gray assumes that Goethe, Hegel, Fichte, Schelling, Schopenhauer, Marx, Wagner, Nietzsche, Mann, and Rilke all had a share in a common aberration that finally produced Hitler. Protected by Christian ethics and the common sense of empiricism, Gray hopes to "divert the immense vitality of recent years away from new catastrophes." He makes the assumption that this task can only be performed by someone who stands outside the German tradition and has not been hoodwinked by it. Early in the book, Gray states that "literary criti-cism in any proper sense scarcely exists in Germany," thus depriving well-meaning Germans of any hope of rehabilitating themselves. I am not sure that Mr. Gray would consider Erich Heller's essays as examples of "proper criticism." His many years in England may not, in Gray's eyes, have been sufficient to cleanse their author, who was educated in Prague, of all traces of mysticism and ob-scurantism.

Yet Heller too seems to take it for granted that a common doom hangs over the whole German tradition, that "another and better answer must be found" to attitudes that "engender . . . many a doubt." His list of culprits would not en-tirely coincide with Gray's; I suppose that Goethe, for instance, would not be in-cluded in it, whereas Schiller (whom Gray lets off rather lightly) certainly is. He also makes it clear that the reaction to the tradition must begin in the wake of the tradition itself, not from the uncontaminated but insular standpoint that Gray oc-cupies. But even for Heller there is little doubt about the unity of this tradition, nor about the fact that recent events (not only Nazism) have discredited it to such an extent that it should now be abandoned.

Only a curiously simplistic notion of the relationship between literary thought and political action could treat literature and politics as being entirely isolated within their own fixed spheres, and yet so closely interrelated that passage can be made from one to the other, as from cause to effect, without trace of mediation. The literary analyses in Gray's book are often excellent; but although they are entirely lacking in sociological and political concerns, they nevertheless lead to the rashest of generalizations about the political responsibilities of the writers. One would think that, after some of the experiences of this century, the complexity of the relationship between thought and action would be better understood. Nazi Germany is a case in point. The discrepancy between intellectual values and actual behavior has rarely been so baffling as in this case. No one could claim (nor does Gray) that the Nazi movement somehow rooted itself in a venerable and mature tradition. It was, if anything, notable for its profound anti-intellectualism and the crude but effective manner in which it played on the most primitive mass instincts, as well as on the shortsighted economic interests of social classes that considered themselves underprivileged. The Nazis received little support from German writers and intellectuals and were not very eager to enlist them in their ranks.

Later on, when the regime was established and in need of respectability, there was a deliberate attempt to interpret certain figures of the German past along hypernationalistic and even racist lines: Goethe, Hölderlin, Kleist, and Nietzsche were most frequently distorted in this fashion. These attempts were often ludicrous, but sometimes effective enough to demand vigorous reaction. Some of these trends persist today, but are no longer left unchallenged. It should be clear to anyone who follows the German critical writing that Mr. Gray annihilates with one stroke, that the poets themselves, in their own works, provide a very adequate defense against such misrepresentations. Contemporary interpreters of Hölderlin, of Kleist, and even of Nietzsche, such as, among others, Karl Löwith, Beda Alleman, or Peter Szondi, have brought this out without much difficulty, although they may still run into surprisingly strong pockets of resistance. These very critics will find little solace in the peremptory manner in which Gray disposes of so complicated a case as Kleist, for instance, by labeling him without further qualification as an example of "insane and brutal nationalism."

If Hitler triumphed in Germany it was in spite of the intellectual tradition of the country, rather than because of it. There was *trahison des clercs* to the precise extent that literary thought and political action had lost contact with each other. The problem is not that a philosophical tradition could be so wrong but that it could have counted for so little when it was most needed. The responsibility rests not with the tradition but with the manner in which it was used or neglected, and this is primarily a sociological problem. Nor was there in this tradition anything that advocated a separation between mind and action; in this respect, German thought of the nineteenth century is rather ahead of French and English thought.

The pessimism and negativeness for which both Heller and Gray seem to indict it so severely may well have been due to a greater awareness of the historical forces that brought about such catastrophes as Nazism. It is not in the power of philosophy or literature to prevent the degradation of the human spirit, nor is it its main function to warn against this degradation; Nietzsche could rightly be criticized for having warned too much and perhaps for not having thought enough. A literature of nihilism is not necessarily nihilistic, and one should be careful about praising or blaming writers for events that took place after they had ceased to exist: it is just as absurd to praise Rousseau for the French Revolution as to blame Nietzsche for Hitler. This does not mean that philosophers and poets have no moral or political responsibility even when their work is apolitical. But it means this responsibility should be evaluated within the full philosophical or literary context of their work, not their lives, still less the effect that their work may or may not have had on other people. The real and difficult problems that the German tradition formulated during the last two hundred years cannot be dismissed because it is supposed to have led to a national catastrophe.

Because Gray's book lacks historical perspective, the general sections remain superficial and inchoate. Erich Heller's essays come much closer to being a real discussion of important issues, but they also suffer from a certain oversensitivity to national characteristics. He overstates the importance of German influence when he claims that "the 'Modern mind' speaks German"; and he directs his criticism at an illusory target when he sees the contents of this mind determined by national traits. National categories applied to literary and philosophical matters always tend to miss the mark; the interstices of the net are both too loose and too tight. They fail to sift out the individual qualities of the writer's mind and neglect the tendency toward universality inherent in philosophy as well as poetry. This is true even of such "nationalistic" periods as the nineteenth century. The aberration that led such a figure as Wagner, or, in a less one-sided way, Stefan George, to adopt nationalistic attitudes can only be understood from a perspective that is no longer national. The confusion stems precisely from the fact that the nation, a perfectly legitimate concept in itself, acts as a substitute for something more fundamental and more encompassing. Figures of the recent German past — one thinks of such divergent writers as Brecht, Walter Benjamin, and Karl Kraus — had already reacted against this confusion of values. The reaction continues in some of the most influential spokesmen of contemporary Germany: Adorno, Ernst Bloch, Günter Grass, etc. Those critics, activity engaged in "demythologizing" national values, have found powerful antecedents among writers who are here, implicitly or explicitly, being attacked: Hölderlin, Kleist, and Nietzsche. But both Gray and Heller are confined within a national point of view to such a degree that they seem unable to participate in this enterprise. Critical nationalism, rare in the United States, is a frequent sin among European critics, just as common in France and England as it is in Germany.

In their analysis of the German tradition, both authors focus on some of the same targets and hint at shortcomings that are not unrelated. Gray reproaches German thought for being excessively fond of polar antitheses and for proceeding from there to sweeping syntheses that disregard the complexity of experience. From Schiller's "naive" and "sentimental" poetry, to Nietzsche's antithetical treatment of the Dionysian and the Apolline, two souls always seem to have been at war within the German, as within Faust's, heart and mind. And German thought proceeds from this polarity to sweeping Hegelian syntheses that disregard the complexity of experience. In this view, Gray echoes a common reproach made in the name of empiricism against idealistic philosophy. Heller singles out "inwardness," "the retreat of the Spirit into human subjectivity," as the main characteristic of the tradition, and interprets it as a deliberate alienation of the consciousness from the outside world. In this he is in close accord with a long line of critics hostile to romanticism and postromanticism. One could easily argue that these characteristics are not specifically German, that just as much system making was going on in France, and that a comparable "inwardness" prevailed in England during the same period. But this argument would evade the central issue at stake in both books. Heller, whose approach is by no means as narrowly national as Gray's, would readily admit that his reservations about the romantic personality are not confined to its German manifestations; his frequent allusions to French and English literature make this clear. Gray, on the other hand, devotes his concluding chapter to demonstrating British immunity to German contamination, treating instances of German influence during the nineteenth century — Coleridge, Carlyle, Pater, Arnold, and others — as if they were the vaccine that made this immunity possible. But when he talks about individual writers, especially those he likes (Kafka, Trakl, Hofmannsthal), he abandons some of his general notions and reveals values of human compassion and humility with which it is easy enough to sympathize. And when Heller, in his chapter on the romantic mind, suggests that a reconciliation between mind and nature can be achieved by moving beyond the extreme point reached in Hegel and Rilke, he offers a cogent alternative to romantic inwardness, thus pursuing and deepening a demonstration begun in his previous collection of essays (*The Disinherited Mind*) and which in this book gains in clarity and elegance.

It does not matter too much, then, if both authors somewhat too readily call "German" a general feature of the romantic and postromantic intellect. If their description of the phenomenon were correct, the name would be of secondary importance. There can be no doubt about the authority with which both approach this complex period, their insight sharpened by a knowledge of the tradition against which they rebel. But one must challenge them on this broader question as well. For all the differences between the two books, both misrepresent the "artist's journey into the interior" on very similar grounds. And their diagnosis arises from a consciousness that has not understood itself as thoroughly as the consciousness of the artists and philosophers it sets out to interpret.

Let us take as an example Heller's and Gray's treatment of Rilke, a poet to whom both give considerable prominence. In many ways, Rilke is highly vulnerable to their statregy, being less resilient than Hegel or Nietzsche, who have a much wider conceptual apparatus at their disposal. Rilke's emotional use of the term "inwardness" provides Heller with an abundance of quotations that sound very convincing. And it seems appropriate that in his discussion of Rilke's imagery Gray reproaches the poet for using words in a manner that does not conform to our experience of the behavior of physical objects. As one of his examples, he cites a famous passage from the Second Duino Elegy in which Rilke, striving to convey the full meaning of his central symbol, the Angel, leads up to it by a series of designations culminating in the italicized word *mirrors:*

> *mirrors,* drawing up their own
> outstreamed beauty into their faces again

> [*Spiegel:* die die enströmte eigene Schönheit
> wiederschöpfen zurück in das eigene Antlitz.]

In ordinary experience, our actual image (which others know more objectively than we do ourselves) is likely to be disappointingly different from our image of ourselves. In this respect, we are not like mirrors, inasmuch as our reality and the reflected consciousness of this reality do not coincide; the discovery of this discrepancy may be a highly unsettling experience, whether it be the experience of "bodily decrepitude" or of moral inadequacy. The creature strong enough not to experience this disappointment would indeed be like a mirror; for the images on both sides of the reflecting surface would be identical. And the beauty, physical or moral, of such a creature would be increased by this self-assurance, exactly in the manner in which some of Rilke's poems describe the beauty of a woman enhanced by the approval she can, for a moment, receive from her own image glimpsed in a mirror:

> Enhanced by your own image, how rich you are.
> Affirming yourself, you affirm your hair and cheek . . .

> [Gesteigert um dein Bild: wie bist du reich.
> Dein Ja zu dir bejaht dir Haar und Wange . . . ]

In this sense, it can be said that the source of beauty resides in the mirrored image and not in the object itself, that the mirror reflects the splendor of the image back upon itself. But Mr. Gray stays with the literal fact that "mirrors do not give and receive back, just the opposite." Rilke has indeed reversed the perspective, because he does not treat the mirror as a mere physical object, but reflects on the manner in which, as a physical object, it differs from the experience we have of ourselves. The way in which he uses language forces us, first of all, to become conscious of the particular oddity of mirrors (objects that have the power to make an object and its reflection identical), then to become conscious by contrast of the discrepancy that exists in ourselves. Moreover, by evoking moments during which this discrepancy disappears, he reveals a hidden potential of our being.

Nothing mystical or weightily philosophical is involved here: it is an attempt to become aware, by means of language, of the relationship between the self and the world that surrounds it. As a result of this effort, the relationship turns out to be so intimate and involved that it can no longer be expressed by the misleading metaphor of an "inner" and an "outer" world. Rilke is trying to move beyond the polarities that are still taken for granted by his critics. This undoubtedly has some affinity with certain aspects of phenomenological thought that were developing around the same time. But Gray would no doubt consider this added proof that "Rilke is doing violence to the external world of things, compelling them to serve the purposes of his 'great Idea' "—all the more since the main proponents of phenomenology, Husserl and Heidegger, are both Germans and the latter politically suspect to boot. Yet phenomenology is precisely the method that holds, with Hegel, that philosophy begins not with a "great Idea" but with a small reality—as Rilke's poetry almost tiresomely does.

Rilke comes at the end of a long withdrawal from the large speculative systems and set aesthetic norms that held sway till well into the eighteenth century. This movement toward greater particularization can indeed be described, in Erich Heller's words, as a "journey into the interior," since the point of departure of contemporary thought is no longer the given order of the natural world but the self in its relation to this world. Heller's stress on inwardness shows considerable progress over many earlier definitions of romanticism as a pantheistic, irrational unity with nature. It is much more difficult to follow him, however, in his account of the reasons that led to this withdrawal. In the work of Rilke, as in that of many of his romantic predecessors, these reasons are lengthily and often convincingly stated. They arise out of a growing awareness of the essential contingency of the human condition, coupled with the realization that many psychological, philosophical, and theological attitudes have no other purpose than to hide this contingency from our insight into ourselves. Rilke's reassertion of the self does not occur as a proud, Promethean (or even Faustian) statement of the power of the mind over nature, but originates in a feeling of loss and bewilderment. The same is true of most of the major poets and thinkers of the period, although the form in which this bewilderment is experienced varies considerably of course from writer to writer. Even Nietzsche's notorious Will to Power designates not the power of the self, but the power of Being in which the self participates in an exceedingly fragmentary and indirect way. What would require extensive demonstration in the work of Nietzsche is quite obvious in Rilke, who identifies power with entities, such as the Angel, that are clearly superhuman. Even if the self can be misled later into another illusory reconciliation with the natural world (and this may well be the case with Rilke) it stands originally clear of such expectations. In all these writers, inwardness always begins as a negative moment, an experience of humility.

Heller makes the opposite claim. His argument suggests that we need only recover from the romantic sin of intellectual pride in order to return to a more harmonious state of being. Hence his strong insistence on Faust as the archetypal romantic hero—in itself a debatable assertion since so many of Goethe's ironies at his hero's expense express the reservations of a modern mind about the illusions of an earlier age. Hence also the entirely misleading confusion created, in the essay "The Realistic Fallacy," between the desire for full "understanding" of the self and of "rational appropriation" of the world, a confusion that short-circuits the tension out of which the masterpieces of realism as well as postromantic symbolism originated. Heller describes the motives that brought the romantic artist back to the self as an arbitrary assertion of freedom, an inability to leave the sovereign goodness of the world undisturbed. Moreover, he strongly suggests that this destructive meddling is actually rooted in weakness, in an impotence that avenges itself by destroying what it cannot possess. In his vision of things, a fundamentally benign and harmonious world in which mind and body are in unison is confronted by a power-hungry Spirit that considers this world "only as a cue to its monologues." The Spirit acting out of a "compulsion that . . . has about it nothing of the feel of necessity" can only come to rest when it has carried out the death sentence it has pronounced on the world of the senses and "amputated it as a limb suffering the disease of healthy, concrete reality." Throughout the book, inwardness is associated with self-willed violence. The romantic artists are "arbitrary sovereigns who wield unpredictable power from their inner courtrooms." Rilke falls prey to "spiritual violence that maintains the good manners and appearances of gentleness" and, in one vast unholy alliance, all of them join in preparing the apocalypse that is about to destroy us all.

In the course of his analysis, Heller cannot avoid coming upon the great negative themes of the romantics—the forces beyond our power that threaten the self, and whose presence reveals so clearly that the romantic movement did not begin in the blindness of pride but in the humility of reflection: the themes of mutability, of time, and of death. To Heller, death seems to be an expression of human will. When he encounters it in Keats's "Ode to a Nightingale," he gives to the famous lines "Now more than ever seems it rich to die . . . " a positive reading that the entire context of the poem denies, and makes Keats sound as if he were Novalis caught in an obvious display of bad faith.

But it is the treatment of romantic neo-Hellenism that his distortion is most clearly visible. By painting a sharp contrast between the harmony of Greek art and the division of the romantic mind, Heller suggests that the romantic attitude toward Greece is one of nostalgic envy, like that of fallen man toward the lost Garden of Eden. This may indeed be the apparent theme in Winckelmann, in the first version of Schiller's *The Gods of Greece,* or in some of George's more programmatic poems; English readers are familiar with the theme from the uncharacteristic sonnet of the least Hellenic of English romantics, William Wordsworth: "The world is too much with us . . . " ("I'd rather be / A pagan suckled in a creed outworn . . . "). But most romantics quickly moved beyond this mood of regret and, in the most deeply Hellenic of them all, Hölderlin, it never appeared in this form. Greece is for them the great elegiac theme, not because they were so naive as to believe that the Greeks were identical with the ideal image projected by their sculpture, but because even the creation of an art great enough to achieve semipermanence did not shelter Greece from division and destruction. The neo-Hellenic theme is for the romantics a special version of the theme of mutability and contingency, not the description of an actual state of being that could be brought back if we only had the strength to do so. The passing of classical art does not demonstrate the perversity of a Spirit that "wants to be rid of all sensuous encumbrance," but reveals the irrevocably negative power of time. Hegel always insisted so strongly on the concrete, incarnate aspect of the Idea and made high claims for art precisely because it necessarily includes a concrete, sensory dimension; he can hardly be defined as the ruthless destroyer of reality that Heller portrays him to be on the strength of a highly one-sided and undialectical reading of a section from the *Lectures of Aesthetics.*

In any interpretation of romanticism, the question of motive is of determining importance: the presence of negative components in the romantic mind becomes indeed a sign of weakness if they are the compensatory fantasies of an overreaching spirit. If, on the other hand, they result from a genuine experience of reality, then we can only praise these writers and thinkers for having come closer to showing us our condition as it really is. The project of moving beyond romanticism will then take on a very different meaning from the one suggested in these essays.

Next to Faust, Heller suggests Hamlet as the romantic prototype; Hamlet is "the man who has bequeathed to modern literature and thought the obsessive preoccupation with 'authenticity.' " This concern, he goes on to say, leads to paralysis "because there is for Hamlet nothing that could possibly be in accord with his inner being. . . . The action chosen would always, whatever he did, crudely diverge from the subtle and illegible text written within." To blame Hamlet for what happens at Elsinore is like blaming the German poets of the nineteenth century for the subsequent murder of their civilization. The "authenticity" that sets Hamlet apart is caused not only by a fastidious desire to make the world accord with his ineffable feeling of selfhood, but by his knowledge of a distressing fact that others seek to conceal. The morbid manner in which he handles this knowledge may well be far from commendable; in the same manner, many romantic and postromantic writers let their original insight become obscured by evasive or obsessive behavior. Still the value of the insight remains: whether we want it or not, we cannot hide from the demands of its "authenticity." The romantic text we confront is indeed subtle, but it will appear illegible only to those interpreters who prefer not to see what it says.

# Madame de Staël and Jean-Jacques Rousseau (1966)

We know that the best means of characterizing the various preromantic thematic structures is to trace them back to the source that almost all of them have in common: the work and thought of Jean-Jacques Rousseau. Thereby we escape the superficiality of positivist histories, since any serious contact with Rousseau necessarily takes the form of a withdrawal into oneself, of an interiorization. The history of an influence then becomes, almost immediately, an internal history. This is certainly the case when we try to understand what Rousseau meant for Madame de Staël.

Rousseau's influence covers the whole of Madame de Staël's work and is to be met with in her works of fiction as well as in her critical and political texts, for it is not possible to separate Rousseau's implicit presence in a narrative like *Zulma* or a novel like *Delphine* from his explicit presence in the many references that abound from the *Lettres sur les écrits de Rousseau* (1788) to *De la littérature*. From the beginning, Rousseau will be for her both a source of inspiration and an object of reflection, an intuitive affinity that operates in the vague and obscure zone constituted, for Madame de Staël, by the seat of the passions, but also a mediating entity that will permit her to establish, with this zone, a relation that belongs to the clarifying world of consciousness. Morever, it is in the ambivalence of this double function that Rousseau always appeared to her as a paradoxical but indestructible combination of passion and reflection, the symbol of an inner life unified by a reflection that knows no other object than the passional self.

The association of Rousseau with passional sensibility has of course nothing surprising about it at the end of the eighteenth century. In Madame de Staël we find all the naive forms of the cult of sensibility from which, at the time, so many versions of the Rousseau myth took their inspiration. Madame de Staël is moved that "Rousseau [had not] found a tender soul who might have been concerned to reassure him, to revive his defeated courage, who might have loved him deeply"; she adheres without hesitation to the legend of suicide, which she accounts for by anguish in the face of solitude; she censures him for having depicted Julie's attitude toward Saint-Preux as too unimpassioned and too methodical. But in the *Lettres sur Rousseau,* there is mixed with this conventional sensibility a reflection that allows her to consider Rousseau as she "observes herself . . . and to paint what she feels" (Introduction to *Zulma*). "Elevation of soul," Madame de Staël says apropos of Rousseau, "is born of self-consciousness." This one phrase would suffice to distinguish her version of Rousseauistic meditation from the dryness with which a certain eighteenth-century mind substitutes for feeling, the conscious will to feel. André Monglond has characterized this false relation between thought and emotion, in which the spirit of analysis gives way to an atrophied sentiment: "an entirely artificial sensibility indulged in by a century that, having abused analysis, vainly attempts by factitious means to recover its lost possessions." This judgment has no application to the relation between Madame de Staël and Rousseau. Madame de Staël's analytic language is capable of the worst aberrations: banality, dissimulation, self-serving sentimentality — but her reflection is inexorably linked, in its origins, to passion, in an alliance so intimate that it becomes impossible to say where the one begins and the other ends. It is this indestructible unity that we want to apprehend, by showing how Madame de Staël recognized herself in Rousseau.

Let us listen to her speak of Rousseau in this highly revealing text, which is to be found in *De la littérature:*

> Only Rousseau (and Goethe) could paint reflective passion, the passion that judges itself without being able to master itself. This scrutiny of its own sensations, made by the very being those sensations are devouring, would chill our interest, if anyone but a man of genius sought to attempt it. But nothing is more moving than this combination of pains and meditations, of observations and delirium, which represents the unhappy man contemplating himself by thought, and succumbing to pain, focusing his imagination upon himself, strong enough to observe himself suffer, and yet incapable of affording his soul any relief whatever.

What is most striking in this passage is the profound association between reflection and suffering: not only does reflection begin in disorder, in a disarray of being, but it is of no help in lightening that pain, whose scope exceeds any possibility of human intervention. Hence it is an avowal of weakness, but of a weakness that nonetheless contains a positive moment. For this pain, which risks toppling us over into nonbeing, must be maintained long enough for reflection to be able to constitute itself. It must be, according to Madame de Staël's expression, "strong enough to observe itself suffer." The strength of reflection is like the strength Baudelaire invokes in his famous lines:

> Ah Seigneur! donnez-moi la force et le courage
> De contempler mon coeur et mons corps sans dégout.

> [Lord give me strength and courage to behold
> my body and my heart without disgust!]

But for this text to yield all it contains, we must juxtapose it to another passage in which Rousseau is no longer in question, but where Madame de Staël justifies the method she has followed in writing her essay *De l'influence des passions:*

> In composing this work, in which I pursue the passions as destructive to happiness . . . it is myself whom I have sought to persuade; I have written in order to regain possession of myself, through so many struggles, to release my faculties from the slavery of the sentiments, to raise myself to a kind of abstraction that allows me to observe the pain of my soul. . . . Absolute distraction being impossible, I have sought whether the very meditation on the objects that concern us did not lead to the same result, and if, by approaching the phantom, it did not vanish, rather than moving away. . . . I have tried this, and I am not certain of having succeeded in the first test of my doctrine upon myself; hence would it be up to me to assert its absolute power? Alas! upon approaching, by reflection, all that constitutes human character, we lose ourselves in the mists of melancholy. Political institutions, civil relations offer us almost certain means of public happiness or misery; but the depths of the soul are so difficult to plumb! . . . Inexplicable phenomenon, this spiritual existence of humanity that . . . seems still to be on the eve of its creation, immured in the chaos that precedes it!

The movement described here, and which is generated by an effort of self-consciousness in the very act of writing, is exactly like that which characterized Rousseau: the same combination of reflection and pain, the same impotence of reflection to conquer the pain that gives birth to it. More explicitly even than in the passage on Rousseau, it appears that this failure is not due to any defective functioning, to some imprecision in the technique of thought, to which it would be possible to apply some remedy. Reflection fails not because it lacks power or effectiveness but, on the contrary, because it succeeds all too well. It succeeds in knowing its object—i.e., the self—for what it is, in all the painful imprecision of its contingency. The cause of reflection's failure resides not in itself but in being, in that "chaos that precedes it" and to which it permits returning. Hence we see Madame de Staël concluding with the same profound truth, independently of whether she turns toward Rousseau or toward herself. Rousseau and her own passional self function in a rigorously interchangeable manner, as if one could be substituted for the other without in any way influencing the content of the truth of which both are the point of departure.

It would be wrong to believe that Madame de Staël's egotism simply substituted her own self for Rousseau's: as a description of what constitutes the irreducible specificity of the author of *La Nouvelle Héloïse*, her observations are wonderfully accurate. We shall find their equivalent, in her period, only in certain notations of Joubert or in the inspired intuitions of Hölderlin. It is a matter of something much more important than a simple substitution of oneself for someone else. We might say quite as validly that in this exchange of subjectivities, it is Rousseau who has been substituted for Madame de Staël's self—quite as much as the converse. It is in the nature of this substitution to be reversible, to proceed from the self toward the other, as well as from the other toward the self. It would be possible for Madame de Staël to assert: "Jean-Jacques Rousseau, c'est moi," without in the least alienating herself from her own nature. For it is precisely this possibility of thus substituting herself for Rousseau that defines her own being.

Moreover, can we assert that this possibility of substitution is based on an identification, on a close coincidence, like that of two forms that overlap at all points? This would fail to recognize that such mutual transparency necessarily implies a distance, and that it is this distance that makes the relation between Rousseau and Madame de Staël the perfect emblem of reflection. Speaking of Rousseau, Madame de Staël does not spare her criticisms or her suggestions; she proposes various options, changes in the elaboration of works, and in general displays the greatest freedom of judgment. It is rather when this distance is lacking that we founder, apropos of Rousseau, in the sentimental platitudes we mentioned earlier. This relative detachment is therefore immensely important, and Madame de Staël knows this very well. Preparing to speak of her favorite work by Rousseau, *La Nouvelle Héloïse,* here is how she puts it: "It is with pleasure that I undertake to retrace the effect this work produced on me; I shall try chiefly to guard against an enthusiasm that might be attributed to my soul's disposition rather than to the talent shown in the work. . . . Hence I shall shift myself some *distance* from the impressions I have received and I shall write about *Héloïse* as I would do, I believe, if time had aged my heart." She will use almost the same terms when she wants to express the point of view she will adopt to speak of the passion that, more than any other, defines her inmost nature. "It is by the aid of reflection, it is by *distancing from me* the enthusiasm of youth that I shall consider love . . . , the highest felicity that can exalt human hopes." Once again, Rousseau's work and intimate passion are interchangeable when it comes to naming an essential movement of consciousness. It appears that the identity between Madame de Staël and Rousseau is based on the possibility of establishing a distance in relation to what, in them, is closest to them. It is because, of all writers, Rousseau is closest to Madame de Staël that she is compelled to observe him, so to speak, at arm's length, to maintain between herself and him that "pious distance" Valéry invokes in his *Fragments de Narcisse:*

Cette tremblante, frêle, et pieuse distance
Entre moi-même et l'onde, et mon âme, et les dieux!

[That frail, tremulous and pious distance
Between myself and the pool, and my soul and the gods!]

Madame de Staël's authentic self is constituted in the space of that distance, a space opened by the act of reflection.

This distance can also be conceived temporally. "There is one age for experience," Rousseau says in the preface to *Julie,* "another for memory. Feeling dies out at the end, but the soul possessed of sensibility *remains* forever." To the link that unites reflection to suffering is joined here the link that unites reflection to duration. Memory, temporal form of self-consciousness, is what confers duration on the soul and characterizes that soul as "possessed of sensibility," with all the period moral and ontological connotations this term implies. Madame de Staël says just this in the sentence already quoted: "Elevation of soul is born of self-consciousness." This ethical language, which risks becoming moralistic and justificatory, must not conceal from us the temporal nature of her assertion. For what Madame de Staël is speaking of in terms of morality in reality designates a certain sentiment of duration, very close to Rousseau's reflective temporality. The origin of suffering—which, it will be recalled, represents for her the fundamental mode of human *Dasein*—resides in an experience of a temporal order: inconstancy.

In Madame de Staël's fictions, inconstancy—which a moralizing bad faith readily transforms into the other person's infidelity, especially that of the beloved man—manifests itself with all the unexpected violence of a divine intervention. It does not result from a psychological disposition of the characters, but is produced like a lightning bolt, like something that entirely escapes our will. Against the fundamental inconstancy of being, the self is defenseless. It can only let itself be driven toward the abyss of its own destruction, hastening if possible the deliberation of physical time by what will it has left. From this point of view, Madame de Staël's fictions, much more than the ironic *Werther,* are an ill-disguised exhortation to suicide. But even in one of her earliest fictions, in the little narrative entitled *Zulma,* the heroine, a victim of infidelity, is allowed the few minutes necessary to interpret her destiny. This duration granted Zulma, which saves her from nothing and in no way diminishes her pain, nonetheless plays an important part: in this brief narrative, it symbolizes the act of literary creation.

In the chapter of Madame de Staäl's essay on the passions, which takes the place initially intended for *Zulma,* this dialectic of inconstancy and duration is asserted even more particularly:

> The indissoluble links are opposed to the heart's free choice; but a degree of independence renders almost impossible a lasting affection; there must be memories to stir the heart, and there are no profound memories, if one does not believe in the rights of the past over the future. . . . There are intervals in all that belongs to the imagination, and if morality does not fill them, in one of these transitory intervals, we shall be separated from each other forever.

All of Madame de Staël's ambivalence lies in the use of the word "morality" in this context. On the practical level, it signifies the play of rights and duties in the concrete circumstances of existence; but on the ontological level, it can designate the reflective relation of the self to being.

In the realm of facts, this duration that "morality" comes to fill can represent Madame de Staël's abusive employment of gratitude to destroy others' freedom; it is at the source of all the ambiguities of pity, of kindness, and of duplicity that abound in her work. But, considered as an ontological temporal structure, this duration is precisely equivalent to the reflective *distance* we were just speaking of. It is the time of the fiction the writer grants herself, the memory of the passion in which the latter is maintained during the time it takes to be enlightened by consciousness, instead of letting oneself be immediately destroyed by the threatening inconstancy. Rousseau's reflective reverie is steeped in a similar duration, which is quite distinct from the physical flow of time, since it is reverie itself that engenders this duration, as a correlative of consciousness.

Yet this fictive duration that Madame de Staël, following Rousseau, discovers as a temporal form of reflection, remains empty of any substantial content. So long as it is oriented toward the past, her reflection can operate on a given content, but it has nothing left to accomplish once this content is exhausted. As soon as her story is over, there is nothing left for Zulma to do but annihilate herself, with an almost comical alacrity. It seems impossible to transform this retrospective temprality into a present temporality, which would be that of the work actually being written. In *Delphine,* in which the form of the epistolary novel necessitates an action articulated in the present, the narrative space the author has opened for herself refuses to be filled. A series of novelistic peripeteias leads to the customary assertion of failure and the pain of love, a failure linked this time to another form of inconstancy, the tyranny of public opinion. But this point is reached relatively early in the novel and leads to a situation comparable to that which will exist between Julie and Saint-Preux, once the father's return prevents the happy union of the two lovers. From this moment, Delphine can say, like Saint-Preux, that henceforth "we are beginning to live again in order to begin suffering again, and the sentiment of our existence is for us only a sentiment of pain" (*La Nouvelle Héloïse,* III).

In Madame de Staël's novel, the many pages that follow this moment are no more than a void that no diversion can fill, a void without, in which even expectation has lost its tension. A monotonous succession of foreseeable catastrophes here engenders only an interminable succession of groans. In contrast, *La Nouvelle Héloïse* only gains in density and in substance as the work approaches its end. This contrast is very suggestive. In the work most directly inspired by her favorite novel, that *Nouvelle Héloïse* of which she so often speaks with perspicacity and on which *Delphine* is modeled, it seems that Rousseau and Madame de Staël come to a parting of the ways. At the risk of seeming to conclude this discussion on a negative note, we must briefly interpret this divergence, not that it leads to a value judgment unfavorable to Madame de Staël, but because it sheds light on an essential aspect of the relation between reflection and literary creation.

In *Delphine,* it is with a presistence bordering on obsession that Madame de Staël places her heroine in situations in which everything guides her toward renunciation. And it is with the same persistence that Delphine rejects each of these occasions. Neither loyalty to a promise given in formal circumstances, nor the concern for another's legitimate happiness—nothing can lead Delphine to renounce the possibility of satisfying here and now her desire for happiness. And when, in her own commentaries on her novel, Madame de Staël suggests an alternative to the attitude of her character, it is not in terms of sacrifice but in terms of propriety: renunciation would not have been desirable in itself, but necessary in the eyes of an all-powerful society. Delphine's persistence thus reflects a parallel decision of the novelist: capable of establishing the distance of reflection in relation to herself, Madame de Staël is incapable, however, of not employing this reflection, if need be, to justify herself in others' eyes. It is no accident that Zulma was already placed in the situation of someone who must convince a tribunal of her innocence.

To shift from self-justification to self-comprehension, reflection must be able to renounce not only the hope of overcoming pain, but even the hope of justifying itself by means of that pain, of making it serve self-glorification. Rousseau knew this well, who put Julie's renunciation at the heart of his novel, and who specifically refused to make this renunciation into a martyrdom. The grim happiness that prevails in the second part of *La Nouvelle Héloïse* is the exact opposite of Delphine's plangent suffering. The ambience of Clarens is that of authentic reflection. By opting for reflection instead of an attachment to the equivocal pleasures of sensuality and heroism, the novelist chose to prefer the success of his fiction to that of his private self. The world of Clarens is an integrally fictive world and based on a difficult knowledge. Here everyone knows that the failure of personal happiness is not due to the intervention of others, but that it reveals the very movement of being. Hence there is no further need to justify oneself before others, nor to hope that happiness can be found in the real world. Far from being an idealization or a compensation, the fiction, by the intermediary of artistic creation, brings the private self closer to being. The same movement occurs in Rousseau when Pygmalion's self, engendering Galatea, permits her to become the self's true center. The priority of the fiction is achieved in self-renunciation. It suffices that Julie-Galatea appears on the scene for the novelistic space to be filled forthwith; she need scarcely make a move and immediately, by her mere presence, a whole world radiates around her, while Delphine, on the contrary, can engender only a void. No matter how much Madame de Staël multiplies peripeteias and piles up complications, nothing can be achieved for a self that remains captive of its "facticity," that believes itself determined in its destiny by entities that belong to its own world.

We must be careful not to blame Madame de Staël for this. Her oeuvre is the kind that allows us a better understanding of the nature of masterpieces. As is indicated only too well by the critical history of *La Nouvelle Héloïse,* Rousseau's apparent positivity risks masking the depth of negativity and renunciation from which his oeuvre derives and at the price of which it could develop. This same negativity provokes us directly into the void that inhabits Madame de Staël's fiction. By its intermediary, we can rediscover the essential role Rousseau's work has played. Ultimately, it is Rousseau who is illuminated by its contact, and not the converse. Here too, the relation between Madame de Staël and Jean-Jacques Rousseau resembles the relation between reflection and being: it is what is reflected that finally becomes, itself, a source of light.

Translated by Richard Howard

# Introduction to the Poetry of
# John Keats (1966)

In the course of time, the reputations of the main English romantic poets have undergone considerable and revealing fluctuations. It would nowadays be considered eccentric to rate Byron above Wordsworth or Blake, yet during his lifetime Byron's fame far surpassed that of his contemporaries. Not till the end of the nineteenth century did Blake begin to receive full recognition, and we are now no longer surprised to find critics give him a central position that none of his contemporaries would have remotely suspected. We may have some difficulty in sharing the excitement with which the young Yeats discovered the audacities of Shelley's more speculative poems, but, on the other hand, Arnold's judgment in rating Wordsworth above Spenser, Dryden, Pope, and Coleridge might again find some support, albeit for reasons that have little in common with Arnold's.

These fluctuations reflect changes in critical temper that are themselves the result of a continued reinterpretation of romanticism. Time and again, literary and critical movements set out with the avowed aim of moving beyond romantic attitudes and ideas; in America alone, Pound's imagism, Irving Babbitt's neohumanism, and the New Criticism of T. S. Eliot are relatively recent instances of such a trend; the same antiromantic (or anti-idealist) bias underlies neorealist and neo-Marxist tendencies here and abroad. But time and again, it turns out that the new conceptions that thus assert themselves were in fact already present in the full context of European romanticism; instead of moving beyond these problems, we are merely becoming aware of certain aspects of romanticism that had remained hidden from our perception. We certainly have left behind the Victorian image of Wordsworth, but Wordsworth himself is far from having been fixed and determined by a poetic or critical itinerary that went beyond him. What sets out as a claim to overcome romanticism often turns out to be merely an expansion of our understanding of the movement, leading inevitably to changes in our images of individual poets.

The poetry of Keats is no exception. As the amount of biographical and critical studies augments in quantity and in quality, our knowledge of Keats has increased considerably, yet many questions remain unresolved, as if the work had not yielded all the possibilities of significance that it may contain. The curve of his reputation shows perhaps less dramatic ups and downs than in the case of Blake or even Shelley: it has constantly risen since his death at the age of twenty-five in 1821. He had already earned the enthusiastic appreciation of several close and loyal friends during his lifetime, but his career was too short to give him the real critical recognition that would have been so useful: Wordsworth paid little attention to him; for all his apparent sympathy, Shelley was deeply uncongenial and remained aloof; Coleridge was already on the decline and Keats hardly knew him; Hazlitt was the object of his admiration rather than a full admirer, and even Hunt's ultimate loyalty went to Shelley rather than to the earlier disciple. Later in the century, the Victorians were never able to forgive Keats his plebeian birth and the unbridled erotic despair of the love letters to Fanny Brawne; Arnold has to strain a great deal to find in the life and letters traces of the moral high seriousness that he cannot fail to detect in the greater poems. Some of this Victorian snobbishness still echoes in Yeats's reference to Keats as a "coarse-bred son of a livery-stable keeper" who made "luxuriant song" out of his frustrations. But the poetry had always found considerable appreciation, not only for its decorative aspects that so delighted the Pre-Raphaelites, but for its thematic depth as well. In our own century, when the relationship between life and work is understood in a somewhat less literal manner, a considerable exegetic effort has been directed especially toward the elucidation of the shorter poems. Continued interest in the biography and in the letters—a new edition of the letters edited by Hyder E. Rollins appeared in 1958 and W. J. Bate's biography appeared in 1963—indicates that the problem that preoccupied the Victorians, the contrast between the banality of Keats's life and the splendor of his work, has not been fully resolved. Arnold's remarks about an element of vulgarity in Keats have cut so deep that recent biographers are still writing polemically in an effort to dispel their effect. This almost always results, even among Keats's warmest admirers, in a trace of condescension or defensiveness, as if one were forced to look for attenuating circumstances. The facts are distorted either by making the life appear darker and more tragic than it was, or by exalting Keats's very genuine courage and self-sacrifice to the point where it obscures his poetry. Except for the last few months, the life is in fact more banal than tragic; it is one of Keats's most engaging traits that he resists all temptation to see himself as the hero of a tragic adventure. The unfavorable circumstances of his birth—he was the eldest of four orphaned children cheated out of their modest inheritance by an unscrupulous guardian—were such that he lived almost always oriented toward the future, keeping his capacity for personal happiness in reserve, so to speak, for the better days he saw ahead. The pathos, of course, is that he never reached these days, but he was no longer able to write by the time he realized this. In reading Keats, we are therefore reading the work of a man whose experience is mainly literary. The growing insight that underlies the remarkably swift development of his talent was gained primarily from the act of writing. In this case, we are on very safe ground when we derive our understanding primarily from the work itself.

The pattern of Keats's work is prospective rather than retrospective; it consists of hopeful preparations, anticipations of future power rather than meditative reflections on past moments of insight or harmony. His poems frequently climax in questions—"Was there a poet born?" "Did I wake or sleep?"—or in statements such as: "and beyond these / I must not think now . . . ", "but now no more, / My wand'ring spirit must not further soar"—that suggest he has reached a threshold, penetrated to the borderline of a new region that he is not yet ready to explore but toward which all his future efforts will be directed. *I Stood Tiptoe* announces *Endymion, Endymion* announces *Hyperion, Hyperion* prefigures *The Fall of Hyperion,* etc.; Keats is steadily moving forward, trying to pull himself up to the level and the demands of his own prospective vision. None of the larger works— and we know that the larger works mattered most to him—can in any sense be called finished. The circle never seems to close, as if he were haunted by a dream that always remains in the future.

The dream is dramatically articulated from the very start, in a naïve but clear mythological outline that even the awkward diction of the early poems cannot altogether hide from sight. It reveals Keats's original conception of the poet's role and constitutes the thematic center around which the history of his development is organized.

In one of Keats's longer early poems, the title line as well as the last word suggest a soaring, Icarus-like urge to "burst our mortal bars" and leave the human world behind. But nothing could be less like Shelley's skylark, a "scorner of the ground," than Keats's young poet. Icarus's rise as well as his fall are acts of overbearing that destroy balance and "burst" beyond natural limits. Even in the earliest poems, Keats never conceives of poetry in this manner: to the contrary, poetry is always the means by which an excess is tempered, a flight checked, a separation healed. In terms of the material sensations toward which Keats's imagery naturally tends, this tendency is expressed in the impression of a temperate breeze that cools excessive heat, but never chills—a sensation so all-pervading throughout the early poems that it cannot be considered merely conventional or derivative:

> . . . pebbly beds;
> Where swarms of minnows show their little heads, . . .
> To taste the luxury of sunny beams
> Tempered with coolness.
>
> (I Stood Tiptoe, lines 71ff.)

> Where had he been, from whose warm head outflew
> That sweetest of all songs, that ever new,
> That aye refreshing, pure deliciousness . . .
>
> (lines 181ff.)

> The breezes were ethereal, and pure,
> And crept through half-closed lattices to cure
> The languid sick; it cooled their fevered sleep . . .
>
> (lines 221ff.)

The early Keats discovers the narrative equivalence of this restoring, balancing power of poetry in the Greek myths, which he interprets at the time as tales in which the distance between mortals and immortals is overcome by an act of erotic union. As a story of love between a goddess and a mortal shepherd, Endymion attracts him even more than Psyche or Narcissus, and he announces it as his main theme before embarking on the narrative poem *Endymion* itself. But the symbolic function of the poet as a narrator of myths immediately widens in significance: since he can "give meek Cynthia her Endymion," he not only restores the natural balance of things, but his exemplary act extends to the whole of mankind. The union between the goddess and the shepherd prefigures directly the communal celebration of mankind liberated from its suffering. By telling "one wonder of [Cynthia's] bridal night," the poet causes the "languid sick" to awake and

> Young men, and maidens at each other gazed
> With hands held back, and motionless, amazed
> To see the brightness in each other's eyes;
> And so they stood, filled with a sweet surprise,
> Until their tongues were loosed in poesy.
> Therefore no lover did of anguish die:
> But the soft numbers, in that moment spoken,
> Made silken ties, that never may be broken.
>
> (I Stood Tiptoe, lines 231ff.)

Here we have Keats's original dream in all its naïve clarity: it is a dream about poetry as a redeeming force, oriented toward others in a concern that is moral but altogether spontaneous, rooted in the fresh sensibility of love and sympathy and not in abstract imperatives. The touching tale of a lovelorn goddess replaces the Ten Commandments, a humanized version of Hellenic myth replaces biblical sternness, in an optimistic belief that the universe naturally tends toward the mood of temperate balance and that poetry can always recapture the freshness of ever-rising springs.

The optimism of this myth is tempered, however, by the negative implications it contains: if poetry is to redeem, it must be that there is a need for redemption, that humanity is indeed "languid sick" and "with temples bursting." The redemption is the happier future of a painful present. One of the lines of development that Keats's poetry will follow reaches a deeper understanding of this pain that, in the earlier texts, is merely a feverish restlessness, a discordance of the sensations that creates a tension between warring extremes of hot and cold. Some of his dissatisfaction with the present is transposed in Keats's image of his own situation as a beginning poet on the contemporary literary scene: the greatness of the major predecessors—Spenser, Shakespeare, and Milton—measures his own inadequacy and dwarfs the present:

> Is there so small a range
> In the present strength of manhood, that the high
> Imagination cannot freely fly
> As she was wont of old?
> (*Sleep and Poetry*, lines 162ff.)

Totally oriented toward the future, Keats cannot draw strength from this past grandeur; his use of earlier models will always be more a sympathetic imitation than a dialogue between past and present, as between Milton and Wordsworth in *The Prelude*. Hence Keats's use of earlier poets is more technical than thematic: however Spenserian or Miltonic the diction of *The Eve of St. Agnes* and *Hyperion* may be, Spenser and Milton are not present as such in the poems; Keats has to derive all his power from energy he finds in himself or in his immediate vicinity. But he experiences his own times as literarily deficient: a curious passage from *Sleep and Poetry*, where the entire movement of the poem, as well as the allegiance to Leigh Hunt, would demand the unmixed praise of contemporary poetry, turns into a criticism of Byron and Wordsworth for failing to deliver the message of hope that Keats would like to hear. As a criticism of *The Excursion* the observation would be valid enough, but it is presented instead as a source of personal discouragement. A certain form of despondency and stagnation seems to threaten Keats from the start and forces him to take shelter in falsely idyllic settings like the one at the end of *Sleep and Poetry*, where the problem that concerns him can be temporarily forgotten but not resolved.

Retreats of this kind recur throughout the work, but they gain in poetic significance as the predicament from which he retreats grows in universality. This progression can be traced in the changed use of Ovidian myth from *Endymion* on, as compared to the earliest poems. Originally, the myths serve to gain access to the idyllic aspects of nature: they are "delightful stories" about "the fair paradise of Nature's light." The sad tales alternate with joyful ones merely for the sake of variety. This, of course, is by no means the dominant mood in Ovid himself, who often reports acts of refined cruelty with harsh detachment. From *Endymion* on, the movement of mythical metamorphosis, practically absent from the early poems, achieves a striking prominence that will maintain itself to the end; the very narrative pattern of *Endymion,* of *Lamia,* and, in a more hidden way, of *Hyperion* and the odes, is based on a series of transformations from one order of being into another. The various metamorphic combinations between the inanimate, the animal, human, and divine world keep appearing, and the moment of transformation always constitutes the dramatic climax toward which the story is oriented. Far from being merely picturesque, the metamorphoses acquire an obsessive intensity in which one recognizes a more mature version of the original happy dream of redemption.

The erotic contact between the gods and man in Ovid is anything but the idyllic encounter between Cynthia and Endymion in *I Stood Tiptoe;* it results instead in the brutal degradation of the human being to a lower order of life, his imprisonment in the rigid forms of the inanimate world: Niobe's "very tongue frozen to her mouth's roof" (*Metamorphoses* VI, line 306), Daphne's "swift feet grown fast in sluggish roots" (I, line 551), Myrrha, the mother of Adonis, watching her skin change to hard bark (X, line 494). This state of frozen immobility, of paralysis under the life-destroying impact of eternal powers, becomes the obsessive image of a human predicament that poetry is to redeem. A long gallery of human beings thus caught in poses of frozen desire appears throughout the work: the lovers in Book III of *Endymion* imprisoned in a sea cave "vast, and desolate, and icy-cold" (III, line 632), the figures on the Grecian Urn, the knight-at-arms of "La Belle Dame sans Merci" caught "On the cold hillside," the knights and ladies at the beginning of *The Eve of St. Agnes* "sculptured dead, on each side, [who] seem to freeze, / Emprisoned in black, purgatorial rails," Saturn at the beginning of *Hyperion* "quiet as a stone, / Still as the silence round about his lair." There hardly exists a single of Keats's important poems in which a version of this recurrent theme fails to appear, though the outward form may vary. It is most frequently associated with the sensation of cold, as if the cooling breeze of *I Stood Tiptoe* heralding the benevolent arrival of the gods had suddenly turned icy and destructive. The myth is a paradoxical version of the mutability theme: the passage of time, the loss of power, death, are the means by which the gods announce their presence; time is the only eternal force and it strips man of his ability to move freely in the direction of his own desire; generations are wasted by old age, "youth grows pale, and specter-thin, and dies" and "Everything is spoiled by use" ("Fancy" line 68). Under the impact of this threat, mankind is made powerless in the stagnation that Keats felt at times in himself and saw around him. Mutability causes paralysis.

His dream then becomes a kind of reversal of the Ovidian metamorphosis, in which man was frozen into a natural form: the poet is the one who can reverse the metamorphosis and reanimate the dead forms into life. Again, Book III of *Endymion* gives a clear mythological outline of this process: by a mere touch of his wand, warmth is restored to the frozen lovers and the reanimated figures rejoice in an exact repetition of the redemption scene from *I Stood Tiptoe* (*Endymion*, III, lines 780ff.). This dream, by which dead nature is restored to life and refinds, as it were, the human form that was originally its own, is Keats's fondest reverie. A large measure of his poetical power stems from this. It allows him to give nature such an immediate and convincing presence that we watch it take on effortlessly human form: the ode "To Autumn" is the supreme achievement of this Ovidian metamorphosis in reverse. His ability to make his conceits and metaphors spring out of a genuine identity of nature with man, rather than out of an intellectual awareness of an analogy between both, is also rooted in this dream. It is so strong that it forces itself upon the narrative of his longer poems, even when the original story does not allow for it. In *Hyperion,* one can never conceive of Apollo as the warring opponent of the Titans. Instead, the story inevitably turns toward a repetition of the Glaucus episode in *Endymion:* Apollo tends to become the young man whose task it is to free and rejuvenate Saturn, the victim of old age. We are dealing with still another version of Keats's humanitarian dream. He will reach maturity at the end of a rather complicated itinerary, when the last trace of naïveté is removed from this vision.

The power by means of which the poet can redeem the suffering of mankind is called love, but love, in Keats, is a many-sided force. On the simplest level, love is merely the warmth of sensation: Endymion's ardor is such that it seems to melt the curse of time away at sheer contact. Till the later "Ode to Psyche," when love has been internalized to such an extent that it bears only the remotest relationship to anything physical, the epithet "warm" associated with Eros, preserves the link with sensation in a world that is otherwise entirely mental.

> A bright torch, and a casement ope at night,
>   To let the warm Love in!
>      ("Ode to Psyche," lines 66–67).

The importance of sensuality to Keats has been abundantly stressed; when some biographers, with the laudable intention of rescuing Keats from the Victorian reproach of coarseness, have tried to minimize the importance of erotic elements in his poetry, they present an oddly distorted picture. Yet, even his most straightforward eroticism easily turns into something more than sensation. First of all, sensuous love for him is more readily imagined than experienced; therefore it naturally becomes one of the leading symbols for the workings of the imagination. One of his most elaborate conceits on the activity of the mind, the final stanza of the "Ode to Psyche," spontaneously associates Eros with fancy; the same is true of the poem "Fancy," in which Eros is present as an activity of the mind. Moreover, since Keats is the least narcissistic of romantic poets, love is easily transferred by him to others and becomes a communal bond: one remembers how the union of Cynthia and Endymion spontaneously turns into a public feast, the kind of Rousseauistic brotherhood that recurs in romantic poetry as a symbol of reconciliation. In *Endymion* also, one passes without tension from love to a communal spirit of friendship with social and political overtones; something of the spirit of the French Revolution still echoes in these passages. In the optimistic world of *Endymion,* love and history act together as positive forces and historical redemption goes hand in hand with sensuous fulfillment.

Another aspect of the love experience, however, leads to more complex involvements. Aside from sensation, love also implies sympathy, a forgetting of the self for the sake of others, especially when the other is in a state of suffering. In the earlier poems, when the poet's sympathy goes out to Narcissus, to Psyche, or to Pan, or even when Endymion is moved to tears over the sad fate of the wood nymph Arethusa, these movements of the heart could still be considered a conventional form of sensibility. But in the recurrent image of frozen immobility, the suffering is not just an arbitrary trick of fate or a caprice of the gods: it becomes the generalized statement of the human predicament, man stifled by the awareness of his mortality. Sympathetic understanding of these threatened figures, the attempt "To think how they may ache in icy hoods and mails" (*St. Agnes*, line 18), tears us away from the safety of everyday experience and forces us to enter a realm that is in fact the realm of death. The ordinary life of consciousness is then suspended and its continuity disrupted. Hence the experience can only be expressed in metaphors such as "trance" or "sleep," suspended states of consciousness in which the self is momentarily absent. The "romantic" setting of certain dream episodes in *Endymion* or in "La Belle Dame sans Merci" should not mislead us into misunderstanding the connection between love and death that prevails here: love is not a temptation to take us out of the finite world of human experiences, still less an impulse toward a platonic heaven. Keats's love impulse is a very human sense of sympathy and pity, chivalrous perhaps, but devoid of transcendental as well as escapist dimensions. Endymion cannot resist the "sorrow" of the Indian maiden, Glaucus is taken in by the feigned tears of Circe, the knight of "La Belle Dame" is definitely lulled to sleep only after his lady has "wept, and sighed full sore," and Lamia, also, woos her lover, Lucius, by appealing to his pity as well as to his senses. Keats's imagination is fired by a mixture of sensation and sympathy in which the dual nature of love is reunited. The sympathy, however, is even more important than the sensation: love can exist without the latter but not without the former, and some of Keats's heroes are motivated by sympathy alone. This adds an important dimension to our understanding of the relationship between love, poetry, and death in his work: because poetry is essentially an act of sympathy, of human redemption, it must move though the deathlike trances that abound in Keats. One misunderstands these moments altogether if one interprets them as a flight from human suffering; to the contrary, they are the unmistakable sign of a sympathetic identification with the human predicament. There are moments of straightforward escape in Keats: we mentioned the end of *Sleep and Poetry* as one instance; several of the more trivial poems fulfill the same function. But the "tranced summer night" of *Hyperion,* the Cave of Quietude in Book IV of *Endymion,* the "drowsy numbness" of the Nightingale Ode, the "cloudy swoon" of *The Fall of Hyperion,* do not stand in opposition to human sympathy; as the subsequent dramatic action of these poems indicates, they represent a necessary first step toward the full unfolding of humanitarian love as it grows into a deeper understanding of the burden of mortality.

This expansion of the theme of love, which takes place without entering into conflict with the other, sensuous aspect of love, leads to a parallel deepening of the theme of history. In the easy simplicity of *Endymion,* Keats can herald, at the opening of Book II, the "sovereign power of love" over history: love suffices to bring about universal reconciliation and to make the slow labor of history superfluous. By the time of *Hyperion,* a considerable change has already taken place: the myth of the defeat of the Titans by a new generation of gods is interpreted as the very movement of history. Oceanus's speech (*Hyperion,* III, lines 114ff.) as well as Mnemosyne's initiation of Apollo to

> Names, deeds, gray legends, dire events, rebellions,
> Majesties, sovran voices, agonies,
> Creations and destroyings . . .
> $\qquad$ (*Hyperion,* III, lines 114ff.)

makes very clear the increased importance of the theme. But it is not till the late *Fall of Hyperion* that Keats's historical consciousness is fully developed. In *Hyperion,* it remains obscure why the knowledge of the historical past that "pours into the wide hollows of [Apollo's] brain" suffices to "make a god of [him]." The corresponding scene in *The Fall of Hyperion* may be confused in some respects, but not as far as the poet's attitude toward history is concerned: history, in its most general aspects, is for him a privileged subject, because the gift of sympathy, which he possesses to a larger degree than any other man, allows him to understand the sacrificial nature of all historical movement, as epitomized in the downfall of Saturn. Far from reasserting the consoling law stated by Oceanus, "That first in beauty should be first in might," (*Hyperion,* II, line 229), the historical awareness in *The Fall* returns to the deeper theme of man's temporal contingency. The poet is the chosen witness of the damage caused by time; by growing in consciousness he gains no new attributes of beauty or might, merely the negative privilege of witnessing the death of those who surpassed him in greatness. The suggestion of a conquering, youthful Apollo has entirely disappeared. The dynamic thrust of history itself is frozen into immobility by the deadly power of time, and the poet now has to expand his capacity for sympathy until it encompasses the full range of this tragedy:

> Without stay or prop
> But my own weak mortality, I bore
> The load of this eternal quietude,
> The unchanging gloom . . .
> *(The Fall of Hyperion,* I, lines 388ff.)

History can only move by becoming aware of its own contingency. From his earliest poems on, Keats had conceived of his own work as a movement of becoming, a gradual widening of his consciousness by successive stages. The pattern is present in the prefigured outline of his own career in *Sleep and Poetry,* in the structure of *Endymion,* which, for all its apparent disorder, is nevertheless organized as a consistent "growth of a poet's mind," in the famous letter to Reynolds of May 3, 1818, on the poet's progress from the thoughtless Chamber to the "Chamber of Maiden-Thought." This prospective scheme now no longer appears as a reassuring projection, since every step in the progression takes on the form of a tragedy beyond redemption, though not beyond the power of understanding. Nowhere does Keats come closer to a historical consciousness that recognizes and names the full power of negativity. Traveling entirely by his own pathways, he comes upon some of the insights that will shape the destiny of the nineteenth and twentieth centuries.

Yet, it seems that Keats never achieves an authority that is commensurate with the quality of this perception. The conception of the poet's role, in *The Fall of Hyperion,* appears at once so lofty in its impersonality and disinterestedness, yet so humane in its concern for the grief of others, that we would expect a more serene tone in Keats's later work. Instead, he frequently sounds the strident note of someone who sees through the fallacy of his own certainties. There seems to be little room for self-deception in the stern wisdom of *The Fall of Hyperion;* where are we to find the point where Keats lies open to his own reproof?

Nothing could be more genuine than the positive aspect of Keats's concern for others: neither in the poetry nor in the letters can one discover a jarring tone that would reveal the presence of affectation or pose in his humanitarian attitude. Keats's generosity is total and all the more admirable since it is never based on an idealization of himself or of others, or on an attempt to emulate a chosen model. Perfect good faith, however, does not shelter us from the intricacies of moral inauthenticity. Keats's gift for sympathy has a negative aspect, and the significance of his complete evolution can only be understood if one takes this into account.

Already in *Endymion,* when Keats is speaking of love and friendship as central formative experiences, he refers to these experiences as "self-destroying":

> But there are
> Richer entanglements, enthrallments far
> More self-destroying, leading, by degrees,
> To the chief intensity: the crown of these
> Is made of love and friendship . . .
>
> (Endymion, I, lines 797ff.)

"Self-destroying" is obviously used in a positive sense here, to designate the moral quality of disinterestedness—yet "destroying" is a curiously strong term. The phrase is revealing, for a recurrent pattern in the poetry indicates a strong aversion to a direct confrontation with his own self; few poets have described the act of self-reflection in harsher terms. For Endymion, the most miserable condition of man is that in which he is left to consider his own self in solitude, even when this avowedly takes him close to teaching the "goal of consciousness" (II, line 283):

> There, when new wonders ceased to float before,
> And thoughts of self came on, how crude and sore
> The journey homeward to habitual self!
> A mad pursuing of the fog-born elf,
> Whose flitting lantern, through rude nettle-brier,
> Cheats us into a swamp, into a fire,
> Into the bosom of a hated thing.
>
> (II, lines 274ff.)

The inward quest for self-knowledge is described here in the very terms used by Milton to represent the triumph of Satanic temptation (*Paradise Lost,* IX, lines 633ff.) The "hated thing" to which Keats refers is the situation, rather than the content of his own consciousness: the condition of the "sole self" is one of intolerable barrenness, the opposite of all that imagination, poetry, and love can achieve. The experience of being "tolled back to one's sole self" is always profoundly negative. He almost succeeds in eliminating himself from his poetry altogether. There is, of course, much that is superficially autobiographical in *Endymion* and even in *Hyperion,* but one never gains an intimate sense of Keats's own selfhood remotely comparable to that conveyed by other romantic poets. The "I" of the Nightingale Ode, for instance, is always seen in the movement that takes it away from its own center. The emotions that accompany the discovery of the authentic self, feelings of guilt and dread as well as sudden moments of transparent clarity, are lacking in Keats. Poetic "sleep" or "trance" is a darkening, growing opacity of the consciousness. Suffering plays a very prominent role in his work, but it is always the suffering of others, sympathetically but objectively perceived and so easily generalized into historical and universal pain that it rarely appears in its subjective immediacy: a passage such as the opening scene of *Hyperion* gains its poetic effectiveness from the controlled detachment of an observer who is not directly threatened. The only threat that Keats seems to experience subjectively is that of self-confrontation.

Keats's sympathetic love thus appears less simple than it may seem at first sight: his intense and altogether genuine concern for others serves, in a sense, to shelter him from the self-knowledge he dreads. He is a man distracted from the awareness of his own mortality by the constant spectacle of the death of others. He can go very far in participating in their agony: he is indeed one "to whom the miseries of the world / Are misery and will not let [him] rest" (*Fall of Hyperion,* I, lines 148–49). But the miseries are always "of the world" and not his own, a distinction that should disappear when the suffering referred to is so general that it designates a universal human predicament. Although it would be entirely false to say of Keats that he escaped out of human suffering into the idealized, trancelike condition of poetry, one can say, with proper caution, that he moves away from the burden of self-knowledge into a world created by the combined powers of the sympathetic imagination, poetry, and history, a world that is ethically impeccable, but from which the self is excluded.

The tension resulting from this ambivalence does not remain entirely hidden. It comes to the surface, for instance, in the difficult choice he has to make in his literary allegiances, when he has to reconcile his admiration for Shakespeare and Milton with his consideration for Wordsworth, whom he considered his greatest contemporary. His own term for the "self-destroying" power of the poetic imagination is "negative capability," the ability of the mind to detach itself from its own identity, and he associates this characteristic of the poetic temperament primarily with Shakespeare. It is typical, in this respect, that he would consider Shakespeare's life as exemplary: "Shakespeare led a life of Allegory" (letter to George Keats, February 19, 1819) in the full figural and Christian sense of the term, when it is precisely a life so buried under the wealth of its own inventions that it has ceased to exist as a particular experience. This stands, of course, in total contrast to what we find in Wordsworth, for whom the determining moment occurs when the mind exists in and for itself, in the transparency of an inwardness entirely focused upon the self. Even in the absence of the posthumously published *Prelude,* Keats knew the direction of Wordworth's thought and felt the challenge it offered to his own orientation. W. J. Bate, in his biography of Keats, has well seen the decisive importance of this confrontation when, in the letter of May 3, 1818, to Reynolds, Keats rates Wordsworth above Milton ("who did not think into the human heart") because he is the poet of the conscious self. But Keats did not choose, at that time, to follow Wordsworth into the "dark passages" that he had begun to explore. The poem that stems from these meditations, the first *Hyperion,* is certainly not Wordsworthian and not altogether Miltonic either: the emphasis on characterization, the deliberate variety of tones, the pageantlike conception of history, are all frankly Shakespearean, and in many ways *Hyperion* resembles an optimistic, humanized version of *Troilus and Cressida* more than *Paradise Lost*. It definitely is a poem founded on negative capability. The sense of human sympathy has grown considerably since *Endymion,* but we are even further removed from real self-awareness than in the early poem. Only at the very end of his career will these unresolved tensions come fully into the open and disrupt the continuity of his development—but this happened, not as a result of literary influence, but under the pressure of outward circumstances.

Interpreters of Keats have difficulty agreeing on the significance of his latest work: after the almost miraculous outburst of creative activity in May 1819, when he wrote practically all the great odes in quick succession, there still followed a period of nearly six months until the final onset of his illness. *The Fall of Hyperion, Lamia,* and several other shorter poems were written at that time. There is some logic in considering the entire period from June till the end of the year as one single unit—the "late" Keats—that includes the poems to Fanny Brawne, dating from the fall of 1819, and frequently considered as poetically unimportant and slightly embarrassing documents written when he was no longer in full control of his faculties. In truth, it is from *The Fall of Hyperion* on that a sharp change begins to take place; it is also from that moment on that the differences among the commentators begin to increase. For all the divergences in the interpretation of the main odes, there exists a clear consensus about the general meaning and merit of these poems; the differences refer to matters of detail and are certainly to be expected in the case of rich and complex poems studied in such great detail. But *The Fall of Hyperion* is considered by some as "the culmination of Keats's work" and the dialogue between Moneta and the poet as a "dialectical victory" over Moneta's attack on poetry; for others, however, the same passage is read as symbolizing "exhaustion and despair" at "seeing the world of poetry doomed to destruction."[1] *Lamia* has also given rise to incompatible readings and to general puzzlement. The hesitations of the critics are the unmistakable sign of a change that is so far-reaching that it requires a radical readjustment on the part of the readers. The particular difficulty and obscurity of *The Fall of Hyperion* and *Lamia* stems from the fact that they are works of transition toward a new phase that is fully revealed only in the last poems Keats wrote.

The striking fact about Keats's last poems is that they contain an attack on much that had been held sacred in the earlier work; one is reminded, at moments, of Yeats's savagely derisive treatment of his own myths in some of the *Last Poems.* There is something indecorous in the spectacle of a poet thus turning against himself, and one can understand the desire of commentators to play down this episode in Keats's history, all the more since illness, poverty, and increased bitterness invaded his life at the time, offering a convenient explanation for this radical change in tone. It would be a reflection, however, on the strength of Keats's earlier convictions if they had not been able to stand up under the pressure of these events, however damaging they may have been. Even among his near contemporaries — one thinks of Hölderlin, Maurice de Guérin, and Gérard de Nerval — some of the most assertive poems are written in a comparable state of physical and mental distress. We must understand that, far from detracting from his stature, the negativity of Keats's last poems shows that he was about to add another dimension to a poetic development that, up till then, had not been altogether genuine.

We can take as an example the poem dated October 1819, and entitled "To — ," sometimes referred to as "Ode" or "Second Ode to Fanny Brawne." The term "Ode" in the title is fitting, for the dramatic organization of the poem is very similar to that of the famous great odes; it is, in fact, the exact negative counterpart of the "Ode to a Nightingale." The paradox that was partly concealed by the richness of the language in the earlier odes is now fully revealed; the poems in fact set out to destroy the entities they claim to praise; or, to put it less bluntly, the ambiguity of feeling toward these entities is such that the poems fall apart. In the October poem, the absurdity of the dramatic situation is apparent from the first lines, in which Keats begs Fanny to assist him, by her presence, in curing a suffering of which this very presence is the sole cause:

> What can I do to drive away
> Remembrance from my eyes? for they have seen,
> Aye, an hour ago, my brilliant queen!
> Touch has a memory. O say, love, say,
> What can I do to kill it and be free
> In my old liberty?
>
> ("To — ," lines 1ff.)

The prospective character of Keats's poetry, which we stressed from the start, stands out here in its full meaning. The superiority of the future over the past expresses, in fact, a rejection of the experience of actuality. Memory, being founded on actual sensations, is for Keats the enemy of poetic language, which thrives instead on dreams of pure potentiality. In the last stanzas, the poem turns from past to future, with all the ardor of the sensuous desire that tormented Keats at the time, and with an immediacy that produces the kind of language that already proved so cumbersome in the erotic passages of *Endymion*:

> O, let me once more rest
> My soul upon that dazzling breast!
> Let once again these aching arms be placed,
> The tender gaolers of thy waist! . . .
> Give me those lips again!
>
> (*ibid.*, lines 48ff.)

The interest of the passage is that the desire it names has already been canceled out by the statement made at the onset of the poem. The passion that produces these lines is precisely what has been rejected at the start as the main obstacle to the "liberty" of poetic creation. Before Fanny's presence had put the poet within "the reach of fluttering love," his poetic faculties could grow unimpaired:

> My muse had wings
> And ever ready was to take her course
> Whither I bent her force, . . .
>
> (lines 11ff.)

This belongs to a past that preceded his involvement; the movement toward the future is checked by the awareness of a contradiction that opposes love to poetry as memory is opposed to dream. Contradicting the prayer for her return, the poem concludes by stating a preference for imaginary passion over actual presence:

> Enough! Enough! it is enough for me
> To dream of thee!

It is certainly true that the poem destroys itself in a hopeless conflict between temptation and rejection, between praise and blame, that no language can hope to resolve. What is so revealing, however, is that the contradiction so crudely manifest here is potentially present in the earlier odes as well.

The difference in situation between this late poem and the odes "On a Grecian Urn" and "To a Nightingale" is obvious enough: the urn and the nightingale are general, impersonal entities, endowed with significance by an act of the poet's imagination; Fanny Brawne, on the other hand, is a highly distinct and specific person whose presence awakens in him an acute sense of threatened selfhood. The temptation she incarnates clashes directly with his desire to forget his own self. In the earlier odes, this conflict is avoided by keeping carefully apart what the urn and the nightingale signify for Keats himself, and what they signify for Keats in relation to humanity in general. The poetic effectiveness of the odes depends entirely on the positive temptation that emanates from the symbolic entities: the world to which they give access is a world of happiness and beauty, and it is by the suggestive evocation of this world that beauty enters the poems. This, in turn, allows for the dramatic contrast with the world of actual experience, caught in the destructive power of mutability and described throughout, in the Grecian Urn as well as in the Nightingale ode, in terms that appeal directly to our moral sympathy:

> Here, where men sit and hear each other groan;
> Where palsy shakes a few, sad, last gray hairs,
> Where youth grows pale, and specter-thin, and dies;

> Where but to think is to be full of sorrow
> And leaden-eyed despairs . . .
>> ("Ode to a Nightingale," lines 24ff.)

The mixture of emotions, in these texts, is subtle and self-deceiving. On the one hand, the poet's sympathy for the suffering of mankind gives him the kind of moral authority that allows him to call for a lucid acceptance of human limitations. It is this morally responsible voice that warns his fellow men against the danger of giving in to the deceptive quality of poetic symbols: they "tease" and "deceive" in foreshadowing an eternity that is not within our reach; the urn and the nightingale finally act as powers of death and, in that sense, these poems are also written against the objects they set out to praise. But Keats does not remain in the barren, impoverished world of human contingency, the world of gray rocks and stones that is the landscape of Wordsworth's *Prelude*. As a poet, he does not seem to share in the torments of temporality. The youth that "grows pale and specter-thin, and dies" in stanza 3 of the Nightingale Ode could not possibly be the same voice that evokes so magnificently the change that comes over the world by losing oneself in the "embalmèd darkness" of the bird's song:

> I cannot see what flowers are at my feet,
> Nor what soft incense hangs upon the boughs,
> But, in embalmèd darkness, guess each sweet
> Wherewith the seasonable month endows
> The grass, the thicket, and the fruit-tree wild . . .
>> (lines 41ff.)

The richness of these most un-Wordsworthian lines can only come into being because Keats's self is in fact dissociated from the suffering mankind with which he sympathizes. As a humanist, he can lay claim to a good conscience and write poems that have reassured generations of readers, willing to be authoritatively told about the limits of their knowledge ("that is all / Ye know on earth, and all ye need to know"); but as a poet, he can indulge in the wealth of a soaring imagination whose power of metamorphosis knows no limits. The poet of the Grecian Urn would hardly be able to evoke the happy world on the urn if he were himself the creature "lowing at the skies" about to be sacrificed.

We can see from the poem "To ——," what happens when this distance between the private self and its moral stance vanishes: the late poem is the "Ode to a Nightingale" with the metamorphic power of the imagination destroyed by a sense of real selfhood. This destruction now openly coincides with the appearance of love on the scene, in an overt admission that, up to this point, the moral seriousness of the poems had not, in fact, been founded on love at all:

> How shall I do
> To get anew

> Those molted feathers, and so mount once more
>   Above, above
>   The reach of fluttering Love
> And make him cower lowly while I soar?
>           ("To —," lines 18ff.)

The violence of the feeling is reminiscent of the hostile language in which Endymion refers to solitary self-knowledge. In the experience of love, the self comes to know itself without mask, and when this happens the carefree movement of the poetic imagination falters. Before, as we know from the Nightingale Ode, the intoxication of the imagination, like that of wine, was able to fuse the familiar Keatsian tension between heat and cold into one single sensation:

> O, for a draught of vintage! that hath been
>   Cooled a long age in the deep-delved earth,
> Tasting of Flora and the country green,
>   Dance, and Provençal song, and sunburned mirth!
>           ("Ode to a Nightingale," lines 11ff.)

But now, in a world ruled by the law of love, such easy syntheses are no longer within our power:

> Shall I gulp wine? No, that is vulgarism,
>   A heresy and schism,
>     Foisted into the canon law of love; —
> No — wine is only sweet to happy men; . . .
>           ("To —," lines 24ff.)

Consequently, the metamorphosis of the landscape, achieved in stanza 5 of the Nightingale Ode under the impact of the trancelike song, fails, and we are confronted instead with the bleakness of a totally demythologized world:

> That monstrous region, whose dull rivers pour,
> Ever from their sordid urns unto the shore,
> Unowned of any weedy-hairèd gods;
> Whose winds, all zephyrless, hold scourging rods,
> Iced in the great lakes, to afflict mankind;
> Whose rank-grown forests, frosted, black, and blind,
> Would fright a Dryad; whose harsh herbaged meads
> Make lean and lank the starved ox while he feeds;
> There bad flowers have no scent, birds no sweet song,
> And great unerring nature once seems wrong.
>           (ibid., lines 34ff.)

The landscape, at last, is that of Keats's real self, which he had kept so carefully hidden up till now under poetic myth and moral generosity. It is still an imagined landscape, but rooted this time in an experience that is both intimate and painful: his brother's financial disaster near the very "Great Lakes" here evoked was caused by such a landscape, and it is certain that Keats equated his own miseries with the calamitous misadventures of his brother in America.[2] This does not make this landscape less "symbolic" than the world of the Nightingale or the Grecian Urn, but it dramatizes the distinction between a symbol rooted in the self and one rooted in an abstract dream.

The power that forces a man to see himself as he really is, is also called "philosophy" in the later Keats; the term receives the same ambiguous value emphasis as does the word "love." In the same poem "To — ," the previous poetry, written when he was free of the burden of love, is called "unintellectual" and the confining power of self-awareness is stressed again in the rhetorical question:

> What seabird o'er the sea
> Is a philosopher the while he goes
> Winging along where the great water throes?
> (lines 15ff.)

We have come a long way since the early days of *Endymion* when Keats thought of philosophy as a means to help him carry out his generous dream of human redemption. Apollonius, the philosopher in *Lamia,* has all the outward attributes of villainy, yet there can be no doubt that truth is on his side: Lucius is about to mistake the seductiveness of a serpent for real love and it is, after all, his own weakness that is to blame for his inability to survive the revelation of the truth. In this poem, Truth and Beauty are indeed at odds, but one may well conjecture that, as Keats's sense of truth grew, he would have been able to discover a beauty that would have surpassed that of Lamia. Fanny Brawne may well have looked to him more like Moneta than like La Belle Dame sans Merci.

With the development that stood behind him, this final step could only take the violently negative form of his last poems. It is morally consistent that he would have rebelled against a generosity that offered more protection than it cost him. After having acted, in all his dreams of human redemption, as the one who rescues others from their mortal plight, his last poem reverses the parts. Taking off from an innocuous line in *The Fall of Hyperion* ("When this warm scribe my hand is in the grave") he now offers his hand no longer in a gesture of assistance to others, but as the victim who defies another to take away from him the weight of his own death:

> This living hand, now warm and capable
> Of earnest grasping, would, if it were cold
> And in the icy silence of the tomb,
> So haunt thy days and chill thy dreaming nights
> That thou wouldst wish thine own heart dry of blood

So in my veins red life might stream again,
And thou be conscience-calmed—see here it is—
I hold it towards you.
                    ("This Living Hand," lines 1–8)

Romantic literature, at its highest moments, encompasses the greatest degree of generality in an experience that never loses contact with the individual self in which it originates. In the *Confessions,* Rousseau tells how an injustice committed at his expense during his youth awakened within him a universal moral sense: "I feel my pulse quicken as I write this; I shall never forget these moments if I live a hundred thousand years. This first experience of violence and injustice remained so deeply engraved on my soul that all ideas related to it take me back to this initial emotion; this experience which, at its origin, existed only for me, has acquired such a strong consistency in itself, and has grown so far away from my own self-interest, that my heart flares up at the sight or at the report of an unjust deed, committed anywhere at anyone's expense, as if it concerned me personally." It is the scope of this generalized passion that makes it possible for Rousseau to be at the same time the poet who wrote *Julie* and the moral philosopher who wrote the *Social Contract.* The same scope is present in Wordsworth and also, at times, in Blake and Coleridge. Nowadays, we are less than ever capable of philosophical generality rooted in genuine self-insight, while our sense of selfhood hardly ever rises above self-justification. Hence our criticism of romanticism so often misses the mark: for the great romantics, consciousness of self was the first and necessary step toward moral judgment. Keats's last poems reveal that he reached the same insight; the fact that he arrived at it by a negative road may make him all the more significant for us.

## Notes

1. Edward E. Bostetter in *The Romantic Ventriloquists* (Seattle: University of Washington Press, 1963), p. 171; the preceding quotation is from Harold Bloom, *The Visionary Company* (New York: Doubleday, 1961), p. 418.

2. Keats's younger brother George emigrated to Illinois, hoping to make a living from land that proved to be untillable; his financial troubles were a constant burden to Keats during the time of his engagement to Fanny Brawne and during his final illness.

# The Riddle of Hölderlin (1970)

When Hölderlin's first works began to circulate in Germany in the 1790s, they met with limited response. Hölderlin was known to be a man of considerable poetic and intellectual power: both Hegel and Schelling, who had been his fellow students at the theological seminary in Tübingen had been struck by his genius, and Schiller had taken it on himself to sponsor the literary beginnings of the younger poet who, like himself, was of Swabian birth. But, from the very beginning, something unsettling in his personality and in his poetry, a combination of tense abstraction and exalted fervor, created a barrier between Hölderlin and his contemporaries, and forced him into isolation. Goethe, dismissing some of his earlier poetic attempts as lacking in humanity and concreteness, paid little attention to him; even Schiller, who had sponsored the publication of the early novel *Hyperion*, lost sight of the man he had considered his most promising disciple.

After a short-lived attempt to launch his own literary review, Hölderlin found himself more and more thrown back on his own resources. He lived a difficult and unsettled life as a private tutor, shuttling back and forth between unsatisfactory posts and leaving most of the poetry he was writing unpublished. By the time he was thirty-five, symptoms of schizophrenia became so obvious that he was unable to lead a normal life. Finally confined in the care of a Tübingen carpenter, he remained there until his death at seventy-three. Thus the creative period of his life lasted hardly more than ten years, of which only six, from 1800 to 1806, can be considered of full poetic maturity.

Throughout the nineteenth century some interest in Hölderlin persisted, based on the semimythical figure of a "mad" poet of exceptional talent, rather than on a knowledge of the work. Nietzsche, one of the few to sense Hölderlin's full importance, rightly complained, in a letter dated October 19, 1861, that his "favorite poet" is "hardly known by the majority of his people." For more than a century, one of the most extraordinary achievements of German poetry was little known and might have become forever forgotten had it not happened that shortly before the First World War a young German scholar, Norbert von Hellingrath, began to work on Hölderlin's manuscripts and brought out the first volumes of a complete critical edition.

Since then Hölderlin's reputation has steadily grown, and he has become one of the main figures in Western poetry. His complex and demanding work has been the focus of unprecedented efforts at exegesis, producing one of the most rapidly increasing bibliographies in German literary studies. From a shadowy and eccentric minor poet Hölderlin has grown, during the last thirty years, into something like an academic institution. Methodological and ideological battles are being fought in his name; ideologists of the left and of the right claim him as one of their precursors. Such is the authority that emanates from his work that it seemed for a while that every German literary critic or historian had to prove himself by demonstrating his ability to cope with Hölderlin. The resulting literature has reached such a degree of inbred polemical and technical intricacy that it has tended to bury the freshly rediscovered work under a heap of glosses. One moved quickly from books on Hölderlin to volumes surveying the secondary literature; and it could rightly be said that the development of German criticism of the last fifty years could best be traced in Hölderlin studies.

A reaction was bound to occur and now, when new translations are making Hölderlin's work available to French- and English-speaking readers, German interest in him has—quantitatively speaking—passed its peak. This is just as well, for what is most needed at this point is a well-informed and thoughtful interpretation of specific texts rather than large generalizations about a poet who remains, in spite of so much analytic effort, enigmatic and little understood. The estrangement that existed between Hölderlin and his contemporaries persists in fact today, in spite of the admiration that now surrounds him. Indeed, when he was little known, his work was sheltered from misinterpretation, but now that all of Hölderlin's writings are studied so closely, they are often admired for the wrong reasons and made to mean something quite different from what they actually do.

One feels almost envious of the American and English readers who, thanks to the recent bilingual edition by Michael Hamburger (*Poems and Fragments* [London: Routledge & Kegan Paul, 1966]), will encounter Hölderlin's poetry for the first time, and feel its power as literature and not as a problem of literary interpretation. They may well be put off by its difficulty and obscurity. The difficulty is not due to arcane knowledge or to anomalies of form, for Hölderlin's erudition derives from classical and biblical sources, while his poetic form uses the neoclassical conventions reintroduced into the German literature by Klopstock. Rather, the obscurity stems from the fact that the poetry seems to contain little that is personal or familiar, and does not describe experiences that are easy to share. The light that hangs over Hölderlin's world is not quite the light of common day.

Goethe missed the presence of a "portrayal of human beings" (*Menschenmalerei*) and found the descriptions of nature that occur often in the poet's work overstylized and overgeneral, not rooted enough in actual observation. Had he read some of the poems written after 1799, instead of the still awkward earlier samples that Schiller sent him, he probably would not have complained about the descriptive passages in Hölderlin's poetry. For these are the passages to which the new reader is most likely to respond, the easiest introduction to Hölderlin's universe. Almost all of Hölderlin's poems contain descriptive sections that are quite specific, not only because they are given precise geographical names — the source of the Danube, the Rhine, various Swabian cities, glimpses of the Alps or of the vineyards near Bordeaux — but because they appear as concrete visual images, representations of reality.

There is a great deal of both suggestive and precise detail in a scene like this description of a nightfall over a city, at the beginning of the poem "Bread and Wine"; I quote the passage in German as well as Mr. Hamburger's translation, for his is not perhaps the ideal rendering for a first encounter:

> Rings um ruhet die Stadt; still wird die erleuchtete Gasse,
>     Und, mit Fakeln geschmükt, rauschen die Wagen hinweg.
> Satt gehn heim von Freuden des Tags zu ruhen die Menschen,
>     Und Gewinn und Verlust wäget ein sinniges Haupt
> Wohlzufrieden zu Haus; leer steht von Trauben und Blumen,
>     Und von Werken der Hand ruht der geschäfftige Markt.
> Aber das Saitenspiel tönt fern aus Gärten; vieleicht, daß
>     Dort ein Liebender spielt oder ein einsamer Mann
> Ferner Freunde gedenkt und der Jugendzeit; und die Brunnen
>     Immerquillend und frisch rauschen an duftenden Beet.
> Still in dämmriger Luft ertönen geläutete Gloken,
>     Und der Stunden gedenk rufet ein Wächter die Zahl.
> Jetzt auch kommet ein Wehn und regt die Gipfel des Hains auf,
>     Sieh! und das Schattenbild unserer Erde, der Mond
> Kommet geheim nun auch; die Schwärmerische, die Nacht kommt,
>     Voll mit Sternen und wohl wenig bekümmert ums uns,
> Glänzt die Erstaunende dort, die Fremdlingin unter den Menschen
>     Über Gebirgeshöhn traurig und prächtig herauf.

In Mr. Hamburger's version:

> Round us the town is at rest; the street, in pale lamplight, grows quiet
>     And, their torches ablaze, coaches rush through and away
> People go home to rest, replete with the day and its pleasures,
>     There to weigh up in their heads, pensive, the gain and the loss,
> Finding the balance good; stripped bare now of grapes and of flowers
>     As of their hand-made goods, quiet the market stalls lie.
> But faint music of strings comes drifting from gardens; it could be
>     Someone in love who plays there, could be a man all alone
> Thinking of distant friends, the days of his youth; and the fountains,
>     Ever welling and new, plash amid fragrance from beds.
> Church-bells ring; every stroke hangs still in the quivering half-light
>     And the watchman calls out, mindful, no less, of the hour.
> Now a breeze rises too and ruffles the crest of the coppice,
>     Look, and in secret our globe's shadowy image, the moon,
> Slowly is rising too; and Night, the fantastical, comes now
>     Full of stars and, I think, little concerned about us,
> Night, the astonishing, there, the stranger to all that is human,
>     Over the mountain-tops mournful and gleaming draws on.

The same precise observation is still present, although in much more compressed form, in later poems such as "Andenken" ("Remembrance").

> Geh aber nun und grüsse
> Die schöne Garonne,
> Und die Gärten von Bourdeaux
> Dort, wo am scharfen Ufer
> Hingehet der Steg und in den Strom
> Tief fällt der Bach, darüber aber
> Hinschauet ein edel Paar
> Von Eichen und Silberpappeln; . . .

> But go now, go and greet
> The beautiful Garonne
> And the gardens of Bordeaux,
> To where on the rugged bank
> The path runs and into the river
> Deep falls the brook, but above them
> A noble pair of oaks
> And white poplars looks out; . . .

This is not descriptive poetry as we would find in Wordsworth or in Coleridge, nor is it the kind of reverie associated with a Rousseauistic response to natural settings. The landscapes are made up of an intricate network of forces whose relations are strongly dramatized. As a result, despite the absence of explicit symbolism or allegory, one feels behind these landscapes a working principle that encompasses mind and nature within a larger element. Like landscapes in a dream, every detail seems to have a meaning, to refer back to a will, to a purpose, even if this purpose remains hidden. Hölderlin modulates almost without transition from nature descriptions to dramatic scenes describing the actions of entities endowed with more than human or natural status. The course of the Rhine becomes the bearing of a demigod; the fall of night over a city the way in which a god ambiguously manifests his presence in withdrawal; a sunrise in the Alps suggests the proper distance between god and man.

In a late eighteenth-century work, such sudden and apparently effortless transitions from nature to divine presences are by no means easy to understand. The word "god" in Hölderlin, in the singular or in the plural, does not have behind it the weight of doctrinal and literary tradition that gives it an anagogic level of meaning as in Dante or in Milton. Nor are we dealing with a humanized and secularized version of Hellenic or Christian symbolism, as when Shelley or Keats represents the historical destiny of mankind in mythological form. It would also be false to think of Hölderlin's poetry as a form of pantheism. He does not reach what he calls "the gods" through the mediation of nature; nature, in his work, is not closer to god than the thoughts and the deeds of man. Least of all does the theocentric vocabulary designate a religious experience in the traditional sense of the term: it refers to no dogma or act of faith. How the more-than-human point of view throughout the poetry is to be interpreted will remain the burden of Hölderlin criticism for many years to come.

The new reader of Hölderlin's poetry does not encounter these questions in their philosophical or theological form, for he has the task first of making sense out of poems that are difficult in syntax and thought. He is likely to respond first of all to the suggestiveness of the landscapes and the descriptions. The mastery of these passages, in which the movement of the verse line matches exactly that of the scene or the object that is being described, should convince him, if need be, that he is dealing with a poetic mind that, as far as control over language is concerned, is anything but arbitrary or unstable.

On the other hand, next to the landscapes, he will encounter compressed and enigmatic statements, highly quotable and suggestive of profundity but so general that they call for more specific interpretation within the context of the poems — lines such as *"Was bleibet aber stiften die Dichter"* (translated by Mr. Hamburger as "But what is lasting the poets provide"); *"Wie du anfiengst wirst du bleiben"* (" . . . as you began, so you will remain"); *"Wozu Dichter in dürftiger Zeit?"* ("Who wants poets at all in the lean years?"); or the famous opening lines of the hymn "Patmos": "*Nah ist / Und schwer zu fassen der Gott*" ("Near is / And difficult to grasp, the God"). Although not in themselves obscure, these pronouncements are like riddles whose answers can only be found in other parts of the poems in which they appear.

Between the concrete descriptions and the abstract maxims appear passages of great dramatic intensity, often relating directly or allusively to historical events of the past or the present—the wars of Troy, the battle of Salamis, as well as such contemporary events as the Napoleonic wars or the Peace of Lunéville—or, with equal frequency and dramatic immediacy, to events from mythology or from the Bible: the wars of the Titans, the birth of Dionysus, the Last Supper, etc. The three levels or, as Hölderlin calls them, "tonalities"—the descriptive, the purely abstract, and the dramatic—are very closely related. They do not alternate at random but are controlled in their order and function by a general design that gives the poetry an unmistakably unified voice (Hölderlin speaks of *Grundton*). This voice remains recognizable in its three different registers, although it is extremely difficult to capture its meaning, i.e., to make explicit the relationship between the descriptive, the philosophical, and the dramatic parts of Hölderlin's poetry.

Whether the readers of Mr. Hamburger's translation will be able to perceive this unifying voice and to interpret its statement remains somewhat doubtful. The edition unquestionably is considerably better than earlier scattered attempts to introduce Hölderlin to English-speaking readers, including Mr. Hamburger's own earlier collection of Hölderlin translations published in 1943. For the first time, we are given a comprehensive selection of the poetry, including two later versions of the unfinished *Empedokles* tragedy.

The French reader is still more fortunate in having in the Bibliothèque de la Pléiade a new edition, edited by Philippe Jaccottet, which includes, besides the poems and the novel *Hyperion* (which is also available in a good English translation by Willard Trask), the important philosophical essays and the letters, not yet available in English. In its typography and appearance Mr. Hamburger's volume resembles Friedrich Beissner's authoritative critical edition of Hölderlin's works published in Stuttgart. The resemblance is somewhat misleading, however, since Mr. Hamburger's is not a scholarly publication but a comprehensive selection of Hölderlin's mature work, without critical apparatus and offering only a few sparse notes that might well have been dispensed with—for if one starts annotating Hölderlin, a great deal more is needed than these few pages. Fortunately, the edition is bilingual and benefits from the care and talent of a translator who knows Hölderlin's work well and makes a valiant effort to master some of the considerable difficulties of his task.

Whether Mr. Hamburger succeeds is difficult to assess. In his preface, he addresses himself to the problem in a modest and sensible way, proclaiming his wish to remain as faithful as possible to the original, respecting the poet's intention wherever he can while still maintaining a diction that is not more unusual in English than Hölderlin's is in German. Mr. Hamburger's mildly polemical remarks aimed at "free" translators who write their own poem about a poem, indicate his moderate stand on the ever-disputed question of the ethics and aesthetics of translation. He rejects absolute literalness as well as the audacity of radical recasting.

The result is a rather colorless copy of the original, which is rarely felicitous but does not introduce major distortions. The opening passage from "Bread and Wine" that I have quoted is a typical example of Mr. Hamburger's craft: clear English, slightly awkward when it tends to pile prepositions on prepositions ("rush through and away . . . "; "There to weigh up . . . "), and sometimes padded to keep the hexameter filled out (the *pale* lamplight, not in the original, or the watchman who "calls out mindful, *no less,* of the hour"). There is one error (*Werken der Hand* translated as "hand-made goods" when Hölderlin means human labor in a general way).

A graver shortcoming is the near total loss of Hölderlin's syntactical constructions, which allow him to convey, in an imitative pattern that links the syntax with the described action, the drama of his scenes. In the opening passage of "Bread and Wine," for example, the German text aims entirely at the climactic effect achieved when the moon and the allegorized Night appear on the scene. A succession of constructions beginning not with the grammatical subject, but with an adverb, take the attention away from a series of diurnal things, put in third place behind adverb and verb: "*still wird . . . (die Gasse), satt gehn . . . (die Menschen), von Werken der Hand ruht . . . (die Markt), still ertönen . . . (die Gloken), der Stunden gedenk rufet . . . (ein Wächter).*"

In contrast, the sound of the violin and of the fountains, both prefiguring night, by being placed at the head of a sentence is given the emphasis of a subject. When the moon finally appears, heralded by a breeze itself introduced by the key verb "comes," it is as a prominent active subject of the sentence that stretches almost over an entire line, in sharp contrast to the subdued subjects of the earlier lines. Its dynamic presence (which so struck Rilke that, in his poem "To Hölderlin," he likened the poet himself to an ever-wandering moon) is conveyed by the verb "come," thrice repeated.

Practically nothing of all this remains in translation. The adverbial constructions have disappeared, with one exception ("quiet the market stalls lie") which, standing alone, fulfills no function; by not repeating the verb, the translator loses the sudden and parallel "coming" of moon and night, and he spoils the dramatic moment by padding with the word "slowly," which is not in the original.

Nor is the translator always successful in the compressed formulations of the more philosophical passages. Such faults are more disquieting, not only because they reveal misconceptions in the understanding of Hölderlin's meaning, but because they cut the thread that ties together the different tonalities. If the philosophical passages are misconstrued, loosened from the descriptive and dramatic context, the entire structure, all the more fragile for being so intricately interconnected, collapses into incoherence.

A brief passage from the hymn "The Rhine" can serve as an example. The fourth strophe of the poem begins, *"Ein Rätsel ist Reinentsprungenes,"* a passage that Mr. Hamburger translates as "A mystery are those of pure origin." The term *Reinentsprungenes* can indeed be considered as a focal point around which a large part of the poem gravitates. The poet himself, introduced in the opening lines of the poem, is seen meditating on the word *Reinentsprungenes,* or, literally, on the source of the river whose name indeed suggests *rein*—pure:

> Im dunkeln Efeu sasz ich, an der Pforte
> Des Waldes, eben, da der goldene Mittag,
> Den Quell besuchend, herunterkam
> Von Treppen des Alpengebirgs, . . .
>
> Jetzt aber, drinn im Gebirg,
> Tief unter den silbernen Gipfeln
> Und unter fröhlichem Grün,
> Wo die Wälder schauernd zu ihm,
> Und der Felsen Häupter übereinander
> Hinabschaun, taglang, dort
> Im kältesten Abgrund hört
> Ich um Erlösung jammern
> Den Jüngling, . . .
>
> Die Stimme wars des edelsten der Ströme,
> Des freigeborenen Rheins, . . .

In Mr. Hamburger's translation:

> Amid dark ivy I was sitting, at
> The forest's gate, just as golden noon,
> To visit the wellspring there, came down
> From steps of the Alpine ranges . . .
>
> But now, within the mountains
> Deep down below the silvery summits
> And in the midst of gay verdure,
> Where shuddering the forests
> And the heads of rocks overlapping
> Look down at him, all day

There in the coldest chasm
I heard the youth implore
Release . . .

The voice it was of the noblest of rivers,
Of free-born Rhine, . . .

The first meaning that readers may associate with the term *Reinentsprungenes* could very possibly be that of the virgin birth, and Mr. Hamburger strengthens a tendency in this direction by his use of the word "mystery"—as one speaks of the "mystery" of the Immaculate Conception or as Yeats, for example, also in reference to the Incarnation, speaks of "the uncontrollable mystery on the bestial floor." Some of the allusive passage later in the hymn can indeed be construed with Christian references, although several other divine or semidivine figures are being alluded to: a single, unnamed god at the beginning of the sixth strophe, Prometheus in strophe 7, Herakles in strophes 5 and 11, Dionysus in strophe 10, etc. On the whole, there are fewer allusions to Christ in this poem than in many others of the same period, whereas a great deal of emphasis falls on natural entities, such as the Rhine, or on historical figures, such as Rousseau.

Nor does Hölderlin speak of "mystery" but of "riddle" (*Rätsel*). If the "pure origin" were a mystery, it would be vain to search for its precise meaning anywhere: the poem would have to be read as a prayer or incantation, a hymn of praise that calls the gods down among mortals and invites them to speak, like the incense burned at the altar, the ritual that surrounds the sacrifice. But if "pure origin" is a "riddle," then the poem has a very different function. A riddle is not, in itself, out of the reach of knowledge, but is temporarily hidden from knowledge by a device of language that can, in turn, be deciphered only by another operation of language. The word "riddle" directs our attention to the need to find the meaning of the word *Reinentsprungenes* in the various devices of the poem's own language. The poem is not ritual, mystery, or prayer, but a text to be interpreted and inviting the reader's answer, as all riddles do.

That the poem provides such an answer is something on which nearly all recent Hölderlin interpreters would agree, although their answers would vary. The question itself is complicated by the contrasting tension between God-as-a-mystery and God-as-a-riddle that is itself part of this poem. For if we attempt to decipher the meaning of "The Rhine," the first answer the poem yields seems to lead us away from the investigation itself. If we ask, for example, why the Rhine can be said to originate "purely," we find instead that the river does not remain at a prudent, questioning distance from the "riddle" of its own origin, but boldly takes the place of the powers by which it has been put on earth. And this boldness is first treated positively: it sets the Rhine apart from other rivers that spring up in the same region but flow passively, by the shortest and straightest road, toward the ocean. By contrast, the Eastern course of the Rhine near the source reveals the river's impatient wish to act as freely and independently as the powers that engendered it:

> Die Stimme wars des edelsten der Ströme,
> Des freigeborenen Rheins,
> Und anderes hoffte der, als droben von den Brüdern,
> Dem Tessin und dem Rhodanus,
> Er schied und wandern wollt', und ungeduldig ihn
> Nach Asia trieb die königliche Seele.

> The voice it was of the noblest of rivers,
> Of free-born Rhine,
> And different were his hopes when up there from his brothers
> Ticino and Rhodanus
> He parted and longed to roam, and impatiently
> His regal soul drove him on towards Asia

At first reading, the purity of the Rhine seems to derive from its willingness to lose itself in the mystery of its origin, and to reject any interference, whether by language or anything else. The river prefers an "Eastern" abandon in the silent depth of mystery to a "Western" rationality, and its superiority seems to be the result of this choice.

The subsequent development of the poem — much too intricate for summary — qualifies this statement to the point of near reversal. The movement of the river toward the East turns out to be a necessary moment in the Rhine's destiny, but also a moment of extreme danger and temptation, which has to be checked if the river is to fulfill its historical function as a founder of cities and of an earth-bound civilization:

> . . . wenn in der Eil'
> Ein Gröszerer ihn nicht zähmt,
> Ihn wachsen läszt, wie der Blitz, musz er
> Die Erde spalten, und wie Bezauberte fliehn
> Die Wälder ihm nach und zusammensinkend die Berge.

> Ein Gott will aber sparen die Söhnen
> Das eilende Leben und lächelt,
> Wenn unenthaltsam, aber gehemmt
> Von heiligen Alpen, ihm
> In der Tiefe, wie jener, zürnen die Ströme.
> In solcher Esse wird dann

Auch alles Lautre geschmiedet,
Und schön ists, wie er drauf,
Nachdem er die Berge verlassen,
Stillwandelnd sich im deutschen Lande
Begnüget und das Sehnen stillt
Im guten Geschäffte, wenn er das Land baut
Der Vater Rhein und liebe Kinder nährt
In Städten, die er gegründet.

   . . . if in his haste
A greater one does not tame him,
But lets him grow, like lightning he
Must rend the earth and like things enchanted
The forests join his flight and, collapsing, the mountains.
A god, however, wishes to spare his sons
A life so fleeting and smiles
When, thus intemperate but restrained
By holy Alps, the rivers
Like this one rage at him in the depth.
In such a forge, then, all
That's pure is given shape
And it is good to see
How then, after leaving the mountains,
Content with German lands he calmly
Moves on and stills his longing
In useful industry, when he tills the land,
Now Father Rhine, and supports dear children
In cities which he has founded.

We move further from mystery and toward a more conscious use of language in the remaining part of the poem, as we go from a natural object devoid of self-awareness like the river, toward increasingly self-conscious entities: first, an unnamed Promethean figure whom the commentators have had difficulty in identifying, but who appears in a setting that suggests the greatness and decline Hölderlin associates with the historical destiny of Greece; then Rousseau, a near contemporary who represents for Hölderlin the essence of the post-Hellenic Western mind in its concentration on self-knowledge, language, and historical understanding as steps away from natural and original conditions. The destinies of these two apparitions follow the same pattern as that of the river: a violent moment of youthful *hybris* is followed by a return to a reflective mood, whereby the earlier impulse is recollected in tranquillity, in a mood that suggests the Wordsworthian definition of the language of poetry.

> Drum wohl ihm, welcher fand
> Ein wohlbeschiedenes Schiksaal,
> Wo noch der Wanderungen
> Und süsz der Leiden Erinnerung
> Aufrauscht am sichern Gestade,
> Dasz da und dorthin gern
> Er sehn mag bis an die Grenzen
> Die bei der Geburt ihm Gott
> Zum Aufenthalte gezeichnet.
> Dann ruht er, seeligbescheiden,
> Denn alles, was er gewollt,
> Das Himmlische, von selber umfängt
> Es unbezwungen, lächelnd
> Jetzt, da er ruhet, den Kühnen.

> So happy he who has found
> A well-allotted fate
> Where still of his wanderings
> And sweetly of his afflictions
> The memory murmurs on banks that are sure,
> So that this way, that way with pleasure
> He looks as far as the bounds
> Which God at birth assigned
> To him for his term and site.
> Then, blissfully humble, he rests,
> For all that he has wanted,
> Though heavenly, of itself surrounds
> Him uncompelled, and smiles
> Upon the bold one now that he's quiet.

The text establishes that the purity in the term *Reinentsprungenes* designates a proper balance between desire and reflection, between instinct and consciousness, between action and interpretation; and that this balance can only be achieved by means of language. The figure that is finally held up as closest to the poet is not a figure of mystery and of Dionysian fervor, in the Nietzschean sense, but that of the riddle-posing and riddle-solving Socrates:

> Denn schwer ist zu tragen
> Das Unglük, aber schwerer das Glük.
> Ein Weiser aber vermocht es
> Vom Mittag bis in die Mitternacht,

Und bis der Morgen erglänzte,
Bein Gastmahl helle zu bleiben.
For hard to bear
Is misfortune, but good fortune harder.
A wise man though, was able
From noon to midnight, and on
Till morning lit up the sky
To keep wide awake at the banquet.

The sentence "*Ein Rätsel ist Reinentsprungenes*" is now seen to mean not only that "pure" origins are enigmatic but also that the quality of pure origins that gave both the Rhine and Rousseau such historical strength and the poet a subject for infinite meditation belongs to the riddle as a paradigmatic form of language. Subject and predicate are reversible: the sentence means not only that "pure origin" is a riddle but that the riddle itself is one of the entities that can lay claim to pure origin. Translating "riddle" as "mystery," and introducing the restrictive "those" in "those of pure origin" (thus making it seem as if only persons or personifications could be *Reinentsprungen,* whereas the quality extends to entities as impersonal as language itself), Mr. Hamburger suppresses the all-important link between origin and language. He makes it seem as if Hölderlin was asserting the existence of a transcendental experience that lies beyond the reach of language, when the entire drift of the poem moves in the opposite direction. A single word change makes an assertion of controlled lucidity into an incomprehensible plea for incomprehensibility. In his 1942 edition of Hölderlin translations Hamburger had translated the same passage, "An enigma are things of pure source," which is, in all respects, better and more accurate than his more recent version.[1]

Dramatic passages, especially in the *Empedokles* tragedy, are much more successfully rendered. The iambic meter is more congenial to English prosody than the hexameter of the elegies and the Pindaric free verse of the hymns, and the pathos of the speeches seems to suit Mr. Hamburger better than the descriptive or meditative language of the later poems. He manages to sustain the tone of tragedy throughout the play, an achievement that unfortunately cannot be illustrated by isolated passages. In the translation of the earlier odes, he misrepresents only when a misplaced fear of abstraction, falsely assumed to be unpoetic, leads him to introduce nonexistent metaphors where Hölderlin deliberately avoids them.

Thus the line in the ode "Rousseau," "*Kennt er im ersten Zeichen Vollendetes schon*" (literally: "In the earliest sign he can already read fulfillment") is translated, "In seed grains he can measure the full-grown plant," a metaphor of Mr. Hamburger's own invention and out of place at this point in the poem. Hölderlin may not have found his ideal translator yet, but this first responsible English edition of his work nevertheless is a great step forward toward breaking the artificial national isolation in which his work has been held until now.

The successful rendering of the dramatic passages, in contrast to the descriptive and philosophical parts, will focus the attention of Mr. Hamburger's readers on the historical themes. This may well encourage a misrepresentation that recurs all too frequently in Hölderlin studies. There has been a persistent tendency to treat Hölderlin as a prophetic and eschatological poet, the precursor of a new historical era that his work helps to prepare. The trend goes back to Stefan George and his circle, who were closely associated with the rediscovery of Hölderlin shortly before World War I. It prevails, in a subtler form, in some of Heidegger's commentaries on Hölderlin's poetry during the thirties, whose ideological and nationalist overtones others, at the same time, were stating much less obliquely. But even when it appears in a nonpolitical or politically acceptable form, the messianic scheme that one tends to associate with Hölderlin's view of history distorts his actual statement.

Hölderlin was indeed a fervent admirer of ancient Greece, which he celebrates, in many poems, as a great historical achievement. On the other hand, he can write negatively about his own times as, for example, near the end of *Hyperion,* or, later, in rare allusions to the solitude and suffering involved in his radical separation from his contemporaries. This suggests a conception of history in which the Hellenic past was a time of fulfillment as compared to the misery in the European present of 1800. History would then consist of alternating periods of light and dark, characterized, in Hölderlin's vocabulary, by the presence or absence of entities referred to as the "gods."

This combination of historical and theocentric references is highly suggestive, since it allows the reader to interpret events according to a grand scheme, while conferring on these events an aura of dramatic or poetic urgency that would be lacking in a technical philosophy of history. Thus the transposition of Hölderlin's philo-Hellenism into a literal historical scheme yields an interpretation of the present that is, to some critics, reassuring; during a period of history that is part of our civilization, men could think of the gods as actual presences from which they were not separated by transcendental distances. If this was possible for a consciousness not essentially different from our own, it follows that the absence of gods, painfully experienced as everyday reality, may be only a passing dark phase between two stages of unity, one past but another still to come.

The harshness of the present can then be seen as, in Matthew Arnold's words, a "wandering between two worlds"; if one of these worlds is indeed dead, then this death was not of our doing, and if the other is "powerless to be born," then the strength necessary for its rebirth may arise at any moment through the will of powers that we do not control. Interpreted in such a literal and historical way, Hölderlin's much-quoted phrase about a barren, empty time (*durftiger Zeit*), uncritically assumed to mean the post-Hellenic world, satisfies our self-pity and impatience, while reaffirming the faith that *"the gods are living / Over our heads . . . in a different world,"* and that *"the Heavenly who once were / Here . . . shall come again, come when their advent is due"* ("Bread and Wine"). Secularized by a crude transposition to the historical world, Hölderlin's eschatological themes, taken out of context, turn into reassuring myths about the certainty of a better future.

In its entirety, however, Hölderlin's work disproves the simplified relationship between poetry and history that is so often attributed to him. The contrast between the German present and the Hellenic past was not for Hölderlin a contrast between divine presence and absence, between unity and division, but a dialogue between two successive modes of consciousness. History plays a prominent part in a poetry that involves the destiny of nations and of eras rather than of particular persons. But the poetry is never positively oriented toward a future historical rebirth prefigured and prepared in the poet's language.

The certainties that Hölderlin's work asserts with ever-increasing control are certainties about the complex and primarily negative relationship prevailing between any kind of reflective language (including that of poetry) and the more immediate experience of reality that is a necessary part of history. History appears to him as the starting point of a reflection, not as an incentive to action. This inner understanding does not alleviate our present predicament, nor does it imply any knowledge or control over what will happen in the future. True wisdom begins in the knowledge of its own historical ineffectiveness. When Hölderlin evokes the possibility of future moments of historical splendor, comparable to what Greece used to be in the past, such evocations are accompanied by the foreknowledge that people will be conscious of the achievement of these periods when they have ceased to be and have become in turn parts of the past. Nothing could be more remote from schemes that conceive of history as either apocalyptic failure or salvation.

The truth of such negative insights is highly repellent to a period like our own, frustrated at finding itself at the same time so advanced in self-awareness and so powerless in its control over events. Hence the alacrity with which Hölderlin's work has been scrutinized for tokens of historical prophecy. Only gradually does it begin to appear that he was saying something more demanding about the transitory nature of all historical achievement, about the difficulty for the mind to maintain its balance in view of the ceaseless erosion of the historical world, and about poetry as a medium in which some degree of lucidity can prevail.

Hölderlin's language, when one can hear and understand the unifying voice that binds the different tonalities together, is not a symbolic or allegorical representation of historical events, but the autonomous movement of a mind that establishes its own domain, at a level that, in its effectiveness, lies well below history but well above it in its wisdom. For a long time, Hölderlin's readers preferred to ignore him; then they glorified him in a manner that his own thought decries, or reduced him to the banality of a psychological case. The new translations and the rigor of some recent studies indicate that the austere task of understanding his real meaning progresses, albeit at the cost of lost illusions that accompanies any increased insight.

## Notes

1. The translation of the line in the French edition of Hölderlin avoids all the pitfalls of Michael Hamburger's later version. Gustave Roud translates: "*Énigme, ce qui naît d'un jaillisement pur!*" which can mean just as well "*ce qui naît d'un jaillisement pur est énigmatique*" as "*l'énigme est ce qui naît d'un jaillissement pur.*" The word *énigme* is as close as French can come to the connotations of the word *Rätsel*.

# Jacques Derrida, *Of Grammatology* (1970)

This work attracted considerable interest from the moment of its publication; indeed its philosophical scope, accommodating in a profoundly original formulation the Nietzschean critique of the polarities governing Western philosophical discourse, tended to eclipse the more strictly exegetical part, which is of the greatest concern to readers of Rousseau. Even livelier was the interest awakened by the polemical portions on Saussure and Lévi-Strauss, and the reading of Rousseau's *Essay on the Origin of Languages,* which in itself takes up more than half the book, risked passing unremarked. Yet far from constituting a simple illustration or, as has been said, a "practical exercise" completing the theoretical part of *Of Grammatology,* this reading is actually its center: the first part of the book must remain closed to those who deny close critical attention to Derrida's reading of Rousseau. This reading marks an important stage in our understanding of Rousseau, which it extends without, however, entirely breaking with the established tradition.

We must confine ourselves to noting two aspects of this interpretation, the first of a methodological nature, the second more substantial. More than in any other commentator in French, we find a true *reading* here, not limiting itself to sketching the features of a thematic narrative that can be organized only by ignoring or masking the discontinuities abounding in Rousseau's discourse but, on the contrary, discerning in these very lacunae the principle of a complication raised to the level of a system. Not a literal reading, then, which would be limited to juxtaposing incompatibilities, nor strictly speaking a symbolic, thematic, or even a dialectical reading, which would attempt to reconcile the different discursive levels among themselves. What is involved here is a truly hermeneutic reading, one that traces the contours of a field of signification by means of the logical points of resistance strewn throughout the text, rather than at their expense. The accusations or apologies of so many of Rousseau's commentators, irritated or baffled by frequently contradictory utterances, become thus superfluous; we ignore Rousseau's chief riches by attempting to reduce him to strict coherence.

Derrida manages to distinguish between Rousseau's explicit meaning (*vouloir dire*) and a more secret one (*dire*), and to produce a reading that derives from the interplay of these two semiological levels, whose irreducible difference governs the movement of the text. Thus he can assume, for instance, the tension that exists in Rousseau between a genealogical mode of thought that seeks out origins, and a more purely structural mode that remains in the discontinuity of more or less arbitrary synchronies. The particularly enlightening analysis of the structure of supplementarity appears as the result of this tension: origin as the privileged principle Rousseau wants to assert is always called into question by utterance itself, which denotes—as though under duress—the existence of a lack, of a void in the plenitude of the initial moment, and refers us to an antecedent at once temporal and logical. This antecedent will be found, in its turn, caught up in a similar interplay. The very fruitful concept of supplementarity is therefore not the result of a thematic reading—it could not be, for supplementarity is precisely what Rousseau cannot assert in the explicit form of a theme—but appears as the result of a method of reading that deconstructs thematic utterance by means of implicit utterance.

Is this method anticipated by Rousseau himself? Or does it derive from Derrida's mainly Nietzschean antecedents and thereby constitute a deliberate violence done to Rousseau by a more radical hermeneutics than his own? This leads us to the substance of Derrida's reading, without our being able to do more than sketch out the schema of a difficult answer to our own question.

Derrida goes very far in attributing to Rousseau a systematic and verified knowledge of the duplicity of his own discourse—further than even the exegetes most disposed to take seriously the importance Rousseau grants to the linguistic sign. A persistent shift has occurred in Rousseau studies, a slippage from what we might call apparent polarities toward more secret ones: thus the very noticeable opposition between Nature and Culture in the *First Discourse* has been gradually elaborated to the point of no longer acknowledging any of the classical polarities opposing a subject to an object. In conceiving the notion of subject more categorically, critics like Marcel Raymond and Georges Poulet have given Rousseauean interiority a virtually absolute meaning that renders secondary any notion of nature as object. Henceforth the polarities are located within the subject, in the relations the subject sustains with himself in the interiority of consciousness or, as Rousseau puts it, of the sentiment of existence. Whence the special interest these critics take in texts such as the *Fifth Reverie,* in privileged moments of the

*Confessions,* or in themes such as tranquility, the pure upsurge of initial sensation, etc. But this hypostasis of the subject also makes that subject particularly vulnerable, since everything henceforth depends, in a sense, on his possibility of existence. Whence the basic fragility of a self that knows it is constantly threatened, first of all, by its own attributes of elasticity and proliferation. Jean Starobinski has drawn attention to this development, emphasizing texts like the preface to *Narcissus,* the letters to Malesherbes, *Pygmalion,* the *Dialogues,* and certain "doubled" passages of the *Confessions,* in order to document this constant "danger of reflection." But to speak of reflection and distance is necessarily to speak of language, and even of language sufficiently advanced as to constitute the infinite complication of the sign. So it is not surprising that, although Starobinski has continued to deal with danger and threat in a largely psychological mode, he has nonetheless very distinctly posited, in *La Transparence et l'obstacle,* the question of the sign's role in Rousseau's thought. The fact that Derrida begins his reading of the *Essay* with the discussion of a philologically oriented remark of Starobinski's — a matter of determining the date of the *Essay on the Origin of Languages* by internal evidence — indicates an affinity rather than a polemic between the two interpreters.

For Derrida makes the problem of language the axis of Rousseau's thought. He confines his account to a reading of the *Essay,* satisfied with illuminating but lateral references to the *Second Discourse,* the beginning of *Emile,* and the texts on music. This way of granting a single text virtually exclusive privileges will no doubt inspire reservations; yet it is quite legitimate in the methodological procedure Derrida has adopted, and can be criticized only if we show a basic incompatibility between his method and Rousseau's thought. Which brings us back to the relations between the theory of writing in Derrida and in Rousseau.

Derrida seeks to make Rousseau into a linguist at least as subtle as Saussure and distinctly more so than Lévi-Strauss:[1] contrary to the latter, Rousseau "had *actually* experienced the disappearance (of fulfilled speech) in speech itself, in the mirage of its immediacy. He had acknowledged and analyzed it with incomparable acuity." Yet Derrida refuses to break with the nearly two-hundred-year-old tradition that interprets Rousseau as a philosopher of immediate presence and which takes quite literally his assertations about the priority of voice over writing, about origin as the subject's presence-to-himself, about the mimetic function of conceptual language over the mode of representation, etc. *Of Grammatology* shows that all these assertions are in fact contested by Rousseau's own language, though without Rouseau's being able to master the fluctuations of meaning that result from them. Derrida attempts to grasp, with great rigor, the specific nuance of the gesture by which Rousseau abdicates before the negative truth of his own discourse, though without abdicating the orthodoxy of his philosophical and historical position. Rousseau continues to belong to what Derrida calls the logocentric tradition, an age-old tradition that asserts the priority of language as reflection of the present substance (*logos*) over language as model of a purely semiotic structure of reality. According to a schema that tends to be repeated in Rousseau studies—though rarely on so advanced a level of understanding—Derrida can therefore deconstruct Rousseau by means of an interpreting metalanguage that asserts it has transcended the perspective of the interpreted language, since it announces the closing of a field of signification that remained open and ambiguous for Rousseau. Derrida can conceive of an ambivalence that remains inconceivable to Rousseau.

A critical reading of Derrida might therefore take two different directions. On the one hand, we might reproach him for giving too much weight to Rousseau's "premodernist" texts and passages, for overemphasizing factors of distance, negativity, and historical arbitrariness that must give way before the massive affirmation of fulfilled presence, in its immediate or elegiac form, found in so many famous pages. We might, in particular, invoke the most strictly "poetic" passages of Rousseau's oeuvre, precisely in the logocentric sense of the word, which appear in the works Derrida neglects (*Julie, Reveries,* certain passages of the *Confessions*). But we might also argue in the opposite direction and show that in these very "poetic" texts appears a conception of language of which Derrida's very account is merely a discursive version. We owe a great deal to Jacques Derrida for having imposed on the interpretation of Rousseau the necessity of making such a choice, and for having designated with an exemplary philosophical lucidity the site where this choice must be made.

Translated by Richard Howard

## Notes

1. See also Jacques Derrida, "La Linguistique de Rousseau," *Revue internationale de Philosophie,* 21 (1967), pp. 443–62.

# Foreword to Carol Jacobs,
## *The Dissimulating Harmony* (1978)

I well remember that, some ten years ago, I had occasion to recommend to an enlightened and benevolent university press the publication of a dissertation that, in my view, had merits of originality and critical insight.[1] It dealt with one particular, rather brief work of a very prolific novelist. It was refused for entirely legitimate (though probably misguided) considerations, because the market could not absorb a book-length study of a single work out of a large canon, especially in the case of a novelist. One could justify a book on Flaubert, say, or on Stendhal, but the public would balk at a volume devoted only to *Novembre,* or to *Henry Brulard.* Shortly afterward, Roland Barthes published *S/Z,* which deals, at some length, with a single short story, and his talent and prestige carried the day for a different type and format of critical essay.

Times have changed, and the publication of books like this one bears witness to renewed possibilities of serious and scrupulous work. Consequently, the expectations of the audience likely to read such a book will also have to undergo some modifications. The publisher's attitude in 1967 was symptomatic of what used to be expected from a critical study — and of what will always remain its principal, though perhaps no longer its only, function. On preparing to read a volume that mentions Nietzsche, Rilke, Artaud, and Benjamin on its title page, one expects a contribution to the general understanding of these prominent authors, in the form either of new data about their history or of original, temporarily definitive readings of their main texts, thoughtfully placed within the context of their complete works. One also expects a justification of this particular grouping of writers, a shared theme or motif or predicament that makes their combined study

218

particularly enlightening, or the usual rationale for comparative studies as giving access to a more refined and universal way of writing literary history. One would certainly expect the book to have something to say about the modernity of these authors (since they are all considered to be, in various ways, innovators) or about the nature of their particular alienations and nostalgias, since they were conspicuous outsiders, and some of them were declared insane.

If these broad characterizations may seem to apply less to Rilke than to the others—since he was publicly highly successful and lived what could be considered, from outward appearances, an exemplary and enviably "poetic" life—then one might perhaps speculate how the three others could be played off against Rilke in what would lead to a diagnosis, positive or negative, of the relationships between literature, society, and history.

At the very least, one would expect the essays to reflect, in their style and in their implicit values, the aesthetic pleasure that is bound to be produced by writers of such considerable gifts, all of them remarkable stylists who, by a consensus that no person of taste would wish to question, write very well and attach great importance to formal effects and devices. The readings should respond to the seductiveness of these devices and be, in fact, guided by them. This combination of aesthetic and historical values, despite their apparent independence from each other, grounds in fact the implicit ontology (or metaphysical specificity) of the literary work under which we operate. It determines how we read, how literature is taught in schools and universities, and how the literary commodity is rated in the marketplace. Such a combination of pleasure and worth (history being predestined, by definition, to be hard-working and severe, but responsible) is almost too good to be true and should certainly not be jettisoned lightly.

Coming to *The Dissimulating Harmony* with such expectations one is likely to be disappointed. Historical and psychological considerations are sparse, as are all synthetic judgments about the authors as a group, about each of them individually, and even about the works that Carol Jacobs has selected for analysis. Neither are the essays easy to read or particularly elegant in the conventional sense. They are quite technical and all appear frustratingly inconclusive, leaving us suspended with unresolved difficulties rather than enriched by a new understanding. They are also strikingly self-conscious, more concerned with the predicament of the commentator than with the intrinsic dimensions of the works or the existential pathos of their creation. What then is at stake here? The author's competence is not in question; some historical observations along the way and some paragraphs in which a more subjective voice is heard demonstrate that she could be very successful at a different, more familiar kind of literary criticism. In the name of what considerations does she forgo possibilities of critical discourse that seem easily available to her and to which her subject matter lends itself exceptionally well? One should perhaps not conclude too soon that it is out of perversity or because the contingencies of her literary education deprived her of happier influences.

A speedy way to at least broach what could become a very far-reaching question is to turn to what Jacobs, in her chapter on Rilke, has to say about paraphrase. Paraphrase is, of course, the mainstay of all critical writing. It is generally, though not necessarily, shorter than the text it claims to elucidate, but what is certain is that it can never be exactly the same. It is always a transposition, a translation from "a situation into a *more familiar* situation . . . , something new expressed in the language of something old and familiar." Paraphrase is, therefore, as in the passage from Nietzsche just quoted, a synonym (or a paraphrase) for understanding. It proceeds by a complex and, in the case of a skillful reader, subtle strategy of expansion and elision, the most important being not so much what one develops, makes explicit, and repeats, but what one omits. The principle of omission is usually quite simple: one omits what one does not understand. Since the author has probably done the same thing, concealing and diverting what stands in the way of his own meaning, the complicity between writer, explicator, and reader is particularly effective. In the name of the integrity of the text—a notion to be understood semantically as a potential singularity of meaning, as well as aesthetically and ethically as the coherence and the good faith of the work— whatever stands in the way of this integrity must be erased. The quality of an interpreter is confirmed by his ability to overlook obstacles to understanding. These obstacles are not always the obvious ones; on the contrary, the tactics of paraphrase consist of facing up to apparent difficulties (be they of syntax, of figuration, or of experience) and of coping with them exhaustively and convincingly. Paraphrase is the best way to distract the mind from genuine obstacles and to gain approval, replacing the burden of understanding with the mimicry of its performance. Its purpose is to blur, confound, and hide discontinuities and disruptions in the homogeneity of its own discourse. The precision of what is being said is not taken too seriously. Is it not, after all, the privilege of the arts, as opposed to the sciences, to play freely with truth and falsehood for the sake of graceful effect?

What would happen if, for once, one were to reverse the ethos of explication and try to be really precise, replacing (or at least trying to replace) paraphrase by what one would have to call genuinely analytic reading, just to see what would ensue? Carol Jacobs's work gives a glimpse of some of the consequences. They are quite unsettling, unless of course the reader tries to paraphrase in his turn Carol Jacobs out of the disasters of her own making, explaining her away in ways that are all too easy to imagine. But if one takes her at her word and tries to read her the way she tries to read her texts, surprising things become evident—and not only with reference to these particular texts, though they certainly do not remain untouched. Many assumptions about the still fundamentally dialectical pattern of Nietzsche's thought, about the prophetic authority of Rilke's poetry, about the depth of the nostalgias that allow Benjamin to assert a historical palingenesis beyond the most radical negations, will no longer be so easy to maintain. Readers of Nietzsche, Rilke, Artaud, and Benjamin will have to decide this for themselves by following Jacobs's reading in detail and by testing in very specific ways whether their own assurances and preconceptions are being dislodged by what she brings out. I, for one, admit to having been thus affected and wish to reflect on the general implications of this experience rather than on its consequences for a given author or text, or on the techniques here used to attempt a reading that would no longer blindly submit to the teleology of controlled meaning. All this would have to be the object of a genuine discussion rather than of a brief introduction. But since it is one of Carol Jacobs's virtues to be admirably discreet about the wider implications of her analytic labors, I feel free to state more crudely some of the things that remain delicately implied.

First of all, consider what was referred to as the ethos of this type of discourse. It would be a mistake to assume, because the readings are technical rather than aesthetically pleasing and because they disrupt some of the assertions that have traditionally excited the admiration of many readers, that this critical reader lacks aesthetic sensitivity or ethical concern. She could not begin to write the way she does if she were not keenly responsive to both. The point is rather whether the epistemology of understanding should be predicated by ethical or aesthetic considerations or the other way around. Is the integrity of understanding a function of the integrity of meaning, or should meaning be allowed to disintegrate under the negative impact of elements in a text, however marginal or apparently trivial, that can only be silenced by suppression? Whatever the answer, the conflict is that of one mode of integrity or sensibility with another, and not a priori proof of its absence in the undoer (nor, for that matter, of its presence in the defender) of the text's stability. Jacobs tries to proceed regardless of the consequences of the understanding she reaches and to be guided first of all by the need for this understanding whatever it may turn out to be—including the hard-earned conviction of its impossibility. In this way, what she wishes is no longer paraphrase but actual reading, productive of its own ethical imperative.

By putting the question thus, it should be clear that there is in fact no real question to be put. For how could a text have its understanding depend on considerations that would not be epistemologically determined? All depends on how one "understands" the relationships between truth and understanding. Understanding is not a version of a single and universal Truth that would exist as an essence, a hypostasis. The truth of a text is a much more empirical and literal event. What makes a reading more or less true is simply the predictability, the necessity of its occurrence, regardless of the reader or of the author's wishes. "Es ereignet sich aber das Wahre" (not *die Wahrheit*), says Hölderlin, which can be freely translated, "What is true is what is bound to take place." And, in the case of the reading of a text, what takes place is a necessary understanding. What marks the truth of such an understanding is not some abstract universal but the fact that it has to occur regardless of other considerations. It depends, in other words, on the rigor of the reading as argument. Reading is an argument (which is not necessarily the same as a polemic) because it has to go against the grain of what one would want to happen in the name of what has to happen; this is the same as saying that understanding is an epistemological event prior to being an ethical or aesthetic value. This does not mean that there can be a true reading, but that no reading is conceivable in which the question of its truth or falsehood is not primarily involved.

It would therefore be naive to make a reading depend on considerations, ethical or aesthetic, that are in fact correlatives of the understanding the reading is able to achieve. Naive, because it is not a matter of choice to omit or to accentuate by paraphrase certain elements in a text at the expense of others. We do not have this choice, since the text imposes its own understanding and shapes the reader's evasions. The more one censors, the more one reveals what is being effaced. A paraphrase is always what we called an analytic reading; that is, it is always susceptible of being made to point out consistently what it was trying to conceal. Knowing this, the difference between Carol Jacobs and other critics (who presumably write paraphrases without worrying about it) is not so great after all, since all of us are always doing what she is doing, whether we know, it or not. But once we know it we cannot go back to our original innocence, for one has to be quite smart in order to pretend convincingly to be dumb.

So, in one respect, the interest of Jacobs's way of reading is that she does openly what we have no choice but to do anyway, when our most cherished certainties about Nietzsche, say, or about Rilke or about ourselves are being dissolved by understanding. But this is only one perspective on a tale that does not stop there. This argument has driven us into a corner, a bind that has to do, as it happens, with the nature of arguments. True reading, as opposed to paraphrase, is an argument; that is, it has the sequential coherence we associate with a demonstration or with a particularly compelling narrative. But what is here being argued (or compellingly told) is precisely the loss of an illusory coherence: the historical consistency of Nietzsche's theory of tragedy or the existential necessity of Rilke's fulfillment by renunciation or Artaud's fulfillment by cruelty, etc.

The argument, assuming it resists attempts to find fault with the details of its articulation, demonstrates the necessary occurrence of this disruption and, what is more, designates it by a variety of specific names: "stammering," "beheading," and finally, the "image." These names are not arbitrary but are literally present in the texts, though muted or disguised: the word "stammer" occurs in Nietzsche in places now shown to be crucial; beheading and castration are explicit in Rilke, albeit disguised at times by various plays of the signifier; "image" (*Bild*) is, like the purloined letter, so literally inscribed in Benjamin's diction (and even in one of his titles) that no one seems to have noticed it until Jacobs came along. This sequence of terms clinches, as the saying goes, the argument, in a well-modulated progression that leads irresistibly to the key term "image." "Image" is now shown to be the term that subsumes the others, and "stammering," "beheading," etc., proven to be mere images for "image." By the same token, the demonstration of this necessary incoherence becomes a remarkably sound narrative, and the entire book can be summarized in the single parable of the last chapter: not just the tale of Rastelli the juggler as told by Benjamin's fictional narrator, but this tale plus the added turn that Carol Jacobs's commentary gives to it. Reading becomes a parable (*Gleichnis*), an allegory of reading as the literal designation of its undoing.

But how is it possible for a literal designation to be an image, that which is never literal? What these essays convincingly demonstrate is that the disruption of meaning occurs when the literal or figural status of the text's central event (its understanding) has to be, and cannot be, decided. What is here astutely called "image" is the necessity for any literal, and therefore comprehensible, meaning to be disguised in a representation that can be called a history, a narrative, an argument, a parable, or an allegory, but that errs to the exact extent that it represents. One will have recognized the not-so-secret theme of Nietzsche's *The Birth of Tragedy*. But whereas the apparent fluidity of Nietzsche's text turns out to be a stammer, the high quality of Carol Jacobs's readings threaten her with a worse danger. She cannot prevent her stammering text from being impeccably fluid. Parable turns into paraphrase after all, even and especially when one is as fully aware as she is of this inconsistency. The result is no longer the birth of something purely tragic, though it is certainly not benign. It may well be the birth of criticism as truly critical reading, a birth that is forever aborted and forever repeated but that, in the meantime, makes for indispensable reading.

## Notes

1. The dissertation de Man refers to here is that of Samuel Weber; it was later published under the title *Unwrapping Balzac: A Reading of "La Peau de Chagrin"* (Toronto: University of Toronto Press, 1979). Carol Jacobs's *The Dissimulating Harmony* was published by Johns Hopkins University Press in 1978. — Ed.

# Sources

# Sources

The following is a list of the original titles, places, and dates of publication of the essays in this collection; they are listed in order of publication and are reprinted by permission of the publishers.

"Montaigne et la transcendance." *Critique*, no. 79 (December 1953), pp. 1011–22.

"The Inward Generation." *Cambridge Review*, 1 (Winter 1955), pp. 41–47.

"Le néant poétique (commentaire d'un sonnet hermétique de Mallarmé)." *Monde Nouveau*, no. 88 (April 1955), pp. 63–75.

"Tentation de la permanence." *Monde Nouveau*, no. 93 (October 1955), pp. 49–61.

"Keats and Hölderlin." *Comparative Literature*, 8 (Winter 1956), pp. 28–45.

"Situation de roman." *Monde Nouveau*, no. 101 (June 1956), pp. 57–60.

"Le Devenir, la poésie." *Monde Nouveau*, no. 105 (November 1956), pp. 110–24.

"La critique thématique devant le thème de Faust." *Critique*, no. 120 (May 1957), pp. 387–404.

"A New Vitalism." Review of Harold Bloom, *The Visionary Company*. *Massachusetts Review*, 3 (Spring 1962), pp. 618–23.

"Giraudoux." Review of Jean Giraudoux, *Three Plays*. *New York Review of Books*, 1 (November 28, 1963), pp. 20–21.

"Heidegger Reconsidered." Review of William Barrett, *What is Existentialism? New York Review of Books*, 2 (April 2, 1964), pp. 14–16.

"Spacecritics." Review of J. Hillis Miller, *The Disappearance of God*, and Joseph Frank, *The Widening Gyre. Partisan Review*, 31 (Fall 1964), pp. 640–50.

"Sartre's Confessions." Review of Jean-Paul Sartre, *The Words. New York Review of Books*, 3 (November 5, 1964), 10–13.

"A Modern Master." Review of Jorge Luis Borges, *Labyrinths* and *Dreamtigers. New York Review of Books*, 3 (November 19, 1964), pp. 8–10.

"Whatever Happened to André Gide?" Review of André Gide, *Marshlands* and *Prometheus Misbound*, and Wallace Fowlie, *André Gide: His Life and Art. New York Review of Books*, 4 (May 6, 1965), pp. 15–17.

"What Is Modern?" Review of Richard Ellmann and Charles Feidelson, eds., *The Modern Tradition*. *New York Review of Books*, 5 (August 26, 1965), pp. 10–13.

"The Mask of Albert Camus." Review of Albert Camus, *Notebooks, 1942–1951*. *New York Review of Books*, 5 (December 23, 1965), pp. 10–13.

"Modern Poetics: French and German." In Alex Preminger, et al., eds., *Princeton Encyclopedia of Poetry and Poetics*, pp. 518–23. Princeton, N.J.: Princeton University Press, 1965; enlarged ed., 1974.

"The Literature of Nihilism." Review of Erich Heller, *The Artist's Journey into the Interior and Other Essays*, and Ronald Gray, *The German Tradition in Literature, 1871–1945*, *New York Review of Books*, 6 (June 23, 1966), pp. 16–20.

"Madame de Staël et Jean-Jacques Rousseau." *Preuves*, 190 (December 1966), pp. 35–40.

Introduction to John Keats, *Selected Poetry*, ed. by Paul de Man. New York: Signet/New American Library, 1966.

"The Riddle of Hölderlin." Review of Friedrich Hölderlin, *Poems and Fragments*. *New York Review of Books*, 15 (November 19, 1970), pp. 47–52.

Review of Jacques Derrida, *De la grammatologie*. *Annales de la societé Jean-Jacques Rousseau*, (Geneva), no. 37 (1966–68; published 1971), pp. 284–88.

Foreword to Carol Jacobs, *The Dissimulating Harmony*. Baltimore/London: The Johns Hopkins University Press, 1978, pp. vii–viii.

# Index

# Index
Compiled by Hassan Melehy

231

# Theory and History of Literature

# Theory and History of Literature

**Paul de Man** was Sterling Professor of Humanities at Yale University, where he taught comparative and French literature from 1970 until his death late in 1983. He also taught at Harvard, Cornell, and Johns Hopkins, and held a chair in comparative literature at the University of Zürich. His books include: *Blindness and Insight* (1971; revised edition, Minnesota, 1983), *Allegories of Reading* (1980), *The Rhetoric of Romanticism* (1984), and *The Resistance to Theory* (Minnesota, 1986). One additional posthumous title is forthcoming from Minnesota: *Aesthetic Ideology*.

**Lindsay Waters** earned his doctorate in English at the University of Chicago and has published essays on English and Italian literature. He was Senior Editor at the University of Minnesota Press, where he worked from 1978 until 1984, and is now General Editor at Harvard University Press. He is editor, with Wlad Godzich, of *Reading de Man Reading* (Minnesota, 1989).